of Congress Cataloging in Publication Data

James Robert.
directors guide-Western Europe.

Moving-picture producers and directors--Europe--
   I. Canham, Kingsley. II. Title.
P3   791. 43'0233'0922   76-1891
8-0908-7

Film Directors (

WESTERN EUI

by

JAMES ROBEI

wi

Kingsley Canhan

Herve Dumont, Pierr

Jeanne Passalacc

Library

Parish,
Film

1.
Registers.
PN1998. A
ISBN 0-810

The

Me

Co

Manu

PREFACE

In this companion volume to FILM DIRECTORS: A Guide to Their American Films (Scarecrow, 1974), the goal is again to provide a single compendium of directors--in this case, those based in Western Europe--who have contributed feature-length productions to the cinema. It is hoped that the following checklists will offer film enthusiasts the needed opportunity to survey a craftsman's output to date and observe the progress and patterns of the subject's motion-picture career.

Entries include only "full-length" films of over four reels or forty minutes and only films in which the subject is at least the principal director, if not the only. So long as the major reputation was first obtained in Europe, directors who made films in the U.S. are included, along with their U.S. credits.

The selection of directors has been based on a desire to offer in a manageably-sized book a wide spectrum of professionals who have been employed in the film industries throughout Western Europe. Naturally the volume does not attempt to be all-inclusive. For the purposes of the present work, Sweden, for example, was considered eastern Europe. Credits relating to Hungarian, Czech, and other eastern European films appear in this volume because of the director's major subsequent identification with western Europe-- e. g. , Germany in a great many cases.

Alphabetization of directors' names that are compounds has been according to one Anglo-American practice--i. e. , that of entry under Da, De, La, etc. --as an aid for those unfamiliar with European practice.

The symbol † next to a country-and-year designation means the film was produced for the individual director's own production company; if in addition the individual was actually the producer, the notation "(also producer)" will appear as well as the †. Sometimes † is modified by the bracketed phrase '[co-production company]," meaning the individual shared its ownership.

The author would be most appreciative of any suggestions, corrections, or additions that any reader may care to provide.

James Robert Parish
300 East 56th Street #9B
New York, N.Y.   10022

EUROPEAN COUNTRIES
NOT COVERED IN THIS VOLUME*

Albania
Bulgaria
Czechoslovakia
Denmark
East Germany
Estonia
Finland
Greece
Hungary

Latvia
Lithuania
Norway
Poland
Sweden
Turkey
USSR
Yugoslavia

*The current work, Film Directors Guide: Western Europe, is the
second in a projected series that will eventually also cover Eastern
Europe (and the USSR), Asia, Africa, and Australia.

ABBREVIATIONS

Note: Only for American- or British-made feature films/documentaries/serials/telefeatures are releasing companies designated; for film products elsewhere only the countries of origin are designated.

AA	Allied Artists Pictures Corporation Anglo-Amalgamated Film Distributors (N. B. some releases bear only "Anglo" as distributors)
ABFD	Associated British Film Distributors
ABP/ABPC	Associated British Picture Corporation
AFU	Army Film Unit
AIP	American International Pictures
AKU	Army Kinematograph Unit
AP & D	Associated Producers and Distributors
Arg	Argentina
Associated FN	Associated First National Pictures, Inc. (later part of Warner Bros., Inc.)
Aus	Austrian
Avco Emb.	Avco Embassy Pictures Corporation
b.	born
B & D	British and Dominions Film Corporation
Bel	Belgian
BFI	British Film Institute
BIED	British Independent Exhibitors' Distributors
BL/BLFC	British Lion Film Corporation
Br	British
Braz	Brazilian
Bry	Bryanston Films
Bul	Bulgarian
Butcher	Butcher's Film Service
BV	Buena Vista Distribution

Can	Canadian
CFF	Children's Film Foundation
CFU	Crown Film Unit
Cin	Cinerama Releasing Corporation
Col	Columbia Pictures Industries, Inc.
CUE	Commonwealth United Entertainment
Czech	Czechoslovakian
d.	died
Dan	Danish
Dut	Dutch
Egy	Egyptian
EL	Eagle Lion Film Distributors
Emb	Embassy Pictures
EMI	Electrical and Musical Industries
Eng	English (the language)
ep	episode
Ex	Exclusive Films
FBO	Film Booking Offices
FN	First National Pictures, Inc. (later part of Warner Bros., Inc.)
FNP	First National-Pathé (British)
FOB	Festival of Britain
Fox	Fox Film Corporation
Fr	French
GB	Great Britain
GEF	Golden Era Film Distributors
Ger	German
GFD	General Film Distributors
GN	Grand National
GPO	General Post Office
Hun	Hungarian
IFD	Independent Film Distributors
IFR	International Film Renters
It	Italian
JMG	Jury-Metro-Goldwyn

Liech	Liechtenstein
LIP	Lippert Pictures, Inc.
	London Independent Producers
Metro-Goldwyn	Metro-Goldwyn Distributing Corporation (later part of Metro-Goldwyn-Mayer, Inc.)
MGM	Metro-Goldwyn-Mayer, Inc.
MOI	Ministry of Information
Mon	Monogram Pictures Corporation
MRA	Moral Rearmament
Par	Paramount Pictures Corporation
PDC	Producers Distributing Corporation
Pol	Polish
Por	Portuguese
PRC	Producers Releasing Corporation
Rep	Republic Pictures Corporation
RFD	Rank Film Distributors
Rus	Russian
SC	Sound City Films
Sp	Spanish
Swe	Swedish
Swi	Swiss
TFD	Twickenham Film Distributors
TV	Television
20th	Twentieth Century-Fox Film Corporation
UA	United Artists Corporation
UNFS/UNESCO	United Nations Film Service
Univ	Universal Pictures, Inc.
US	United States
W & F	Woolf and Freedman Film Service
W Ger	West Germany
WB	Warner Bros. Inc.
WB-7 Arts	Warner Bros.-Seven Arts, Inc.
WPD	Warner-Pathé Distributors
Yug	Yugoslavian
†	denotes film was made for the director's own production company

ACKNOWLEDGMENTS

Ruud Bischoff

Francis Bolen

Felix Bucher

Jean Canham

Cinemathèque Royale de Belgique (Jacques Ledoux)

John Robert Cocchi

Godefroid Courtmans

Peter Cowie

Jorge Palayo

Francisco Rialp

Mel Schuster

Henri Sonet

Tantivy Press

Theatre Collection at Lincoln Center Library for the Performing Arts (Paul Myers and his staff)

THE GUIDE

ACHE, CLAUDE, b. Belgium
  Fredaines (Bel 1961)
  Ricochets (Bel 1963)

AKERMAN, CHANTAL, b. June 6, 1950, Brussels
  Hotel Monterey (Bel 1971) (also script)
  Yonkers [Hanging out 1973] (Bel 1973) (also script)
  Le 15 du 18 (Bel 1973) (also co-script, co-camera, co-editor)
    (with Samy Szlingerbaum)
  Je, tu, il, elle (Bel 1974) (also script, actor)

ALESSANDRINI, GOFFREDO, b. Nov. 19, 1904, Cairo, Egypt
  Sole e terra madre (It 1928)
  Diga di Maghmod (It 1929)
  La segretaria privata (It-Ger 1931)
  Seconda B (It 1934)
  Don Bosco (It 1935)
  Cavalleria (It 1936)
  Luciana Serra, pilota (It 1938)
  Abunas Messias (It 1939)
  Noi vivi (It 1942)
  Furia (It 1942)
  L'Ebreo errante (It 1948)
  Sangue sul sagrata (It 1952) (in collaboration with Michele Nesce
    Umbria)
  Camicie rosse [Anita Girabaldi] (It 1952)

ALLEGRET MARC, b. Dec. 22, 1900, Basle, Switzerland
  Voyage au Congo (Fr 1926) (with André Gide)
  Papoul (Fr 1930)
  La Meilleure Bobonné (Fr 1930)
  J'ai quelque chose à vous dire (Fr 1930)
  Le Blanc et le noir (Fr 1931) (with Robert Florey)
  Les Amants de minuit (Fr 1931) (with Augusto Genina)
  Mam'selle Nitouche (Fr 1931)
  La Petite Chocolatière (Fr 1931)
  Fanny (Fr 1932)
  Lac-aux-dames (Fr 1934) (also co-script)
  L'Hotel du libre échange (Fr 1934)
  Sans famille (Fr 1934)
  Zouzou (Fr 1934)
  Les Beaux Jours (Fr 1935)

1

Marc Allegret with Valerie Hobson visiting the set of <u>Blanche Fury</u> (1948).

Sous les yeux d'occident (Fr 1936)
Les Amants terribles (Fr 1936)
Aventure à Paris (Fr 1936)
Orage (Fr 1937)
La Dame de Malacca (Fr 1937)
Gribouille (Fr 1937)
Entrée des artistes (Fr 1938)
Le Corsaire (unfinished-Fr 1939)
Jeunes filles de France (Fr 1940) (with Etienne Lallia)
Parade en sept nuits (Fr 1941)
L'Arlésienne (Fr 1942)
Félicie Nanteuil/Histoire comique (Fr 1942)
La Belle Aventure (Fr 1942)
Les Petites du quai aux fleurs (Fr 1943)
Lunegarde (Fr 1945)
Pétrus (Fr 1946) (also co-script)
Blanche Fury (GB) (GFD 1948)
Maria Chapdelaine [The Naked Heart] (Fr 1950) (also co-script)
Le Demoiselle et son revenant (Fr 1951)
Avec André Gide (Fr 1952) (two versions)
Blackmailed (GB) (GFD 1951)
Le Film de Jean (Fr 1953)
Julietta (Fr 1953)
L'Amante de Paride [The Face That Launched a Thousand Ships]

(It 1953) (also co-script)
Eterna femmina (It 1953) (with Edgar G. Ulmer)
Futures vedettes [Sweet Sixteen] (Fr 1954) (also co-producer, co-script)
L'Amant de Lady Chatterley (Fr 1955) (also co-adaptor)
En effeuillant la marguerite [Mam'zelle Striptease] (Fr 1956) (also co-adaptor)
Ma femme, mon gosse et moi/L'Amour est en jeu (Fr-It 1957)
Sois belle et tais-toi [Blonde for Danger] (Fr 1958) (also co-story, co-script)
Un Drôle de dimanche (Fr 1959)
Les Affreux (Fr 1959)
Les Démons de minuit [Demons at Midnight] (Fr-It 1961) (also co-script) (with Charles Gérard)
Les Parisiennes [Tales of Paris] (ep "Sophie") (Fr-It 1961)
L'Abominable homme des douanes (Fr 1963) (also co-script)
Début de siècle (Fr 1968) (also script)
Le Bal du Comte d'Orgel (Fr 1970) (also script)

ALLEGRET, YVES, b. Oct. 13, 1907, Paris
Vous n'avez rien à déclarer? (Fr 1936) (with Leo Joannon)
L'Emigrante (unfinished Fr 1939) (also co-script) (with Leo Joannon)
La Roue tourne (unfinished Fr 1941)
Tobie est un ange (Fr 1941) (destroyed)
Les Deux Timides (Fr 1942) (also script) (under alias of "Yves Champlain")
La Bôite aux rêves (Fr 1943) (also co-script) (begun by Jean Choux)
Les Démons de l'aube (Fr 1945)
Dédée d'Anvers [Dedee] (Fr 1947) (also co-script)
Une si jolie petite plage [Such a Pretty Little Beach] (Fr 1948)
Manèges [The Wanton] (Fr 1949)
Les Miracles n'ont lieu qu'une fois (Fr 1950)
Nez de Cuir, gentilhomme d'amour (Fr 1951) (also adaptor)
Les Sept Péchés capitaux [Seven Capital Sins] (ep "La luxure") (Fr 1951)
La Jeune Folle [A Kiss for a Killing] (Fr 1952)
Mam'zelle Nitouche [Oh No, Mam'zelle] (Fr-It 1953) (also co-script)
Les Orgueilleux [The Proud Ones] (Fr-Mex 1953) (also co-script)
Oasis (Fr-Ger 1954)
La Meilleure Part (Fr-It 1955) (also co-script)
Quand la femme s'en mêle (Fr-It-W Ger 1957)
Méfiez-vous fillettes [Young Girls Beware] (Fr 1957)
La Fille de Hambourg [The Girl from Hamburg] (Fr 1958) (also co-script)
L'Ambitieuse [The Climbers] (Fr-It-Australian 1959)
La Chien de pique [The Jack of Spades] (Fr 1961) (also co-dialogue)
Germinal (Fr-It 1962)
Terreur sur la Savane [Konga-Yo] (Congo 1962) (also co-script)
Johnny Banco (Fr-It-W Ger 1966) (also co-script)
L'Invasion (Fr-It 1970)

ALLIO, RENE, b. March 8, 1924, Marseille
La Vieille Dame indigne [The Shameless Old Lady] (Fr 1964)
(also script)
L'Une et l'autre (Fr 1967) (also script)
Pierre et Paul (Fr 1968) (based on his novel, co-script, also actor)
Les Camisards (Fr 1970) (also producer, co-script)
Rude journeé pour la reine (Fr 1973) (producer, also actor, script)

AMENDOLA, MARIO (a. k. a. Irving Jacobs) b. Dec. 8, 1910, Genoa, Italy
I peggiori anni della nostra vita (It 1950)
Il tallone di Achille (It 1952)
Finalmente libero (It 1953)
Bertoldo, Bertoldino e Cacasenno (It 1954)
La campana di San Giusto (It 1954)
I dritti (It 1957)
Le dritte (It 1958)
I prepotenti (It 1958)
L'amore nasce a Roma (It 1959)
A qualcuno piace (It 1959)
Simpatico mascalzone (It 1959)
La banda del buco (It 1960)
Caravan petrol (It 1960)
Il terrore dell'Oklahoma (It 1960)
Cacciatori di dote (It 1962)
Toto di notte n. 1 (It 1962)
Il duca nero [The Black Duke] (It 1963)
Toto sexy (It 1963)
Vino, whisky e acqua salata (It 1963)
I due gladiatori (It 1964)
Maciste gladiatore di Sparta (It 1965)
Soldati e caporali (It 1965)
Cuore matto ... matto da legare (It 1967)
Trappola per sette spie (It 1967)
... Da nemici mi guardo io (It 1969)
Pensiero d'amore (It 1969)

ANDERSEN, WIES, b. Feb. 6, 1936, Belgium
Johnny en Jessy (Bel 1972)

ANDERSON, LINDSAY, b. April 17, 1923, Bangalore, India
This Sporting Life (RFD 1963)
The White Bus (UA 1967) (also co-producer)
If (Par 1968) (also co-producer)
O Lucky Man! (WB 1973) (also co-producer, actor)

ANDERSON, MICHAEL, b. Jan. 30, 1920, London
Private Angelo (ABP 1949) (also co-script) (with Peter Ustinov)
Waterfront [Waterfront Women] (GFD 1950)
Hell Is Sold Out (Eros 1951)
Night Was Our Friend (Monarch 1951)

Lindsay Anderson with Sean Bory on the set of If (1969).

Will Any Gentleman? (ABP 1953)
The House of the Arrow (ABP 1953)
The Dam Busters (ABP 1955)
1984 (ABP 1956)
Around the World in 80 Days (UA 1957)
Yangtse Incident [Battle Hell] (BL 1957)
Chase a Crooked Shadow (ABP 1958)
Shake Hands with the Devil (UA 1959)
The Wreck of the Mary Deare (MGM 1959)
All the Fine Young Cannibals (MGM 1960)
The Naked Edge (UA 1961)
Wild and Wonderful (Univ 1964)
Flight from Ashiya (US-Jap) (UA 1964)
Operation Crossbow (GB-It) (MGM 1965)
The Quiller Memorandum (GB-USA) (RFD 1966)
Eye of the Devil (MGM 1966) (uncredited with J. Lee Thompson)
The Shoes of the Fisherman (MGM-EMI 1968)
Pope Joan (Col 1972)

ANNAKIN, KEN, b. Aug. 10, 1914, Beverley, Yorkshire, England
Holiday Camp (GFD 1947)
Miranda (GFD 1948)
Broken Journey (GFD 1948)
Here Come the Huggetts (GFD 1948)

Quartet (ep "The Colonel's Lady") (GFD 1948)
Vote for Huggett (GFD 1949)
The Huggetts Abroad (GFD 1949)
Landfall (ABP 1949)
Double Confession (ABP 1950)
Trio (eps "The Verger"; "Mr. Knowall") (GFD 1950)
Hotel Sahara (GFD 1951)
The Planter's Wife [Outpost in Malaya] (GFD 1952)
The Story of Robin Hood and His Merrie Men (RKO 1952)
The Sword and the Rose (RKO 1953)
You Know What Sailors Are (GFD 1954)
The Seekers [Land of Fury] (GFD 1954)
Value for Money (RFD 1955)
Three Men in a Boat (IFD 1956)
Loser Takes All (BL 1956)
Across the Bridge (RFD 1957)
Nor the Moon By Night [Elephant Gun] (RFD 1958)
Third Man on the Mountain (BV 1959)
Swiss Family Robinson (BV 1961)
Very Important Person [A Coming Out Party] (RFD 1961) (also
    co-script)
The Hellions (Col Br 1961)
Crooks Anonymous (AA 1962)
The Fast Lady (RFD 1962)
The Longest Day (20th 1962) (with Bernard Wicke; uncredited,
    Darryl F. Zanuck)
The Informers [Underworld Informers] (RFD 1963)
Those Magnificent Men in Their Flying Machines (20th 1965)
    (also co-script)
Battle of the Bulge (WB 1965)
The Long Duel (RFD 1967) (also producer)
The Biggest Bundle of Them All (MGM 1967)
Quei Temerari Sulle Loro Pazze, Scatenate, Scalcinate Carriele
    [Monte Carlo or Bust!/Those Daring Young Men in Their
    Jaunty Jalopies] (It-Fr 1969) (also producer, co-script)
Ruf der Wildnis [Call of the Wild] (W Ger-Br-Sp-It-Fr 1972)

ANTONIONI, MICHELANGELO, b. Sept. 29, 1912, Ferrara, Italy
Cronaca di un amore (It 1950) (also story, co-script)
I vinti (ep) (It 1953) (also co-script)
La signora senza camelie (It 1953) (also story, co-script)
L'amore in città [Love in the City] (ep "Tentato suicidio") (It
    1953)
Le amiche (It 1955) (also co-script)
Il grido [The Outcry] (It 1957) (also story, co-script)
Nel segno di Roma (It 1958) (uncredited, with Riccardo Freda)
L'avventura (It-Fr 1960) (also story, co-script)
La notte [The Night] (It 1961) (also story, co-script)
L'eclisse [The Eclipse] (It 1962) (also co-script)
Deserto Rosso [Red Desert] (It 1964) (also co-script)

Facing page: Antonioni (on camera) filming Blow-Up (1966).

I tre volti (ep "Prefazione") (It 1965)
Blow-Up (MGM 1967) (also co-script)
Zabriskie Point (USA) (MGM 1970)

ARANDA, VICENTE, b. 1926, Barcelona
Brilliante porvenir (Sp 1964) (with Roman Gubern)
Fata Morgana (Sp 1965) (also script)
Las crueles (Sp 1969)
El cadaver exquisito (Sp 1969)

ARDAVIN, CESAR (Cesar Fernandez Ardavin), b. Sept. 23, 1923,
  Madrid
La Llamada de Africa (Sp 1952)
Crimen imposible (Sp 1953)
La puerta abierta (Sp 1956)
... Y eligio el infierno (Sp 1957)
El Lazarillo de Tormes (Sp 1959)
Schwarze Rose, Rosemarie [Festival] (Sp-Ger 1960)
Cerca de la Estrellas (Sp 1961)
La Frontera de Dios (So 1963)
Confidencias de un marido (Sp 1963) (also supervisor, producer,
  script with Francisco Prosper)
Don Quijote, ayer y hoy (Sp 1964)
La Celestina (Sp-Ger 1968) (also script, art director)
Hembra [Prohibidd] (Sp 1970) (also co-script)

ARIEN, GASTON, b. Belgium
Baas Ganzendonck (Bel 1945) (also co-script)

ARLISS, LESLIE (Leslie Andrews), b. 1901, London
The Farmer's Wife (Pathe 1941) (also co-script) (with Norman
  Lee)
The Night Has Eyes [Terror House] (Pathe 1942) (also co-
  script)
The Man in Grey (GFD 1943) (also co-script)
Love Story [A Lady Surrenders] (EL 1944) (also co-script)
The Wicked Lady (EL 1945) (also co-script)
A Man About the House (BL 1947) (also co-script)
Idol of Paris (WB Br 1948)
Saints and Sinners (BL 1949) (also producer, co-script)
The Woman's Angle (ABP 1952) (also co-script)
See How They Run (BL 1955) (also co-script)
Miss Tulip Stays the Night (Adelphi 1955)

ARNOULD, RIGO (Rigobert Arnould), b. Belgium
Yser (Bel 1925)
La Fosse ardente (Bel 1933)

ARTHUYS, PHILIPPE, b. 1928, Paris
La Cage de verre (Fr-Israel 1964) (also script, music) (with
  Jean-Louis Lévi-Alvarès)
Des Christs par milliers (Fr 1969) (also script)
Dieu a choisi Paris [God Chose Paris] (Fr 1969) (also co-script)
  (with Gilbert Prouteau)

ASQUITH, ANTHONY HON, b. Nov. 9, 1902, London, d. Feb. 20, 1968
   Shooting Stars (New Era 1928) (also author, co-script) (with
      A. V. Bramble)
   Underground (Pro Patria 1928) (also script)
   The Runaway Princess (Ger) (JMG 1929) (also script) (with
      Frederick Wendhausen)
   A Cottage on Dartmoor [Escaped from Dartmoor] (Pro Patria
      1929) (also script)
   Tell England [The Battle of Gallipoli] (Wardour 1931) (with
      Geoffrey Barkas) (also co-script)
   Dance Pretty Lady (Wardour 1932) (also script)
   The Lucky Number (Ideal 1933)
   The Unfinished Symphony (GB-Ger) (Gaumont 1934) (also adaptor)
      (with Willi Forst)
   Moscow Nights [I Stand Condemned] (GFD 1935) (also co-script)
   Pygmalion (GFD 1938) (with Leslie Howard)
   French Without Tears (Par 1939)
   Freedom Radio [A Voice in the Night] (Col 1941)
   Quiet Wedding (Par 1941)
   Cottage to Let [Bombsight Stolen] (GFD 1941)
   Uncensored (GFD 1942)
   The Demi-Paradise [Adventure for Two] (GFD 1943)
   We Dive at Dawn (GFD 1943)
   Welcome to Britain (MOI 1943) (with Burgess Meredith)
   Fanny by Gaslight [Man of Evil] (GFD 1944)
   The Way to the Stars [Johnny in the Clouds] (UA 1945)
   While the Sun Shines (Pathé 1947)
   The Winslow Boy (BL 1948) (also co-script)
   The Woman in Question [Five Angles on Murder] (GFD 1950)
   The Browning Version (GFD 1951)
   The Importance of Being Earnest (GFD 1952) (also adaptor)
   The Net [Project M7] (GFD 1953)
   The Final Test (GFD 1953)
   The Young Lovers [Chance Meeting] (GFD 1954)
   Carrington V. C. [Court-Martial] (IFD 1954)
   Orders to Kill (BL 1958)
   The Doctor's Dilemma (MGM 1959) (also co-producer)
   Libel (MGM 1959)
   The Millionairess (20th 1960)
   Guns of Darkness (WPD 1962)
   The V. I. P's (MGM Br 1963)
   An Evening with the Royal Ballet (U 1963) (with Anthony Have-
      lock-Allan)
   The Yellow Rolls Royce (MGM Br 1964)

ASTRUC, ALEXANDRE, b. July 13, 1923, Paris
   Le Rideau cramoisi [The Crimson Circle] (Fr 1952) (also script)
   Les Mauvaises Rencontres (Fr 1955) (also co-script)
   Une Vie (Fr-It 1958) (also co-script)
   La Proie pour l'ombre (Fr 1960) (also script co-dialogue)
   L'Education sentimentale (Fr-It 1961)
   La Longue Marche (Fr 1966) (also co-script)
   Flammes sur l'Adriatique (Fr-Yug 1968) (also co-script)

ATTENBOROUGH, RICHARD, b. Aug. 29, 1923, Cambridge, England
   Oh! What a Lovely War (Par 1969) (also co-producer)
   Young Winston (Col 1972)

AUREL, JEAN, b. 1925, Rumania/Paris(?)
   14-18 (Fr 1962) (also co-editor)
   La Bataille de France (Fr 1963) (also co-editor)
   De l'amour [All About Loving] (Fr-It 1964) (also co-script)
   Lamiel (Fr-It 1967) (also co-script)
   Manon 70 (Fr-It- W Ger 1968) (also co-script)
   Les Femmes (Fr 1969) (also co-script)
   Etes-vous fiancée à un marin grec ou à pilote de ligne? (Fr
      1970) (also co-script)
   Comme un pot de fraises (Fr 1974) (also co-script)

AUTANT-LARA, CLAUDE, b. Aug. 5, 1903, Luzarches, Seine-et-
      Oise, France
   Buster se marié (Fr version of Parlor, Bedroom and Bath)
      (Fr 1930)
   Le Plombier amoureux (Fr version of The Passionate Plumber)
      (Fr 1931)
   Le Fils du royal (Fr version of Son of India) (Fr 1931)
   La Pente (Fr 1931)
   Pur sang (Fr 1931)
   L'Athlète incomplet (Fr 1932)
   Le Gendarme est sans pitié (Fr 1932)
   Un Chien sérieux (Fr 1932)
   Monsieur le duc (Fr 1932)
   La Peur des coups (Fr 1932)
   Invité monsieur à dîner (Fr 1932)
   Ciboulette (Fr 1933) (also co-script, co-costume designer)
   The Mysterious Mr. Davis [My Partner, Mr. Davis] (RKO
      1936) (also co-script)
   Le Mariage de Chiffon (Fr 1942)
   Lettres d'amour (Fr 1942)
   Douce (Fr 1943)
   Sylvie et le fantôme (Fr 1944)
   Le Diable au corps [The Devil in the Flesh] (Fr 1947)
   Occupe-toi d'Amélie [Keep an Eye on Amelia] (Fr 1949)
   L'Auberge rouge [The Red Inn] (Fr 1951) (also co-adaptor, co-
      dialogue)
   Les Sept Péchés capitaux [Seven Capital Sins] (ep "L'orgueil")
      (Fr-It 1951) (also co-script)
   Le Bon Dieu sans confession (Fr 1953) (also co-script)
   Le Blé en herbe (Fr-It 1953)
   Le Rouge et le noir [The Red and the Black] (Fr-It 1954)
   Marguerite de la nuit (Fr-It 1956)
   La Traversée de Paris [Pig Across Paris] (Fr-It 1956)
   En cas de malheur [Love Is My Profession] (Fr-It 1958)
   Le Joueur [The Gambler] (Fr-It 1958)
   La Jument verte [The Green Mare's Nest] (Fr-It 1959) (also
      producer)

Les Régates de San Francisco (Fr-It 1960)
Les Bois des amants [Between Love and Desire] (Fr-It 1960)
Tu ne tueras point [Non uccidere/Thou Shalt Not Kill] (It-Yug-
    Liech 1961) (also co-producer)
Le Comte de Monte Cristo [The Story of the Count of Monte
    Cristo] (Fr-It 1961)
Vive Henri IV, vive l'amour (Fr-It 1962)
Le Meurtrier [Rough Rope] (Fr-It-W Ger 1963)
Le Magot de Joséfa (Fr-It 1964) (also co-script)
Humour noir (ep "La Fourmi") (Fr-It 1964)
Le Journal d'une femme en blanc [Woman in White] (Fr-It 1965)
Une Femme en blanc se révolte (Fr-It 1966)
Le Plus Vieux Métier du monde [The Oldest Profession] (ep
    "Aujourd'hui") (Fr- W Ger-It 1967)
Le Franciscain de Bourges (Fr 1968)
Les Patates (Fr 1969) (also co-script)
Le Rouge et le blanc (Fr 1972)

BABUT DU MARES, MICHEL, b. Feb. 6, 1936, Antwerp, Belgium
La Vénus d'Ille (Bel 1962) (also script)
Le Compensateur (Bel 1968) (also script)
L'Expérience (Bel 1970) (also script)

BAKER, ROY WARD, b. 1916, London
The October Man (GFD 1947)
The Weaker Sex (GFD 1948)
Paper Orchid (Col 1949)
Morning Departure [Operation Disaster] (GFD 1950)
Highly Dangerous (GFD 1950)
The House in the Square [I'll Never Forget You] (20th 1951)
Don't Bother to Knock (20th 1952)
Night Without Sleep (20th 1952)
Inferno (20th 1953)
White Witch Doctor (20th 1953) (resigned, replaced by Henry
    Hathaway)
Passage Home (GFD 1955)
Jacqueline (RFD 1956)
Tiger in the Smoke (RFD 1956)
The One That Got Away (RFD 1957)
A Night to Remember (RFD 1958)
The Singer Not the Song (RFD 1961) (also producer)
Flame in the Streets (RFD 1961) (also co-producer)
The Valiant (UA 1962)
Two Left Feet (BL 1963) (also producer, co-script)
Quatermass and the Pit [Five Million Years to Earth] (WPD
    1967)
The Anniversary (WPD 1967)
Moon Zero Two (WPD 1969)
The Vampire Lovers (MGM-EMI 1970)
Dr Jekyll & Sister Hyde (MGM-EMI 1971)
Asylum (CI 1972)
Vault of Terror (20th Rank, 1973)
The Legend of the Golden Vampires (GB-Hong Kong) (WB 1974)

BAKY, JOSEF VON, b. March 23, 1902, Zombor, Hungary, d.
    1966
    Intermezzo (Ger 1936)
    Die Frau am Scheidewege (Ger 1938)
    Die kleine und die grosse Liebe (Ger 1938)
    Menschen vom Variété (Ger 1939)
    Ihr erstes Erlebnis (Ger 1939)
    Der Kleinstadtpoet (Ger 1940)
    Annelie (Ger 1941)
    Münchhausen (Ger 1943)
    Via Mala (Ger 1945)
    ... Und über uns der Himmel (Ger 1947)
    Der Ruf (Ger 1949)
    Die seltsame Geschichte des Brandner Kaspar (Ger 1949)
    Das doppelte Löttchen (Ger 1950)
    Der träumende Mund (Ger 1952)
    Tagebuch einer Verliebten [Diary of a Married Woman] (Ger
        1953)
    Hotel Adlon (Ger 1955)
    Dunja (Ger 1955)
    Fuhrmann Henschel (Ger 1956)
    Robinson soll nicht sterben (Ger 1957)
    Die Frühreifen (Ger 1958)
    Gestehen Sie, Dr. Corda! (Ger 1958)
    Stefanie (Ger 1958)
    Der Mann, der sich verkaufte (Ger 1958)
    Die ideale Frau (Ger 1959)
    Marili (Ger 1959)
    Sturm in Wasserglas (Ger 1960)
    Die seltsame Gräfin (Ger 1961)

BALDI, FERNANDO, b. Italy
    Il prezzo dell'onore (It 1953)
    Ricordami (It 1956)
    Amarti e il mio destino (It 1957)
    Assi alla ribotta (It 1959)
    Due selvaggi a corte (It 1959)
    David e Golia [David and Goliath] (It 1960) (with Richard Pottier)
    I tartari (It 1961) (with Richard Thorpe)
    Orazio e curiazi (It 1962)
    Sfida al re di Castiglia (It-Sp 1964)
    Il figlio di Cleopatra (It-GB 1964)
    Tiki (It 1965)
    Preparati la bara (It 1968)
    Afyon (It 1972)
    Carambola (It 1974)

BALDI, MARCELLO, b. Aug. 1, 1923, Trento, Italy
    Italia k2 (It 1955)
    Il clandestino (It 1957)
    La morte ha viaggiato con me (It 1957) (in Coll.)
    Il raccomandato di ferro (It 1959)
    Marte, dio della guerra (It 1962)

13   BARATIER

Il criminale (It 1963)
Giacobbe, l'Uomo che lottò con Dio (It 1963)
Saul e David (It 1965)
I grandi condottieri (It-Sp 1966) (in collaboration)
Inferno a Caracas (It-Ger 1966)
Stuntman (It-Fr 1968)

BARATIER, JACQUES, (Jacques Baratier de Rey), b. 1918, Mont-
pelier (Hérault), France
Goha (Fr-Tunisia 1957)
La Poupée [He, She or It] (Fr 1962)
Dragées au poivre [Sweet and Sour] (Fr-It 1963) (also co-script)
L'Or du duc (Fr-It 1965) (also script, co-dialogue)
Le Désordre à vingt ans [Voila l'ordre] (Fr 1967) (also co-
script)
Piège (Fr 1969) (also script)
La Décharge (F-W Ger 1970) (also actor, co-script)
Cinéma différent 3 (Fr-W Ger 1972) [ep combining footage from
Piège (1968) and a short Prologue (1969)]
Vous intéressez-vous à la chose? [First Time with Feeling]
(Fr-W Ger 1973) (also co-script)

BARBONI, ENZO (a. k. a. E. B. Clucher), b. July 10, 1922, Rome
Lo chiamavano Trinità (It 1970) (also script)
Continuavano a chiamarlo Trinità (It 1971) (also script)
Gli fumavano le Colt ... lo chiamavano Camposanto (It 1971)
(script only)
Anche gli angeli mangiano fagioli (It-Fr-Sp 1972) (also script)

BARDEM, JUAN ANTONIO, (Juan Antonio Munoz), b. June 2, 1922,
Madrid
Paseo sobre una guerra antigua (Sp 1949) (also co-script) (with
Luis G. Berlanga) [silent short incorporated in feature, La
honradez de la cerradura, d. Luis Escobar]
Esa pareja feliz (Sp 1951) (also co-script) (with Luis G. Ber-
langa)
Comicos (Sp 1954) (also script)
Felicies Pascuas (Sp 1954) (also co-script)
Muerte de un ciclista [Death of a Cyclist] (Sp 1955) (also script)
Calle mayor [Grand' Rue] (Sp-Fr 1956)
La muerte de Pio Baroja (Unreleased Sp 1957)
La venganza (Sp 1957) (also script)
Sonatas (Sp 1959) (also script)
A las cinco de la tarde (Sp 1960) (also co-script)
Los inocentes (Arg 1962) (also co-script)
Nunca pasa nada (Sp 1963) (also co-script)
Los pianos mecanicos [The Uninhibited] (Sp 1964) (also script)
El último dia de la guerra [The Last Day of the War] (Sp 1969)
(also co-script)
Variétés (Sp 1971) (also script)
La corrupción de Chris Miller (Sp-US 1974) (also co-script)
La Isla misteriosa [The Mysterious Island) (Sp-US 1974) (also
co-script)

BAVA, MARIO (a. k. a. John M. Old), b. July 31, 1914, San Remo,
    Italy
    La battaglia di Maratona (It 1959) (also camera) (uncredited,
        with Jacques Tourneur, Bruno Vailati)
    La maschera del demonio [Black Sunday] (It 1961) (also cam-
        era) (with Raoul Walsh)
    Esther e il re [Esther and the King] (It 1961) (also camera)
        (with Raoul Walsh)
    Ercole al centro della terra [Hercules in the Haunted World]
        (It 1961) (also co-script, camera)
    Gli invasori [Fury of the Vikings] (It 1961) (also co-script,
        camera)
    La ragazza che sapeva troppo [The Evil Eye] (It 1962) (also
        co-script, camera)
    Le meraviglie di Aladino [The Wonders of Aladdin] (It 1962)
        (with Henry Levin)
    La frusta e il corpo [Son of Satan] (It-Fr 1963) (also producer)
    Sei donne per l'assassino [Blood and Black Lace] (It-Fr-Ger
        1964) (also co-script)
    Terrore nello spazio [Planet of Vampires] (It 1965)
    Raffica di Coltelli (It 1965)
    Dr. Goldfoot and the Girl Bombs [Dr. G. and the Love Bombs]
        (It 1966)
    Operazione paura [Curse of the Dead] (It 1966) (also co-script)
    Diabolik [Danger Diabolik] (It-Fr 1967) (also co-script)
    Cinque bambole per la luna di Agosto (It 1969)
    Il rosso segna della follia [Un hacha para la luna de miel] (It-
        Sp 1969)
    Roy Colt and Winchester Jack (It 1970)
    Ecologia del delitto (It 1970)

BECKER, JACQUES, b. Sept. 15, 1906, Paris; d. Nov. 21, 1960
    Le Commissaire est bon enfant/ Le gendarme est sans pitié
        (Fr 1935) (co-story, co-script, actor) (with Pierre Prévert)
    Tête de Turc [Un Tête qui rapporte] (Fr 1935) (also co-script)
    L'Or du Cristobal (Fr 1939) (film begun by Becker but com-
        pleted by Jean Stelli, who took full credit)
    Dernier atout (Fr 1942) (also co-script)
    Goupi mains rouges (Fr 1943) (also co-script)
    Falbalas (Fr 1945) (also co-story, co-script)
    Antoine et Antoinette (Fr 1946) (also co-story, co-script, co-
        dialogue)
    Rendez-vous de Juillet (Fr 1948) (also co-story, co-script, co-
        dialogue)
    Edouard et Caroline [Edward and Caroline] (Fr 1951) (also co-
        script)
    Casque d'or [Golden Helmet] (Fr 1952) (also co-script, dia-
        logue)
    Rue de l'Estrapade [Francoise Steps Out] (Fr 1953) (also co-
        dialogue)
    Touchez pas au grisbi [Honor Among Thieves] (Fr 1954) (also
        co-script)
    Ali Baba et les quarantes voleurs [Ali Baba] (Fr 1954) (also

co-story, co-script)
Les Aventures d'Arsène Lupin (Fr-It 1956) (also co-script,
   actor)
Montparnasse 19 [The Lovers of Montparnasse] (Fr-It 1957)
   (also script)
Le Trou [The Hole] (Fr-It 1959) (also co-script, co-dialogue)

Jacques Becker

BECKER, JEAN, b. May 10, 1933, Paris
   Un Nommé la Rocca (Fr-It 1961) (also script)
   Echappement libre [Backfire] (Fr-Sp-It 1964) (also script)
   Pas de caviar pour Tante Olga (Fr 1965) (also co-adaptor)
   Tendre voyou (Fr 1967) (also co-adaptor)

BECKER, WOLFGANG, b. 1921
   Liebe--wie die Frau sie wünscht (Ger 1957)
   Peter Voss, der Millionendieb (Ger 1958)
   Ich war ihm hörig (Ger 1958)
   Italienreise--Liebe inbegriffen (Ger 1958)
   Alle lieben Peter (Ger 1959)
   Der lustige Krieg des Hauptmann Pedro (Ger 1959)
   Kein Engel ist so rein (Ger 1960)
   Die Letzten drei der Albatross [Mutiny in the South Seas]

(Ger-It-Fr 1965)
Ein Ferienbett mitt 100 PS (Ger 1965)
Ellenbogenspiele (Ger 1969)
Ich Schlafe mit meinem Mörder (Ger-Fr 1970)

BEJART, MAURICE, b. 1927, France
Le Sacre du printemps (Bel 1968) (also co-script)
Bhakti (Bel 1969) (also script)

BELLOCCHIO, MARCO, b. 1940, Placenza, Italy
I pugni in tasca [Fist in His Pocket] (It 1965) (also story,
    script)
La Cina è Vicina [China Is Near] (It 1969) (also co-story,
    script)
Amore e rabbia (ep "Discutiamo, discutiamo") (It 1969)
In nome del Padre (It 1972) (also script)

Marco Bellocchio

BENAZERAF, JOSE, b. 1922, Casablanca
Le Cri de la chair [Eternity for Us] (Fr 1962)
La Drogue du vice [Concerto de la peur] (Fr 1963)
24 heures d'un Americain a Paris (Fr 1964)
Cover Girls (It-Fr 1965) (also co-script) (filmed in 1963)
L'Enfer sur la plage (Fr 1965)
L'Enfer dans la peau (Fr 1965)
Joe Caligula (Fr 1966)
Du suif chez les dabs (Fr 1966)
St Pauli zwischen Nacht und Morgen (W Ger 1966)
Un Epais manteau de sang (Fr 1967) (also script)
Le Désirable et le sublime (Fr 1970) (also script)
Frustration (Fr 1971) (also producer, co-script)
Adolescence pervertie (Fr 1973) (also script)
The French Love (Fr 1973) (also script)
Un Homme sa penche sur son destin (Fr 1973) (also script)
Le Bordel (Fr 1974) (also script)

BENE, CARMELO, b. 1937, Lecce, Italy
Nostra signora dei Turchi (It 1968)
Capricci (It 1969)
Don Giovanni (It 1970)
Salomé (It 1971)

BENIEST, HEIN, b. Belgium
Jongens Zoals Wij (Bel 1956) (also script)
Moeder Wat Zijn Wij Rijk (Bel 1957) (also script)
Kinderen in Gods Hans (Bel 1958) (also script)
Brigands voor Outer en Heerd (Bel 1961) (also script)
Zomercapriolen (Bel 1962)

BENNETT, COMPTON (Robert Compton-Bennett), b. Jan. 15, 1900,
     Tunbridge Wells, Kent, England
The Seventh Veil (GFD 1943)
The Years Between (GFD 1946)
Daybreak (GFD 1946)
My Own True Love (Par 1948)
That Forsyte Woman [The Forsyte Saga] (MGM 1949)
King Solomon's Mines (MGM 1950) (with Andrew Marton)
So Little Time (ABP 1952)
The Gift Horse [Glory at Sea] (IFD 1952)
It Started in Paradise (GFD 1952)
Desperate Moment (GFD 1953)
That Woman Opposite [City After Midnight] (Monarch 1957)
After the Ball (IFD 1957)
The Flying Scot [Mailbag Robbery] (AA 1957) (also producer)
Beyond the Curtain (RFD 1960) (also co-script)
How to Undress in Public without Undue Embarrassment (Mon-
     arch 1965) (also producer, script)

BENNO, ALEX (Benjamin Bonefang), b. Nov. 2, 1873, Oberhausen,
     Germany, d. Apr. 2, 1952
Kee en Janus naar Berlijn (Dut 1922)

Bleeke Bet (Dut 1923)
Kee en Janus naar Parijs (Dut 1924)
Mooi Juultje van Volendam (Dut 1924)
Oranke Hein (Dut 1925)
Revue artistique (Dut 1926)
Moderne Landhaaien (Dut 1926)
Op hoop van zegen (Dut 1934)
Bleeke Bet (Dut 1934) (with Richard Oswald)
Amsterdam bij nacht (Dut 1937)

BENOIT, NORBERT (Norbert Vanpeperstraete), b. 1912, Belgium
    Péché mortel (Bel 1942) (also script)
    La Maudite (Bel 1948) (with E. G. De Meyst)
    Je n'ai que toi au monde [Les Anges sont parmi nouse] (Bel
        1949) (with E. G. De Meyst)

BERGER, LUDWIG (Ludwig Bamberger), b. Jan. 6, 1892, Mainz,
        Germany; d. 1969
    Der Richter von Zalamea (German 1920) (also script)
    Der Roman der Christine von Herre (Ger 1920) (also script)
    Ein Glas Wasser (Ger 1922) (also co-script)
    Das Spiel der Königin (Ger 1923) (also co-script)
    Ein Waltzertraum (Ger 1925)
    Der Meister von Nürnberg (Ger 1927) (also co-script)
    Liebe, Liebe (Ger 1928)
    Das brennende Herz [The Burning Heart] (Ger 1928)
    The Woman from Moscow (USA) (Par 1928)
    Sins of the Father (USA) (Par 1928)
    The Vagabond King (USA) (Par 1930)
    The Playboy of Paris (USA) (Par 1930)
    Le petit cafe [French version of The Playboy of Paris] (USA)
        (Par 1930)
    Ich bei Tag und du bei Nacht (Ger 1932)
    Moi le jour, toi la nuit [Fr version of Ich bei Tag und du bei
        Nacht] (Ger 1932)
    Early to Bed [Eng version of Ich bei Tag und du bei Nacht]
        (Ger 1932)
    Walzerkrieg (Ger 1933)
    La Guerre des valses [French version of Walzerkrieg] (Ger
        1933)
    Pygmalion (Dut 1937)
    Trois Valses (Fr 1938)
    The Thief of Bagdad (UA 1940) (with Michael Powell, Tim
        Whelan)
    Ballerina (Fr 1950)

BERGONZELLI, SERGIO (a. k. a. Serge Bergon)
    Gli avventurieri dei tropici (It 1960)
    Uno straniero a sacramento (It 1965)
    Una colt in pugno al diavolo (It 1967)
    Silvia e l'amore (It 1968)
    Le dieci meraviglie dell'amore (It-Ger 1969)
    Nelle piege della carne (It-Sp 1970)

Io, Cristiana studentessa degli scandali (It 1971)
Cristina monaca indemoniata (It 1972) (also script)
La cognatina (It 1974)

BERKENMAN, PAUL, b. May 12, 1926, Ghent, Belgium
    Prelude Tot de Dageraad (Bel 1958) (also co-script, co-camera)
        (with Raymond Cogen, Marcel de Backer)
    Want Allen Hebben Gezondig (Bel 1961) (also co-script) (with
        Raymond Cogen, Antoon Carette)
    Novemberspelen [Amours d'automne) (Bel 1962) (also co-script)
        (with Raymond Cogen)
    Une Demoiselle sans bagage (Bel 1963) (also co-script) (with
        Raymond Cogen)

BERLANGA, LUIS G., b. June 12, 1921, Valencia, Spain
    Esa pareja feliz (Sp 1951) (with Juan Antonio Bardem) (also co-
        story, co-script)
    Bienvenido, Mister Marshall! (Sp 1952) (also co-story, co-
        script)
    Novio a la vista (Sp 1953) (also co-script)
    Calabuch (Sp-It 1956) (also co-script)
    Los Yueves, Milagro (Sp-It 1957) (also story, co-script)
    Plácido (Sp 1961) (also co-story, co-script)
    Les Quatres Vérités (ep "La Muerte y el Lenador") (Fr-It-Sp
        1962) (also co-story, co-script)
    El verdugo [Not on Your Life] (Sp-It 1963) (also co-script)
    La boutique (Sp 1967) (also co-story, co-script)
    ¡Vivan los novios! (Sp 1969) (also co-script)
    Life Size Grandeur Nature (Sp-Fr-It 1974) (also co-story, co-
        script)

BERNARD, RAYMOND, b. Oct. 10, 1891, Paris
    Le Ravin sans fond (Fr 1917) (with Jacques Feyder)
    Le Gentilhomme commerçant (Fr 1918)
    La Traitement du Hoquet (Fr 1918)
    Le Petit Café (Fr 1919) (also co-script)
    Le Secret de Rosette Lambert (Fr 1920)
    La Maison vide (Fr 1921)
    Triplepatte (Fr 1922)
    Le Costaud des Epinettes (Fr 1923)
    L'Homme inusable (Fr 1923)
    Décadence et grandeur (Fr 1923)
    Le Miracle des loups [The Miracle of the Wolves] (Fr 1924)
        (also producer)
    Le Joueur d'échecs (Fr 1927)
    Tarakanova (Fr 1930)
    Faubourg Montmartre (Fr 1932)
    Les Croix de bois (Fr 1932)
    Les misérables [Part 1: Fantine] (Fr 1934) (also co-script)
    Les misérables [Part 2: Les Thénardier] (Fr 1934) (also co-
        script)
    Les misérables [Part 3: Liberté, liberté, Chérie!] (Fr 1934)
        (also co-script)

Tartarin de Tarascon (Fr 1934) (also adaptor)
Amants et voleurs (Fr 1935)
Le Coupable (Fr 1936)
Anne-Marie (Fr 1936)
Marthe-Richard--Au service de la France (Fr 1937)
J'étais une aventurière (Fr 1938)
Les Otages (Fr 1939)
Cavalcade d'amour (Fr 1939)
Un Ami viendra ce soir (Fr 1945) (also co-script)
Adieu Chérie (Fr 1945) (also co-script)
Le Jugement de Dieu (Fr 1949) (also co-adaptor)
Maya (Fr 1949) (also co-adaptor)
Le Cap de l'Espérance (Fr 1951)
La Dame aux camélias (Fr 1952) (also co-script)
La Belle de Cadix (Fr 1953) (also co-script)
Les Fruits de l'été (Fr 1954) (also co-script)
Le Septième Commandment (Fr 1957) (also co-story, co-script, co-dialogue)
Le Septième Ciel (Fr 1958) (also co-script, co-dialogue)

BERNHARDT, CURTIS (Kurt Bernhardt), b. April 15, 1899, Worms, Germany
Qualen der Nacht [Torments of the Night] (Ger 1926) (also co-script)
Die Waise von Lowood (Ger 1926)
Kinderseelen Klagen euch an (Ger 1927)
Das Mädchen mit den Fünf Nullen [Das Grosse Los] (Ger 1927)
Schinderhannes [The Prince of Rogues] (Ger 1928) (also co-script)
Das letzte Fort (Ger 1928)
Die Frau, nach der Man sicht sehnt [Three Loves] (Ger 1929)
Die letzte Kompagnie [Thirteen Men and a Girl] (Ger 1930)
Der Mann, der den Mord beging [Nachte am Bosporus] (Ger 1931)
L'Homme qui assassina [Fr version of Der Mann, der den Mord beging] (Ger 1931)
Der Rebell (Ger 1932) (with Luis Trenker)
Der grosse Rausch (Ger 1932)
Der Tunnel (Ger and Fr versions 1933)
L'Or dans la rue (Fr 1934)
Le Vagabond bien-aimé (Fr 1936)
The Beloved Vagabond [version of Le Vagabond Bien-Aimé] (Col Br 1936)
Carrefour (Fr 1938)
Nuit de Décembre (Fr 1939)
My Love Came Back (USA) (WB 1940)
The Lady with Red Hair (USA) (WB 1940)
Million Dollar Baby (USA) (WB 1941)
Juke Girl (USA) (WB 1942)
Happy Go Lucky (USA) (Par 1943)
Conflict (USA) (WB 1945)
Devotion (USA) (WB 1946)
My Reputation (USA) (WB 1946)

A Stolen Life (USA) (WB 1946)
Possessed (USA) (WB 1947)
The High Wall (USA) (MGM 1949)
The Doctor and the Girl (USA) (MGM 1949)
Payment on Demand (USA) (RKO 1950) (also co-script)
Sirocco (USA) (Col 1951)
The Blue Veil (USA) (RKO 1951)
The Merry Widow (USA) (MGM 1952)
Miss Sadie Thompson (USA) (Col 1953)
Beau Brummel (USA) (MGM 1954)
Interrupted Melody (USA) (MGM 1955)
Gaby (USA) (MGM 1956)
Damon and Pythias (MGM 1963)
Stefanie in Rio (Casino 1963)
Kisses for My President (USA) (WB 1964) (also producer)

BERRI, CLAUDE (Claude Langman), b. July 1, 1934, Paris
    Les Baisers (ep "Baiser de 16 ans") (Fr-It 1964) (also script)
    La Chance et l'amour (ep "La chance du guerrier") (Fr-It
        1964) (also script)
    Le Vieil Homme et l'enfant [The Two of Us] (Fr 1966) (also
        adaptor)
    Mazel tov ou le mariage [Marry Me, Marry Me] (Fr 1968)†
        (also script, actor)
    Le Pistonné [The Man with Connections] (Fr 1970)† (also script)
    Le cinéma de Papa [Le cancre] (Fr 1970)† (also script, actor)
    Sex shop (Fr-It-W Ger 1972)† (also script, actor)
    Le Mâle du siècle (Fr 1974) (also co-script, co-dialogue)

BERTHOMIEU, ANDRE, b. Feb. 16, 1903, Rouen, France
    Pas si bête (Fr 1927)
    Ces dames aux chapeaux verts (Fr 1929)
    Rapacité (Fr 1930)
    Mon ami Victor (Fr 1930)
    La Femme idéale (Fr 1933)
    Gagne ta vie (Fr 1933)
    Mon coeur et ses millions (Fr 1933)
    Coquecignole (Fr 1933)
    Baranc (Fr 1933)
    Le Crime du bouif (Fr 1933)
    Mademoiselle Josette ma femme (Fr 1933)
    Le Crime de Sylvestre Bonnard (Fr 1933)
    Les Ailes brisées (Fr 1933)
    N'aimer que toi (Fr 1934)
    L'Aristo (Fr 1934)
    Jim, la houlette roi des voleurs (Fr 1935)
    L'Amant de Madame Vidal (Fr 1935)
    Le Secret de Polichinelle (Fr 1936)
    La Flamme (Fr 1936)
    Le Mort en fuite (Fr 1936)
    La Chaste Suzanne (Fr 1937)
    Porte-veine (Fr 1937)
    Les Nouveaux Riches (Fr 1938)

Eusèbe député (Fr 1938)
Le Train pour Venise (Fr 1938)
L'Inconnue de Monte-Carlo (Fr 1939)
Dédé la musique (Fr 1939)
La Neige sur les pas (Fr 1941)
Promesse à l'inconnue
La Croisée des chemins (Fr 1942)
L'Ange de la nuit (Fr 1942)
Le Secret de Madame Clapain (Er 1943)
J'ai 17 ans (Fr 1945)
Peloton d'exécution (Fr 1945)
Gringalet (Fr 1946) (also story, script)
Pas si bête (Fr 1946)
Amours, délices et orgues (Fr 1946) (also script)
Carré de valets (Fr 1947) (also script)
Blanc comme neige (Fr 1947) (also script)
La Coeur sur la main (Fr 1948) (also script)
Le Bal des pompiers (Fr 1948) (also script)
L'Ombre (Fr 1948) (also script)
Le Roi Pandore (Fr 1949) (also script)
La Petit Chocolatière (Fr 1949) (also script)
La Femme nue (Fr 1949) (also script)
Mademoiselle Josette ma femme (Fr 1950) (also script)
Pigalle-Saint-Germain-des-Prés (Fr 1950) (also script)
Les Roi des Camelots (Fr 1950) (also script)
Chacun son tour (Fr 1951) (also script)
Jamais deux sans trois (Fr 1951) (also script)
Allô, je t'aime (Fr 1952) (also script)
Belle mentalité (Fr 1952) (also script)
Le Dernier Robin des bois (Fr 1952) (also script)
Le Portrait de son père (Fr 1953) (also script)
L'Oeil en coulisses (Fr 1953) (also script)
Scènes de ménage (Fr 1954) (also script)
Les Deux font la paire (Fr 1954) (also script)
Quatre jours à Paris (Fr 1955) (also script)
Les Duratons (Fr 1955) (also script)
La Joyeuse Prison (Fr 1956) (also script)

BERTOLUCCI, BERNARDO, b. March 16, 1941, Parma, Italy
La commare secca (It 1962) (also co-script)
Prima della rivoluzione (It 1964)
La via del petrolio (It TV 1965-1966) (also script)
Amore e rabbia [Love and Anger] (ep "L'agonia") (It 1967) (also
script for ep) (released in 1969)
Partner (It 1968) (also co-script)
Strategia del ragno [The Spider's Web] (It 1969) (also co-script)
Il conformista [The Conformist] (It 1970)
Ultimo Tango a Parigi [Last Tango in Paris] (It-Fr 1973) (also
story-script)

BIANCHI, GIORGIO, b. Feb. 18, 1904, Rome
La maestrina (It 1942)
Il mondo vuole così (It 1946)

23   BILLINGTON

La resa di Tití (It 1946)
Cronaca nera (It 1947)
Fatalità (It 1947)
Che tempi! (It 1949)
Una lettera all'alba (It 1949)
Vent'anni (It 1949)
Il caimano del Piave (It 1950)
Cuori sul mare (It 1950)
Porca miseria (It 1951)
Amor non ho ... però però (It 1952)
La nemica (It 1954)
Scampolo '53 (It 1954)
Via Padova [Lo scocciatore] (It 1954)
Accadde al penitenziàrio (It 1955)
Buonanotte ... avvocato! (It 1955)
Graziella (It 1955)
Io piaccio [La via del successo con le donne] (It 1955)
Non c'è amore più grande (It 1955)
L'ombra (It 1955)
Il conte Max (It 1957)
Gli zitelloni (It 1958)
Brevi amori a Palma di Maiorca (It 1959)
Il moralista (It 1959)
La nipote Sabella (It 1959)
Uomini e nobiluomini (It 1959)
Chiamate 22-22 tenente Sheridan (It 1960)
Femmine di lusso (It 1960)
Le olimpiadi dei mariti (It 1961)
Gli attendenti (It 1961)
Mani in alto (It 1961)
Il cambio della guardia (It 1962)
Il mio amico Benito (It 1962)
Peccati d'estate (It 1962)
Totò e Peppino divisi a Berlin (It 1962)
I quattro tassisti (It 1964)
Sedotti e bidonati (It 1964)
Assicurasi vergine (It 1967)
Quando dico che ti amo (It 1967)

BILLINGTON, KEVIN, b. 1934, Warrington, Lancashire, England
Interlude (Col 1968)
The Rise and Rise of Michael Rimmer (WB 1970) (also co-
script)
The Light at the Edge of the World [La Luz del fin del mundo]
(USA-Sp-Liech) (MGM 1971)
Voices (Hemdale 1973)

BINGER, MAURITS HERMAN, b. Apr. 5, 1868, Haarlem, Nether-
lands, d. Apr. 9, 1923
Gouden ketenen (Dut 1915)
Majoor Frans (Dut 1916)
Het geheim van den Vuurtoren (Dut 1916)
American Girls (Dut 1918)

De Kroon der Schande (Dut 1918)
Op Hoop van Zegen (Dut 1918)
Toen het Licht Verdween (Dut 1918)
Het Goudvisje (Dut 1919)
Een Carmen van het Noorden (Dut 1919)
Joy (Dut 1919)
Ulbo garvems (Dut 1917)
De Leugen van Pierrot (Dut 1920)
Schakels (Dut 1920)
As God Made Her (Dut-Br 1920) (with B. E. Doxat-Pratt)
Fate's Plaything (Dut-Br 1920) (with B. E. Doxat-Pratt)
The Little Hour of Peter Wells (Dut-Br 1920) (with B. E.
     Doxat-Pratt)
Sister Brown (Dut-Br 1920) (with B. E. Doxat-Pratt)
De Jantjes (Dut 1922)
Onder Spiritistiche Dwang (Dut 1922)
Mottige Janus (Dut 1922)

BITSCH, CHARLES, b. April 23, 1931, Mulhouse, France
Les Baisers (ep "Cher baiser") (Fr-It 1964) (also script)
La Chance et l'amour (ep "Lucky la chance") (Fr-It 1964)
     (also script)
Le Dernier Homme [The Last Man] (Fr 1969) (also script)

BLASETTI, ALESSANDRO, b. July 3, 1900, Rome
Sole (It 1928) (also co-script, editor)
Resurrectio (It 1930) (also co-story, script, co-editor)
Nerene (It 1930) (also co-editor)
Terra madre (It 1930) (also co-script, co-editor)
Palio (It 1932) (also co-script, co-editor)
La tavola dei poveri (It 1932) (also co-script, co-editor)
1860 (It 1933) (also co-script, co-editor)
Il caso Haller (It 1933) (also co-editor)
L'impiegata di papa (It 1933) (also co-editor)
Vecchia guardia (It 1934) (also co-script, co-editor)
Aldebaràn (It 1935) (also co-script, actor)
La contessa di Parma (It 1937) (also co-script, co-editor)
Ettore Fieramosca (It 1938) (also co-script, co-editor)
Retroscena (It 1939) (also co-story, co-script, co-editor)
Un'avventura di Salvator Rosa (It 1940) (also co-script, co-
     editor)
La corona di ferro (It 1941) (also co-story, co-script) (with
     Renato Castellani)
La cena delle beffe (It 1941) (also co-script)
Quattro passi fra le nuvole [Four Steps in the Clouds] (It 1942)
     (also co-script, actor)
Nessuno torna indietro (It 1943) (also co-script)
Un giorno nella vita (It 1946) (also co-story, co-script)
Il testimone (It 1946) (supervisor, co-script only)
Fabiola (It 1949) (also co-script)
Prima comunione [Father's Dilemma] (It 1950) (also co-producer
Bellissima (It 1951) (actor only)
Altri tempi [Infidelity] (It 1952) (also co-story, co-script)

La fiammata (It 1952) (also co-script)
Tempi nostri [Anatomy of Love] (It 1954) (also co-script)
Peccato che sia una canaglia [Too Bad She's Bad] (It 1955) (also co-script)
La fortuna di essere donna [Lucky to Be a Woman] (It 1956) (also co-script)
Amore e chiacchiere (It 1957) (also co-script)
Europa di notte [European Nights] (It 1959) (also co-script)
Io amo, tu ami [I Love, You Love] (It 1960)
Le quattro verità (ep "La Lepre e la tartaruga") (It-Fr-Sp 1963)
Liola (It 1964) (also co-script)
Io, Io, Io ... e gli altri [Me, Me, Me ... and the Others] (It 1966) (also co-script)
La ragazza del bersagliere (It 1967) (also co-script)
Simón Bolívar (It-Sp-Venez 1968) (also co-script)

BOCCA, TONIO (a. k. a. Amerigo Anton)
Traguardi de gloria (It 1957)
Arriva la banda (It 1958)
Il conquistatore d'Oriente (It 1961)
Sansone contro il Pirata (It 1963)
Il dominatore del deserto (It 1964)
Maciste all corte dello Zar (It 1964)
I predoni della steppa (It 1964)
La rivinta di Ivanhoe (It 1965)
Agente X-I-7, operazione Oceano (It-Sp 1966)

BOESE, CARL, b. Aug. 26, 1887, Berlin; d. 1958
Nocturno der Liebe (Ger 1918)
Die Geisha und der Samurai (Ger 1919)
Drei Nächte (1920)
Der Golem, wie er in die Welt kam (Ger 1920) (with co-director)
Die Herren vom Maxim (Ger 1920)
Das Floss der Töten (Ger 1921)
Die rote Mühle (Ger 1921)
Die Tänzerin Barberina (Ger 1921)
Das Auge der Toten (Ger 1922)
Gespenster (Ger 1922)
Die grosse Lüge (Ger 1922)
Landstreicherin Courage (Ger 1922)
Das ungeschriebene Gesetz (Ger 1922)
Graf Cohn (Ger 1923)
Ein Kind--ein Hund (Ger 1923)
Maciste und die chinesische Truhe (Ger 1923)
Die Frau im Feuer (Ger 1924)
Sklaven der Liebe (Ger 1924) (also co-script)
Die drei Portiermädel (Ger 1925)
Die eiserne Braut (Ger 1925)
Grüss mir das blonde Kind am Rhein (Ger 1925)
Heiratsschwindler (Ger 1925)
Krieg im Frieden (Ger 1925)

... Und es lockt ein Ruf aus sundiger Welt (Ger 1925)
Wenn Du eine Tante hast (Ger 1925)
Es blasen die Trompeten (Ger 1926)
Kubinke, der Barbier, und die drei Dienstmädchen (Ger 1926)
Ledige Töchter (Ger 1926)
Die letzte Droschke von Berlin (Ger 1926)
Der Mann ohne Schlaf (Ger 1926)
Nanette macht alles (Ger 1926)
Der Seekadett (Ger 1926)
Die sporckschén Jäger (Ger 1926) (also co-script)
Das edle Blut (Ger 1927)
Die Elf Teufel (Ger 1927)
Die indiskrete Frau (Ger 1927)
Schwere Jungens--leichte Mädchen (Ger 1927)
Die weisse Spinne (Ger 1927)
Eve in Seide (Ger 1928) (also co-script)
Kinder der Strasse (Ger 1928)
Lemkes seltsam Witwe (Ger 1928) (also co-script)
Ossi hat die Hosen an 28 (Ger 1928) (also producer)
Der Piccolo vom goldenen Löwen (Ger 1928) (also producer)
Wenn die Mutter und die Tochter ... (Ger 1928) (also producer)
Alimente (Ger 1929)
Bobby der Benzinjunge (Ger 1929)
Geschminkte Jugend (Ger 1929)
Der Detektiv des Kaisers (Ger 1920)
Ehestreik (Ger 1930)
O Mädchen, mein Mädchen, wie lieb' ich Dich! (Ger 1930)
Drei Tage Mittelarrest (Ger 1930)
Komm mit mir zum Rendezvous (Ger 1930) (also co-script)
Kasernenzauber (Ger 1930)
Bockbierfest (Ger 1930)
Der ungetreue Ekkehart (Ger 1931)
Der Schrecken der Garmison (Ger 1931)
Der schönste Mann im Staate (Ger 1931)
Vater geht auf Reisen (Ger 1931)
Die schwebende Jungfrau (Ger 1931)
Meine Cousine aus Warschau (Ger 1931)
Dienst ist Dienst (Ger 1931)
Grock (Ger 1931)
Man bracht kein Geld (Ger 1931)
Keine Feier ohne Meyer (Ger 1931)
Die Herren vom Maxim (Ger 1932)
Annemarie, die Braut der Kompanie (Ger 1932)
Theodor Körner (Ger 1932)
Der Frechdachs (Ger 1932) (with Heinz Hille)
Drei von der Kavallerie (Ger 1932)
Paprika (Ger 1932)
Lumpenkavaliere (Ger 1932)
Gruss und Kuss, Veronika! (Ger 1933)
Die Unschuld vom Lande (Ger 1933)
Roman einer Nacht (Ger 1933)
Das Lied vom Glück (Ger 1933)
Eine Frau wie Du (Ger 1933)

Heimkehr ins Glück (Ger 1933)
Die kalte Mamsell (Ger 1933)
Drei blaue Jungs--ein blondes Mädel (Ger 1933)
Gretel zieht das grosse Los (Ger 1933) (also script)
Schutzenkönig wird der Felix (Ger 1934)
Liebe dumme Mama (Ger 1934)
Fräulein Frau (Ger 1934)
Wenn ein Mädel Hochzeit macht (Ger 1934)
Das Blumenmädchen vom Grand Hotel (Ger 1934)
Der Schrecken vom Heidekrug (Ger 1934)
Meine Frau, die Schutzenkönigin (Ger 1934)
... Heute Abend bei mir (Ger 1934)
Herz ist Trumpf (Ger 1934)
Eine Nacht an der Donau (Ger 1935)
Der Gefangene des Königs (Ger 1935)
Ein falscher Fuffziger (Ger 1935)
Ein ganzer Kerl (Ger 1935)
Die Fahrt in die Legend (Ger 1935)
Der verkannte Lebemann (Ger 1936)
Dahinten in der Heide (Ger 1936)
Engel mit kleinen Fehler (Ger 1936)
Männer vor der Ehe (Ger 1936) (also co-script)
Mädchen für alles (Ger 1937)
Abenteuer in Warschau (Ger 1937)
Eine Nacht mit Hindernissen (Ger 1937)
Wie der Hase läuft (Ger 1937)
Heiraten--aber wen? (Ger 1938)
Steputat & Co. (Ger 1938)
War es der im 3. Stock? (Ger 1938)
Fünf Millionen suchen einen Erben (Ger 1939)
Schwarzfahrt ins Gluck (Ger 1938)
Meine Tante--Deine Tante (Ger 1939)
Drei Vater um Anna (Ger 1939)
Hallo, Janine! (Ger 1939)
Polterabend (Ger 1940)
Hochzeitsnacht (Ger 1941)
Familienanschluss (Ger 1941)
Alles für Gloria (Ger 1941) (also co-script)
Um 9 kommt Harald (Ger 1942)
Leichtes Blut (Ger 1942)
... und die Musik spielt dazu (Ger 1943) (also script)
Das Hochzeitshotel (Ger 1944)
Der Posaunist (Ger 1945) (also co-script)
Beate (Ger 1948) (also script)
Wenn manner schwindeln (Ger 1950) (also co-script)
Das Mädchen aus der Konfektion (Ger 1951) (also co-script)
Der keusche Lebemann (Ger 1952)
Der Onkel aus Amerika (Ger 1952)
Der keusche Josef (Ger 1953)
Das Nachtgespenst (Ger 1953)
Die spanische Fliege (Ger 1955)
Meine Tante--Deine Tante (Ger 1956)
Vater macht Karriere (Ger 1957)

BOIGELOT, JACQUES, b. Aug. 23, 1929, Brussels
Charles Dekeukeleire (Bel TV 1960)
Paix sur les champs (Bel 1970) (also script)

BOISROND, MICHEL, b. Oct. 9, 1921, Châteauneuf-en-Taymerais,
France
Cette sacrée gamine [Mademoiselle Pigalle] (Fr 1955) (also co-
script, co-dialogue)
C'est arrivé à Aden [It Happened in Aden] (Fr 1956) (also co-
script)
Lorsque l'enfant paraît [Blessed Events] (Fr 1956)
Une Parisienne (Fr-It 1957) (also co-script, co-adaptor)
Faibles femmes [Women Are Weak] (Fr 1958) (also co-script)
Les Chemin des écoliers (Fr 1959)
Voulez-vous danser avec moi? [Come Dance with Me] (Fr-It
1959) (also co-script)
La Française et l'amour [Love and the Frenchwoman] (ep "La
virginite") (Fr 1960)
Un Soir sur la plage [Violent Summer] (Fr 1961)
Les Amours célèbres (Fr-It 1961)
Les Parisiennes [Tales of Paris] (Fr-It 1961) (with Marc Allé-
gret, Claude Barma, Jacques Poitrenaud)
Comment réussir en amour? (Fr-It 1962)
Comment trouvez-vous ma soeur? (Fr 1963)
Comment épouser un première ministre? (Fr-It 1964)
Cherchez l'idole [The Chase] (Fr-It 1964)
Atout coeur à Tokyo pour O. S. S. 117 [Terror in Tokyp] (Fr-It
1966)
L'Homme qui valait des millards [Million Dollar Man] (Fr-It
1967) (also co-script)
La Leçon particulière [The Private Lesson] (Fr 1968) (also co-
script)
On est toujours trop bon avec les femmes (Fr 1971) (also
adaptor)
Le Petit Poucet (Fr 1972) (also co-script)
Dis-moi que tu m'aimes (Fr 1974) (also co-script, co-adaptor,
co-dialogue)

BOISSET, YVES, b. 1939, France
Coplan sauve sa peau [The Devil's Garden] (Fr-It 1967) (also
co-script)
Cran d'arrêt (Fr-It 1969) (also co-script)
Un Condé (Fr-It 1970) (also co-script)
Le Cobra/Le Saut de l'ange (Fr 1971) (also co-script)
R. A. S. (Fr-It 1973) (also co-script)

BOLOGNINI, MAURO, b. June 28, 1922, Pistoia, Italy
Ci troviamo in galleria (It 1953)
I cavalieri della regina (It 1955) (also co-script)
Gli innamorati (It 1955) (also co-script)
La vena d'oro (It 1955) (also co-script)
Guardia, guardia scelta, brigadiere e maresciallo (It 1956)
Marisa la civetta (It 1957) (also co-script)

Giovani mariti [Young Husbands] (It 1958) (also co-script)
Arrangiatevi (It 1959)
La notte brava [Night Heat] (It 1959) (also co-script)
I bell' Antonio (It 1960)
La giornata balorda [From a Roman Balcony] (It 1960)
La viaccia [The Love Makers] (It-Fr 1961)
Senilità (It 1961)
Agostino (It 1961) (also actor)
La corruzione (It 1963)
La mia signora (eps "I Miei cara" and "Luciana") (It 1964)
Le bambole [Four Kinds of Love] (ep "Monsignor Cupido") (It
    1965)
I tre volti (ep "Gli amanti celebri") (It 1965)
La donna e una cosa ureravigliosa (It 1966)
Le fate [Sex Quartet] (ep "terzo") (It 1966)
Madamigella di Maupin (It-Sp 1967)
Arabella (It 1967)
L'amore attraverso i secoli (ep "Notti romane") (It 1967)
Le streghe [The Witches] (ep "senso civico") (It 1967)
Capriccio all'italiano (eps "Perche" and "La gelosa") (It 1968)
Un bellissimo novembre (It 1969)
L'assoluto naturale (It 1969)
Metello (It 1969) (also co-script)
Bubû di Montparnasse (It 1969)
Imputazione di omicidio per uno studente (It 1971)
Libera, amore mio (It 1972)
Fatti di gente per bene (It 1974)
Per Le Antioche Scale [Down the Ancient Stairs] (It 1974)

BONNARD, MARIO, b. June 12, 1889, Rome; d. March 22, 1965
    L'altro io (It 1917) (also actor)
    Pupille nell'ombre (It 1917) (also actor)
    Passa la ruina (It 1917) (also story, actor)
    Il rifugio dell'alba (It 1918) (also actor)
    Mentre il pubblico ride (It 1919)
    Germana (It 1919) (also actor)
    Il fauno di marmo (It 1919) (also actor)
    L'amica (It 1920) (also actor)
    Papa Lebonnard (It 1920) (also actor)
    La stretta (It 1920) (also actor)
    Le rouge et le noir (It 1920) (also actor)
    Il milione (It 1920) (also actor)
    La gerla di papa Martin (It 1921)
    La morte piange (It 1921) (also actor)
    Ride e poi ... s'annoia (It 1921) (also actor)
    Il trittico (It 1923) (also actor)
    A morte!, Signor ladro (It 1923) (also actor)
    Il tacchino (It 1923) (also actor)
    I promessi sposi (It 1923)
    La maschera che ride (It 1924) (also actor)
    Teodoro e socio (It 1924)
    La monaca silenziosa [Die schweigende Nonne] (Ger 1925)
    Der goldene Abgrund (Ger 1927)

Mauro Bolognini

Russia (Ger 1937)
Rapa-Nui [Atlantis] (Ger 1928)
Schuss in der Opera [La tragedia dell'Opera] (Ger 1928)
Der Kampf ums Matterhorn [La grande conquista] (Ger 1928)
    (with N. Malasomma)
Das letzte Souper [Fante di cuori] (Ger 1928)
Der Ruf des Nordens [Legione bianca] (Ger 1929) (with N.
    Malasomma)
Der Sohn der Weissen Berge [I cavalieri della montagna] (Ger
    1930)
Die Heiligen drei Brunnen (Ger 1930)
Fra Diavolo (Fr-Ger 1931)
Pas de femmes (Fr 1932)
Tre uomini in frack [Trois hommes en habit] (It-Fr 1932)
Cinque a zero (It 1932)
Il trattato scomparso [Le Masque qui tombe] (It-Fr 1933)

Eve cherche un père (Fr 1933)
Marcia nuziale [La Marche nuptiale] (It-Fr 1934)
Milizia territoriale (It 1935)
Trenta secondi d'amore (It 1936)
L'alberto di Adamo (It 1936)
Il feroce Saladino (It 1937)
Il conte di Brechard (It 1938)
Jeanne Doré (It 1938)
Io, suo padre (It 1939)
Papa per una notte (It 1939)
Frenesia (It 1939)
Il ponte dei sospiri (It 1940)
La gerla di Papa Martin (It 1940)
La fanciulla di Portici (It 1940)
L'uomo del romanza (It 1940)
Marco Visconti (It 1940)
Il re si diverte (It 1941)
Rossini (It 1942)
Avanti c'è posto (It 1942)
Campo del Fiori (It 1943)
Che distinta famiglia (It 1943)
Il ratto delle Sabine (It 1945)
Addio mia bella Napoli (It 1946)
La città dolente (It 1949)
Margherita da Cortono (It 1950)
Stasera sciopero (It 1951)
Il voto (It 1952)
I figli non si vendono (It 1952)
L'ultima sentenza (It 1952)
Frine, cortigiana d'Oriente (It 1953)
Tormento del passato (It 1954)
Tradita (It 1955)
Hanno rubato un tram (It 1955)
La ladra (It 1956)
Mi permette, babbo? (It 1956)
Afrodite, dea dell'amore (It 1958)
Gli ultimi giorni di Pompei [Last Days of Pompeii] (It 1959)
Gastone (It 1960)
I masnadieri (It 1962)

BOORMAN, JOHN, b. Jan. 18, 1933, Shepperton, Middlesex, England
Catch Us If You Can [Having a Wild Weekend] (WPD-AA 1965)
Point Blank (MGM 1967)
Hell in the Pacific (Cin 1968)
Leo the Last (UA 1970)† [co-production company] (also co-script)
Deliverance (WB 1972) (also producer)
Zardoz (20th-Rank 1974)† (also producer, script)

BOROWCZYK, WALERIAN, b. 1923, Kwilcz, Poland
Theatre de Monsieur et Madame Kabal (Fr 1967) (also story, script designer, animator, sound effects)

John Boorman

Goto, l'île d'amour (Fr 1968) (also script, co-dialogue)
Blanche (Fr 1971) (also script, co-art director, editor)
Contes immoraux [Immoral Tales] (Fr 1973) (also script, art
   director, editor)

BOULTING, JOHN, b. Nov. 21, 1913, Bay, Buckinghamshire, Eng-
   land
Journey Together (RKO 1945) (also producer, script)
Brighton Rock [Young Scarface] (Pathé 1947)†
Seven Days to Noon (BL 1950)†
The Magic Box (BL 1951)
Seagulls over Sorrento [Crest of the Wave] (MGM Br 1954) (also
   co-producer) (with Roy Boulting)
Private's Progress (BL 1956)† (also co-script)

Lucky Jim (BL 1957)†
I'm All Right Jack (BL 1959)† (also co-script)
Suspect [The Risk] (BL 1960)† (also co-producer, co-script)
    (with Roy Boulting)
Heavens Above! (BL-Romulus 1963)† (also co-script)
Rotten to the Core (BL 1965)† [co-production company]

John Boulting (left) with Peter Sellers on the set of Heavens Above!
(1963).

BOULTING, ROY, b. Nov. 21, 1913, Bray, Buckinghamshire, Eng-
    land
    Trunk Crime [Design for Murder] (Angelo 1939)†
    Inquest (GN 1939)†
    Pastor Hall (GN 1940)†
    Thunder Rock (MGM 1942)† (also editor)
    Desert Victory (AFU 1943) (also supervising editor)
    Tunisian Victory (AFU 1943) (with Frank Capra)
    Burma Victory (AFU 1945) (also supervising editor, co-com-
        mentary)
    Fame Is the Spur (GFD 1947)†
    The Guinea Pig [The Outsider] (Pathé 1948)† (also co-script)
    High Treason (GFD 1951) (also co-story, co-script)
    Single-Handed [Sailor of the King] (20th 1953)
    Seagulls over Sorrento [Crest of the Wave] (MGM Br 1954) (also
        co-producer, co-script) (with John Boulting)

Josephine and Men (BL 1955)† (also co-script, co-adaptor)
Run for the Sun (UA 1956) (also co-script)
Brothers in Law (BL 1957)† (also co-script)
Happy Is the Bride (BL 1958) (also co-script)
Carlton-Browne of the F. O. [Man in a Cocked Hat] (BL 1959)
    (with Jeffrey Dell)† (also co-story, co-script)
A French Mistress (BL 1960)† (also co-script, lyrics)
Suspect [The Risk] (BL 1960)† (also co-script, co-dialogue)
    (with John Boulting)
The Family Way (BL 1966) (also co-adaptor)
Twisted Nerve (BL 1968)† (also co-script)
There's A Girl in My Soup (Col 1970)†
Mr. Forbush and the Penguins (BL 1971) (uncredited with Al
    Viola)
Soft Beds, Hard Battles (Col 1973)† (also co-script, co-music)

BOURGUIGNON, SERGE, b. Sept. 3, 1928, Maignelay (Oise),
    France
Sikkim, terre secrète (Fr 1956)
Les Dimanches de Ville d'Avray [Sundays and Cybele] (Fr 1962)
The Reward [USA] (20th 1965) (also co-script)
A Coeur joie [Two Weeks in September] (Fr-GB 1967) (also co-
    script)
The Picasso Summer [USA] (WB 1970) [begun as TV feature in
    1967 by Bourguignon but finished by and credited to Robert
    Sallin]

BOX, MURIEL, b. 1905, New Malden, Surrey, England
The Happy Family [Mr. Lord Says No] (Apex 1952) (also co-
    script)
Street Corner [Both Sides of the Law] (GFD 1953) (also co-
    script)
To Dorothy a Son [Cash on Delivery] (IFD 1954)
The Beachcomber (GFD 1954)
Simon and Laura (RFD 1955)
Eyewitness (RFD 1955)
The Passionate Stranger [A Novel Affair] (BL 1957) (also co-
    script)
The Truth About Women (BL 1958) (also co-script)
Subway in the Sky (Britannia 1959)
This Other Eden (RFI 1959)
Too Young to Love (RFD 1960) (also co-script)
The Piper's Tune (CFF 1962)
Rattle of a Simple Man (WPD 1964)

BRAGAGLIA, CARLO LUDOVICO, b. July 8, 1894, Frosinone, Italy
La borsa o la vita (It 1932) (also co-script)
Non son gelosa (It 1932)
Un cattivo soggetto (It 1933)
Quelle vecchia canaglia (It 1934)
Frutto acerbo (It 1934)
Amore (It 1935)
La fossa degli angeli (It 1936)

Animali pazzi (It 1939)
Belle o brutte si sposan tutte (It 1939)
L'amore si fa così (It 1939)
Pazza di gioia (It 1940) (also story, script)
Un mare di guai (It 1940) (also story, script) (with Amleto
  Pallermi)
Una famiglia impossibile (It 1940)
Il prigioniero di Santa Cruz (It 1940)
La forza bruta (It 1941)   1903783
Alessandro, sei grande! (It 1941)
Barbablù (It 1941)
Due cuori sotto sequestro (It 1941) (also script)
L'allegro fantasma (It 1941) (only story)
La scuola dei timidi (It 1942)
Violette nei capelli (It 1942) (also script)
Se io fossi onesto (It 1942) (also script)
La guardia del corpo (It 1942) (also script)
Non ti pago! (It 1942)
Casanova farebbe così (It 1942)
Fuga a due voci (It 1943)
Il fidanzato di mia moglie (It 1943)
Non sono superstizioso, ma ... (It 1943)
Tutta la vita in ventiquattr'oe (It 1943)
La vita è bella (It 1944) (also script)
Pronto, chi parla? (It 1945)
Lo sbaglio di essere vivo (It 1945)
Torna a Sorrento (It 1946)
Albergo Luna, camera 34 (It 1947)
L'altra (It 1947)
La primula bianca (It 1947)
Totò le Mokò (It 1949)
Il falco rosso (It 1950)
Figaro qua, Figaro là (It 1950)
47 morto che parla (It 1950)
Le sei mogli di Barbablù (It 1950)
Totò cerca moglie (It 1950)
L'eroe sono io (It 1951)
Una bruna indiavolata (It 1953)
Don Lorenzo (It 1953)
A fil di spada (It 1953)
Il segreto delle tre punte [Secret of 3 Points] (It 1953)
Orient Express (It Ger Fr 54)
La cortigiana di Babilonia [Queen of Babylon] (It 1955)
Il falco d'oro (It 1956)
Gerusalemme liberata [Mighty Crusader] (It 1957)
Lazzarella (It 1957)
Caporale di giornata (It 1958)
E permesso maresciallo? (It 1958)
Io, mammeta e tu (It 1958)
Annibale [Hannibal] (It 1959) (uncredited, with Edgar G. Ulmer)
La cameriere (It 1959)
La spada e la croce (It 1959)
Gli amori di Ercole [The Loves of Hercules] (It 1960)

Le vergini di Roma [The Warrior Women] (It 1960) (uncredited,
   with Vittorio Cottafavi)
Pastasciutta nel deserto [Spaghetti in the Desert] (It 1960)
I quattro monaci [The Four Monks] (It 1962)
Ursus nella valle dei leoni [Ursus in the Valley of the Lions]
   (It 1962)
I quattro moschettieri [The Four Musketeers] (It 1963)

BRASS, TINTO (Giovanni Brass), b. March 26, 1933, Milan
   Chi lavora è perduto [In capo al mondo] (It 1963) (also story,
      editor)
   Il disco volante (It 1964)
   La mia signora (eps "L'uccellino," "I miei cari") (It 1964)
   Ça ira [Il fiume della rivolta] (It 1965)
   Yankee (It 1966)
   Col cuore in gola (It 1967) (also story, co-script, editor)
   Nero su bianco [Black on White] (It 1969)
   L'urlo (It 1969)
   Dropout (It 1970)
   La vacanza (It 1971) (also story, co-script, editor)

BRAUN, HARALD, b. 1901, Berlin; d. April 26, 1960
   Zwischen Himmel und Erde (Ger 1942) (also co-script)
   Hab' mich lieb (Ger 1942)
   Träumerei (Ger 1944) (also co-script)
   Nora (Ger 1944) (also co-script)
   Der stumme Gast (Ger 1945) (also co-script)
   Zwischen Gestern und Morgen (Ger 1947) (also co-script)
   Das verlorene Gesicht (Ger 1947) (also co-script)
   Nachtwache (Ger 1949) (also co-script)
   Der Mann der zweimal leben wollte (Ger 1950) (only co-script)
   Der fallende Stern (Ger 1950) (also co-script)
   Herz der Welt (Ger 1951) (also co-script)
   Vater braucht eine Frau (Ger 1952)
   Solange Du da bist (Ger 1953)
   Königliche Hoheit (Ger 1953)
   Der letzte Sommer (Ger 1954) (also co-script)
   Der letzte Mann (Ger 1955)
   Regine (Ger 1955)
   Herrscher ohne Krone (Ger 1957)
   Der glaserne Turm [The Glass Tower] (Ger 1957) (also co-
      script)
   Buddenbrooks (only co-script)
   Die Botschafterin (only co-script)

BREL, JACQUES, b. April 8, 1929, Brussels
   [a photograph of Brel as an actor appears near the CARNE
      entry]
   Franz (Bel 1972) (also co-script)
   Le Far-West (Bel 1973) (also co-script)

BRESSON, ROBERT, b. Sept. 25, 1907, Bromont-Lamontie (Puy-de-Dôme), France
Les Affaires publiques (Fr 1934) (also script, co-camera, editor)
Les Anges du péché (Fr 1943) (also co-script)
Les Dames du Bois de Boulogne (Fr 1945) (also script, adaptor)
Journal d'un curé de campagne (Fr 195) (also script, adaptor, dialogue)
Un Condamné à mort s'est échappé (Fr 1956) (also script, adaptor, dialogue)
Pickpocket (Fr 1959) (also story, script, adaptor, dialogue)
Procès de Jeanne d'arc (Fr 1962) (also script, adaptor, dialogue)
Au hasard Balthazar (Fr 1966) (also story, script, dialogue, art director)
Mouchette (Fr 1967) (also script, adaptor, dialogue, actor)
Une Femme douce [A Gentle Creature] (Fr 1969) (also script, adaptor, dialogue)
Quatre nuits d'un rêveur [Four Nights of a Dreamer] (Fr-It 1971) (also script, adaptor, dialogue)
Lancelot-du-Lac (Fr-It 1974) (also script, adaptor, dialogue)

BRIDGES, ALAN, b. Sept. 28, 1927, London
Act of Murder (WPD-AA 1964)
Invasion (WPD-AA 1966)
The Hireling (Col 1973)

BRIGNONE, GUIDO, b. Dec. 6, 1887, Milan; d. 1959
Odette (It 1915)
Le perle di Cleopatra (It 1920)
I due sergenti (It 1922)
Le sorprese del divorzio (It 1923)
Saetta, impara a vivere! (It 1924)
Maciste imperatore (It 1924)
Maciste nella gabbia dei leoni (It 1926)
Maciste all'inferno (It 1926)
Vite ... embrassez-moi! (Fr 1928)
Das Erlebnis einer Nacht (Ger 1929)
Corte d'assise (It 1930)
Rubacuori (It 1931)
Teresa Confalonieri (It 1934)
Passaporto rosso (It 1935)
Ginevra degli Almieri (It 1935)
Vivere (It 1936)
Cantatae con me (It 1936)
Mamma (It 1941)
Maria Malibran (It 1942)
Il romanzo di un giovane povere (It 1942)
Il fiore sotti gli occhi (It 1943)
Canto, ma sottovoce (It 1946)
Monaca santa (It 1948)
La sepolta viva (It 1949)

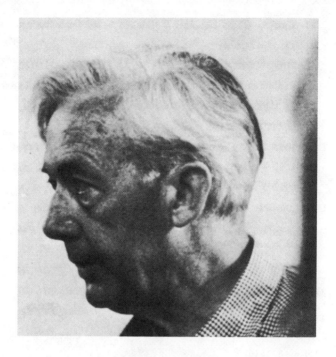

Robert Bresson

Santo disonore (It 1949)
Il barone Carlo Mazza (It 1949)
Il bacio di una morta (It 1949)
Il nido di Falasco (It 1950)
Il conte di Sant-Elmo (It 1951)
Core'ngrato (It 1951)
Bufere (It 1953)
Processo contro ignoti (It 1953)
Inganno (It 1953)
Noi peccatori (It 1953)
Ivan, il figlio del diavolo bianco (It 1954)
Quando tramonta il sole (It 1956)
Papà Pacifico (It 1956)
Il vetturale del Moncenisio (It 1956)
Le schiave di Cartagine (It 1956)
Nel segno di Roma (It 1959)

BRISMEE, JEAN, b. Aug. 20, 1926, Pipaix, Belgium
Au service du diable (Bel 1971)
Approche des difficultés scolaires (Bel 1974)

BROCA, PHILIPPE DE, b. March 15, 1933, Paris
  Les Jeux de l'amour [Playing at Love] (Fr 1960) (also co-
    script)
  Le Farceur [The Joker] (Fr 1960) (also co-script)
  L'Amant de cinq jours [The Five-Day Lover] (Fr-It 1961) (also
    co-script)
  Les Sept Péchés capitaux [Seven Capital Sins] (ep "La gour-
    mandise") (Fr-It 1961)
  Cartouche [Swords of Blood] (Fr-It 1961) (co-script, also actor)
  Les Veinards (ep "La vedette") (Fr 1962) (also co-script)
  L'Homme de Rio [That Man from Rio] (Fr-It 1963) (also co-
    script)
  Un Monsieur de compagnie [Male Companion] (Fr-It 1964) (also
    co-adaptor)
  Les Tribulations d'un Chinois en Chine [Up to His Ears] (Fr-It
    1965) (also co-script)
  Le Roi de coeur [King of Hearts] (Fr-It 1966) (also co-script)
  Le Plus Vieux Métier du monde [The Oldest Profession] (ep
    "Mademoiselle Mimi") (Fr-It 1967)
  Le Diable par la queue (Fr-It 1968)†
  Les Caprices de Marie [Give Her the Moon] (Fr-It 1969) (also
    co-script)
  La Poudre d'escampette (Fr 1971) (also co-script)
  Chère Louise [Louise] (Fr-It 1972)
  Le Magnifique [How to Destroy the Reputation of the Greatest
    Secret Agent in the World] (Fr-It 1973) (also actor)

BROOK, PETER, b. March 21, 1925, London
  The Beggar's Opera (BL 1953)
  Moderato cantabile [Seven Days, Seven Nights] (Fr) (Raoul J.
    Levy-Mondian 1961)
  Lord of the Flies (BL 1963)
  The Persecution and Assassination of Jean-Paul Marat as Per-
    formed by the Inmates of the Asylum of Charenton under the
    Direction of the Marquis de Sade [Marat/Sade] (UA 1966)
  Tell Me Lies (London Continental 1968) (also co-producer,
    script)
  King Lear (GB-Dan) (Col 1971)

BROWNLOW, KEVIN, b. 1938, Crowborough, Sussex, England
  It Happened Here (UA 1963) (also co-producer, story, co-
    script, co-camera)
  Abel Gance--The Charm of Dynamite (Hunter 1968)

BRUNEL, ADRIAN, b. 1892, Brighton, Sussex, England; d. Feb.
    18, 1958
  The Cost of a Kiss (Mirror 1917)
  The Man without Desire (Novello-Atlas 1923) (also actor)
  Lovers in Araby (Novello-Atlas 1924) (also co-script, actor)
  Blighty (W & F 1927)
  The Vortex (W & F 1927)
  The Constant Nymph (W & F 1928)
  A Light Woman (W & F 1928) (also co-script)

The Crooked Billet (W & F 1928)
Elstree Calling (Wardour 1930) (also co-script) (with Andre
  Charlot, Jack Hulbert, Alfred Hitchcock, Paul Murray)
Taxi to Paradise (Fox Br 1933) (also co-script)
I'm an Explosive (Fox Br 1933) (also script)
Follow the Lady (Fox Br 1933) (also script)
Little Napoleon (Fox Br 1933) (also script)
Two Wives for Henry (Fox Br 1933) (also script)
The Laughter of Fools (Fox Br 1933) (also script)
Important People (MGM Br 1934)
Badger's Green (B & D-Par Br 1934)
Sabotage [When London Sleeps] (Reunion 1934)
Variety (Butcher 1935) (also co-script)
The City of Beautiful Nonsense (Butcher 1935)
Cross Currents (B & D-Par Br 1935) (also co-script)
While Parents Sleep (UA 1935)
Vanity (Col Br 1935)
The Invader [An Old Spanish Custom] (MGM Br 1936)
Prison Breaker (Col Br 1936)
Love at Sea (B & D-Par Br 1936)
Rebel Son (UA 1939) (uncredited, with Albert De Courville)
The Lion Has Wings (UA 1939) (also co-script) (with Brian
  Desmond Hurst, Michael Powell)
The Girl Who Forgot (Butcher 1939)

BRUSSE, KEES, b. Feb. 26, 1925, Rotterdam
Kermis in de Regen (Dut 1962)
Mensen van Morgen (Dut 1964)
Een Stukje Noord-Holland (Dut 1974)

BRUYNINCKX, JEF, b. Aug. 13, 1919, Belgium
't Is Wreed in der Wereld (Bel 1953) (with Joris Diels)
De Roof van Hop-Marianneke (Bel 1954)
De Klucht van de Brave Moordenaar (Bel 1955) (also co-script)
Vuur, Liefde en Vitamine (Bel 1956)
Wat Doen We met de Liefde? (Be 1957)
Het Geluk Komt Morgen (Bel 1958)
Voor Elk Wat Wils (Be 1958)
Vrijgezel met 40 Kinderen (Bel 1958)

BUCHET, JEAN MARIE, b. Feb. 24, 1938, Jemappes, Belgium
La Fugue de Suzanne (Bel 1973)

BUCHOWETSKI (Buchowetzki), DIMITRI, b. 1895, Russia, d. 1932
Anita Jo (Ger 1919)
Die letzte Stunde (Ger 1920)
Danton [All for a Woman] (Ger 1920)
Sappho [Mad Love] (Ger 1921) (also script)
Der Galiläer (Ger 1921)
Othello [The Moor] (Ger 1921) (also script)
Peter der Grosse (Ger 1922)
Das Laster des Spiels (Ger 1923)
Das Karussel des Lebens (Ger 1923) (also co-script)

Man (USA) (Par 1924) (also story)
Lily of the Dust (USA) (Par 1924)
The Swan (USA) (Par 1925) (also script)
Graustark (USA) (FN 1925)
The Crown of Lies (USA) (Par 1926)
The Midnight Sun (USA) (Univ-Jewel 1926)
Valencia (USA) (MGM 1926) (also co-story)
Love (USA) (MGM 1927) (replaced by Edmund Goulding)
Weib im Dschungel (USA) [Ger version of The Letter] (Par 1930)
Le Réquisitoire (USA) [Fr version of Manslaughter] (Par 1930)
Die Nacht der Entscheindung (USA) [Ger version of The Virtuous Sin] (Par 1931)
Stamboul (Par Br 1931)

BUÑUEL, LUIS, b. Feb. 22, 1900, Calanda, Spain
Un Chien andalou (Fr 1928) (also producer, co-story, co-script, editor, actor)
L'Age d'or (Fr 1930) (also co-story, co-script, music editor, editor)
Las Hurdes (Sp 1932) (also story, co-commentary, editor)
Don Quintin el amargo (Sp 1935) (also executive producer, production supervisor) (uncredited with Luis Marquina)
La hija de Juan Simón (Sp 1935) (also executive producer, production supervisor, actor) (uncredited with José Luis Sáenz de Heredia)
Quién me quiere a mi? (Sp 1936) (also executive producer, production supervisor) (uncredited with José Luis Sáenz de Heredia)
Centinela alerta! (Sp 1936) (executive producer, production supervisor, actor) (uncredited with Jean Grémillon)
Gran Casino [Tampico/En el viejo Tampico] (Mex 1946)
El gran calavera (Mex 1949)
Los olvidados (Mex 1950) (also co-script, co-story)
Susana [Demonio y carne] (Mex 1950)
La hija del engaño [Don Quintin el amargo] (Mex 1951)
Una mujer sin amor [Destino de una mujer/Cuando los hijos nos juzgan] (Mex 1951)
Subida el cielo (Mex 1951) (also co-adaptor)
El bruto [The Brute] (Mex 1952) (also co-story, co-script)
Las aventuras de Robinson Crusoe [The Adventures of Robinson Crusoe/Robinson Crusoe] (Mex 1952) (also co-script, dialogue)
El (Mex 1952) (also co-script)
Abismos de pasión/Cumbres borrascosas (Mex 1953) (also co-script)
La ilusión viaja en tranvía (Mex 1953) (also co-script)
El río y la muerte (Mex 1954) (also co-script)
Ensayo de un crimen [The Criminal Life of Archibaldo de la Cruz] (Mex 1955) (also co-script)
Cela s'appelle l'aurore (Fr-It 1955) (also co-adaptor, co-script)
La Mort en ce jardin [La muerte en este jardin] (Fr-Mex 1956) (also co-adaptor, co-script)
Nazarin (Mex 1958) (also co-script)

La Fièvre monte à El Paso [Los ambiciosos/Republic of Sin]
(Fr-Mex 1959) (also co-adaptor, co-script)
La joven [The Young One] (Mex 1960) (also co-script)
Viridiana (Sp-Mex 1961) (also story, co-script)
El angel exterminador [The Exterminating Angel] (Mex 1962)
(also script, co-adaptor)
Le Journal d'une femme de chambre [Diary of a Chambermaid]
(Fr-It 1963) (also co-script, co-adaptor, co-dialogue)
Simón del desierto (Mex 1965) (also story, co-script)
Belle de jour (Fr-It 1967) (also actor, co-adaptor, co-dialogue,
co-script)
La Voie lactée (Fr-It 1968) (also story, co-adaptor, co-dia-
logue, co-script, musical soundtrack)
Tristana (Sp 1970) (also co-script)
Le Charme discret de la bourgeoisie [The Discreet Charm of
the Bourgeoisie] (Fr 1972) (also co-story, co-adaptor, co-
dialogue, co-script, music soundtrack)
Le Fantôme de la liberté (Fr 1974) (also co-story, co-script,
co-dialogue)

BUYENS, FRANS, b. Feb. 2, 1924, Belgium
Vechten voor Onze Rechten (Bel 1962)
August Vermeylen (Bel 1962)
Deutschland--Endstation Ost (Bel 1964)
Meer of Minder Mens (Bel 1967) (also script)
Frans Masereel--Ik Houd van Zwart en Wit (Bel 1969)
Eens Mens Genaamd Paul Ghysbrecht (Bel TV 1971)
Een Mens Genaamd Rik Poot (Bel TV 1971)
Ieder van Ons (Bel 1971) (also script, narrator)
Breendonck: Open dialoog 70 (Bel 1971)
Een Mens Genaamd Ernest Mandel (Bel 1972)
Een Mens Genaamd Hubert Buntinx (Bel TV 1972)
Vrouw en Arbeid (Bel TV 1972)
Een Mens Genaamd Walter Beckers (Bel TV 1972)
In Liefde Bloiende (Bel 1972)
Het Dwaallicht (Bel 1973) (also script)
Waar de Vogeltjes Hoesten (Bel 1974) (also script)
Wonder Shop (Bel 1974)

CALIF, HENRI, b. Jul. 27, 1910, Philipoli, Bulgaria
L'Extravagante mission (Fr 1945)
Jericho (Fr 1945)
Les Chouans (Fr 1946)
La Maison sous la mer (Fr 1946)
Les Eaux troubles (Fr 1948)
Bagarres [The Wench] (Fr 1948)
La Souricière (Fr 1949)
Ombres et lumière (Fr 1950)
La Passante (Fr 1950)
Le Carrefour des passions [Gli nomini sono nemici] (Fr-It 1951)
(completed by Ettore Grannini)
Les Amours finissient a l'aube (Fr 1952)
Le Secret d'Helene Mariwron (Fr-It 1953)

Les Violets (Fr 1953)
L'Heure de la vérité (Fr 1964)
Féminin-Féminin (Fr 1971)

CALSTER, OG (A. M. van Calster), b. Belgium
J'ai gagné un million (Bel 1935)
Le Roi soldat (Bel 1937)

CAMERINI, MARIO, b. Feb. 6, 1895, Rome
Jolly, clown da circo (It 1923) (also co-script)
La casa dei pulcini (It 1924) (also story)
Voglia tradire mi marito (It 1925)
Maciste contro lo sceicco (It 1925) (also story)
Saetta, principe per un giorno (It 1925)
Kiff Tebbi (It 1927)
Rotaie (It 1929)
La riva dei bruit (It 1930)
Figaro e la sua gran giornata (It 1931)
L'ultima avventura (It 1932) (also co-script)
Gli uomini, che mascalzoni! (It 1932) (also co-story, co-script)
T'amero sempre (It 1933) (also story)
Cento di questi giorni (It 1933) (also story) (with Augusto Camerini)
Giallo (It 1933)
Come le foglie (It 1934) (also co-script)
Il cappello a tre punte [Three-Cornered Hat] (It 1934)
Daro un milione (It 1935) (also co-script)
Ma non è una cosa seria (It 1936)
Il grande appello (It 1936) (also story, co-script)
Der Mann, der Nicht nein sagen kann (Ger version of Ma non
  è una cosa seria) (It 1937)
Il signor Max (It 1937) (also co-script)
Batticuore (It 1938) (also co-script)
I grandi magazzini (It 1939) (also co-story, co-script)
Il documento (It 1939) (also co-script, co-editor)
Centomila dollari (It 1940) (also co-script)
Una romantica avventura (It 1940) (also co-script)
I promessi sposi (It 1941) (also co-script)
Una storia d'amore (It 1942) (also co-story, co-script)
T'amero sempre (It 1943) (also story, co-script)
Due lèttere anonime (It 1945) (also co-script)
L'angelo è il diavolo (It 1946) (also co-script)
La figlia del capitano [The Captain's Daughter] (It 1947) (also
  co-script)
Molti sogni per le strade (It 1948) (also co-script)
Il brigante musolino [The Fugitive] (It 1950) (also co-script)
Due moglie sono troppe [Honeymoon Deferred] (It-GB 1951)
  (also co-script)
Moglie per una notte (It 1952)
Gli eroi della domenica (It 1952) (also co-story, co-script)
Ulisse [Ulysses] (It 1954)
La bella mugnaia [The Miller's Wife] (It 1955) (also co-script)
Suor letizia [When Angeles Don't Fly] (It 1956) (also co-script)

Vacanze a Ischia (It 1957) (also co-script)
Primo amore (It 1958) (also co-story, co-script)
Via Margutta [Run with the Devil] (It-Fr 1959) (also story, co-script)
Crimen [Killing at Monte Carlo] (It 1960)
I briganti italiani [Seduction of the South] (It 1961) (also co-script)
Kali-Yug, la dea della vendetta (It 1963)
Il mistero del tempio indiano (It 1964)
Delitto quasi perfetto (It 1966)

CAMPOGALLIANI, CARLO, b. October 10, 1885, Modena, Italy
Il cortile (It 1930)
Medico per forza (It 1931)
La lanterna del diàvolo (It 1931)
Stadio (It 1934)
I quattro moschettieri (It 1936)
Montevergine (It 1939)
La notte della beffe (It 1940)
Cuori nella tormenta (It 1941)
Il cavaliere di Kruja (It 1941)
Il bravo di Venezia (It 1941)
Perdizione (It 1942)
Musica proibita (It 1942)
Treno crociato (It 1943)
Silenzio, si gira! (It 1943)
L'innocente Casimiro (It 1945)
La gondola del diavolo (It 1946)
La mano della mort (It 1949)
Bellezze in bicicletta (It 1951)
La figlia del mendicante (It 1951)
Bellezze in motoscooter (It 1953)
La canzone del cuore (It 1955)
Foglio di via (It 1955)
L'orfana del ghetto (It 1955)
Torna, piccina mia! (It 1955)
L'angelo delle Alpi (It 1957)
Ascoltami (It 1957)
Mamma sconosciuta (It 1957)
Serenatella, sciué, sciué (It 1957)
Capitan fuoco (It 1959)
Il terrore dei barbari [Goliath and the Barbarians] (It 1959)
Fontana di Trevi (It 1959)
Maciste nella valle dei re [Son of Samson] (It 1960)
Ursus, Alboino e Rosmunda [Sword of the Conqueror] (It 1961)
Il ponte dei sospiri (It 1964) (only script)

CAMUS, MARCEL, b. April 21, 1912, Chappes, France
Renaissance du Havre (Fr 1948) (also co-script)
Mort en fraude [Fugitive in Saigon] (Fr 1957) (also co-script)
Orfeu negro [Black Orpheus] (Fr-It-Brazil 1958) (also co-adaptor, co-dialogue)
Os Bandeirantes (Fr-It 1960) (also script, co-adaptor,

co-dialogue)
L'Oiseau de paradis [Dragon Sky] (Fr-It 1962) (also co-adaptor, co-dialogue)
Le Chant du monde (Fr 1965) (also script)
Vivre la nuit (Fr-It 1968) (also co-script)
Le Mur de l'Atlantique (Fr-It 1970) (also co-adaptor, co-dialogue)
Un Eté sauvage (Fr-It 1970) (also co-script)

CAMUS, MARIO, b. 1935, Santander, Spain
Los Farsantes (Sp 1963)
Young Sanchez (Sp 1963)
Muere una mujer (Sp 1964)
La visita que no toco el timbre (Sp 1965)
Con el viento solano (Sp 1965)
Cuando tu no estas (Sp 1966)
Volver a vivir (Sp 1966)
Al ponerse el sol (Sp 1967)
Digan lo que digan (Sp 1967)
Esa Mujer (Sp 1969)
La colera del viento (Sp-It 1971) (also co-script)

CAPITANI, GIORGIO, b. Italy
Delirio (It 1954) (with co-director)
Il piccolo vetraio (It 1955)
Piscatore è Pusilleco (It 1955)
La trovatella di Milano (It 1956)
Teseo contro il Minotauro (It 1962) (second unit dir.)
L'affondamento della valiant (It 1962)
Ercole, Sansone, Maciste e Ursus: gli invincibili (It 1963)
Che notte, ragazzi! (It-Sp 1966)
La notte è fatta per ... rubare (It 1966)
Ognuno per se (It 1968)
L'arcangelo (It 1969)

CAPUANO, LUIGI (a. k. a. Lewis King), b. July 13, 1904, Naples, Italy
Legge di sangue (It 1948)
Rondini in volo (It 1950)
La strada finisce sul fiume [Stormbound] (It 1950)
La rossa (It 1951)
Vertigine d'amore (It 1951)
Condannatelo (It 1953)
Ergastolo (It 1953)
Gli innocenti pagano (It 1953)
I misteri della giungla nera (It 1953)
Ballata tragica (It 1955)
Cuore di mamma (It 1955)
Luna nuova (It 1955)
Suor Maria (It 1955)
Maruzzella (It 1956)
Scapricciatiello (It 1956)
Serenata a Maria (It 1957)

Carosello di canzoni (It 1958)
Sorrisi e canzoni (It 1958)
Amaramente (It 1959)
Il conte di Matera (It 1959)
Il mondo dei miracoli (It 1959)
Onore e sangue (It 1960)
Il terrore della maschera rossa (It 1960)
Una spada nell'ombra (It 1961)
La vendetta di Ursus (It 1961)
Drakut il vendicatore (It 1962)
Zorro alla corte di Spagna (It 1962)
La tigre dei sette mari (It 1963)
Il boia di Venezia (It 1964)
Il leone di San Marco (It 1964)
Sandokan alla riscossa [Sandokan Fights Back] (It 1964)
L'avventuriero della Tortuga (It-Sp 65)
Sandokan contro il leopardo di Sarawak (It 1965)
Il magnifico texano (It 1967)
Perry Grant, agente di ferro (It 1967)
Un corpo caldo per l'inferno (It 1969) (only co-story)
Sangue chiama sangue (It 1969)

CARDIFF, JACK, b. Sept. 18, 1914, Yarmouth
Intent to Kill (20th 1958)
Beyond This Place [The Web of Evidence] (AA 1959)
Scent of Mystery (Todd Enterprises 1960)
Sons and Lovers (20th Br 1960)
My Geisha (USA) (Par 1962)
The Lion (20th Br 1962)
The Long Ships (Col 1964)
Young Cassidy (MGM Br 1965) (replaced ill John Ford)
The Liquidator (MGM Br 1966)
The Mercenaries [Dark of the Sun] (MGM Br 1968)
Girl on a Motorcycle (BL 1968) (also adaptor)
Scalawag (USA) (Par 1972) (also camera) (with Kirk Douglas)
The Mutations (USA) (Col 1973)
Penny Gold (RFD 1973)

CARMINEO, GIULIANO (a. k. a. Anthony Ascott)
Panic Button ... operazione fisco [Panic Button] (It-US 1962)
Joe ... cercati un posto per morire (It 1968)
Il momento di uccidere (It-Ger 1968)
Sono Sartana, il vostro becchino (It 1969)
Buon funerale, amicos! ... page Sartana (It 1970)
Una nuvola di polvere ... un grido di morte ... arriva Sartana
    (It-Sp 1971)
Gli fumavano le Colt ... lo chiamavano Camposanto (It 1971)
Lo chiamavano Spirito Santo (It-Sp 1971)
Testa t'ammazzo, croce ... sei morto ... mi chiamano Alle-
    luja (It 1971)
Fuori uno, sotto un altro, arriva "Il Passatore" (It-Sp 1972)

Jack Cardiff in 1951 (as lighting cameraman).

CARNE, MARCEL, b. Aug. 18, 1909, Paris
Jenny (Fr 1936)
Drôle de drame (Fr 1937)
Le Quai des brumes (Fr 1938)
Hôtel du Nord (Fr 1939) (also co-adaptor)
Le Jour se lève (Fr 1939)
Les Visiteurs du soir (Fr 1942)
Les Enfants du paradis [Children of Paradise] (Fr 1944-45) (also co-script)
Les Portes de la nuit (Fr 1946) (also co-script)
La Fleur de l'âge [unfinished] (Fr 1947)
La Marie du port (Fr 1949) (also co-script)
Juliette ou la clef des songes (Fr 1951) (also co-script) (begun in 1942)
Thérèse Raquin [The Adulteress] (Fr-It 1953) (also co-script)
L'Air de Paris (Fr-It 1954) (also co-script)
Le Pays d'où je viens (Fr 1956) (also co-adaptor)
Les Tricheurs (Fr 1958) (also co-script)

Terrain vague (Fr 1960) (also co-adaptor, co-dialogue)
Du mouron pour les petits oiseaux (Fr-It 1963) (also co-adaptor)
Trois chambres à Manhattan [Three Rooms in Manhattan] (Fr
   1965) (also co-adaptor)
Les Jeunes Loups [The Young Wolves] (Fr 1968) (also co-
   script)
Les Assassins de l'ordre (Fr 1971) (also co-adaptor)
La Merveilleuse Visite (Fr 1974) (also co-script)

Marcel Carné (right) with actor Jacques Brel on the set of Les Assassins de l'ordre (1971).

CARRERAS, MICHAEL
   The Steel Bayonet (UA 1957) (also producer)
   Visa to Canton [Passport to China] (Col Br 1960) (also pro-
      ducer)
   Maniac (Col Br 1962)
   The Savage Guns (Capricorn-MGM Br 1962) (also co-producer)
   What a Crazy World (WPD 1963) (also producer, co-script)
   The Curse of the Mummy's Tomb (Col Br 1964) (also producer)
   Slave Girls [Prehistoric Women] (WPD 1966) (also producer,
      script)
   The Lost Continent (WPD 1968) (also co-producer)
   Blood From the Mummy's Tomb (MGM-EMI 1971) (completed
      film after death of Seth Holt)

CARSTAIRS, JOHN PADDY, b. 1910, London; d. Dec. 12, 1970
    Paris Plane (MGM Br 1933)
    Holiday's End (B & D-Par Br 1937)
    Double Exposures (Par Br 1937)
    Night Ride (B & D-Par Br 1937)
    Missing, Believed Married (B & D-Par Br 1937)
    Incident in Shanghai (B & D-Par Br 1938)
    Lassie from Lancashire (ABPC 1938)
    The Saint in London (RKO Br 1939)
    Meet Maxwell Archer [Maxwell Archer Detective] (RKO Br
        1939)
    The Second Mr. Bush (Anglo 1939)
    Spare a Copper (ABFD 1940)
    He Found a Star (GFD 1941)
    Dancing with Crime (Par Br 1947)
    Sleeping Car to Trieste (GFD 1948)
    Fools Rush In (GFD 1949)
    The Chiltern Hundreds [The Amazing Mr. Beecham] (GFD 1949)
    Tony Draws a Horse (GFD 1950)
    Talk of a Million [You Can't Beat the Irish] (ABP 1951)
    Treasure Hunt (IFD 1952)
    Made in Heaven (GFD 1952)
    Top of the Form (GFD 1953) (also co-script)
    Trouble in Store (GFD 1953) (also co-script)
    Up to His Neck (GFD 1954) (also co-script)
    One Good Turn (GFD 1954) (also co-script)
    Man of the Moment (RFD 1955) (also co-script)
    Jumping for Joy (RFD 1956)
    Up in the World (RFD 1956)
    The Big Money (RFD 1956)
    Just My Luck (RFD 1957)
    The Square Peg (RFD 1958)
    Tommy the Toreador (WPD 1959)
    Sands of the Desert (WPD 1960) (also co-script)
    A Weekend with Lulu (Col Br 1961)
    The Devil's Agent (BL 1962)

CASS, HENRY, b. 1902, London
    Lancashire Luck (B & D-Par Br 1937)
    29 Acacia Avenue [The Facts of Love] (Col Br 1945)
    The Glass Mountain (Renown 1949) (also co-script)
    No Place for Jennifer (ABP 1950)
    Last Holiday (ABP 1950)
    Young Wives' Tale (ABP 1951)
    Castle in the Air (ABP 1952)
    Father's Doing Fine (ABP 1952)
    The Reluctant Bride [Two Grooms for a Bride] (Eros 1955)
    No Smoking (Eros 1955)
    Bond of Fear (Eros 1956)
    Breakaway (RKO Br 1956)
    The High Terrace (RKO Br 1956)
    The Crooked Sky (RFD 1957)
    Booby Trap (Eros 1957)

Professor Tim (RKO Br 1957)
Blood of the Vampire (Eros 1958)
The Hand (Butcher 1960)
Boyd's Shop (RFD 1960)
The Man Who Couldn't Walk (Butcher 1960)
Mr. Brown Comes Down the Hill (MRA 1966) (also producer,
 script)
Happy Deathday (MRA 1970) (also script)
Give a Dog a Bone (MRA 1972) (also producer, script)

CASTELLANI, RENATO, b. Sept. 4, 1913, Savona, Italy
La corona di ferro (It 1941) (also story, script) (with Ales-
 sandro Blasetti)
Un colpo di pistola [A Pistol Shot] (It 1941) (also co-script)
Zaza (It 1942) (also script)
La donna della montagna (It 1942) (also co-script)
Mio figlio professore [My Son, the Professor] (It 1946) (also
 co-script)
Sotto il sole di Roma (It 1948) (also co-story, co-script)
E primavera [Springtime in Italy] (It 1949) (also co-story, co-
 script)
Due soldi di speranza [Two Pennyworth of Hope] (It 1951) (also
 co-story, co-script)
Giulietta e Romeo [Romeo and Juliet] (It-GB 1954) (also co-
 story, co-script)
I sogni nel cassetto (It 1957) (also story, script)
Nella città l'inferno [And the Wild Wild Women] (It 1958) (also
 co-script)
Il brigante [Italian Brigands] (It 1961) (also co-script)
Mare matto [Crazy Sea] (It 1963) (also co-story, co-script)
Tre notte d'amore (ep "La vedova") (It 1964)
Controsesso (ep "Una donna d'affari") (It 1964) (also co-story,
 co-script of episode)
Questi fantasmi [Ghosts, Italian Style] (It 1967) (also co-script)
Una breva stagione [A Brief Season] (It 1969)

CASTILLO, ARTURO RUIZ, b. Dec. 9, 1910, Madrid
La inquietudes de Shanti-andia (Sp 1946)
Obsesion (Sp 1947)
La Manigua sin dios (Sp 1947)
El santurio no se rinde (Sp 1949)
Maria antonia [La Caramba] (Sp 50)
Catalina de Inglaterra (Sp 1951)
El cerco del diablo (Sp 1952)
La Laguna Negra (Sp 1952)
Dos Caminos (Sp 1953)
Los Ases buscan la Paza (Sp 1954)
El guardian del paraiso (Sp 1955)
Pasion en el Mar (Sp 1956)
Culpables (Sp 1958)
Carta Al Cielo (Sp 1958)
Bajo el cielo Andaluz (Sp 1959)
Pachin (Sp 1960)

Llovidos del cielo (Sp 1962)
El secreto del Capitan O'Hara (Sp 1964)

CAUVIN, ANDRE, b. Feb. 12, 1907, Belgium
Congo, terre d'eaux vives (Bel 1939)
Nos soldats d'Afrique (Bel 1939)
Congo (Bel 1944)
L'Equateur aux cent visages (Bel 1948)
Bongolo (Bel 1952)
Bwana Kitoko (Bel 1952)
Manganga (Bel 1957)
Agadir, minuit moins le quart (Bel 1959)
L'île de paix (Bel 1969)
Une Journée a l'université de paix (Bel 1969)

CAVALCANTI, ALBERTO, b. Feb. 6, 1897, Rio de Janiero
Le Train sans yeux (Fr 1925-6) (also editor)
Rien que les heures (Fr 1926) (also producer, co-script)
En rade (Fr 1927) (also co-script, editor)
Yvette (Fr 1927) (also script, editor)
La P'tite Lili (Fr 1927) (also script)
La Jalousie du barbouillé (Fr 1927) (also script, decorator,
    editor)
Le Capitaine fracasse (Fr 1928) (also co-script, editor)
Le Petit Chaperon rouge (Fr 1929) (also co-adaptor, co-dia-
    logue, decorator, editor)
Vous verrez la Semaine prochaine (Fr 1929) (also script)
Toute sa vie (Fr 1930)
A Cançăo do Bereo (Por 1930) (Por version of Toute sa Vie)
Les Vacances du diable (Fr 1930)
A mi-chemin du ciel (Fr 1930)
Dans une île perdue (Fr 1931)
En lisant le journal (Fr 1932)
Le Jour du frotteur (Fr 1932) (also script, editor)
Revue Montmartroise (Fr 1932)
Nous ne ferons jamais de cinéma (Fr 1932)
Le Truc du brésilien (Fr 1932)
Le Mari Garçon [Le garçon divorcé] (Fr 1932)
Coralie et Cie (Fr 1933) (also script)
Le Tour de chant (Fr 1933) (also script)
Pett and Pott (GPO 1934) (also script, editor)
SOS Radio Service (GPO 1934)
New Rates (GPO 1934)
Line to Tcherva Hut (GPO 1936)
We Live in Two Worlds (GPO 1937)
Who Writes to Switzerland? (GPO 1937)
Four Barriers (GPO 1937)
Happy in the Morning (GPO 1938) (also producer, script)
Men of the Alps (GPO 1939)
Midsummer's Day's Work (GPO 1939)
Film and Reality (1942)
Alice in Switzerland (MOI, 1942)
Went the Day Well? [48 Hours] (UA Br 1942)

Watertight (MOI 1943) (also script)
Champagne Charlie (Ealing 1944)
Dead of Night (eps "The Christmas Story," "The Ventriloquist's
    Dummy") (EL 1945)
Nicholas Nickleby (GFD 1947)
They Made Me a Fugitive [I Became a Criminal] (WB Br 1947)
The First Gentleman [Affairs of a Rogue] (Col Br 1948)
For Them That Trespass (ABP 1949)
Simão, o Coaltta (Bra 1952) (also producer)
O Canto do mar (Bra 1953-4) (also producer, co-story)
Mulher de verdare (Bra 1954) (also producer)
Herr Puntila und sein Knecht (Aus 1955) (also co-adaptor)
Die Windrose (Aus 1956) (Supervising director only)
La prima notte (Fr-It 1958)
The Monster of Highgate Ponds (CFF 1961)
Story of Israel: Thus Spake Theodor Herzl (1967) (also script)

CAVALIER, ALAIN, b. Sept. 14, 1931, Vendôme, France
Le Combat dans l'île (Fr 1961) (also co-script)
L'Insoumis (Fr-It 1964) (also co-script)
Mise à sac [Pillaged] (Fr-It 1967) (also co-script)
La Chamade [Heartbeat] (Fr-It 1968) (also co-script)

CAVANI, LILIANA, b. 1938, Modena, Italy
Francesco d'Assisi (It 1966)
Galileo (It 1968)
I cannibali (It 1969)
L'ospite (It 1971)
Il portiere di notte [The Night Porter] (It 1973) (also script)

CAVENS, ANDRE, b. Oct. 1, 1912, Brussels; d. April 9, 1971
Il y a un train toutes les heures (Bel 1962)
Michaella (Bel 1968) (also co-script)

CAYATTE, ANDRE, b. Feb. 3, 1909, Carcassonne, France
La Fausse Maîtresse (Fr 1942) (also script)
Au bonheur des dames (Fr 1942) (also co-script)
Pierre et Jean (Fr 1943) (also co-script)
Le Dernier Sou (Fr 1944) (also script)
Sérénade aux nuages (Fr 1945) (also co-script)
Roger-la-Honte (Fr 1945) (also script)
La Revanche de Roger-la-Honte (Fr 1946) (also script)
La Chanteur inconnu (Fr 1947)
Le Dessous des cartes (Fr 1947) (also co-script)
Les Amants de Vérone (Fr 1948) (also script)
Retour à la vie (ep "Le retour de Tante Emma") (Fr 1949)
Justice est faite [Let Justice Be Done] (Fr 1950)
Nous sommes tous des assassins [We Are All Murderers] (Fr
    1952) (also co-script)
Avant le déluge (Fr-It 1953) (also co-script)
Le Dossier noir (Fr-It 1955) (also co-script)
Oeil pour oeil (Fr-It 1956) (also co-script)
La Miroir à deux faces [The Mirror Has Two Faces] (Fr-It

1958) (also co-script, adaptor)
Le Passage du Rhin [The Crossing of the Rhine] (Fr-W Ger
    1960) (also co-script)
Le Glaive et la balance [Two Are Guilty] (Fr-It 1962) (also
    script)
La Vie conjugale: Françoise (Fr-It 1963) (also co-adaptation,
    script)
La Vie conjugale: Jean-Marc (Fr-It 1963) (also co-adaptation,
    script)
Piège pour Cendrillon [A Trap for Cinderella] (Fr-It 1965) (also
    co-adaptor)
Les Risques du métier (Fr 1967) (also co-script)
Les chemins de Khatmandu [The Road to Katmandu] (Fr-It 1969)
    (also script, co-adaptor)
Mourir d'aimer (Fr 1971) (also co-script)
Il n'y a pas de fumée sans feu (Fr-It 1973) (also co-script)
Verdict (Fr-It 1974) (also co-script)

CERCHIO, FERNANDO (a. k. a. Fred Ringoold), b. August 7, 1914,
    Turin, Italy
Cenerentola (It 1949)
Gente così (It 1950)
Il bivio (It 1952)
Il figlio di Lagardère (It 1952)
Il bandolero stanco (It 1952)
Lulú (It 1953)
Addio mia bella signora (It 1954)
Il visconte di Bragelonne (It 1955)
I quattro del getto tonante (It 1955)
I misteri di Parigi (It 1958)
Erode il grande [Herod The Great] (It 1958)
Amanti del deserto (It 1959)
Giuditta ed Oloferne [Head of a Tyrant] (It 1959)
Il sepolcro dei re (It 1961)
Totò contro Maciste (It 1962)
Col ferro e col fuoco (It 1962)
Lo sceicco rosso (It 1962)
Nefertite regina del Nilo [Nefertite Queen of the Nile] (It 1962)
Totò e Cleopatra (It 1963)
Totò contro il pirata nero (It 1964)
Per un dollaro di gloria (It 1966)
Segretissimo (It 1966)
Il marcho di Kriminal (It 1967)
La morte sull'alta collina (It-Sp 1969)

CHABROL, CLAUDE, b. June 23, 1930, Sardent, France
Le beau Serge (Fr 1958)† (also script, dialogue, actor)
Les cousins (Fr 1959)† (also script)
A Double Tour [Leda] (Fr 1959) (also actor)
Les Bonnes Femmes (Fr 1959) (also story, actor)
Les Godelureaux (Fr 1961) (also co-adaptor, actor)
Les Sept Péchés capitaux [Seven Capital Sins] (ep "L'Avarice")
    (Fr-It 1962) (also actor)

L'Oeil du malin [The Third Lover] (Fr-It 1962) (also script)
Ophélia (Fr-It 1962) (also co-adaptor, co-dialogue)
Landru (Fr-It 1962) (also uncredited co-script)
Les Plus Belles Escroqueries du monde (ep "L'Homme qui
  vendit la Tour Eiffel") (Fr-It-Japan 1964) (also script)
Paris vu par ... (ep "La Muette") [Six in Paris] (Fr 1964)
  (also script, actor)
Le Tigre aime la chair fraîche [The Tiger Likes Fresh Blood]
  (Fr-It 1964)
Marie-Chantal contre le Docteur Kah (Fr-It-Morocco 1965)
  (also co-script, actor)
Le Tigre se parfume à la dynamite [An Orchid for the Tiger]
  (Fr-Sp-It 1965) (also actor)
La Ligne de démarcation (Fr 1966) (also adaptor, dialogue)
Le Scandale [The Champagne Murders] (Fr 1967) (2 versions)
La Route de Corinthe [The Road to Corinth] (Fr-It-Gr 1967)
  (also actor)
Les Biches [The Does] (Fr-It 1968) (also co-script, actor)
La Femme infidèle (Fr-It 1968) (also script)
Que la bête meure [Killer!] (Fr-It 1969) (also script)
Le Boucher [The Butcher] (Fr-It 1969) (also script)
La Rupture (Fr-It-Belg 1970) (also script, actor)
Juste avant la nuit [Just Before Nightfall] (Fr-It 1971) (also
  script)
La Decáde prodigeuse [Ten Days' Wonder] (Fr 1971) (also
  script) (2 versions)
Docteur Popaul (Fr-It 1972) (also co-song)
Les Noces rouges [Blood Wedding] (Fr-It 1973) (also script)
Nada (Fr-It 1973)
De Grey (Fr TV 1973)
Le Banc de la désolation (Fr TV 1973)
Partie de plaisir (Fr 1974)
Monsieur Bébé (Fr TV 1974)

CHAFFET, DON, b. Aug. 5, 1917, Hastings, Sussex, England
  The Mysterious Poacher (GFD 1950)
  The Case of the Missing Scene (GFD 1951)
  Skid Kids (ABFD-CFF 1953)
  Time Is My Enemy (IFD 1954)
  The Secret Tent (BL 1956)
  The Girl in the Picture (Eros 1957)
  The Flesh is Weak (Eros 1957)
  A Question of Adultery (Eros 1958)
  The Man Upstairs (BL 1958) (also co-script)
  Danger Within (BL 1959)
  Dentist in the Chair (Renown 1960)
  Lies My Father Told Me (Eire 1960) (also co-producer)
  Nearly a Nasty Accident (Brittania 1961)
  Greyfriars Bobby (BV 1961)
  A Matter of Who (MGM Br 1962)
  The Prince and the Pauper (BV 1962)
  The Webster Boy (RFI 1963)
  The Horse Without a Head (BV 1963)

Jason and the Argonauts (Col Br 1963)
A Jolly Bad Fellow (Par Br 1963)
The Three Lives of Thomasina (BV 1964)
The Crooked Road (Br-Yug 1966) (made in 1964)
One Million Years B. C. (WPD 1966)
The Viking Queen (WPD 1967)
A Twist of Sand (UA Br 1967)
Creatures the World Forgot (Col Br 1970)
Clinic Xclusive (Doverton 1972)
Charley-One-Eye (Saga 1974) (made in 1972)
Persecution (Doverton 1974)

CLAIR, RENE (René Chomette), b. Nov. 11, 1898, Paris
Paris qui dort (Fr 1923) (also script)
Entr'acte (Fr 1924)
Le Fantôme du Moulin Rouge (Fr 1924) (also script)
Le Voyage imaginaire (Fr 1925) (also script)
La Proie du vent (Fr 1926) (also script)
Un Chapeau de paille d'Italie [The Italian Straw Hat] (Fr 1927)
    (also script)
Les Deux Timides (Fr 1928) (also script)
Sous les toits de Paris (Fr 1930) (also script)
Le Million (Fr 1931) (also script)
A nous la liberté (Fr 1931) (also script)
Quatorze Juillet (Fr 1932) (also script)
Le Dernier Milliardaire (Fr 1934) (also script)
The Ghost Goes West (UA Br 1936)
Break the News (GFD 1938)† (also co-script)
Air pur (Unfinished Fr 1939) (also script, co-dialogue)
The Flame of New Orleans (Univ 1940)
Forever and a Day (USA) (RKO 1943) (also co-producer) (with
    Edmund Goulding, Cedric Hardwicke, Frank Lloyd, Victor
    Saville, Robert Stevenson, Herbert Wilcox)
I Married a Witch (USA) (Par 1942)
It Happened Tomorrow (USA) (UA 1944) (also co-script)
And Then There Were None [Ten Little Niggers] (USA) (20th
    1945)
Le Silence est d'or (Fr 1947) (also script)
La Beauté du diable (It-Fr 1949) (also co-script, co-dialogue)
Les Belles de nuit (Fr-It 1952) (also script, dialogue)
Les Grandes Manœuvres (Fr-It 1955) (also co-script, co-dia-
    logue)
Porte des Lilas (Fr-It 1957) (also co-script)
La Française et l'amour [Love and the Frenchwoman] (ep
    "Le Mariage") (also script)
Tout l'or du monde [All the Gold in the World] (Fr-It 1961)
    (also co-script)
Les Quatre Vérités (ep "Les deux pigeons") (Fr-It-Sp 1962)
    (also script)
Les Fêtes galantes (Fr-Rumanian 1965) (also script, dialogue)

CLAUS, HUGO, b. April 5, 1929, Bruges, Belgium
Cri et connaissance (Bel 1963) (with Paul Haesaerts)
De Vijanden (Bel 1967) (also script)

CLAYTON 56

CLAYTON, JACK, b. Feb. 6, 1921, London
   Room at the Top (IFD 1959)
   The Innocents (20th Br 1961) (also co-producer)
   The Pumpkin Eater (Col Br 1964)
   Our Mother's House (MGM Br 1967) (also co-producer)
   The Great Gatsby (USA) (Par 1974) (also uncredited co-script)

CLEMENT, RENE, b. March 18, 1913, Bordeaux
   La Bataille du rail (Fr 1946) (also co-script)
   La Belle et la bête [Beauty and the Beast] (Fr 1946) (only as
      technical adviser to Jean Cocteau)
   Le Père tranquille (Fr 1946)
   Les Maudits (Fr 1947) (also co-script, co-adaptor)
   Au-dela des grilles (It-Fr 1949)
   Le Château de verre (Fr-It 1950) (also co-adaptor)
   Jeux interdits [Forbidden Games] (Fr 1952) (also co-adaptor,
      co-dialogue)
   Monsieur Ripois [Lovers, Happy Lovers, Knave of Hearts]
      (Fr-GB 1954) (also co-adaptor)
   Gervaise (Fr 1956)
   Barrage contre le Pacifique [La Diga sul Pacifico, The Sea
      Wall] (Fr-It 1958) (also co-adaptor, co-dialogue)
   Plein soleil [Purple Noon] (Fr-It 1959) (also co-adaptor, co-dia-
      logue)
   Che gioia vivere [Quelle joie de vivre] (It-Fr 1961) (also co-
      script, co-adaptor)
   Le Jour et l'heure [The Day and the Hour] (Fr-It 1963) (also
      co-adaptor)
   Les Félins [The Love Cage/Joy House] (Fr 1963) (also co-
      adaptor)
   Paris brûle-t-il? [Is Paris Burning?] (Fr 1966)
   Le Passager de la pluie [Rider on the Rain] (Fr-It 1969)
   La Maison sous les arbres [The Deadly Trap] (Fr-It 1971) (also
      co-adaptor)
   La Course du lièvre a travers les champs [And Hope to Die]
      (Fr-US 1972)

CLOUZOT, HENRI-GEORGES, b. Nov. 20, 1907, Niort, France
   L'Assassin habite au 21 (Fr 1942) (also co-adaptor, dialogue)
   Le Corbeau [The Crow] (Fr 1943) (also co-adaptor, co-dialogue)
   Quai des Orfèvres (Fr 1947) (also co-adaptor, co-dialogue)
   Manon (Fr 1949) (also co-adaptor, co-dialogue)
   Retour à la vie (ep "La retour de Jean") (Fr 1949) (also co-
      script, co-dialogue)
   Miquette et sa mère (Fr 1949) (also co-adaptor, dialogue)
   Le Salaire de la peur [The Wages of Fear] (Fr-It 1953) (also
      co-adaptor, co-dialogue)
   Les Diaboliques [The Fiends] (Fr 1955) (also adaptor, dialogue)
   Le Mystère Picasso (Fr 1956) (also script, actor)
   Les Espions [The Spies] (Fr 1957) (also co-adaptor, co-dia-
      logue)
   La Vérité [The Truth] (Fr 1960) (also co-script, co-adaptor,
      co-dialogue)

René Clement (center, kneeling) on the set of <u>Jeux Interdits</u> (1948).

La Prisonnière [Woman in Chains] (Fr-It 1968) (also co-script)
Messa da requiem (Swi-W Ger 1969)

COCTEAU, JEAN, b. July 5, 1889, Maisons-Lafitte, France; d.
    Oct. 10, 1963
    Le sang d'un poète (Fr 1930-1932) (also script, editor)
    L'eternel retour (Fr 1943) (also script, dialogue) (uncredited,
        with Jean Delannoy)
    La Belle et la bête [Beauty and the Beast] (Fr 1946) (also
        script, dialogue) (with René Clement as technical advisor)
    L'Aigle à deux têtes (Fr 1947) (also based on his play, script,
        dialogue)
    Les Parents terribles (Fr 1948) (also script dialogue)
    Orphée (Fr 1950) (also script, dialogue)
    Le Testament d'Orphée (Fr 1959) (also script, dialogue)

COLETTI, DUILIO, b. Dec. 28, 1908, Pescara, Italy
    Il signore desidera? (It 1934) (only script)
    Pierpin (It 1935) (also script)
    La sposa dei re (It 1938) (also script)
    Il fornaretto di Venezia (It 1939)
    Capitan Francassa (It 1940) (also script)
    La maschera di Cesare Borgia (It 1941)
    Il mercante di schiave (It 1942) (also script)
    Tre ragazze cercano marito (It 1943)
    L'adultera (It 1946)

Il passatore (It 1947)
Cuore (It 1948)
Il grido della terra (It 1949)
Il lupo della Sila [Lure of the Sila] (It 1949)
Romanzo d'amore [All for Love] (It 1950)
Miss Italia [My Beautiful Daughter] (It 1951)
Libera uscita (It 1951)
E arrivato l'accordatore (It 1952)
Wanda la peccatrice (It 1952)
I sette dell'Orsa maggiore [Hell Raiders of the Deep] (It 1953)
La grande speranza (It 1954)
Divisione folgore (It 1955)
Bella non piangere (sup. only) (It 1955)
Londra chiamo Polo Nord [House of Intrigue] (It 1957)
Gli italiani sono matti (It 1958)
Sotto dieci bandiere [Under 10 Flags] (It 1960)
Il re di Poggioreale (It 1961)
Lo sbarco di Anzio [Anzio] (It 1968) (with Edward Omytryk)
Valdez il Mezzo sangue [Valdez, the half-breed] (It-Sp-Fr 1972)
   (with John Sturges)

COLL, JULIO, b. 1919, Caprodon, Spain
Nunca es demasiado tarde (Sp 1955)
La carcel de cristal (Sp 1956)
Dustrito Quinto (Sp 1957)
Un vaso de whiskey (Sp 1958)
El Traje de Oro (Sp 1959)
Los Cuervos (Sp 1961)
La cuarta ventana (Sp 1962)
Ensayo general para la muerte (Sp 1962)
Los muertos no perdonan (Sp 1963)
Fuego [Pyro!] (Sp 1964)
Las Viudas (ep El aniversario) (Sp 1966)
Comando de asesinos [Week-end mit dem Tode] (Sp-Ger 1966)
La familia Colon (Sp TV 1966)
Persucucion hasta Valencia (Sp 1967)
El mejor de Todos (Sp 1968)
El mejor del Mundo (Sp-Mex 1970)
La araucana (Sp-It 1971)

COLLET, PAUL, b. May, 1941, Antwerp, Belgium
Cash? Cash! (Bel 1968) (also co-script) (with Pierre Drouot)
L'Etreinte (Bel 1969) (also co-script) (with Pierre Drouot)
Louisa, een Woord van Liefde [Louisa, un mot d'amour] (Bel
   1972) (also co-script) (with Pierre Drouot)

COLLINSON, PETER, b. 1938, Lincolnshire, England
The Penthouse (Par Br 1967) (also script)
Up the Junction (Par Br 1968)† [co-production company]
The Long Day's Dying (Par Br 1968)
The Italian Job (Par Br 1968)
You Can't Win 'em All (Col Br 1970)
Fright (BL 1971)

Paul Collet with Alison Nacro and Pierre Drouet (co-director) on
the set of Louisa, een Woord van Liefde (1972).

Straight On Till Morning (MGM-EMI 1972)
Innocent Bystanders (Scotia-Barber 1972)
The Man Called Noon (GB-Sp-It 1973)

COMENCINI, LUIGI, b. June 8, 1916, Brescia, Italy
    Proibito rubare [Birth of Boys Town] (It 1948)
    L'imperatore di Capri (It 1949)
    Persiane chiuse (It 1951)
    La tratta delle bianche [Girls Marked Danger] (It 1952)
    Pane, amore e fantasia [Bread, Love and Dreams] (It 1953)
    La valigia dei sogni (It 1954)
    Pane, amore e gelosia [Frisky] (It 1954)
    La bella di Roma (It 1955)
    La finestra sul luna park (It 1957)
    Mariti in città (It 1957)
    Mogli pericolose (It 1958)
    Und das am Montagmorgen (It 1959)
    Le sorprese dell'amore (It 1959)
    Tutti a casa (It 1960)

Luigi Comencini (left) with Stefania Sandrelli and Giuliano Gemma
on the set of Delitto d'amore (1974).

A cavallo della tigre (It 1961)
Il commissario (It 1962)
La ragazza di Bube [Bebo's Girl] (It 1963)
Tre notti d'amore (ep "Fate bene fratelli") (It 1964)
La mia signora (ep "Eritrea") (It 1964)
Le bambole (ep "Il trattato di eugenètica") (It 1965)
La bugiarda (It 1965)
Il compagno don Camillo (It 1965)
Incompreso (It 1967)
Italian secret service (It 1968)
Infanzia, vocazione e prime esperienze di Giacomo Casanova,
   Veneziano (It 1969)
Senza sapere niente di lei (It 1969)
Delitto d'amore (It 1974)
La carne grida e comanda (It 1974)

COMFORT, LANCE (Lancelot Foster Comfort), b. 1908, Harrow,
   Middlesex, England; d. Aug. 25, 1966
   Penn of Pennsylvania [The Courageous Mr. Penn] (Anglo 1941)

Hatter's Castle (Par Br 1941)
Those Kids from Town (Anglo 1942)
Squadron Leader X (RKO Br 1942)
Old Mother Riley Detective (Angle 1943)
When We Are Married (Anglo 1943)
Escape to Danger (RKO Br 1943) (with Mutz Greenbaum)
Hotel Reserve (RKO Br 1944) (with Mutz Greenbaum)
Great Day (RKO Br 1945)
Bedelia (GFD 1946)
Temptation Harbour (Pathe 1947)
Daughter of Darkness (Par 1948)
Silent Dust (ABP 1949)
Portrait of Clare (ABP 1950)
Girl on the Pier (Apex 1953) (also co-producer)
Eight O'Clock Walk (BL 1954)
Bang! You're Dead [Game of Danger] (BL 1954) (also producer)
The Man in the Road (GN 1956)
At the Stroke of Nine (GN 1957)
Face in the Night [Menace in the Night] (GN 1957)
Man from Tangier [Thunder over Tangier] (Butcher 1957)
Make Mine a Million (BL 1959)
The Ugly Duckling (Col Br 1959)
The Breaking Point (Butcher 1961)
Rag Doll (Butcher 1961)
Pit of Darkness (Butcher 1961) (also producer, script)
The Break (Planet 1962)
The Painted Smile (Planet 1962)
Tomorrow at Ten (Planet 1962)
Touch of Death (Planet 1962)
Live It Up [Sing and Swing] (RFD 1963) (also producer)
Blind Corner (Mancunian 1963)
Devils of Darkness (Planet 1964)
Be My Guest (RFD 1965) (also producer)

CORBUCCI, BRUNO, b. Italy
I due pompieri (It 1968)
Zum zum zum n. 2 (It 1969)
Due bianchi nell'Africa nera (It 1970)
Io non spezzo ... rompo (It 1970)
Lisa dagli occhi blù
Boccaccio (It-Fr 1970)
Il furto è l'anima del commercio (It-Fr 1971)
Quando gli uomini armarono la clava e con le donne fecero din
  don (It 1971)
Tutti per uno, botte per tutti (It-Ger-Sp 1972)

CORBUCCI, SERGIO [a.k.a. Stanley Corbett], b. Dec. 6, 1927,
    Rome
Salvate mia figlia (It 1951)
La peccatrice dell'isola [Island Sinner] (It 1953)
Terra straniera [Land of Destin] (It 1953)
Baracca e burattini (It 1954)
Acque amare (It 1955)

Carovana di canzoni (It 1955)
Suonno d'amore (It 1955)
Lacrime di sposa (It 1955)
A vent'anni è sempre festa (It 1957)
Suprema confessione (It 1958)
I ragazzi dei Parioli (It 1959)
Chi si ferma è perduto (It 1961)
Totò, Peppino e la dolce vita (It 1961)
Romolo e Remo [Duel of the Titians] (It 1961)
I due marescialli (It 1961)
Il figlio di Spartacus (It 1962)
Lo smemorato di Collegno (It 1962)
Il giorno più corto (It 1963)
Il monaco di Monza (It 1963)
Gli onorevoli (It 1963)
Massacro al Grand Cañón (It 1964) (with Alfredo Antonini)
Danza macabra (It 1964)
Minnesota Clay (It 1964)
I figli del leopardo (It 1965)
Django (It 1966)
I crudeli (It 1966)
Johnny Oro (It 1966)
Navajo Joe (It 1966)
L'uomo che ride (It 1967)
Bersaglio mobile (It 1967)
Il grande silenzio (It 1968)
Il mercenario (It 1968)
Gli specialisti (It-Fr-Ger 1969)
Vamos a matar, compañeros! (It-Fr-Ger 1970)
Er più [Storia d'amore e di coltello] (It 1971)
Che c'entriamo noi con la rivoluzione? (It-Sp 1972)
J. and S. --Storia criminale del Far West (It-Sp-Ger 1972)

CORNELIUS, HENRY, b. Aug. 18, 1913, South Africa, d. May 3,
    1958
    Passport to Pimlico (GFD 1949)
    The Galloping Major (IFD 1951) (also co-script)
    Genevieve (GFD 1953) (also producer)
    I Am a Camera (IFD 1955)
    Next to No Time (BL 1958) (also script)

COSTA, MARIO, b. June 1, 1908, Rome
    Fontane di Roma (It 1938)
    La sua strada (It 1943)
    Il barbiere di Siviglia [Barber of Seville] (It 1946)
    L'elisir d'amore [This Wine of Love] (It 1947)
    Il segreto di don Giovanni (It 1947)
    Follie per l'opera [Mad About Opera] (It 1948)
    Pagliacci [Love of a Clown] (It 1949)
    Cavalcata d'eroi (It 1951)
    Canzone di primavera (It 1951)
    Trieste mia! (It 1951)

Città canora (It 1952)
Perdonami (It 1953)
Ti ho sempre amato (It 1954)
Per salvarti ho peccato (It 1954)
Pietà per chicade (It 1954)
Gli amori di Manon Lescaut (It 1955)
Prigionieri del male (It 1956)
Arrivano i dollari (It 1957)
Addio per sempre (It 1958)
La belle dell'aria (It 1958)
Via col ... paravento (It 1958)
Il cavaliere del castello maledetto (It 1959)
I reali di Francia (It 1960)
La Venere dei pirati (It 1960)
Il conquistatore di Corinto (It 1962)
Gordon il pirata nero (It 1962)
Il figlio dello sceicco (It 1962)
Il gladiatore di Roma (It 1962)
Il terrore dei mantelli rossi (It 1963)
Gli amanti latini (It 1965)
Buffalo Bill, l'eroe del Far West (It 1965)

COSTA-GAVRAS [Konstantinos Gavras], b. 1933, Athens
Compartiment tueurs [The Sleeping Car Murders] (Fr 1965)
    (also co-script)
Un Homme de trop (Fr 1966) (also script)
Z (Fr-Algeria 1968) (also co-script)
L'Aveu [The Confession] (Fr-It 1970)
Etat de siège [State of Siege] (Fr-It-W Ger 1973) (also co-script)
Section spéciale (Fr 1974)

COTTAFAVI, VITTORIO, b. Jan. 30, 1914, Modena, Italy
Abuna Messias (It 1939) (only co-script)
Nozze di sangue (It 1940) (only co-script)
Quelli della montagna (It 1942) (only co-script)
I nostri sogni (It 1943) (also script)
Lo sconosciuto di San Marino (It 1947) (with M. Waszinsky)
Fantasmi del mare (It 1948)
La fiamma che non si spegne (It 1949)
Messalina (It 1951)
Una donna ha ucciso (It 1952) (also co-script)
La grande strada (It 1952) (with M. Waszinsky)
Il boia di Lilla (It 1953)
Il cavaliere di Maison Rouge (It 1953)
Traviata '53 (It 1953)
In amore si pecca in due (It 1954)
Avanza di galera (It 1954)
Fiesta brava (It 1955) (Unfinished) (also co-script)
Nel gorgo del peccato (It 1955)
Una donna libera (It-Fr 1956)
La rivolta dei gladiatori [The Warrior and the Slave Girl] (It-Sp 1958)

Le legioni di Cleopatra [Legions of the Nile] (It-Fr-Sp 1960)
La vendetta di Ercole [Goliath and the Dragons] (It-Fr 1960)
Ercole alla conquista di Atlantide [Hercules and the Captive
   Women] (It-Fr 1961)
Le vergini di Roma (It-Fr 1961)
I cento cavalieri [The Hundred Horsemen] (It-Sp 1965) (also co-
   script)

COURNOT, MICHEL, b. 1922(?)
Les Gauloises bleues (Fr 1968) (also script)

COUSTEAU, JACQUES-YVES, b. June 11, 1910, Saint-André,
   France
Par dix-huit mètres de fond (Fr 1943) (also producer)
Epaves (Fr 1945) (also producer)
Paysages du silence (Fr 1947) (also producer)
Au large des côtes Tunisiennes (Fr 1948-1949)
Autour d'un récif (Fr 1949) (also producer)
Les Phoques du Rio d'Oro (Fr 1949) (also producer)
Dauphins et Cétacés (Fr 1949) (also producer)
Une Sortie du "Rubis" (Fr 1950) (also producer)
Carnet de plongée (Fr 1950) (also producer)
La Mer Rouge (Fr 1952) (also producer)
Un Musée dans la mer (Fr 1953) (also producer)
Le monde du silence [The Silent World] (Fr 1956) (also pro-
   ducer) (with Louis Malle)
Le Monde sans soleil [World without Sun] (Fr-It 1964) (also
   producer, script, photography) (with co-director)

COWARD, NOEL, b. Dec. 16, 1899, Teddington, England; d. March
   26, 1973
In Which We Serve (BL 1942) (with David Lean) (also producer,
   script, actor)

CRABTREE, ARTHUR, b. Nov. 29, 1900, Shipley, Yorkshire, Eng-
   land
Madonna of the Seven Moons (EL 1944)
They Were Sisters (GFD 1945)
Caravan (GFD 1946)
Dear Murderer (GFD 1947)
The Calendar (GFD 1948)
Quartet (ep "The Kite") (GFD 1948)
Don't Ever Leave Me (GFD 1949)
Lilli Marlene (Monarch 1950)
Hindle Wakes [Holiday Week] (Monarch 1952)
The Wedding of Lilli Marlene (Monarch 1953)
West of Suez [Fighting Wildcats] (Astral 1957)
Morning Call (Astral 1957)
Death Over My Shoulder (Orb 1958)
Fiend without a Face (Eros 1958)
Horrors of the Black Museum (AA 1959)

Noël Coward, as actor, on the set of Bunny Lake Is Missing (1965).

CRICHTON, CHARLES, b. Aug. 6, 1910, Wallasey, England
    For Those in Peril (Ealing 1944)
    Painted Boats [The Girl on the Canal] (Ealing 1945)
    Dead of Night (ep "The Golfing Story") (EL 1945)
    Hue and Cry (GFD 1947)
    Against the Wind (GFD 1948)
    Another Shore (GFD 1948)
    Train of Events (GFD 1949) (with Sidney Cole, Basil Dearden)
    Dance Hall (GFD 1950)
    The Lavendar Hill Mob (GFD 1951)
    Hunted [The Stranger in Between] (GFD 1952)
    The Titfield Thunderbolt (GFD 1953)
    The Love Lottery (GFD 1954)
    The Divided Heart (GFD 1954)
    The Man in the Sky [Decision Against Time] (MGM 1957)
    Law and Disorder (BL 1958)
    Floods of Fear (RFD 1958) (also co-script)
    Battle of the Sexes (Bry 1959)
    The Boy Who Stole a Million (Bry 1961) (also co-script)

The Third Secret (20th 1964)
He Who Rides a Tiger (BL 1965)

CURTIZ, MICHAEL (Mihaly Kertesz), b. Dec. 24, 1888, Budapest;
    d. April 11, 1962
Az Utolso Bohem (Hun 1912)
Ma es Holnap (Hun 1912) (also co-script, actor)
Rablelek (Hun 1913)
Hazasokik Az Uram (Hun 1913)
Az Eiszaka Rabja (Hun 1914) (also story)
Aranyaso (Hun 1914)
Bank Ban (Hun 1914)
A Tolonc (Hun 1914)
A Kolesonkert Csecsemok (Hun 1914)
A Hercegno Pongyolaban (Hun 1914)
Akit Ketten Szeretnek (Hun 1915) (also actor)
A Karthauzi (Hun 1916)
Makkhetes (Hun 1916)
A fekete Szivarvany (Hun 1916)
Doktor Ur (Hun 1916)
A Magyar Fold Ereje (Hun 1916)
A Medikus (Hun 1916)
Zoard Mester (Hun 1917)
A Vötös Samson (Hun 1917)
Az Utolso Hajnal (Hun 1917)
A Senki Fia (Hun 1917)
A Szentjobi Erdo Titka (Hun 1917)
A Kuruzslo (Hun 1917)
A Halazcsengo (Hun 1917)
A Föld Embre (Hun 1917)
Az Ezredes (Hun 1917)
Egy Drajcar Törenete (Hun 1917)
A Beke Utja (Hun 1917)
Az Ardenda Zsido (Hun 1917)
Tatarjaras (Hun 1917) (also script)
Az Orvos (Hun 1918)
Tavasz a Telben (Hun 1917)
A Napraforgos Holgy (Hun 1918)
Lulu (Hun 1918)
Kilencven Kilenc (Hun 1918)
Az Ordog (Hun 1918)
Judas (Hun 1918)
A Csunya Fiju (Hun 1918)
Alraune (Hun 1918)
A Vig Ozvegy (Hun 1918)
Varazskeringö (Hun 1918)
Lu, a Kokott (Hun 1918)
Liliom (Hun 1918) (unfinished)
Jön Az Ocsem (Hun 1919)
Wellington Rejtely (Swed 1919)
Odette et l'histoire des femmes illustrés (Swe 1919)
Die Dame mit dem schwarzen Handschuh (Aus 1919)
Der Stern von Damaskus (Aus 1919)

Die Gottesgeissel (Aus 1920)
Die Dame mit den Sonnenblumen (Aus 1920)
Labyrinth des Grauens (Aus 1920)
Wege des Schreckens (Aus 1921)
Frau Dorothys Bekenntnis (Aus 1921)
Miss Tutti Fruitti (Aus 1921)
Herzogin Satanella (Aus 1921)
Sodom und Gomorrha (Aus) (part one 1922) (part two 1923)
Die La vine (Aus 1923)
Der junge Medardus (Aus 1923) (with Sascha Kolowrat)
Samson und Dalila (Aus 1923)
Namenlos (Aus 1923)
Ein Spiel ums Leben (Aus 1924)
General Babka (Aus 1924)
The Uncle from Sumatra (Aus 1924)
Avalanche (Aus 1924)
Harun Al Raschid (Aus 1924)
Die Slavenkönigin [Moon of Israel] (Aus 1924)
Das Spielzeug von Paris [Red Heels] (Ger-Aus 1925)
Der goldene Schmetterling [The Road to Happiness] (Ger-Aus
     1926)
Flaker Nr. 12 (Aus-Ger 1926)
In the U.S.A. :
     The Third Degree (WB 1926)
     The Million Bid (WB 1927)
     The Desired Woman (WB 1927)
     Good Time Charley (WB 1927)
     Tenderloin (WB 1928)
     Noah's Ark (WB 1928)
     Hearts in Exile (WB 1929)
     Hearts in Exile (WB 1929)
     Glad Rag Doll (WB 1929)
     Madonna of Avenue A (WB 1929)
     The Gamblers (WB 1929)
     Mammy (WB 1920)
     Under a Texas Moon (WB 1930)
     The Matrimonial Bed (WB 1930)
     Bright Lights (WB 1930)
     A Soldier's Plaything (WB 1930)
     River's End (WB 1930)
     Dämon des Meeres (Ger version of Moby Dick) (WB 1931)
     God's Gift to Women (WB 1931)
     The Mad Genius (WB 1931)
     The Woman from Monte Carlo (FN 1932)
     Alias the Doctor (FB 1932)
     The Strange Love of Molly Louvain (FN 1932)
     Doctor X (FN 1932)
     The Cabin in the Cotton (FN 1932) (with William Keighley)
     20,000 Years in Sing Sing (FN 1933)
     The Mystery of the Wax Museum (FN 1933)
     The Keyhole (WB 1933)
     Private Detective 62 (WB 1933)
     Goodbye Again (FN 1933)

The Kennel Murder Case (WB 1933)
Female (FN 1933)
Mandalay (FN 1934)
British Agent (FN 1934)
Jimmy the Gent (WB 1934)
The Key (WB 1934)
Black Fury (WB 1935)
The Case of the Curious Bride (WB 1935)
Front Page Woman (WB 1935)
Little Big Shot (WB 1935)
Captain Blood (WB 1935)
The Walking Dead (WB 1936)
The Charge of the Light Brigade (WB 1936)
Mountain Justice (WB 1937)
Stolen Holiday (WB 1937)
Kid Galahad (WB 1937)
The Perfect Specimen (WB 1937)
Gold Is Where You Find It (WB 1938)
The Adventures of Robin Hood (WB 1938) (with William Keigh-
   ley)
Four Daughters (WB 1938)
Four's a Crowd (WB 1938)
Angels with Dirty Faces (WB 1938)
Dodge City (WB 1939)
Daughters Courageous (WB 1939)
Four Wives (WB 1939)
The Private Lives of Elizabeth and Essex (WB 1939)
Virginia City (WB 1940)
The Sea Hawk (WB 1940)
The Santa Fe Trail (WB 1940)
The Sea Wolf (WB 1941)
Dive Bomber (WB 1941)
Captains of the Clouds (WB 1942)
Yankee Doodle Dandy (WB 1942)
Casablanca (WB 1943)
Mission to Moscow (WB 1943)
This Is the Army (WB 1943)
Passage to Marseille (WB 1944)
Janie (WB 1944)
Roughly Speaking (WB 1945)
Mildred Pierce (WB 1945)
Night and Day (WB 1946)
Life With Father (WB 1947)
The Unsuspected (WB 1947)
Romance on the High Seas (WB 1948)
My Dream Is Yours (WB 1948) (also producer)
Flamingo Road (WB 1949)
The Lady Takes a Sailor (WB 1949)
Young Man with a Horn (WB 1950)
Bright Leaf (WB 1950)
The Breaking Point (WB 1950)
Jim Thorpe--All American (WB 1951)
Force of Arms (WB 1951)

I'll See You in My Dreams (WB 1952)
The Jazz Singer (WB 1953)
The Story of Will Rogers (WB 1952)
Trouble Along the Way (WB 1953)
The Boy from Oklahoma (WB 1954)
The Egyptian (Fox 1954)
White Christmas (Par 1954)
We're No Angels (Par 1955)
The Scarlet Hour (Par 1956) (also producer)
The Vagabond King (Par 1956)
The Best Things in Life Are Free (Fox 1956)
The Helen Morgan Story (WB 1957)
The Proud Rebel (BV 1958)
King Creole (Par 1958)
The Hangman (Par 1959)
The Man in the Net (UA 1959)
The Adventures of Huckleberry Finn (MGM 1960)
A Breath of Scandal (Par 1960)
Francis of Assisi (Fox 1961)
The Comancheros (Fox 1961)

CUTTS, GRAHAM, b. 1885; d. 1958
Cocaine [While London Sleeps] (Astra 1922)
The Wonderful Story (Astra-National 1923)
Flames of Passion (Astra 1922)
Paddy the Next Best Thing (Graham-Wilcox 1923)
Woman to Woman (W & F 1924)
The Passionate Adventure (Gaumont 1924)
The Blackguard (GB/Ger) (W & F 1925)
The Rat (W & F 1925)
The Sea Urchin (W & F 1926) (also co-script)
The Triumph of the Rat (W & F 1926) (also co-script)
The Queen Was in the Parlour [Forbidden Love] (GB/Ger) (W
    & F 1927) (also script)
The Rolling Road (W & F 1927)
Confetti (FNP 1927)
God's Clay (FNP 1928)
The Return of the Rat (W & F 1929)
The Temperance Fete (MGM 1932)
The Sign of Four (Radio 1932) (with Rowland V. Lee)
Love on the Spot (Radio 1932)
Looking on the Bright Side (Radio 1932) (with Basil Dean)
As Good as New (WB Br 1933)
Three Men in a Boat (ABFD 1933)
Oh! Daddy! (Gaumont 1935) (with Austin Melford)
Car of Dreams (Gaumont 1935) (with Austin Melford)
Aren't Men Beasts! (ABPC 1937)
Let's Make a Night of It (ABPC 1937)
Over She Goes (ABPC 1937)
Just William (ABPC 1939) (also co-script)
She Couldn't Say No (ABPC 1939)

CZINNER, PAUL, b. 1890, Budapest; d. June 22, 1972
  Homo Immanis [Der Unmensch] (Aus 1919)
  Inferno (Aus 1920)
  Nju (Ger 1924) (also script)
  Der Geiger von Florenz (Ger 1926) (also script)
  Liebe (Ger 1926) (also script)
  Dona Juana (Ger 1927) (also co-script)
  Fräulein Else (Ger 1929) (also script)
  The Woman He Scorned (WB Br 1929) (also author)
  Ariane [The Loves of Ariane] (Ger/GB 1931) (also co-script, producer)
  Der Träumende Mund (Ger 1932) (also co-script)
  Catherine the Great (UA 1934)
  Escape Me Never (UA 1935)
  As You Like It (20th Br 1936) (with Dallas Bower)
  Dreaming Lips (UA 1937) (with Lee Garmes) (also co-producer)
  Melo (Fr 1938)
  Stolen Life (Par Br 1939)
  Don Giovanni (Maxwell 1955) (with Maxwell Travers) (also co-producer)
  The Bolshoi Ballet (RFD 1957) (also co-producer)
  The Royal Ballet (RFD 1960) (also producer)
  Der Rosenkavalier (RFD 1962) (also producer)
  Romeo and Juliet (RFD 1966) (also producer)

DAALDER, RENE, b. Mar. 3, 1944, Texel, Netherlands
  De Blanke Slavin (Dut 1969)

DA CUNHA TELLES, ANTONIO, b. 1933, Portugal
  O cerco (Por 1969) (also script, editor)
  Meus Amigos (Por 1974)

DALLAMANO, MASSIMO (a.k.a. Max Dillmann), b. April 17, 1917, Milan
  Bandidos (It 1968)
  La morte non ha sesso (It 1968)
  Il dio chiamato Dorian (It-Ger 1970)
  Si puo essere più bastardi dell'ispettore Cliff? (It 1972)
  La polizia chiede aiuto (It 1974)

DAMIANI, DAMIANO, b. July 23, 1922, Pasiano (Udine) Italy
  Il rossetto [Red Lips] (It-Fr 1960) (also co-script)
  Il sicario (It 1961) (also co-script)
  L'isola di Arturo (It 1963) (also co-script)
  La rimpatriata (It 1963) (also co-script)
  La noia [The Empty Canvas] (It 1963) (also co-script)
  Aura, la strega in amore [The Witch in Love] (It 1966)
  Il giorno della civetta [Mafia] (It 1968) (also co-script)
  ¿Quién Sabe? [A Bullet for the General] (Sp-It 1968)
  Una regazza piuttosto complicata (It 1969)
  Confessione di un commissario di polizia al procuratore della repubblica (It 1970) (also co-script)
  Ma moglie più bella (It 1970)

António da Cunha Telles

L'istruttoria è chuiso (It 1971)
Il sorriso del grande tentatore (It 1972)
Morte di un magistrato (It 1974)

DAQUIN, LOUIS, b. 1908, Calais
Nous les gosses (Fr 1941)
Madame et le mort (Fr 1942)
Le Voyageur de la Toussaint (Fr 1942)
Premier de cordée (Fr 1943)
Patrie (Fr 1945)
Les Frères Bouquinquant (Fr 1947)
Le Point du jour (Fr 1948)
Le Parfum de la dame en noir (Fr 1949)
Maître après Dieu [Skipper Next to God] (Fr 1950)
Bel Ami (Fr-Aus 1954)
Les Chardons du Baragan (Fr 1957)
Les Arrivistes [Trübe Wasser] (Fr-E Ger 1959)
Le Foire aux cancres (Fr 1962)

DASKALIDES, JEAN, b. Dec. 23, 1924, Istanbul
  6, Kruiswegstraat (Bel 1973)

DAVIS, DESMOND, b. 1928, London
  Girl with Green Eyes (UA 1964)
  The Uncle (BL 1964) (also co-script)
  I Was Happy Here (RFD 1965) (also co-script)
  Smashing Time (Par Br 1967)

DAY, ROBERT, b. Sept. 11, 1922, London
  The Green Man (BL 1956)
  Stranger's Meeting (RFD 1957)
  Grip of the Strangler [The Haunted Strangler] (Eros 1958)
  Corridors of Blood (MGM Br 1958)
  First Man into Space (MGM Br 1959)
  Life in Emergency Ward 10 (Eros 1959)
  Bobbikins (20th Br 1959)
  Two-Way Stretch (BL 1960)
  Tarzan the Magnificent (Par 1960)
  The Rebel (WPD 1961)
  Operation Snatch (RFI 1962)
  She (WPD 1965)
  Tarzan and the Valley of Gold (US/Sw) (WPD-AA 1966)
  Tarzan and the Great River (Par 1967)

DEAN, BASIL, b. 1888, Croydon
  Escape (Radio 1930) (also producer, script)
  Birds of Prey [The Perfect Alibi] (Radio 1930) (also producer, co-script)
  Nine Till Six (Radio 1932) (also producer)
  The Impassive Footman [Woman in Bondage] (Radio 1932) (also producer)
  Looking on the Bright Side (Radio 1932) (also producer, co-script) (with Graham Cutts)
  Loyalties (ABFD 1933) (also producer)
  The Constant Nymph (Gaumont 1933) (also co-script)
  Autumn Crocus (ABFD 1934) (also producer, script)
  Sing As We Go (ABFD 1934) (also producer)
  Lorna Doone (ABFD 1935) (also producer)
  Look Up and Laugh (ABFD 1935) (also producer)
  Whom the Gods Love [Mozart] (ABFD 1936) (also producer)
  The Show Goes On (ABFD 1937) (also producer, story)
  21 Days [21 Days Together] (Col 1939) (filmed in 1937)

DEARDEN, BASIL, b. Jan. 1, 1911, Westcliff-on-Sea, Essex, England, d. March 24, 1971
  The Black Sheep of Whitehall (UA 1941) (with Will Hay)
  The Goose Steps Out (UA 1942) (with Will Hay)
  The Bells Go Down (UA 1943)
  My Learned Friend (Ealing 1943) (with Will Hay)
  Halfway House (Ealing 1944)
  They Came to a City (Ealing 1944) (also co-script)
  Dead of Night (eps "The Linking Story," "The Hearse Driver")

(EL 1945)
The Captive Heart (GFD 1946)
Frieda (GFD 1947)
Saraband for Dead Lovers (GFD 1948) (with Michael Relph)
Train of Events (GFD 1949) (with Sidney Cole, Charles Crich-
    ton) (also co-script)
The Blue Lamp (GFD 1950)
Cage of Gold (GFD 1950)
Pool of London (GFD 1951)
I Believe in You (GFD 1952) (also co-script)
The Gentle Gunman (GFD 1952)
The Square Ring (GFD 1953)
The Rainbow Jacket (GFD 1954)
Out of the Clouds (GFD 1955)
The Ship That Died of Shame [PT Raiders] (GFD 1955) (also
    co-script)
Who Done It? (RFD 1956)
The Smallest Show on Earth (BL 1957)
Violent Playground (RFD 1958)
Sapphire (RFD 1959)
The League of Gentlemen (RFD 1960)
Man in the Moon (RFD 1960)
The Secret Partner (MGM Br 1961)
Victim (RFD 1961)
All Night Long (RFD 1962)
Life for Ruth [Walk in the Shadow] (RFD 1962)
The Mind Benders (AA 1962)
A Place to Go (Bry 1963)
Woman of Straw (UA 1964)
Masquerade (UA 1964)
Khartoum (UA 1965) (with Eliot Elisofen, Yakima Canutt)
Only When I Larf (Par 1968)
The Assassination Bureau (Par 1969)
The Man Who Haunted Himself (WPD 1970)

DE BARROS, JOSE LEITÃO see LEITÃO DE BARROS

DE CAMPOS, HENRIQUE (Henrique Xavier de Oliveira Campos),
    b. Feb. 9, 1909
Um homem do Ribatejo (Por 1946)
Ribatejo (Por 1949) (also script)
Cantiga da rua (Por 1949)
Duas causas (Por 1952)
Rosa de Alfama (Por 1953)
Quando o mar Galgou a terra (Por 1954)
Perdeu-se um marido (Por 1957)
O homem do dia (Por 1958)
A Luz Vem do Alto (Por 1959)
Canção da suadade (Por 1964)
Pão, amor e ... Totobola (Por 1964)
Estrada da vida (Por 1968)
O Ladrão de quem se fala (Por 1969)
O destino marca a hora (Por 1970)

A maluquinha de arroios (Por 1970)
Os Toiros de Mary Foster (Por 1972)

Henrique de Campos

DECOIN, HENRI, b. March 18, 1896, Paris; d. July, 1969
Toboggan (Fr 1933) (also script, dialogue)
Le Domino vert (Fr 1933) (also co-script) (with Henri Selpin)
Je vous aimerai toujours (Fr 1933)
Les Bleus du ciel (Fr 1933) (also script, dialogue)
Mademoiselle ma mère (Fr 1936)
Abus de confiance (Fr 1937)
Retour à l'aube (Fr 1938) (also co-script)
Battements de coeur (Fr 1939)
Premier rendez-vous (Fr 1941)
Les Inconnus dans la maison (Fr 1941)

Le Bienfaiteur (Fr 1942) (also script)
Mariage d'amour (Fr 1942)
L'Homme de Londres (Sp) (Fr 1943) (also script)
Je suis avec toi (Fr 1943)
La Fille du diable (Fr 1946)
Non coupable (Fr 1947) (also script)
Les Amants du Pont Saint Jean (Fr 1947)
Les Amoureux sont seuls au monde (Fr 1948)
Entre onze heures et minuit (Fr 1949) (also script)
Au Grand balcon (Fr 1949)
Trois télégrammes [Paris Incident] (Fr 1950) (also co-script)
    (with Lucien Arman, Leon Berton, Paul Bisciglia)
Clara de Montargis (Fr 1951) (also story, script, dialogue)
Le Désir et l'amour [Love and Desire] (Fr-Sp 1951) (also
    script, dialogue)
La Vérité sur Bébé Douge [The Truth of Our Marriage] (Fr
    1951)
Les Amants de Tolède [The Lovers of Toledo] (Sp-Fr-It 1952)
Le Dortoir des grandes [Girls' Dormitory] (Fr 1953) (also co-
    script)
Secrets d'alcôve [The Bed] (ep "Le Billet de logement") (Fr-It
    1954)
Les Intrigantes [The Plotters] (Fr 1954)
Bonnes à tuer [One Step to Eternity] (Fr 1954) (also co-dia-
    logue, co-script)
Razzia sur la chnouf [Chnouf] (Fr 1955) (also co-script)
Affaire des poisons (Fr-It 1955) (also co-script)
Folies Bergère (Fr 1956)
Le Feu aux poudres (Fr-It 1956) (also co-script)
Tous peuvent me tuer [Anyone Can Kill Me] (Fr-It 1957) (also
    co-script)
Charmants garçons (Fr 1957)
La Chatte [The Face of the Cat] (Fr 1958) (also co-script)
Pourquoi viens-tu si tard? (Fr 1958)
Nathalie, agent secret (Fr 1959)
La Chatte sort ses griffes [The Cat Shows Her Claws] (Fr 1959)
    (also co-adaptor)
La Française et l'amour [Love and the Frenchwoman] (ep "L'en-
    fance") (Fr-It 1960)
Tendre et violent Elizabeth [Passionate Affair] (Fr 1960) (also
    co-adaptor)
Le Pavé de Paris [The Pavements of Paris] (Fr-It 1960) (also
    co-adaptor)
Maléfices [Where the Truth Lies] (Fr 1961) (also co-script)
La Masque de fer (Fr-It 1962)
Noches de Casablanca (Sp-Fr 1963)
Les Parias de la Gloire (Fr-Sp-It 1964)
Nick Carter va tout casser (Fr-It 1964)

DE COURVILLE, ALBERT, b. 1887, London, d. March 15, 1960
    Wolves [Wanted Men] (W & F 1930)
    77 Park Lane (UA 1931)
    Night Shadows (UA 1931) (Never released)

There Goes the Bride (Ideal 1932)
The Midshipmaid (W & F 1932)
This Is the Life (BL 1933)
Wild Boy (Gaumont 1934) (also co-author)
Things Are Looking Up (Gaumont 1935) (also co-author)
The Case of Gabriel Perry (BL 1935)
Charing Cross Road (BL 1935)
Seven Sinners [Doomed Cargo] (Gaumont 1936)
Strangers on a Honeymoon (Gaumont 1936)
Clothes and the Woman (ABPC 1937)
Oh Boy! (ABPC 1938)
Star of the Circus [Hidden Menace] (ABPC 1938)
Crackerjack [The Man with a Hundred Faces] (GFD 1938)
The Lambeth Walk (MGM 1939)
An Englishman's Home [Madmen of Europe] (UA 1939)
Rebel Son (UA 1939) (with uncredited Adrian Brunel)

DE GARCIA, CHIANCA, b. April 14, 1898, Lisbon
Ver e Amar (Por 1930)
O trevo de quatro folhas (Por 1936)
Rosa do Adro (Por 1936) (also adaptation)
A Aldeia da roupa branca (Por 1938) (also co-script)
Pureza (Braz 1939)
24 horas de sonho (Braz 1941)

DEGELIN, EMILE, b. July 16, 1926, Diest, Belgium
Si le vent te fait peur (Bel 1959) (also script)
Leven en Dood Op het Land (in two parts) (Bel 1963) (also
    script)
Beatrice (Bel 1963) (also co-script)
¿Y Mañana? (Sp-Bel 1966) (also script)
Palaver (Bel 1969) (also script)

DE HEREDIA, JOSE LUIS SAENZ, b. Apr. 10, 1911, Madrid
Patricio Miro una Estrella (Sp 1934)
La hija de Juan Simon (Sp 1935) (with Luis Buñuel)
¿Quien me quiere a mi? (Sp 1936) (with Luis Buñuel)
Raza (Sp 1941)
El Escandalo (Sp 1943)
Bambu (Sp 1945)
El destino se disculpa (Sp 1945)
Mariona rebull (Sp 1946)
La mies es mucha (Sp 1947)
Las Aguas bajan turbias (Sp 1948)
Don Juan (Sp 1950) (also producer)
Los ojos dejan huellas (Sp 1952) (also producer)
Todo es posible en Granada (also producer, script)
Historias de la radio (Sp 1955) (also producer)
Faustina (Sp 1956) (also producer)
Diez fusiles esperan (Sp 1958) (also producer)
El indulto (Sp 1960)
El grano de mostaza (Sp 1962)
Los derechos de la mujer (Sp 1962)

La verbena de la Paloma (Sp 1963)
Historias de la television (Sp 1964)
Franco ese hombre (Sp 1964) (with Ozores)
Fray Torero (Sp 1965)
Relaciones casi publicas (Sp 1968)
Se armo el Belen (Sp 1969)
Cita a las cuatro (Sp 1969)
Juicio de faldas (Sp 1969)
El alma se serena (Sp 1969)
La decente (Sp 1970)
El taxi de los conflictos (Sp 1969)
Don erre que erre (Sp 1970) (also co-script)
Me debes un muerto (Sp 1971)

DE HERT, ROBBE, b. 1942, Belgium
S. O. S. Fonske (Bel TV 1968) (also script) (with Guido Henderick,
   Patrick Le Bon)
De Dood van een sandwichman (Bel 1971) (also co-script) (with
   Guido Henderickx)
Kamera-Sutra of de Bleeke Gezichten (Bel 1972) (also script)
Le Filet américain (Bel 1974)

DE HEUSCH, LUC, b. May 7, 1927, Brussels
La Fête chez les Hamba (Bel 1955)
Ruanda (Bel 1955)
Jeudi, on chantera comme dimance (Bel 1967) (also co-script)
Libre examen (Bel TV 1968) (also script)

DEKEUKELEIRE, CHARLES, b. Feb. 25, 1905, Belgium; d. 1971
Impatience (Bel 1928) (also script)
Histoire de détective (Bel 1928) (also script)
Terres brûlées (Bel 1935) (also script)
Het Kwade Oog (Bel 1937) (also co-script)
Emily Dickenson (Bel TV 1962) (also script)

DE LA PARRA, PIM, Jan. 5, 1940, Paramaribo (Surinam), Dutch
   Guiana
Heart Beat Fresco (Dut 1966)
Confessions of Loving Couples (Dut 1967) (with Wim Verstappen)
Tag der offenen Tür (Ger TV 1967) (with Wim Verstappen)
Jongens, Jongens, Wat een Medi (Dut 1968)
Obsessions (Dut 1969) (also co-script)
Frank & Eva, Living Apart Together (Dut 1973)
Dakota (Dut 1973)
Convent of Doom (Dut-GB 1974)

DELIRE, JEAN, b. March 24, 1930, Châtelet, Belgium
Entre chiens et loups (Bel TV 1959)
La Cruche cassée (Bel TV 1962) (also co-script)
Belle (Bel TV 1967)
Une Certaine Belgique (Bel TV 1967)
Chalet 1 (Bel TV 1968)
Magic City (Bel TV 1969)

Trois étranges histoires (Bel 1969)
Plus jamais seuls (Bel 1972)

DELOUCHE, DOMINIQUE, b. 1931, Paris
  24 Heures de la vie d'une femme [24 Hours in a Woman's Life]
    (Fr-W Ger 1968)
  L'Homme de désir (Fr 1970) (also producer, script)

DELVAUX, ANDRE, b. March 21, 1926, Heverlee, Belgium
  Federico Fellini (Bel TV 1960)
  Jean Rouch (Bel TV 1960)
  Cinéma polonais (Bel TV 1964)
  De Man die Zijn Haar Kort Liet Knippen (Bel 1966) (also co-
    script)
  Un Soir, un train (Bel 1968) (also script)
  Rendez-vous à Bray (Bel 1971) (also script)
  Belle (Bel 1973) (also script)

DE MACEDO, ANTONIO, b. Portugal
  Verso Coincidente (Por 1962)
  Nicotiana (Por 1963)
  Domingo a tarde (Por 1965) (also script, dialogue, sound, edi-
    tor)
  Alta velocidade (Por 1967)
  Fado (Por 1968)
  Almada negrieres, vivo, hoje (Por 1968)
  Historia breva de madeira aglomerada (Por 1970)
  Quatro temas para refinaria e quarteto (Por 1971)
  Nojo Aos Caes (Por 1971)
  A Promessa (Por 1972) (also script)

DE MEYST, EMILE G., b. 1902, Brussels
  La Brabançonne (Bel 1931) (also co-script)
  L'Amour en six jours (Bel 1932) (also co-script)
  Les Péperbol a l'exposition (Bel 1935) (also co-script)
  Ça viendra (Bel 1936) (also co-script)
  Le Mort (Bel 1937) (also co-script)
  Les Gangsters de l'Expo (Bel 1937)
  H'voula (Unfinished--Bel 1939) (also co-script)
  Soldats sans uniforme (Bel 1944) (also co-script) (with George
    Lust)
  Baraque Nº 1 (Bel 1945) (also co-script)
  Forçats d'honneur (Bel 1945) (also co-script)
  Le Cocu magnifique (Bel 1946) (also co-script)
  Les Atouts de Monsieur Wens (Bel 1946) (also co-script)
  Passeurs d'or (Bel 1948) (also co-script)
  Je n'ai que toi au monde [Les Anges sont parmi nous!] (Bel
    1949) (also co-script)
  La Maudite [La Belle de nulle part] (Bel 1949) (also co-script)
    (with Norbert Benoit)
  Ah, qu'il fait bon chez nous (Bel 1950) (also co-script) (with
    Jacques Loar)
  La Tricheuse (Bel 1960) (also co-script)
  Filles de fraudeurs (Bel 1961)

António de Macedo

DEMY, JACQUES, b. June 5, 1931, Pont Château, France
  Lola (It-Fr 1960) (also script, dialogue)
  Les Sept Péchés capitaux (ep "La Luxure") (Fr-It 1962) (also
    script, dialogue)
  La Baie des Anges (Fr 1963) (also script, dialogue)
  Les Parapluies de Cherbour [Umbrellas of Cherbour] (Fr-W
    Ger 1964) (also script, dialogue)
  Les Demoiselles de Rochefort [The Young Girls of Rochefort]
    (Fr 1966) (also script, dialogue)
  Model Shop (USA) (Col 1968) (also producer, script, co-English
    dialogue)
  Peau d'âne [Magic Donkey] (Fr 1971) (also script)
  The Pied Piper (GB) (Scotia-Barber 1972) (also script)
  L'Evénement le plus important depuis que l'homme a marché
    sur la lune [The Slightly Pregnant Man] (Fr-It 1973) (also
    script)

DENHAM, REGINALD, b. 1894, London
  Called Back (Radio 1933) (with Jack Harris)
  The Jewel (Par 1933)

Jacques Demy

Lucky Loser (B & D-Par Br 1934)
Brides to Be (B & D-Par Br 1934)
The Primrose Path (B & D-Par Br 1934)
Death at Broadcasting House (ABFD 1934)
Borrow a Million (Fox Br 1934)
The Price of Wisdom (B & D-Par Br 1935)
The Village Squire (B & D-Par Br 1935)
The Silent Passenger (ABFD 1935)
Lucky Days (B & D-Par Br 1935)
Lieutenant Daring, RN (Butcher 1935)
The Crimson Circle (Wainwright 1936)
Calling the Tune (ABFD 1936)
The House of the Spaniard (ABFD 1936)
Dreams Come True (Reunion 1936)
Kate plus Ten (GFD 1938)
Flying Fifty-Five (RKO Br 1939)
Blind Folly (RKO Br 1939)

DE OLIVEIRA, MANUEL (Manuel Candido Pinto de Oliveira), b.
Dec. 12, 1908, Passamanarias, Portugal
Douro, faina fluvial (Por 1931) (also script)
Miramar, praia das rosas (Por 1939) (also script)
Em Portugal também se fabricam automoveis (Por 1939) (also
script)
Famalição (Por 1941)
Aniki-Bobo (Por 1942) (also script, dialogue)
O pintor e a cidade (Ger 1954) (also story, co-camera)
O coração (Por 1958)
O Pão (Por 1959)
Acto da primavera (Por 1962) (also camera)
Auto da paixão (Por 1962)
A caça (Por 1963) (also camera)
O passado e o presente (Por 1972)

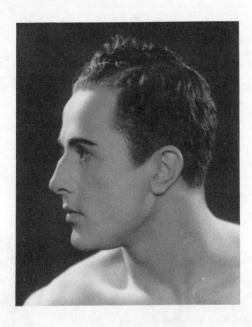

Manuel de Oliveira

DE ORDUÑA, JUAN, b. Dec. 27, 1900, Madrid
Porque te villoras (Sp 1941)
¡A mi la legion! (Sp 1942)
El frente de los suspiros (Sp 1942)
Rosas de Otono (Sp 1943)
La vida empieza a medianoche (Sp 1943)
Tuvo la culpa adan (Sp 1943)
Deliciosamente tontos (Sp 1943)

Yo no me caso (Sp 1944)
Ella, el y sus millones (Sp 1944)
Mi enemigo el doctor (Sp 1945)
Mision blanca (Sp 1946)
Un drama nuevo (Sp 1946)
Serenata Española (Sp 1947)
Locura de amor (Sp 1948)
Tempestad en el alma (Sp 1949)
Agustina de aragon (Sp 1950)
Pequences (Sp 1950)
La leona de Castilla (Sp 1951)
Alba de america (Sp 1951)
Canas y barro (Sp 1953) (also producer)
El padre Pitillo (Sp 1953) (also producer)
Zalacain el aventurero (Sp 1954) (also producer)
El ultimo cuple (Sp 1957) (also producer)
La Tirana (Sp 1958) (also producer)
Musica de ayer (Sp 1958) (also producer)
El amor de los Amores (Sp 1960) (also producer)
Teresa de Jesus (Sp 1961)
Bochorno (Sp 1962) (also producer)
Abajo Espera la muerte (Sp 1964)
Nobleza Baturra (Sp 1964) (also producer)
Anonima de asesionos (Sp 1965) (also producer)
Despedida de casada (Sp 1966) (also producer)
Bohemios (Sp 1967)
La cancion del olvido (Sp 1967)
Maruxa (Sp 1968)
El Huesped del Sevillano (Sp 1968)
La tonta del bote (Sp 1970)

DERAY, JACQUES, b. 1929, Lyon, France
Le Gigolo [Gigolo] (Fr 1960) (also co-script)
Rififi à Tokyo (Fr-It 1961) (also co-adaptor)
Symphonie pour un massacre [The Corrupt] (It-Fr 1963) (also
    co-script)
Par un beau matin d'été (Fr-Sp-It 1964) (also co-script)
Avec la peau des autres [To Skin a Spy] (Fr-It 1964) (also co-
    script)
L'Homme de Marrakech (Fr-Sp-It 1966) (also co-script) (begun
    by Robert Siodmak)
La Piscine [The Swimming Pool] (Fr-It 1969) (also co-adaptor,
    co-dialogue)
Borsalino (Fr-It 1970) (also co-script)
Doucement les basses! (Fr 1971)
Un Peu de soleil dans l'eau froide [Sunlight on Cold Water]
    (Fr 1971) (also co-script)
Un Homme est mort [The Outside Man] (Fr-It 1973) (also co-
    story, co-script)
Borsalino & Cie (Fr-It-W Ger 1974) (also co-script, co-dia-
    logue)

DE ROBERTIS, FRANCESCO, b. Oct. 11, 1902, San Marco, Italy;
    d. Feb. 3, 1959
  Mine in vista (It 1941) (also script)
  Uomini sul fondo (It 1941)† (also script, music)
  Alfa Tau (It 1942) (also script)
  Marina senza stella (It 1943) (also script)
  Uomimi e cieli (It 1943) (also script, music)
  La vite semplice (It 1945) (also script)
  La voce di Paganini (It 1945) (also co-script)
  Fantasmi del mare (It 1948)
  Il murato (It 1949) (also script)
  Gli amati di Ravello (It 1951) (also script)
  Carica eroica [Heroic Charge] (It 1952) (also script)
  Mizar (It 1952) (also script)
  Uomini ombra (It 1955) (also script)
  La donna che venna dal mare (It 1957) (also story, co-script)
  Ragazzi della marina (It 1958)
  Yalis, la vergine del Roncador (It 1961)

DEROISY, LUCIEN, b. Feb. 3, 1912, Namêche, Belgium; d. 1972
  Le Rôle humain de l'électricité (Bel 1958)
  Les Gommes (Bel 1969)
  Autour de René Magritte (Bel 1969) (also script)

DE SANTIS, GIUSEPPE, b. Feb. 11, 1917, Fondé, Italy
  Caccia tragica (It 1948)
  Riso amaro (It 1949)
  Non c'è pace tra gli ulivi (It 1950)
  Roma ore undici (It 1952)
  Un marito per Anna Zaccheo (It 1953)
  Giorni d'amore (It 1955)
  La strada lunga d'un anno (It 1958)
  La garçonniere (It 1960)
  Italiani brava gente (It 1964)
  La giornata di dolore dell'Avvocato Arcuri (It 1971)

DE SETA, VITTORIO, b. Oct. 15, 1923, Palermo, Italy
  Banditi a Orgosolo (It 1961)
  Un uomo a meta (It 1966)
  L'invitata (It 1970)

DE SICA, VITTORIO, b. July 7, 1901, Sera, Italy; d. Nov. 13,
    1974
  Rose Scarlatte (It 1940) (also actor)
  Maddalena zero in condotta (It 1940) (also co-script, actor)
  Teresa venerdì (It 1941) (also co-script, actor)
  Un Garibaldino al convento (It 1941) (also co-adaptor, actor)
  I bambini ci guardano [The Children Are Watching Us] (It 1942)
    (also co-script)
  La porta del cielo (It 1945) (also co-adaptor)
  Sciuscià [Shoeshine] (It 1946) (also co-script)
  Ladri di biciclette [Bicycle Thief] (It 1948) (also producer, co-
    adaptor)

Miracolo a Milano [Miracle in Milan] (It 1951) (also producer, co-adaptor)
Umberto D (It 1952) (also co-producer, co-adaptor)
Stazione termini [Indiscretion of an American Wife] (It 1953) (also co-producer)
L'oro di Napoli [The Gold of Naples] (It 1954) (also co-script, actor)
Il tetto [The Roof] (It 1956)
La Ciociara [Two Women] (It 1960) (also co-script)
Il Giudizio universale (It 1961) (also actor)
Boccaccio '70 (ep "La riffa") (It 1961)
I sequestrati di Altona [The Condemned of Altona] (It 1963)
Il boom (It 1963)
Ieri, oggi e domani [Yesterday, Today and Tomorrow] (It 1963)
Matrimonio all'Italiana [Marriage, Italian Style] (It 1964)
Caccia alla volpe [After the Fox] (It 1966)
Un mondo nuovo (It-Fr 1966)
Le streghe [The Witches] (ep "Una sera come le altre") (It 1967)
Sette volte donna [Woman Times Seven] (It 1967)
Gli amanti [A Place for Lovers] (It 1968)
I girasoli [Sunflower] (It 1970)
Il giardino dei Finzi-Contini [The Garden of the Finzi-Contini] (It 1970)
Le coppie (ep "Il Leone") (It 1971)
Una breva vacanza [Brief Vacation] (It 1972)

DEVILLE, MICHEL, b. 1931, Boulogne-sur-Seine, France
Une Balle dans le canon [A Slug in the Heater] (Fr 1958) (also co-script) (with Charles Gérard)
Ce soir ou jamais [Tonight or Never] (Fr 1961) (also co-script)
Adorable menteuse (Fr 1961) (also co-script)
A cause, à cause d'une femme (Fr 1962) (also co-script)
L'Appartement des filles (Fr-It-W Ger 1963) (also co-script)
Lucky Jo (Fr 1964) (also co-script)
Le Voleur de la Joconde (Fr-It 1965) (also co-script)
Martin soldat [Kiss me General] (Fr 1966)
Benjamin ou les mémoires d'un puceau [Benjamin] (Fr 1968) (also co-script)
Bye Bye Barbara (Fr 1969) (also co-script)
L'Ours et la poupée (Fr 1969) (also co-script)
Raphael ou le débauché (Fr 1971) (also co-script)
La Femme en bleu (Fr-It 1973) (also adaptation, script, co-adaptor, co-dialogue)
Le Mouton enragé (Fr-It 1973) (also co-script)

DE WAVRIN, ROBERT, b. 1888, Belgium; d. 1971
Au pays du scalp (Bel 1930)
Venezuela, paradis terrestre [Venezuela, petite Venise] (Bel 1936)

DEWEVER, JEAN, b. 1927, Paris
Les Honneurs de la guerre (Fr 1960)
César Grandblaise (Fr 1971) (also co-adaptor)

D'HOOP, MICHEL, b. July 29, 1935, Brussels
    Les Chrysalides (Bel 1966) (also script)
    J'Etais une jeune targuia nomade (Bel 1969) (also script,
        camera, narrator)

DICKINSON, THOROLD, b. Nov. 16, 1903, Bristol, England
    The High Command (ABFD 1937)
    Spanish ABC (Br 1938)
    The Arsenal Stadium Mystery (GFD 1939) (also co-script)
    Gaslight [Angel Street] (Anglo 1940)
    The Prime Minister (WB Br 1941)
    The Next of Kin (UA Br 1942) (also co-script)
    Men of Two Worlds (GFD 1946) (also co-script)
    The Queen of Spades (ABP 1949)
    Secret People (GFD 1952) (also co-story, co-script)
    Hill 24 Doesn't Answer (Israel 1954)
    Overture (UNFS 1958)
    Power Among Men (UNFS 1959)

Thorold Dickinson (with glasses)

DIETERLE, WILLIAM (WILHELM DIETERLE), b. July 15, 1893,
    Ludwigshafen, Germany; d. Dec. 16, 1972
    Der Mensch am Wege (Ger 1923) (also script, actor)
    Das Geheimnis des Abbe X (Ger 1927) (also script, actor)
    Die Heilige und ihr Narr (Ger 1928) (also actor)
    Geschlecht in Fesseln (Ger 1928) (also actor)
    Frühlingsrauschen (Ger 1929) (also actor)
    Ich Lebe für Dich (Ger 1929) (also actor)
    Ludwig der zweite König von Bayern (Ger 1929) (also actor)
    Eine Stunde glück (Ger 1920) (also actor)
In the U. S. A.
    Der Tanz geht weiter [Ger version of Those Who Dance] (FN
      1930) (also actor)
    Die Maske fallt (Ger version of The Way of All Men) (FN 1930)
    Kismet [Ger version of Kismet] (FN 1931)
    The Last Flight (FN 1931)
    Her Majesty Love (FN 1931)
    Man Wanted (WB 1932)
    Jewel Robbery (WB 1932)
    The Crash (FN 1932)
    Scarlet Dawn (WB 1932)
    Six Hours to Live (Fox 1932)
    Lawyer Man (WB 1932)
    Grand Slam (WB 1933)
    Adorable (Fox 1933)
    The Devil's in Love (Fox 1933)
    From Headquarters (WB 1933)
    Fashions of 1934 (WB 1934)
    Fog Over Frisco (FN 1934)
    Madame Dubarry (WB 1934)
    The Firebird (WB 1934)
    The Secret Bride (WB 1934)
    Dr. Socrates (WB 1935)
    A Midsummer Night's Dream (WB 1935) (with Max Reinhardt)
    The Story of Louis Pasteur (WB 1936)
    The White Angel (WB 1936)
    Satan Met a Lady (WB 1936)
    The Great O'Malley (WB 1937)
    Another Dawn (WB 1937)
    The Life of Emile Zola (WB 1937)
    Blockade (UA 1938)
    Juarez (WB 1939)
    The Hunchback of Notre Dame (RKO 1939)
    Dr. Ehrlich's Magic Bullet (WB 1940)
    A Dispatch from Reuter's (WB 1940)
    All That Money Can Buy [The Devil and Daniel Webster] (RKO
      1941) (also producer)
    Syncopation (RKO 1942) (also producer)
    Tennessee Johnson (MGM 1942)
    Kismet (MGM 1944)
    I'll Be Seeing You (UA 1944)
    Love Letters (Par 1945)
    This Love of Ours (Univ 1945)
    The Searching Wind (Par 1946)

Duel in the Sun (SRO 1946) (uncredited, with King Vidor, and
    uncredited Josef von Sternberg, William Cameron Menzies,
    Otto Brower, Sidney Franklin)
Portrait of Jenny (SRO 1949)
The Accused (Par 1949)
Volcano (UA-It 1949) (also producer)
Rope of Sand (Par 1949)
Paid in Full (Par 1950)
Dark City (Par 1950)
September Affair (Par 1951)
Peking Express (Par 1951)
Boots Malone (Col 1952)
Red Mountain (Par 1952)
The Turning Point (Par 1952)
Salome (Col 1953)
Elephant Walk (Par 1954)
Magic Fire (Rep 1956) (also producer)
Omar Khayyam (Par 1957)
Herrin der Welt (Ger-It 1959) (released in two parts)
Il vindicatore (Ger-It 1959) (also actor)
Die Fastnachtsbeichte (Ger 1960)
The Confession (Golden Eagle 1965)

DITVOORST, ADRIAAN, b. Jan. 23, 1940, Bergen op Zoom, Neth-
    erlands
Paranoia (Dut 1967)
Antenna (Swi 1970) (also script)
De Blinde Fotograaf (Dut 1973)

DO CANTO, JORGE BRUM, b. Feb. 10, 1910, Lisbon
A dança dos paroxismos (Por 1930) (also script, actor)
Paisagem (Por 1931) (unfinished)
A canção da terra (Por 1938) (also co-producer, script)
João ratso (Por 1940) (also co-script)
Lobos da serra (Por 1942) (also script)
Fatima, terra de fe (Por 1943) (also co-script)
Un homen as direitas (Por 1945) (also co-script, editor)
Ladrão, precisa-se! (Por 1946) (also co-script)
Chaimite (Por 1953) (also script, actor)
Retalhos da vida dum medico (Por 1962) (also script)
Fado corrido (Por 1964) (also co-script, co-adaptor, co-addi-
    tional dialogue, editor, actor)
Cruz de ferro (Por 1968) (also co-script, co-adaptor, editor,
    actor)

DONIOL-VALCROZE, JACQUES, b. 1920, Paris
L'Eau à la bouche [The Game of Love] (Fr 1959) (also script)
Le Coeur battant (Fr 1960) (also script)
La Dénonciation (Fr 1961) (also script)
Le Viol [A Question of Rape] (Sw-Fr 1967) (also script)
La Maison des Bories (Fr 1970)
L'Homme au cerveau greffé (Fr-It-W Ger 1971) (also adaptor,
    dialogue)
Une Femme fatale (Fr-W Ger 1974) (also adaptor, co-dialogue)

Jorge Brum do Canto

DONNER, CLIVE, b. 1926, London
   The Secret Place (RFD 1957)
   Heart of a Child (RFD 1958)
   Marriage of Convenience (AA 1960)
   The Sinister Man (AA 1961)
   Some People (AA 1962)
   The Caretaker [The Guest] (BL 1963)
   Nothing But the Best (AA 1963)
   What's New Pussycat? (US-Fr) (UA 1965)
   Luv (Col 1967)
   Here We Go Round the Mulberry Bush (UA 1967) (also co-pro-
      ducer)
   Alfred the Great (MGM 1969)

DOUGLAS, BILL, b. England
   My Childhood (BFI 1972) (also script)

DRACH, MICHEL, b. 1930, Paris
   On n'enterre pas le dimanche (Fr 1960) (also co-script, co-
      dialogue)
   Amélie ou le temps d'aimer [Amelie] (Fr 1961) (co-producer,
      script, dialogue, actor)
   La Bonne Occase [Les Belles Conduites] (Fr 1964)
   Safari diamants (Fr-W Ger 1966) (also co-script)
   Elise ou la vraie vie (Fr-Algerian 1970) (also co-script)
   Les violons du bal (Fr 1973) (also script)

DROUOT, PIERRE, b. Nov. 4, 1943, Oudenaade, Belgium
   [A photograph of Drouot appears near the COLLET entry]
   Cash? Cash! (Bel 1968) (also co-script) (with Paul Collet)
   L'Etreinte (Bel 1969) (also co-script) (with Paul Collet)
   Louisa, een Word van Liefde (Bel 1972) (also co-script) (with
       Paul Collet)

DUARTE, ARTUR (Artur de Jesus Pinto Pacheco Duarte), b. Oct.
   17, 1895, Lisbon
   O castelo de chocolate (Por 1924)
   Os fidalgos da Casa Mourisca (Por 1938)
   O costa do castelo (Por 1943)
   A menina da radio (Por 1944)
   E perigoso debruçar-se (Por-Sp 1945)
   O hospede do quarto no. 13 (Por-Sp 1945)
   Fogo (Por-Sp 1946)
   Nuvens de verão (Por-Sp 1946)
   O leão da estrela (Por 1947)
   O grande Elias (Por 1950)
   A garça e a serpente (Por 1952)
   O noivo das caldas (Por 1956)
   Dois dias no paraiso (Por 1957)
   Encontro com a vida (Por 1961)
   Encontro com a morte (Braz ?1963)

DUDOW, SLATAN, b. Jan 30, 1903, Zaribrod, Bulgaria; d. Aug.
   12, 1963
   Kühle Wampe (Ger 1932)
   Seifenblasen (Ger 1933)
   Unser täglich Brot (Ger 1949) (also co-script)
   Familie Benthin (Ger 1950) (with Kurt Maltzig) (also co-script)
   Frauenschicksale (Ger 1952) (also co-script)
   Stärker als die Nacht (Ger 1954)
   Der Hauptmann von Köln (Ger 1956) (also co-script)
   Verwirrung der Liebe (Ger 1959) (also co-script)
   Christine (Ger 1963) (unfinished)

DUFFELL, PETER, b. England
   Partners in Crime (AA 1961)
   The House that Dripped Blood (Cin 1971)
   England Made Me (Hemdale 1972) (also co-script)

DULAC, GERMAINE (Charlotte Elisabeth Germaine Saisset-
       Schneider), b. 1882, Amiens, France; d. July, 1942
   Les sœurs ennemies (Fr 1915)
   Géo le mystérieux (Fr 1916)
   Vénus victrix (Fr 1916)
   Dans l'ouragan de la vie (Fr 1916)
   Ames des fous (Fr 1917) (also script)
   Le Bonheur des autres (Fr 1918)
   La Fête espagnole (Fr 1919)
   La Cigarette (Fr 1919) (also co-script)
   Malencontre (Fr 1920)

Artur Duarte

La Belle Dame sans merci (Fr 1920)
La Mort du soleil (Fr 1921)
Werther (Unfinished Fr 1922) (also script)
La Souriante Madame Beudet [The Smiling Madame Beudet] (Fr 1923) (also script)
Gossette (Fr 1923)
Le Diable dans la ville (Fr 1924)
Ame d'artiste (Fr 1925) (also co-script)
La Folie des vaillants (Fr 1925) (also script)
Antoinette Soubrier (Fr 1926) (also script)
La Coquille et le clergyman [The Seashell and the Clergyman] (Fr 1927)
L'Invitation au voyage (Fr 1927) (also script)
Le Cinéma au service de l'histoire (Fr 1927)
La Princesse Mandone (Fr 1928) (also script)
Germination d'un haricot (Fr 1928)
Mon Paris (Fr 1928) (with Albert Guyet)
Les 24 Heures du Mans (Fr 1930)
Le Picador (Fr 1932) (with Jaquelux)
Le Cinéma au service de l'histoire (Fr 1937)

DUPLESSY, ARMAND (Armand Duplessïs or Armand de Prins), b. July 19, 1883, Brussels; d. Feb. 1924
Les Trois Flambeaux de la mort (Bel 1919)

La Petite Chanteuse des rues (Bel 1920)
La Conscrit (Bel 1921)
Gabrielle Petit (Bel 1921)
La Dentellière de Bruges (Bel 1921)
La Rose des Flandres (Bel 1921)
La Petite Filles et la vieille horloge (Bel 1921)
La Libre Belgique (Bel 1921)
Ame Belge (Bel 1921)
Le Caporal Trésignies (Bel 1921)
Le Gentilhomme pauvre (Bel 1921)
Knock-out (Bel 1922)
Le Collier de la momie (Bel 1923)
Destinée (Bel 1923)
Le Mariage de minuit (Bel 1923)
Un Héritage de 500 millions (Bel 1923)
Les Demi-vierges (Bel 1923)
Suprême sacrifice (Bel 1923)

DUPONT, E. A. (Ewald Andre Dupont), b. Dec. 25, 1891, Leitz,
    Germany; d. Dec. 12, 1956
Europa postlagernd (Ger 1918) (also script)
Mitternacht (Ger 1918) (also script)
Der Schatten (Ger 1918)
Der Teufel (Ger 1918)
Die Japanerin (Ger 1918) (also script)
Das Geheimnis der Amerika--Docks (Ger 1918) (also script)
Die Apachen (Ger 1919)
Die Maske (Ger 1919)
Die Spione (Ger 1919)
Das Derby (Ger 1919)
Der Würger der Welt (Ger 1919)
Das Grand Hotel Babylon (Ger 1919)
Der weisse Pfau [Tragödie einer Tänzerin] (Ger 1920) (also co-
    script)
Whitechapel [Eine Kette vom Perlen und Abenteuern] (Ger 1920)
Herztrumpf (Ger 1920)
Der Mord ohne Täter (Ger 1920) (also co-script)
Die GeierWally (Ger 1921) (also script)
Kinder der Finsternis [Part I: Der Man aus Neapel; Part II:
    Kämpfende Welten] (Ger 1921) (also co-script)
Sie und die Drei (Ger 1922)
Das alte Gesetz [Baruch] (Ger 1923)
Die grüne Manuela (Ger 1923)
Der Demütige und die Sängerin (Ger 1925) (also co-script)
Variété (Ger 1925) (also script)
Love Me and the World Is Mine (Univ 1927) (also co-script)
Moulin Rouge (BIP 1928) (also producer, script)
Piccadilly (BIP 1928) (also producer)
Atlantic (BIP 1929) (also producer)
Atlantik (Ger version of Atlantic) (Ger 1929)
Atlantique (Fr version of Atlantic) (with Jean Kemm) (Fr 1929)
Two Worlds (BIP 1930) (also producer, co-story)
Zwei Welten (Ger version of Two Worlds) (Ger 1930)

Cape Forlorn [Love Storm] (BIP 1930)
Menschen in Käfig (Ger version of Cape Forlorn) (Ger 1930)
Salto mortale [Trapeze] (Ger 1931)
Salto mortale (Fr version of Salto mortale) (Fr 1931)
Peter Voss der Millionendieb (Ger 1932) (also co-script)
Der Läufer von Marathon (Ger 1933)
In the U. S. A.
Ladies Must Love (Univ 1933)
The Bishop Misbehaves (MGM 1935)
A Son Comes Home (Par 1936)
Forgotten Faces (Par 1936)
A Night of Mystery (Par 1936)
On Such a Night (Par 1937)
Love on Toast (Par 1937)
Hell's Kitchen (WB 1939) (with Lewis Seiler)
The Scarf (UA 1951) (also script)
Problem Girls (Col 1953)
The Neanderthal Man (UA 1953)
The Steel Lady (UA 1953)
Return to Treasure Island (UA 1954)

DURAS, MARGUERITE (Marguerite Donnadieu), b. 1914, Giadinh,
Indochina [South Vietnam]
La Musica (Fr 1966) (also script) (with Paul Seban)
Détruire, dit-elle [Destroy She Said] (Fr 1969) (also script)
Jaune le Soleil (Fr 1971) (also script)
Natalie Granger (Fr 1972) (also script)
India Song (Fr 1974) (also script, adaptor, dialogue)

DURVIVIER, JULIEN, b. Oct. 8, 1896, Lille, France; d. Oct 29,
1967
Haceldama [Le Prix du sang] (Fr 1919) (also script)
La Réincarnation de Serge Renaudier (Fr 1920) (also script)
(negative destroyed in fire)
Les Roquevillard (Fr 1922) (also script)
L'Ouragan sur la montagne (Fr 1922) (also script)
Der Unheimliche Gast (Ger 1922)
Le Reflet de Claude Mercuoer (Fr 1923) (also script)
Credo ou la tragédie de Loudres (Fr 1923) (also script)
Coeurs farouches (Fr 1923) (also script)
La Machine à refaire la vie (Fr 1924) (with Henry Lepage)
L'Oeuvre immortelle (Bel 1924)
L'Abbé Constantin (Fr 1925)
Poil de carotte (Fr 1925) (also co-script)
L'Agonie de Jérusalem (Fr 1926) (also script)
L'Homme à Hispano (Fr 1926)
Le Mariage de Mademoiselle Beulemans (Fr 1927) (also script)
Le Mystère de la Tour Eiffel (Fr 1927) (Other sources credit
the direction to Marcel Vandal)
Le Tourbillon de Paris (Fr 1928)
La Vie miraculeuse de Thérèse Martin (Fr 1929) (also script)
La Divine Croisière (Fr 1929) (also script)
Maman Colibri (Fr 1929) (also co-script)

Au bonheur des dames (Fr 1929) (also co-script)
David Golder (Fr 1930) (also script)
Le Cinq Gentlemen maudits (Fr 1931) (also script)
Allo, Berlin? Ici, Paris (Fr 1932) (also script)
Poil de carotte (Fr 1932) (also script)
La Vénus du collège (Fr 1932)
La Tête d'un homme (Fr 1932) (also co-script)
Le Petit Roi (Fr 1933) (also script)
Le Paquebot "Tenacity" (Fr 1934) (also co-script)
Maria Chapdelaine (Fr 1934) (also co-script)
Golgotha (Fr 1935) (also co-script)
La Bandera (Fr 1935) (also script)

Julien Duvivier

Le Golem [The Legend of Prague] (Fr-Czech 1936) (also co-
    script)
La Belle Equipe (Fr 1936) (also co-script)
Pépé le Moko (Fr 1936) (also co-script)
L'Homme du jour (Fr 1936) (also co-script)
Un Carnet de bal [Christine] (Fr 1936) (also co-script)
The Great Waltz (USA) (MGM 1938) (with uncredited Josef von
    Sternberg)

La Fin du jour (Fr 1939) (also script)
La Charmette fantôme (Fr 1939) (also co-script)
Untel, père et fils [Heart of a Nation] (Fr-US 1940) (also co-script)
Lydia (USA) (UA 1941) (also co-author)
Tales of Manhattan (USA) (RKO 1942) (with René Clair, Edmund Goulding, Cedric Hardwicke, Frank Lloyd, Victor Saville, Robert Stevenson, Herbert Wilcox)
Flesh and Fantasy (USA) (Univ 1943) (also co-producer)
The Imposter/Strange Confession (USA) (Univ 1943) (also producer, co-script)
Panique (Fr 1946) (also co-script)
Anna Karenina (GB) (BL 1948) (also co-script)
Aux royaume des cieux [Woman Hunt] (Fr 1949) (also co-script)
Black Jack [Captain Blackjack] (Fr-US 1950) (also co-script)
Sous le ciel de Paris [Under the Paris Sky] (Fr 1950) (also co-script)
Le petit monde de Don Camillo [The Little World of Don Camillo] (It-Fr 1951) (also co-script)
La Fête à Henriette [Holiday for Henriette] (Fr 1952) (also co-script)
Le retour de Don Camillo [The Return of Don Camillo] (Fr-It 1953) (also co-script)
L'Affaire Maurizius [On Trial] (Fr-It 1953) (also script)
Marianne de ma jeunesse (Fr-Ger 1954) (also script)
Voici les temps des assassins [Deadlier Than the Male] (Fr 1955) (also script)
L'Homme à l'imperméable [The Man in the Raincoat] (Fr-It 1956) (also co-script)
Pot-Bouillé [The House of Lovers] (Fr-It 1957) (also co-script)
La Femme et le pantin [A Woman Like Satan] (Fr-It 1958) (also co-script)
Marie-Octobre (Fr 1958) (also co-script)
Das kunstseidene Mädchen (W Ger-Fr 1959) (also co-script)
Boulevard (Fr 1960) (also co-script)
La Chambre ardente [The Curse and the Coffin] (Fr-It-W Ger 1961) (also co-script)
Le Diable et les dix commandements [The Devil and the Ten Commandments] (Fr-It 1962) (also co-script)
Chair de poule [Highway Pickup] (Fr-It 1963) (also co-script)
Diaboliquement vôtre [Diabolically Yours] (Fr-It-W Ger 1967) (also co-script)

EADY, DAVID, b. April 22, 1924, London
Bridge of Time (195?)
Road to Canterbury (195?)
Three Cases of Murder (ep "You Killed Elizabeth") (BL 1955)
The Heart Within (RFD 1957)
The Man Who Liked Funerals (RFD 1959)
The Crowning Touch (Butcher 1959)
In the Wake of a Stranger (Butcher 1959)
Faces in the Dark (RFD 1960)
The Verdict (AA 1964)

Operation Third Form (CFF 1966) (also co-story)
Scramble (CFF 1971)† (co-production company)
Hide and Seek (CFF 1972)† (co-production company)
Anoop and the Elephant (CFF 1973)
Where's Johnny? (CFF 1974)† [co-production company] (also co-producer)

ECEIZA, ANTONIO, b. 1935
De cuerpo presente (Sp 1965)
El ultimo encuentro (Sp 1966)
Las secretas intenciones (Sp 1970)

EDWARDS, HENRY, b. 1883, Weston-super-Mare, England; d. Nov. 1, 1952
A Welsh Singer (Butcher 1915) (also co-script)
Doorsteps (Hepworth 1916) (also based on his play)
East Is West (Butcher 1916) (also script)
Merely Mrs. Stubb (Butcher 1917) (also script)
Dick Carson Wins Through (Butcher 1917) (also script)
Broken Threads (Butcher 1917)
The Hanging Judge (Moss 1918) (also script)
Towards the Light (Moss 1918) (also script)
His Dearest Possession (Hepworth 1919)
The Kinsman (Butcher 1919) (also script)
Possession (Butcher 1919)
The City of Beautiful Noises (Butcher 1919)
A Temporary Vagabond (Butcher 1920) (also script)
Aylwin (Hepworth 1920)
The Amazing Quest of Mr. Ernest Bliss (Imperial 1920)
John Forrest Finds Himself (Hepworth 1920)
The Lunatic at Large (Hepworth 1921)
The Bargain (Hepworth 1921) (also co-story)
Simple Simon (Hepworth 1922) (also co-story)
Tit for Tat (Hepworth 1922) (also co-story)
Lily of the Alley (Hepworth 1923) (also script)
Boden's Boy (Hepworth 1923)
The Naked Man (Ideal 1923) (also script)
The World of Wonderful Reality (Hepworth 1924) (also script)
Owd Bob (Novello-Atlas 1923)
King of the Castle (Stoll 1925)
A Girl of London (Stoll 1925)
One Colombo Night (Stoll 1926)
The Island of Despair (Stoll 1926)
The Girl in the Night (Wardour 1931)† (also producer, story)
Stranglehold (WB Br 1931) (also producer, script)
Brother Alfred (Wardour 1932) (also co-script)
The Flag Lieutenant (W & F 1932) (also actor)
The Barton Mystery (B & D-Par Br 1932)
Discord (B & D-Par Br 1933)
One Precious Year (Par Br 1933)
Lord of the Manor (B & D-Par Br 1933)
Anna One Hundred (B & D-Par Br 1933)
Purse Strings (B & D-Par Br 1933)

General John Regan (B & D-Par Br 1933)
The Man Who Changed His Name (Univ Br 1934)
The Lash (Radio 1934)
Lord Edgware Dies (Radio 1934)
Are You a Mason? (Univ Br 1934)
D'Ye Ken John Peel? [Captain Moonlight] (AP & D 1935)
The Rocks of Valpre [High Treason] (Radio 1935)
The Lad (Univ Br 1935)
Squibs (Gaumont 1935)
Vintage Wine (Gaumont 1935)
Scrooge (TFD 1935)
The Private Secretary (TFD 1935)
Eliza Comes to Stay (TFD 1936)
In the Soup (TFD 1936)
Juggernaut (Wardour 1936)
Beauty and the Barge (Wardour 1937)
Song of the Forge (Butcher 1937)
The Vicar of Bray (ABPC 1937)

EICHBERG, RICHARD, b. 1888, Berlin; d. 1952
Strohfeuer (Ger 1914)
Kinder der Landstrasse (Ger 1919)
Nonne und Tänzerin (Ger 1919)
Sklaven fremden Willens (Ger 1919)
Sünde der Eltern (Ger 1919)
Jugend (Ger 1920)
Der Tanz auf dem Vulkan (Ger 1920)
Der lebende Propeller (Ger 1921)
Die Liebesabenteuer der schönen Evelyn (Ger 1922) (only pro-
    ducer)
Monna Vanna (Ger 1922)
Das Strassenmädchen von Paris (Ger 1922)
Fräulein Raffke (Ger 1923)
Die Motorbraut (Ger 1924)
Die schönste Frau der Welt (Ger 1924)
Die Frau mit dem Etwas (Ger 1925)
Die Kleine vom Bummel (Ger 1925)
Leidenschaft (Ger 1925)
Liebes und Trompetenbasen (Ger 1925)
Durchlaucht Radieschen (Ger 1926)
Die keusche Susanne (Ger 1926)
Der Prinz und die Tänzerin (Ger 1926)
Der Fürst von Pappenheim (Ger 1927)
Die Leibeigenen (Ger 1927)
Die tolle Lola (Ger 1927)
Das Girl von der Revue (Ger 1928)
Rutschbahn (Ger 1928)
Song (Ger 1928)
Grosstadtschmetterling (Ger 1929)
Wer wird denn weinen, wenn man auseinandergeht (Ger 1929)
Hai-Tang (Ger 1930)
Der Greifer (Ger 1930)
Night Birds (Eng version of Der Greifer) (Ger 1930)

Der Draufgänger (Ger 1931) (also co-script)
Trara um Liebe (Ger 1931)
Die Bräutigamswitwe (Ger 1931)
Die unsichtbare Front (Ger 1932)
Früchtchen (Ger 1934) (also script)
Die Katz' im Sack (Ger 1935)
Der Schlafwagenkontrolleur (Ger 1935)
Der Kurier des Zaren (Ger-Fr 1936)
Es geht um mein Leben (Ger 1936) (also co-script)
Der Tiger von Eschnapur (Ger 1937) (also co-script)
Die Reise nach Marrakesch (Ger 1949)

ELVEY, MAURICE (William Seward Folkard), b. 1887, Darlington,
      England; d. Aug. 28, 1967
Home (Ideal 1915) (also producer)
Love in a Wood (Jury 1915) (also producer)
Meg the Lady (Jury 1915) (also producer)
Driven [Desperation] (Jury 1915) (also producer, script)
Motherlove (Jury 1916) (also producer)
When Knights Were Bold (Jury 1916) (also producer)
The Princess of Happy Chance (Jury 1916) (also producer)
The Grit of a Jew (Butcher 1917) (also producer)
The King's Daughter (Jury 1917) (also producer)
Smith (Jury 1917) (also producer)
The Woman Who Was Nothing (Butcher 1917) (also producer)
Flames (Butcher 1918) (also producer)
The Gay Lord Quex (Ideal 1918) (also producer)
Dombey and Son (Ideal 1918) (also producer)
Mary Girl (Butcher 1918) (also producer)
Hindle Wakes (Royal 1918) (also producer)
Goodbye Justice (Ideal 1918) (also producer)
Adam Bede (International Exclusives 1918) (also producer)
The Story of David Lloyd George or The Man Who Saved the
      Empire (made for Ideal in 1918 but never shown)
Nelson (Apex 1919)
The Victory Leaders (Stoll 1919)
Comradeship (Stoll 1919) (also producer)
The Keeper of the Door (Stoll 1919)
The Rocks of Vengeance (Stoll 1920) (released as The Rocks of
      Valpre)
God's Good Men (Stoll 1920)
Mr Wu (Stoll 1920)
The Swindler (Stoll 1920)
The Elusive Pimpernel (Stoll 1920)
The Amateur Gentleman (Stoll 1921)
Bleak House (Ideal 1921) (also producer) (probably made ca.
      1919)
At the Villa Rose (Stoll 1921)
The Hundredth Chance (Stoll 1921)
Innocent (Stoll 1921)
A Question of Trust (Stoll 1921) (also producer)
The Tavern Knight (Stoll 1921) (also producer)
A Gentleman of France (Stoll 1921)

The Hound of the Baskervilles (Stoll 1921)
The Adventures of Sherlock Holmes (series of 15) (Stoll 1921)
The Fruitful Vine (Stoll 1922)
The Man and His Kingdom (Stoll 1922)
Dick Turpin's Ride to York (Stoll 1923) (also producer)
Running Water (Stoll 1923) (also producer)
The Sign of Four (Stoll 1923) (also producer, script)
The Passionate Friends (Stoll 1923)
A Debt of Honour (Stoll 1923)
The Wandering Jew (Stoll 1923) (also producer)
Guy Fawkes (Stoll 1923) (also producer)
The Royal Oak (Stoll 1924) (also producer)
Don Quixote (Stoll 1924) (also producer)
Sally Bishop (Stoll 1924) (also producer)
Henry, King of Navarre (Stoll 1924) (also producer)
Slaves of Destiny (Stoll 1924) (also producer)
Curley Top (USA) (Fox 1924)
My Husband's Wives (USA) (Fox 1924)
The Folly of Vanity (USA) (Fox 1924)
The Love Story of Aliette Brunton (Stoll 1925)
She Wolves (USA) (Fox 1925)
Every Man's Wife (USA) (Fox 1925)
The Haunted Castles (series of six) (W & F 1926)
Human Law [Tragodie Einer Ehe] (GB-Ger) (Astra-National
    1927)
The Woman Tempted (Wardour 1927)† (also co-producer)
Mademoiselle from Armentieres (Gaumont 1927) (also co-pro-
    ducer)
The Flight Commander (Gaumont 1927) (also co-producer)
Hindle Wakes [Fanny Hawthorne] (Gaumont 1927) (also co-pro-
    ducer)
The Flag Lieutenant (Gaumont 1927)
The Glad Eye (Gaumont 1928) (also co-adaptor, co-producer)
Quinneys (Gaumont 1928)
Roses of Picardy (Gaumont 1928) (co-producer)
You Know What Sailors Are (Gaumont 1928) (also co-producer)
Mademoiselle Parley Voo (Gaumont 1928)
Palais De Danse (Gaumont 1929) (also co-producer)
High Treason (Gaumont 1929)
Balaclava [Jaws of Hell] (W & F 1930) (with Milton Rosmer)
    (made in 1928 as silent, release delayed for additional sound
    sequences not filmed by Elvey)
The School for Scandal (Par Br 1931) (also producer)
Sally in Our Alley (Radio 1932) (with uncredited Basil Dean)
A Honeymoon Adventure (Radio Br 1932)
Potiphar's Wife [Her Strange Desire] (FN-Pathe 1932)
Frail Women (Radio Br 1932)
In a Monastery Garden (AP & D 1932)
The Water Gipsies (Radio Br 1932)
The Marriage Bond (Radio Br 1932)
Diamond Cut Diamond [Blame the Woman] (MGM 1932) (with
    Fred Niblo)
The Lodger [The Phantom Fiend] (W & F 1932)

Soldiers of the King [The Woman in Command] (W & F 1933)
This Week of Grace (Radio Br 1933)
The Lost Chord (AP & D 1933)
I Lived with You (W & F 1934)
The Wandering Jew (Gaumont 1934)
Love, Life and Laughter (ABFD 1934)
Road House (Gaumont 1934)
Lily of Killarney [Bride of the Lake] (AP & D 1934)
Princess Charming (Gaumont 1934)
My Song for You (Gaumont 1934)
Heat Wave (Gaumont 1935)
The Clairvoyant (Gaumont 1935)
The Tunnel (Gaumont 1936) (Br version of Ger film made the
    previous year; later shown in USA as Transatlantic Tunnel)
Spy of Napoleon (Wardour 1937)
The Man in the Mirror (Wardour 1937)
Change for a Sovereign (FN Br 1938)
A Romance in Flanders [Lost on the Western Front] (BL 1938)
Who Killed John Savage? (WB Br 1938) (also producer)
Melody and Romance (BL 1938)
Lightning Conductor (GFD 1938)
Who Goes Next? (Fox Br 1938)
The Return of the Frog (BL 1938)
Sword of Honour (Butcher 1939) (also producer)
The Spider (GFD 1939)
Sons of the Sea (GN 1939) (also co-script)
For Freedom (GFD 1940) (with Castleton Knight)
Room for Two (GN 1940)
Under Your Hat (BL 1940)
Salute John Citizen (Anglo 1942)
The Gentle Sex (GFD 1943) (with Leslie Howard)
The Lamp Still Burns (GFD 1943)
Medal for the General (Anglo 1944)
Strawberry Roan (Anglo 1945)
Beware of Pity (EL 1946)
The Late Edwina Black [Obsessed] (IFD 1951)† [co-production
    company]
The Third Visitor (Eros 1951)† [co-production company]
My Wife's Lodger (Adelphi 1952)
House of Blackmail (Monarch 1953)
The Great Game (GN 1953)
Is Your Honeymoon Really Necessary? (GN 1953)
The Gay Dog (Eros 1954)
The Haunted Hero (ABP 1954)
What Every Woman Wants (Adelphi 1954)
The Happiness of Three Women (Adelphi 1954)
You Lucky People (Adelphi 1955)
Room in the House (Monarch 1955)
Fun at St Fanny's (BL 1956)
Stars in Your Eyes (Bl 1956)
Dry Rot (IFD 1956)
Second Fiddle (BL 1957)

EMO, E. W. (Emerich Josef Wojtek), b. Seebarn, Austria, 1898
   Flitterwoohen (Ger 1928)
   Polnische wirtschaft (Ger 1928)
   Spelunke (Ger 1928)
   Im Prater Blühn wieder die Bäume (Ger 1929)
   Zwischen vierzehn und siebzehn (Ger 1929)
   Der Hampelmann (Ger 1930)
   Was kostet Liebe? (Aus 1930)
   Heute nacht-Eventuell (Ger 1930)
   Zweimal Hochzeit (Ger 1930)
   Der Storch streikt [Siegfried der Matrose] (Ger 1931)
   Der unbekannte Gast (Ger 1931)
   Ich heirate meinen Mann [German version of Her Wedding Night]
      (Ger 1931)
   Das Testament des Cornelius Gulden [Eine erbschaft mit Hinder-
      nissen] (Ger 1932)
   Der Frauendiplomat (Ger 1932)
   Fräulein--falsch Verbunden (Ger 1932)
   Una notte con te (It-Ger 1932)
   Marion, das gehort Sichnicht (Ger 1932)
   Moderne Mitgift (Ger 1932)
   Kleines Madel--grosses Glück (Ger 1933)
   Und wer küsst mich? (Ger 1933)
   Cercasi Modella (It-Aus 1933)
   Paprika (It-Ger 1934)
   Lisetta (It-Ger 1934)
   Dar Harr ohne Wohnung (Aus 1934)
   Der Doppelgänger (Ger 1934)
   Gern hab'ich die frau'n geküsst [Paganini] (Ger 1934)
   Jungfrau gegen Mönch (Ger 1934)
   Petersburger nachte [Waltzer an der Newa] (Ger 1934)
   Der vogelhändler (Ger 1935)
   Endstation (Ger 1935)
   Familie Schmiek (Ger 1935)
   Der Himmel auf Erden (Aus 1935)
   Zirkus Saran [Knox und die lustigen Vagabunden] (Aus 1935)
   Die Puppenfee (Aus 1936)
   Wer zuletzt küsst [Ungeküsst soll Man nicht schlafen geh'n]
      (Aus 1936)
   Drei mäderl um Schubert [Dreimäderlhaus] (Ger 1936) (also co-
      script)
   Fiakerlied (Ger 1936) (also co-script)
   Schabernack (Ger 1936)
   Die Austernlilli (Ger 1937)
   Der Mann, von demman spricht (Aus 1937)
   Musik für dich (Aus 1937)
   Die verschwundene Frau (Ger 1937)
   Die unentschuldigte Stunde (Aus 1937) (also producer)
   Dreizehn stühle (Aus 1938) (also producer, co-script)
   Der Optimist (Aus 1938) (also producer)
   Anton, der letzte (Aus 1939)
   Unsterblicher Waltzer (Aus 1939)
   Meine Tochter lebt in Wien (Aus 1939)

Der liebe Augustin (Aus 1940)
Liebe ist zollfrei (Aus 1941)
Wien 1910 (Aus 1942)
Reisenbekanntschaft (Aus 1943)
Schwarz auf Weiss (Aus 1943)
Zwei glückliche Menschen (Aus 1943)
Freunde (Aus 1944)
Alles Lüge (Aus 1948)
Kleine Melodie aus Wien (Aus 1948) (also co-script)
Es lebe das Leben (Aus 1949)
Nichts als Zufälle (Ger 1949) (also co-script)
Un eine Nasenlange (Ger 1949)
Es schlägt dreizhen (Aus 1950)
Der Theodor im Fussballtor (Ger 1950) (also co-script)
Hilfe, ich bin unsichtbar! (Ger 1951)
Schäm Dich, Brigitte! (Aus 1952) (also co-script)
Fräulein Casanova (Aus 1953)
Damenwahl (Ger 1953)
Irene in Nöten (Aus 1953)
Ihr Korporal [Husarenmanöver] (Aus-Ger 1956)
K. U. K. feldmarschall (Aus 1956)
Ober, zahlen! (Aus 1957)
Wenn die Bombe platzt (Aus 1958)

ENDFIELD, CY (Cyril Raker Endfield), b. Nov. 10, 1914
Gentleman Joe Palooka (USA) (Mon 1946) (also script)
Stork Bites Man (USA) (UA 1947)
The Argyle Secrets (USA) (Film Classics 1948) (also story,
    script)
Joe Palooka in the Big Fight (USA) (Mon 1949)
The Underworld Story [The Whipped] (USA) (UA 1950)
Try and Get me [The Sound of Fury] (USA) (UA 1951)
Tarzan's Savage Fury (USA) (RKO 1952)
The Limping Man (Eros 1953) (with Charles de la Tour)
The Master Plan (GN 1954) (under alias "Hugh Raker") (also
    co-script)
Impulse (Eros 1955) (also co-script under alias "Jonathan
    Roach") (with Charles de la Tour)
The Secret (Eros 1955) (also script) (with Charles de la Tour)
Child in the House (Eros 1956) (also script) (with Charles de
    la Tour)
Hell Drivers (RFD 1957) (also co-script)
Sea Fury (RFD 1958) (also co-script)
Jet Storm (Britannia 1959) (also co-script)
Mysterious Island (Col Br 1962)
Hide and Seek (Albion 1963)
Zulu (Par 1963) (also co-producer, co-script)
Sands of the Kalahari (USA) (Par-Emb 1965) (also co-producer,
    script)
De Sade [Der Marquis de Sade] (US-W Ger) (AIP 1969) (with
    uncredited Roger Corman, Gordon Hessler)
Universal Soldier (Hemdale 1972) (also script, actor)

Cy Endfield (right) with Ian Carmichael on the set of Hide and Seek (1963).

ENGEL, ERICH, b. 1891, Hamburg; d. 1966
 Wer nimmt die Liebe ernst? (Ger 1931)
 Fünf von der Jazzband (Ger 1932)
 Inge und die Millionen (Ger 1933)
 Pechmarie (Ger 1934) (also co-script)
 Hohe Schule [Riding School] (Aus 1934) [Also known as Das
  Geheimnis des Carlo Cavelli or The Secrets of Cavelli]
 Pygmalion (Ger 1935)
 ... nur ein Komödiant (Aus 1935)
 Ein Hochzeitstraum (Ger 1936)
 Die Nacht mit dem Kaiser (Ger 1936)
 Mädchenjahre einer Königin (Ger 1936)
 Gefährliches Spiel (Ger 1937)
 Der Maulkorb (Ger 1938)
 Hotel Sacher (Ger 1939)
 Der Weg zu Isabell (Ger 1939)
 Ein hoffnungsloser Fall (Ger 1939)
 Nanette (Ger 1939)
 Unser Fräulein Doktor (Ger 1940)

Viel Lärm um Nixi (Ger 1942)
Sommerliebe (Ger 1942)
Altes Herz wird wieder jung (Ger 1943)
Man rede mir nicht von Liebe (Ger 1943)
Es lebe die Liebe (Ger 1944)
Wo ist Herr Belling? (Unfinished Ger 1945)
Fahrt ins Glück (Ger 1945)
Affäre Blum [The Blum Affair] (Ger 1948)
Der Biberpelz (Ger 1948)
Das seltsame Leben des Herrn Bruggs (Ger 1951)
Kommen Sie am Ersten (Ger 1951)
Unter den tausend Laternen (Ger 1952) (also co-script)
Der fröhliche Weinberg (Ger 1952)
Der Mann meines Lebens (Ger 1953)
Konsul Strotthoff (Ger 1954)
Du bist die Richtige (Ger-Aus 1955)
Liebe ohne Illusion (Ger 1955)
Vor Gott und den Menschen (Ger 1955)
Geschwader Fledermaus (Ger 1959)

ENGELS, ERICH, b. 1889, Remscheid, Germany
Das Millionentestament (Ger 1932)
Das Geheimnis des blauen Zimmers (Ger 1932)
Kriminalreporter Holm (Ger 1932)
Die Nacht im Försthaus (Ger 1933)
Das lustige Kleeblatt (Ger 1933)
Peter, Paul and Nanette (Ger 1934) (also script)
Kirschen in Nachbars Garten (Ger 1935) (also co-script)
Donner, Blitz und Sonnenschein (Ger 1936) (also co-script)
Sherlock Holmes (Ger 1937) (also co-script)
Mordsache Holm (Ger 1938)
Im Namen des Volkes (Ger 1939) (also co-script)
Zentrale Rio (Ger 1939)
Das himmelblaue Abenkleid (Ger 1941) (also co-script)
Dr. Crippen an Bord (Ger 1942) (also co-script)
Die goldenne Spinne (Ger 1943) (also co-script)
Freitag, der 13 (Ger 1944)
Mordprozess Dr. Jordan (Ger 1951) (also co-script)
Keine Angst vor Schwiegermüttern (Ger 1954) (also co-script)
Kirschen in Nachbars Garten (Ger 1956) (also co-script)
Dr. Crippen lebt (Ger 1957) (also co-script)
Witwer mit fünf Tochtern (Ger 1957) (also co-script)
Grabenplatz 17 (Ger 1958) (also co-script)
Vater, Mutter und neun Kinder (Ger 1958) (also co-script)
Natürlich die Autofahrer (Ger 1959)
Im Namen einer Mutter (Ger 1960)

ENRICO, ROBERT, b. 1931, Liévin, France
Au coeur de la vie (Fr 1962) (also script)
La Belle Vie [The Good Life] (Fr 1963) (also script)
Les Grandes Gueules [Wise Guys] (Fr-It 1966) (also co-script)
Les Aventuriers [The Last Adventure] (Fr-It 1966) (also co-script)

Tante Zita [Zita] (Fr 1967) (also co-adaptor)
Ho! [ep "Criminal Face"] (Fr-It 1968) (also co-script)
Un Peu, beaucoup, passionnément (Fr 1971) (also co-script)
Boulevard du rhum (Fr 1972) (also co-script)
Les Caïds [The Hell Below] (Fr 1972)
Le Secret (Fr 1974) (also co-adaptor)

EPSTEIN, JEAN, b. 1897, Warsaw; d. 1953
Pasteur (Fr 1922) (with Jean Benoit-Levy)
L'Auberge rouge (Fr 1923) (also adaptor)
Coeur fidèle (Fr 1923) (also co-script)
La Montagne infidèle (Fr 1923)
La Belle Nivernaise (Fr 1923) (also adaptor)
La Goutte de sang (Fr 1924) (with Maurice Mariaud)
Le Lion des Mogols (Fr 1924)
L'Affiche (Fr 1924)
Le Double Amour (Fr 1925)
Les Aventures de Robert Macaire (Fr 1925)
Mauprat (Fr 1926)
Six et demi-onze (Fr 1927)
La Glace a trois faces (Fr 1927)
La Chute de la Maison Usher (Fr 1928)
Finis terrae (Fr 1929)
Sa tête (Fr 1929)
Mor' Vran/La Mer des corbeaux (Fr 1930)
L'Or des mers (Fr 1932)
L'Homme à l'Hispano (Fr 1933)
La Chatelaine du Liben (Fr 1933)
Chanson d'armor (Fr 1934)
Coeur de gueux (Fr-It 1936) (both versions)
La Bretagne (Fr 1936)
La Bourgogne (Fr 1936)
Vive la vie (Fr 1937)
La Femme du bout du monde (Fr 1937)
Les Bâtisseurs (Fr 1938)
La Eau-vive (Fr 1938)

ESTEVA, JACINTO, b. 1936, Barcelona
Lejos de los árboles (Sp 1966) (also story, script)
Dante no es únicamente severo (Sp 1967) (with Joaquin Jorda) (also co-story, co-script)
Despué del diluvio (Sp 1968) (also co-story, co-script)
Metamorfosis (Sp 1972) (also story, co-script)

ETAIX, PIERRE, b. Nov. 23, 1928, Roanne, France
Le Soupirant (Fr-It 1962) (also co-script, actor)
Yoyo (Fr 1965) (also co-script, actor)
Tant qu'on a la santé (Fr-It 1966) (also co-script, actor)
Le Grand Amour (Fr-It 1969) (also co-script, actor)
Pays de cocagne (Fr 1971) (also conception)

EUSTACHE, JEAN, b. 1938
Les Mauvaises Fréquentations (Fr 1964)

Le Père Noël a les yeux bleus [Father Christmas Has Blue
   Eyes] (Fr 1966) (also script)
La Rosière de Pessac [The Virgin of Pessac] (Fr 1969)† [co-
   production company]
Le Cochon (Fr 1970) (with Jean-Michel Barjol)
La maman et la putain (Fr 1973)
Mes Petites Amoureuses (Fr 1974) (also script, dialogue)

FANCK, ARNOLD, b. March 6, 1889, Frankenthal, Germany
   Das Wunder des Schneeschuhs (Part 1, Ger 1921) (also co-
      story, co-script, actor) (with Dr. Tauern)
   Im kampf mit dem Berge (Ger 1921) (also script, co-camera)
   Das Wunder des Schneeschuhs (Part 2, Ger 1922) (also co-
      story, co-script) (with Dr. Tauern)
   Eine Fuchsjagd auf Skiern durchs Engadin (Ger 1922) (also
      script, co-camera)
   Der Berg des Schicksals (Ger 1924) (also producer, script,
      co-camera)
   Der heilige Berg (Ger 1926) (also script)
   Der grosse Sprung (Ger 1927) (also script)
   Die weisse Hölle vom Piz Palü (Ger 1929) (also co-script) (with
      G. W. Pabst)
   Sturme über dem Montblanc (Ger 1930) (also script)
   Der weisse Rausch (Ger 1931) (also script)
   SOS Eisberg (Ger 1933) (also co-script) (with Tay Garnett)
   Der ewige Traum (Ger 1934) (also script)
   Balmat (Ger 1934)
   Die Tochter des Samurai (Ger 1937) (also script)
   Ein Robinson [Das Tagebuch eines Matrosen] (Ger 1940) (also
      co-script)

FASSBINDER, RAINER WERNER, b. May 31, 1946, Bad Woriss-
   hofen, Germany
   Der amerikanische Soldat (Ger 1970)
   Götter der Pest (Ger 1970)
   Liebe ist kälter als der Tod (Ger 1970)
   Warum läuft Herr R. Amok (Ger 1970)
   Warnung vor einer heiligen Nutte (Ger 1971)
   Die bitteren Tränen der Petra Von Kant (Ger 1972)
   Der Händler der vier Jahreszeiten (Ger 1972)

FELLINI, FEDERICO, b. Jan. 20, 1920, Rimini, Italy
   Luci del varietà [Variety Lights] (It 1951) (also co-script) (with
      Alberto Lattuada)
   Lo sceicco bianco [The White Sheik] (It 1952) (also co-script)
   I vitelloni [The Young and the Passionate] (It 1953)
   Amore in città [Love in the City] (ep "Un'agenzia matrimoniale")
      (It 1953) (also co-script)
   La strada (It 1954) (also co-script)
   I bidone [The Swindle] (It 1955) (also co-script)
   Le notti di Cabiria [Nights of Cabiria] (It 1957) (also co-script)
   Fortunella (It 1960) (only story, script)
   La dolce vita (It 1960) (also co-script)

Boccaccio '70 (ep "Le tentazioni del dottor Antonio") (It 1961)
(also co-script)
Otto e mezzo [8 1/2] (It 1963) (also co-script)
Giulietta degli spiriti [Juliet of the Spirits] (It 1967) (also co-script)
Histoires Extraordinaires (ep "Toby Dammit") (It 1968) (also co-script)
Fellini-Satyricon (It-Fr 1969) (also co-script, co-decorator)
I Clowns (It 1970) (also co-script)
Fellini-Roma (It-Fr 1971) (also co-script)
Amarcord (It 1973) (also co-script)

FERRERI, MARCO, b. May 11, 1928, Milan
El pisito (Sp 1958)
Los chicos (Sp 1959) (also co-script)
El cochecito (Sp 1960)
Le italiane e l'amore [Latin Lovers] (ep "Infedeltà coniugale]
(It 1961)
Una storia moderna [The Conjugal Bed] (It 1962)
Mafioso (It 1962) (only co-story)
L'ape regina [The Ape Woman] (It 1963) (also co-script)
Controsesso (ep "Il professore") (It 1964) (also co-script of
episode)
Marcia Nuziale (It 1966) (also co-script)
L'Harem (It 1967)
L'Uomo dai palloncini [Breakup] (It 1968) (also co-script)
Dillinger è Morto (It 1968)
Il seme dell'uomo (It 1969) (also co-script)
L'udienza (It 1970)
La cagna (It 1971)
La grande bouffe (Fr-It 1973)
Touche pas à la Femme blanche (Fr-It 1974)

FERRONI, GIORGIO (a. k. a. Calvin Jackson Padget), b. April 12,
1908, Perugio, Italy
Casello N. 3 (It 1945)
Pian delle stelle (It 1947)
Tombolo, paradiso nero (It 1947)
Marechiaro (It 1949)
Vivere a Sbafo (It 1950)
Vertigine bianca (It 1956)
L'oceano ci chiama (It 1957)
Il mulino delle donne di pietra [Mill of the Stone Women] (It
1960)
Le baccanti (It-Fr 1961)
Le guerra di Troia [The Trojan Horse] (It-Fr 1961)
Ercole contro Moloch (It 1964)
Il leone di Tebe (It 1964)
Coriolano, Eroe senza patria (It 1965)
Un dollaro bucato (It 1965)
New York chiama Superdrago (It 1960)
Per pochi dollari ancora (It 1966)
Wanted (It 1967)

La battaglia di El Alamein (It 1967)
L'arciere di fuoco (It-Fr-Sp 1970)
La notte dei diavoli (It-Sp 1971)

FESCOURT, HENRI, b. Nov. 23, 1880, Béziers, France; d. 1966
Fantasie de milliardaire (Fr 1913)
La Lumière qui tue (Fr 1913)
La Mort sur Paris (Fr 1913)
La Menace (Fr 1914)
Mathias Sandorf [a serial] (Fr 1918-19)
La Nuit du 13 (Fr 1921-22)
La Poupée du milliardaire (Fr 1922)
Les Grands (Fr 1924)
Les Misérables (Fr 1925) [3 parts]
La Glu (Fr 1926)
La Maison du maltais (Fr 1926)
L'Occident (Fr 1927)
Le Comte de Monte Cristo (Fr-Ger 1927)
La Maison de la flèche (Fr 1930)
Serments (Fr 1931)
Service de nuit (Fr 1932)
L'Occident (Fr 1938)
Le Bar du Sud (Fr 1938)
Vous seule que j'aime (Fr 1939)
Retour de flamme (Fr 1942)

FESTA CAMPANILE, PASQUALE, b. July 28, 1927, Melfi, Italy
Un tentativo sentimentale (It 1963) (also co-script, co-adaptor)
(with Massimo Francisco)
Le voci bianchi [White Voices] (It 1963) (also co-script) (with
Massimo Francisco)
La costanza della ragione (It 1965) (also co-script)
Una vergine per il principe [A Virgin for the Prince] (It 1965)
(also co-script)
Adulterio all'italiano [Adultery Italian Style] (It 1966) (also
story, co-script)
La cintura di castia [On My Way to the Crusades I Met a Girl
Who, also The Chastity Belt] (It 1967) (also script)
La rabazza e il generale (It 1968)
Il marito e mio e l'ammazzo quando mi pare (It 1968) (also
script)
La matriarca (It 1968) (also script)
Dove vai tutta nuda? (It 1969) (also script)
Scacco alla regina (It 1969) (also script)
Con quale amore, con quanto amore (It 1969) (also co-script)
Quando le donne avevano la coda (It 1970) (also co-script)
Il merlo maschio (It 1970) (also co-script)
Quando le donne persero la caod (It 1971) (also co-script)
La calandria (It 1972)
L'emigrante (It-Sp-Ger 1972) (also co-script)
Jus primae noctis (It 1972)
Rugantino (It 1973)
La sculacciata (It 1974)

FEUILLADE, LOUIS, b. 1874, Lunel (Hérault), France; d. Feb. 1925
    Les Films esthetiques (Fr 1909-10) [series of 12]
    Bébé (Fr 1910-12) [series of 26]
    La Vie telle qu'elle est (Fr 1911-13) [series of 30]
    Le Proscrit (Fr 1912)
    La Vie drôle (Fr 1913-14) [series of 4]
    Bout-de-Zan (Fr 1913-15) [series of 18]
    La Gardienne du Feu (Fr 1913)
    Le Secret du Porçat (Fr 1913)
    Severo torelli (Fr 1914)
    L'Aventure des Millions (Fr 1916)
    Un Mariage du Raison (Fr 1916)
    Notre pauvre couer (Fr 1916)
    L'Autre (Fr 1917)
    Fantômes [a serial] (Fr 1915)
    Les Vampires [a serial] (Fr 1915)
    Judex [a serial] (Fr 1916)
    La Nouvelle Mission de Judex [a serial] (Fr 1917)
    Le Bandeau sur les yeux (Fr 1917)
    Déserteuse (Fr 1917)
    Le Passe de Monique (Fr 1917)
    La Fugue de Lily (Fr 1917)
    Les Petites marionnettes (Fr 1918)
    Vendémiaire [a serial] (Fr 1918)
    Tih-Minh [a serial] (Fr 1918)
    Le Nocturne [a serial] (Fr 1919)
    L'Homme sans visage [a serial] (Fr 1919)
    Enigme [a serial] (Fr 1919)
    Barrabas [a serial] (Fr 1919)
    Les Deux Gamines [a serial] (Fr 1920)
    L'Orpheline [a serial] (Fr 1921)
    Parisette [a serial] (Fr 1921)
    Le Fils du flibustier [a serial] (Fr 1922)
    Vindicta [a serial] (Fr 1923)
    La Gamin de Paris (Fr 1923)
    La Gosseline (Fr 1923)
    L'Orpheline de Paris [a serial] (Fr 1923)
    Pierrot pierrette (Fr 1924)
    Lucette (Fr 1924)
    Le Stigmate [a serial] (Fr 1925) (completed by Maurice Chapman)

FEYDER, JACQUES, b. July 21, 1888, Ixelles, Belgium; d. May 25, 1948
    M. Pinson, policier (Fr 1915) (also script) (with Gaston Ravel)
    Le Pied qui étreint (Fr 1916) (also script)
    L'Instinct est maître (Fr 1916)
    Le Ravin sans fond (Fr 1917) (with Raymond Bernard)
    L'Atlantide [Missing Husbands] (Fr 1921) (also script)
    Crainquebille (Fr 1923) (also script, production design)
    Visages d'enfants (Fr 1923) (also script, production design) (with Françoise Rosay)

L'Image (Fr 1925) (also co-story, script)
Gribiche (Fr 1926) (also script)
Carmen (Fr 1927) (also co-editor, script) (with Françoise
   Rosay)
Au Pays du roi lépreux (Fr 1927) (also script)
Thérèse Raquin [Shadows of Fear] (Fr 1928) (also adaptor)
Les Nouveaux Messieurs (Fr 1929) (also co-script)
The Kiss (USA) (MGM 1929) (also co-script)
Anna Christie (Ger version) (MGM 1930)
Le Spectre vert (Fr version of The Unholy Night) (USA) (MGM
   1930)
Si l'empereur savait ça! (Fr version of His Glorious Night)
   (USA) (MGM 1930)
Son of India (USA) (MGM 1931)
Daybreak (USA) (MGM 1931)
Le Grand Jeu (Fr 1934) (also co-script)
Pension Mimosas (Fr 1935) (also co-script)
La Kermesse héroïque (Fr 1936) (also co-script)
Die klugen Frauen (Ger 1936) (Ger version of La Kermesse
   héroïque)
Les Gens du voyage (Fr 1937)
Knight Without Armour (GB) (UA Br 1937)
Fahrendes Volk (Ger version of Les Gens du Voyage) (Ger 1938)
La Loi du Nord (Fr 1939) (also co-script)
Une Femme disparaît (Swiss 1942) (also co-producer, script,
   actor)
Macadam (Fr 1946) (died during filming, completed by M.
   Blistène)

FIDANI, DEMOFILO (a.k.a. Miles Deem, Dick Spitfire), b. Italy
   Sedia elettrica (It 1969)
   E vennero in 4 ... per uccidere Sartana (It 1969)
   Arrivano Django e Sartana ... è la fine (It 1970)
   Inginocchiati straniero ... i cadaveri non fanno ombra! (It 1970)
   Era Sam Wallash ... lo chiamavano "Così sia" (It 1971)
   Karzan, il favoloso uomo della giungla (It 1971) (also co-script)
   Per una bara piena di dollari (It 1971)

FISHER, TERENCE, b. 1904, London
   A Song for Tomorrow (GFD 1948)
   Colonel Bogey (GFD 1948)
   To the Public Danger (GFD 1948)
   Portrait from Life [The Girl in the Painting] (GFD 1948)
   Marry Me (GFD 1949)
   The Astonished Heart (GFD 1950) (with Anthony Darnborough)
   So Long at the Fair (GFD 1950) (with Anthony Darnborough)
   Home to Danger (Eros 1951)
   The Last Page [Manbait] (Ex 1952)
   Stolen Face (Ex 1952)
   Wings of Danger [Dead on Course] (Ex 1952)
   Distant Trumpet (Apex 1952)
   Mantrap [Woman in Hiding] (Hammer 1953) (also co-script)
   Four Sided Triangle (Ex 1953) (also co-script)

Spaceways (Ex 1953)
Blood Orange (Ex 1953)
Face the Music [The Black Glove] (Ex 1954)
The Strangler Came Home [The Unholy Four] (Ex 1954)
Final Appointment (Monarch 1954)
Mask of Dust [Race for Life] (Ex 1954)
Children Galore (GFD 1954)
Murder by Proxy [Blackout] (Ex 1955)
Stolen Assignment (BL 1955)
The Flaw (Renown 1955)
The Last Man to Hang? (Col Br 1956)
Kill Me Tomorrow (Renown 1957)
The Curse of Frankenstein (WB Br 1957)
Dracula [Horror of Dracula] (Univ Br 1958)
The Revenge of Frankenstein (Col Br 1958)
The Hound of the Baskervilles (UA Br 1959)
The Man Who Could Cheat Death (Par Br 1959)
The Mummy (Univ Br 1959)
The Stranglers of Bombay (Col Br 1959)
The Brides of Dracula (Univ Br 1960)
The Two Faces of Dr Jeryll [House of Fright] (Col Br 1960)
Sword of Sherwood Forest (Col Br 1960)
The Curse of the Werewolf (Univ Br 1961)
The Phantom of the Opera (Univ Br 1962)
Sherlock Holmes und das Halsband des Todes [Sherlock Holmes
    and the Deadly Necklace] (W. Ger-Fr-It 1962)
The Horror of It All (20th Br 1964)
The Earth Dies Screaming (20th Br 1964)
The Gorgon (Col Br 1964)
Dracula - Price of Darkness (WPD 1965)
Island of Terror (Planet 1966)
Frankenstein Created Woman (WPD 1967)
Night of the Big Heat (Planet 1967)
The Devil Rides Out [The Devil's Bride] (WPD 1968)
Frankenstein Must Be Destroyed (WPD 1969)
Frankenstein and the Monster from Hell (Avco-Emb 1974)

FLEMYNG, GORDON, b. March 7, 1934, Glasgow, Scotland
Solo for Sparrow (AA 1962)
Just for Fun (Col Br 1963)
Five to One (AA 1963)
Dr. Who and the Daleks (RFI 1965)
Daleks--Invasion Earth 2150 A D (BL 1966)
The Split (MGM 1968)
Great Catherine (WPD 1968)
The Last Grenade (CIRO 1970)

FLON, PAUL, b. Oct. 6, 1898, Brussels
Un Homme a passé par là (Bel 1920)
La Petite Martyre belge (Bel 1921) (with Francis Martin)
Belgique (Bel 1922) (with Charles Tutelier)
Un Soldat inconnu (Bel 1922) (with Francis Martin)
A la manière de Zorro (Bel 1923)

Dans Bruges la morte (Bel 1924)
Un Gamin de Bruxelles (Bel 1924) (with Francis Martin)
Un Foyer sans maman (Bel 1925)
Les Croix de l'Yser (Bel 1928) (with Gaston Schoukens)
La Famille Klepkens (Bel 1929) (with Gaston Schoukens)
Fête de quartier (Bel 1954)

FONS, ANGELINO, b. 1936, Madrid
La busca (Sp 1966) (also script)
Cantando a la vida (Sp 1969) (also co-script)
Fortunata y Jacinta (Sp 1970) (also script)
La primera entrega (Sp-It 1972) (also script)
Mi hijo no es lo que parece (Sp 1973) (also script)
Separation Matrimonial (Sp 1973) (also script)

FONSECA E COSTA, JOSE, b. 1933, Angola
O recado (Por 1971)
Mephistopheles et Maria Antonia (Por 1974)

FORBES, BRYAN, b. July 22, 1926, Stratford-atte-Bow, England
Whistle down the Wind (RFD 1961)
The L-Shaped Room (BL 1962)
Seance on a Wet Afternoon (RFD 1964) (also co-producer)
Of Human Bondage (MGM Br 1964) (uncredited, with Ken
    Hughes, uncredited Henry Hatahway)
King Rat (USA) (Col 1965)
The Wrong Box (Col Br 1966) (also co-producer)
The Whisperers (UA 1966)
Deadfall (20th Br 1967)
The Madwoman of Chaillot (WB-7 Arts 1969) (with John Huston)
The Raging Moon (MGM-EMI 1970)
The Stepford Wives (USA) (Col 1975)

FORDE, WALTER, b. 1897, Bradford
Wait and Sea (Butcher 1928) (also co-script, actor)
What Next? (Butcher 1928) (also co-script, actor)
The Silent House (Butcher 1929)
Would You Believe It? (Butcher 1929) (also co-script, actor)
Red Pearls (Butcher 1930)
You'd Be Surprised (Butcher 1930) (also co-script, actor)
The Last Hour (Butcher 1930)
Lord Richard in the Pantry (WB Br 1930)
Bed and Breakfast (Gaumont 1930)
The Ringer (Ideal 1931)
Third Time Lucky (W & F 1931)
The Ghost Train (W & F 1931)
Splinters in the Navy (W & F 1931)
Condemned to Death (W & F 1932)
Lord Babs (Ideal 1932)
Jack's the Boy [Night and Day] (W & F 1932)
Rome Express (Gaumont 1932)
Orders Is Orders (Ideal 1933)
Jack Ahoy! (Gaumont 1934)

Chu Chin Chow (Gaumont 1934)
Bulldog Jack [Alias Bulldog Drummond] (Gaumont 1935)
Forever England [Born for Glory] (Gaumont 1935)
King of the Damned (Gaumont 1936)
Land Without Music [Forbidden Music] (GFD 1936)
Kicking the Moon Around (GFD 1938)
The Gaunt Stranger [The Phantom Strikes] (ABFD 1938)
Let's Be Famous (ABFD 1939)
The Four Just Men [The Secret Four] (ABFD 1939)
Cheer Boys Cheer (ABFD 1939)
Inspector Hornleigh on Holiday (20th Br 1939)
Charley's Big-Hearted Aunt (GFD 1940)
Saloon Bar (ABFD 1940)
Sailors Three [Three Cockeyed Sailors] (ABFD 1940)
Gasbags (GFD 1940) (?uncredited with Marcel Varnel)
Neutral Port (GFD 1940) (?uncredited with Marcel Varnel)
The Ghost Train (GFD 1941)
Inspector Hornleigh Goes to It [Mail Train] (20th British 1941)
Atlantic Ferry [Sons of the Sea] (WB Br 1941)
The Peterville Diamond (WB-FN Br 1942)
Flying Fortress (WB-FN Br 1942)
It's That Man Again (GFD 1943)
Time Flies (GFD 1944)
Master of Bankdam (GFD 1947) (also co-producer)
Cardboard Cavalier (GFD 1949) (also producer)

FORST, WILLI (Willi Frohs), b. 1903, Vienna
Leise flehen meine Lieder (Ger-Aus 1933) (also script)
Maskerade (Aus 1934) (also script)
Mazurka (Ger 1935)
Burgtheater (Aus 1936) (also co-script)
Allotria (Ger 1936) (also co-script)
Serenade (Ger 1937) (also co-script)
Capriolen (Ger 1939) (only co-script)
Ich bin Sebastian Otto (Ger 1939) (also actor) (with Viktor
    Becker)
Bel ami (Ger 1939) (also co-script, actor)
Operette (Ger 1940) (also co-script, actor)
Wiener Blut (Ger 1942) (also actor)
Frauen sind keine Engel (Ger 1943)
Wiener Mädeln (Ger 1945) (also co-script, actor)
Die Sünderin [The Sinner] (Ger 1950) (also co-script)
Es geschehen noch Wunder (Ger 1951) (also co-script, actor)
Dieses Lied bleibt bei Dir (Ger 1954)
Die Drei von der Tankstelle (Ger 1955) (only supervisor)
Kaiserjäger (Aus 1956)
Die unentschuldigte Stunde (Aus 1957)
Wien, du Stadt meiner Träume (Aus 1957) (also co-script)

FRANCIS, FREDDIE, b. 1917, London
Two and Two Makes Six (Bry 1962)
Day of the Triffids (RFD 1962) (uncredited, with Steve Sekely)
Vengeance (Garrick 1962)

Paranoiac (Univ Br 1963)
Nightmare (Univ Br 1963)
The Evil of Frankenstein (Univ Br 1964)
Hysteria (MGM Br 1964)
Dr. Terror's House of Horros (RFI 1964)
Traitor's Gate (Col Br 1964)
The Skull (Par Br 1965)
The Psychopath (Par Br 1966)
The Deadly Bees (Par Br 1967)
Torture Garden (Col Br 1967)
They Came from Beyond Space (Planet 1967)
Dracula Has Risen from the Grave (WB Br 1968)
Mumsy, Nanny, Sonny & Girly (Cin 1969)
Trog (WB Br 1970)
The Happening of the Vampire [Gebissen wire dur Nachts] (GB-
    W Ger 1971)
Tales from the Crypt (Cin Br 1972)
The Creeping Flesh (Tigon 1972)
Tales that Witness Madness (Par Br 1973)
Craze (EMI 1974)

FRANCISCI, PIETRO, b. Sept. 9, 1906, Rome
    Io t'ho incontrata a Napoli (It 1946)
    Natale al camp [Escape into Dreams] (It 1949)
    Antonio da Padova (It 1949)
    Le meravigliose avventure di Guerrìn Meschino (It 1951)
    Il leone di Amalfi (It 1951)
    La regina di Saba (It 1951)
    Attila (It 1955)
    Orlando e i paladini di Francia (It 1958)
    Le fatiche di Ercole (It 1958)
    Ercole e la regina di Lidia (It 1959)
    L'assedio di Siracusa (It 1960)
    Saffo, Venere di Lesbo (It 1960)
    Ercole sfida Sansone (It 1964)
    2 plus 5, missione Hydra (It 1967)

FRANJU, GEORGES, b. April 12, 1912, Fougères (Brittany),
    France
    La Tête contre les murs (Fr 1958)
    Les Yeux sans visage [Eyes Without a Face] (Fr 1959) (also
        co-adaptor)
    Pleins feux sur l'assassin (Fr 1961) (also co-script)
    Thérèse Desqueyroux (Fr 1962) (also co-adaptor)
    Judex (Fr-It 1963)
    Thomas l'Imposteur (Fr 1965) (also co-adaptor)
    La Faute de l'Abbé Mouret (Fr 1971) (also co-adaptor)
    L'Homme sans visage (Fr-It TV 1974) (also music)

FRANK, CHARLES, b. Belgium
    De Ordonnans [Cafe Zonder Bier] (Bel 1961) (also co-script)
        (with Trevor Peacock)
    At the Drop of a Head (English version of De Ordonnans) (Bel
        1961)

Freddie Francis (center), with George Chakiris, Nina Parry and Ambrosine Philpotts, directing Two and Two Make Six (1962).

FRANKEL, CYRIL, b. 1921
  Man of Africa (BL 1953)
  Devil on Horseback (BL 1954)
  Make Me an Offer (BL 1954)
  It's Great to Be Young (ABP 1956)
  No Time for Tears (ABP 1957)
  She Didn't Say No (ABP 1958)
  Alive and Kicking (ABP 1958)
  Never Take Sweets from a Stranger [Never Take Candy from a
    Stranger] (Col Br 1960)
  Don't Bother to Knock (WPD 1961)
  On the Fiddle (AA 1961)
  The Very Edge (Garrick 1963)
  The Witches (WPD 1966)
  The Trygon Factor (RFD 1967)

FRANKEN, MANUS, b. Switzerland; d. 1954
  Pareh--het Lied van de Rijst [Song of the Rice] (Swi 1936)
  Tanah Sabrang (Swi 1938-1939)

115   FREDA

FREDA, RICCARDO (a. k. a.   Robert Hampton, George Lincoln), b.
    Feb. 24, 1909, Alexandria, Egypt
    Piccoli Naufraghi (It 1938) (also co-script)
    Don Cesare di Bazan (It 1942) (also co-script)
    Non canto più (It 1943) (also co-script)
    Tutta la città canta (It 1943) (also co-script, editor)
    Aquila nera (It 1946) (also co-script)
    I miserabili (in two parts) (It 1948) (also co-script)
    Il cavaliere misterioso (It 1949) (also co-script)
    Guarany (It 1950) (also co-script)
    Il conte Ugolino (It 1950) (also co-script)
    Il figlio di d'Artagnan (It 1950) (also script)
    O cacoulha do barulho (It 1950) (also editor)
    Il tradimento (It 1951) (also co-script)
    Vedi Napoli e poi muori (It 1952) (also co-songs)
    La vendetta di aquila nera (It 1952) (also co-script)
    La leggenda del Piave (It 1952) (also story, co-script)
    Spartaco (It 1953) (also co-script)
    Teodora, imperatrice di Bisanzio (It 1953) (also co-adaptor, co-
        script)
    Da qui all'eredità (It 1956) (also co-script)
    Beatrice Cenci (It 1956) (also co-script, co-editor)
    I vampiri (It 1957) (also co-script, actor)
    Agguato a Tangeri (It 1958) (also co-script)
    Agi Murad, il diavolo bianco (It 1959)
    Caltiki il mostro immortale (It 1959)
    I giganti della Tessaglia (It 1961) (also co-script)
    I Mongoli [The Mongols] (It 1961) (with Andre de Toth)
    Maciste alla corte del Gran Khan (It 1961)
    Pax Caccia all'uomo (It 1961)
    Le Sette spade del vendicatore [The Seventh Sword] (It 1962)
        (also co-script)
    Maciste all'inferno (It 1962)
    L'orribile segreto del dottor Hichcock (It 1962)
    Solo contra Roma (It 1962) (with Herbert Wise)
    Oro per i Cesari (It 1963) (with Andre de Toth)
    Lo spettro (It 1963)
    Giulietta e Romeo [Romeo and Juliet] (It-GB 1964)
    Il magnifico avventuriero (It 1964)
    Coplan FX 18 casse tout (Fr-It 1965)
    Roger la honte (Fr 1966)
    Coplan ouvre le feux à Mexico (Fr-It 1966)
    La morte non conta i dollari (It 1967)
    Moresque, obbiettivo allucinante (It 1967)
    Due pistole e un Vigliacco (It 1967)
    A doppia Faccia (It 1969)
    Tamar (It 1970)

FRENCH, HAROLD, b. April 23, 1897, London
    The Cavalier of the Streets (B & D-Par Br 1937)
    Dead Men Are Dangerous (B & D-Par Br 1939)
    House of the Arrow [Castle of Drimes] (ABPC 1940)
    Major Barbara (GFD 1941) (with Gabriel Pascal, David Lean)

Riccardo Freda directing <u>Maciste alla corte del Gran Khan</u> (1961).

Jeannie (GFD 1941)
Unpublished Story (Col Br 1942)
The Day Will Dawn [The Avengers] (GFD 1942)
Secret Mission (GFD 1942)
Dear Octopus [The Randolph Family] (GFD 1943)
English Without Tears [Her Man Gilbey] (GFD 1944)
Mr Emmanuel (EL 1944)
Quiet Weekend (Pathe 1946)
White Cradle Inn [High Fury] (BL 1947) (also co-script)
My Brother Jonathan (Pathe 1948)
The Blind Goddess (GFD 1948)
Quartet (ep "The Alien Corn") (GFD 1948)
Adam and Evelyne [Adam and Evalyn] (GFD 1949) (also pro-
    ducer)
The Dancing Years (ABP 1950)
Trio (ep "Sanatorium") (GFD 1950)
Encore (ep "The Ant and the Grasshopper") (GFD 1951)
The Hour of Thirteen (MGM Br 1952)
The Man Who Watched Trains Go By [Paris Express] (Eros
    1953)
Isn't Life Wonderful? (ABP 1953)
Rob Roy the Highland Rogue (RKO Br 1953)
Forbidden Cargo (GFD 1954)
The Man Who Loved Redheads (BL 1955)

FREND, CHARLES, b. Nov. 21, 1909, Pulborough, Sussex, England
    The Big Blockade (UA 1942) (also co-script)
    The Foreman Went to France [Somewhere in France] (UA 1942)
    San Demetrio--London (Ealing 1943) (also co-script)
    Johnny Frenchman (EL 1945)
    Return of the Vikings (Ealing 1945)
    The Loves of Joanna Godden (GFD 1947)
    Scott of the Antarctic (GFD 1948)
    A Run for Your Money (GFD 1949) (also co-script)
    The Magnet (GFD 1950)
    The Cruel Sea (GFD 1953)
    Lease of Life (GFD 1954)
    The Long Arm [The Third Key] (RFD 1956)
    Barnacle Bill [All at Sea] (MGM Br 1957)
    Cone of Silence [Trouble in the Sky] (Bry 1960)
    Girl on Approval (Bry 1962)
    The Sky Bike (CFF 1967) (also script)

FRENKEL, SR., THEO[DORUS MAURITS], b. July 14, 1871, Rotterdam; d. Sept. 20, 1956
    Fatum (Dut 1915)
    Genie Tegen Geweld (Dut 1916)
    Levensschaduwen (Dut 1917)
    De Duivel (Dut 1917)
    Mea Culpa (Dut 1918)
    Het Proces Begear (Dut 1918)
    Pro Domo (Dut 1918)
    Zonnestraal (Dut 1919)
    De Duivel in Amsterdam (Dut 1919)
    Helleveeg (Dut 1920)
    Geeft Ons de Kracht (Dut 1920)
    Menschenwee (Dut 1921)
    Alexandra (Ger 1922)
    Ein neues Leben (Ger 1922)
    Frauenmoral (Ger 1923)
    Schande (Ger 1923)
    De Bruut (Dut-Ger 1923)
    Amsterdam bij Nacht (Dut 1924)
    Cirque Hollandais (Dut 1924)
    De Cabaret Prinses (Dut 1925)
    Bet Naar de Olympiade (Dut 1928)

FREUND, KARL, b. January 16, 1890, Königshof, Bohemia; d. May 3, 1969
    The Mummy (Univ 1932)
    Moonlight and Pretzels (Univ 1933)
    Madame Spy (Univ 1934)
    The Countess of Monte Cristo (Univ 1934)
    Uncertain Lady (Univ 1934)
    Gift of Gab (Univ 1934)
    I Give My Love (Univ 1934)
    Mad Love (MGM 1935)

FRIJDERS, FRANCOIS, b. Belgium
Leentje van de Zee (Bel 1927)

FROELICH, CARL, b. Nov. 15, 1875, Berlin; d. Feb. 12, 1953
Zu spät (Ger 1911)
Richard Wagner (Ger 1913)
Der Schirm mit dem Schwan (Ger 1915)
Der Liebesroman der Käthe Keller (Ger 1919)
Die Verführten (Ger 1919)
Die Bruder Karamasoff (Ger 1920) (with co-director)
Die Toteninsel (Ger 1920) (also co-script)
Irrende Seelen (Ger 1921) (also co-script)
Don Correa (Ger 1922)
Josef und seine Brüder (Ger 1922) (also script)
Luise Millerin (Ger 1922)
Der Taugenichts (Ger 1922) (also co-script)
Der Wetterwart (Ger 1923)
Mutter und Kind (Ger 1924)
Das Abenteuer der Sybille Brandt (Ger 1925)
Im Banne der Kralle (Ger 1925)
Kammermusik (Ger 1925)
Tragödie (Ger 1925)
Die Flammen lügen (Ger 1926)
Rosen aus dem Süden (Ger 1926)
Wehe, wenn sie losgelassen (Ger 1926) (also co-script)
Die grosse Pause (Ger 1927)
Meine Tante--Deine Tante (Ger 1927)
Violantha (Ger 1927)
Liebe im Kuhstall (Ger 1928)
Liebe und Diebe (Ger 1928)
Liebfraumilch (Ger 1928)
Lotte (Ger 1928)
Zuflucht (Ger 1928)
Die Frau, die jeder liebt, bist Du! (Ger 1929)
Die Nacht gehört uns (Ger 1929)
Brand in der Oper (Ger 1930)
Hans in allen Gassen (Ger 1930)
Mitternachtsliebe (Ger 1931) (with A. Genina)
Luise, Königin von Preussen (Ger 1931)
Mieter Schulze gegen allen (Ger 1932)
Die--oder keine (Ger 1932)
Liebe auf den ersten Ton (Ger 1932)
Gitta entdeckt ihr Herz (Ger 1932)
Volldampf voraus (Ger 1933) (also co-scripted)
Reifende Jugend (Ger 1933)
Der Choral von Leuthen (Ger 1933)
Ich für Dich--Du für mich (Ger 1933)
Krach um Iolanthe (Ger 1934)
Frühlingsmärchen (Ger 1934)
Liselotte von der Pfalz (Ger 1935) (also co-script)
Oberwachtmeister Schwenke (Ger 1935)
Ich war Jack Mortimer (Ger 1935)
Wenn wir alle Engel wären (Ger 1936)

Traumulus (Ger 1936)
Wenn der Hahn kräht (Ger 1936)
Die grossen Torheiten (Ger 1937)
Heimat (Ger 1938)
Die vier Gesellen (Ger 1938)
Die Umwege des schönen Karl (Ger 1938)
Es war eine rauschende Ballnacht (Ger 1939)
Das Herz einer Königin (Ger 1940)
Der Gasmann (Ger 1941)
Hochzeit auf Bärenhof (Ger 1942)
Familie Buchholz (Ger 1944)
Neigungsehe (Ger 1944)
Komplott auf Erienhof (Ger 1950)
Stips (Ger 1951)

FUEST, ROBERT, b. 1927, London
    Just Like a Woman (Monarch 1966) (also script)
    And Soon the Darkness (WP 1970)
    Wuthering Heights (AIP Br 1971)
    The Abominable Dr. Phibes (AIP Br 1971)
    Dr. Phibes Rises Again (AIP 1972) (also co-script)
    The Final Programme [Last Days of Man on Earth] (AIP Br
       1973) (also script)

FULCI, LUCIO, b. June 17, 1927, Rome
    I ladri (It 1959) (also script)
    Ragazzi del juke-box (It 1959) (also script)
    Urlatori alla abarra (It 1960) (also script)
    Colpo gobbo all'italiana (It 1962) (also script)
    I due della legione (It 1962) (also script)
    Le massaggiatrici (It 1962) (also script)
    Gli imbroglioni (It 1963) (also script)
    Uno strano tipo (It 1963) (also script)
    I due evasi di Sing Sing (It 1964) (also script)
    I maniaci (It 1964) (also script)
    I due pericoli pubblici (It 1965) (also script)
    Come inguaiamo l'esercito (It 1965) (also script)
    022, operazione luna (It 1965) (also script)
    Come svaligiamo la Banca d'Italia (It 1966) (also script)
    I due para (It 1966) (also script)
    Tempo di massacro (It 1966) (also script)
    Come rubamo la bomba atòmica (It 1967) (also script)
    Il lungo, il corto, il gatto (It 1967) (also script)
    Operazione San Pietro (It 1968) (also script)
    Una sull'altra (It-Fr-Sp 1969) (also script)
    Beatrice Cenci (It 1969)
    Una lucertola con la pelle di donna (It-Fr-Sp 1970) (also script)
    All'onorevole piacciono le donne (It-Fr 1971) (also script)
    Zanna bianca (It-Sp-Fr 1972) (also script)

FURIE, SIDNEY J., b. Feb. 28, 1933, Toronto, Ontario
    A Dangerous Age (Can 1957) (also producer, script)
    A Cool Sound from Hell (Can 1959) (also producer, script)

Dr. Blood's Coffin (UA 1961)
During One Night (Gala 1961) (also co-producer, script)
The Snake Woman (UA 1961)
Three on a Spree (Gala 1961)
The Young Ones (WPD 1961)
The Boys (Gala 1962) (also co-producer)
The Leather Boys (Garrick 1963)
Wonderful Life (Elstree 1964)
The Ipcress File (Rank-Univ 1965)
The Appaloosa [Southwest to Sonora] (USA) (Univer 1966)
The Naked Runner (WB-7 Arts 1967)
The Lawyer (USA) (Par 1968)
Little Fauss and Big Halsy (USA) (Par 1970)
Lady Sings the Blues (Par 1972)† [co-production company]
Hit! (USA) (Par 1973)

GALLONE, CARMINE, b. Sept. 18, 1886, Taggia, Italy; d. March
   11, 1973
Turbine d'odio (It 1914)
La donna nuda (It 1914)
Avatar (It 1915)
Fior di male (It 1915)
Marcia muziale (It 1915)
Redenzione (It 1915)
Maria di Magdala (It 1915)
Senza colpa (It 1915)
La falena (It 1916)
Malombra (It 1916)
Storia dei tredici (It 1916)
Maman Popee (It 1919)
Il bacio di Cirano (It 1919)
Amleto e il suo clown (It 1921)
Nemesi (It 1921)
Marcella (It 1922)
I volti dell'amore (It 1923)
La cavalcata ardente (It 1923)
Il corsaro (It 1924) (with Augusto Genina)
Gli ultimi giorni di Pompei (It 1926)
Celle qui domine (It 1928) (with co-director)
Schiff in Not SOS (Ger 1928)
Terra senza donne [Das Land ohne Frauen] (Ger 1929)
City of Song [Farewell to Love] (Eng-Fr-It 1931)
Un Soir de rafle (Fr 1931)
Un Fils d'Amérique (Fr 1932)
Le Chant du marin (Fr 1933)
Eine Nacht in Venedig (Ger 1933)
King of the Ritz (Eng 1933)
For Love of You (Eng 1933)
Going Gay (Eng 1933)
Two Hearts in Waltz Time (Gaumont 1934)
Casta Diva (It 1935)
The Divine Spark (Eng version of Casta Diva) (Univ Br 1935)
In Sonnenschein (Ger 1936)

E luce alle stelle (It 1936)
Wenn die Musik nicht wär' [Das Lied der Liebe] (Ger 1935)
Scipione l'Africano (It 1937)
Mutterlied (Ger-It 1937)
Solo per te (It 1938)
Manege (It 1938)
Marionette (It 1938)
Giuseppe Verdi (It 1938)
Il sogno di Butterfly (It 1939)
Manon Lescaut (It 1939)
Oltre l'amore (It 1940)
Melodie eterne (It 1940)
Amami, Alfredo! (It 1940)
L'amante segreta (It 1941)
Primo amore (It 1941)
La Regina di Navarra (It 1941)
Le due orfanelle (It 1942)
Odessa in fiamme (It 1942)
Harlem [Knock Out] (It 1942)
Tristi amori (It 1943)
Il canto della vita (It 1945)
Dayanti a lui tremava tutta Roma [Before Him All Rome
    Trembled] (It 1947)
Biraghin (It 1946)
Rigoletto (It 1947)
La signora dalle camelie [The Lost One] (It 1948)
La leggende di Faust [Faust and the Devil] (It 1949)
Il trovatore (It 1949)
La forza del destino (It 1950)
Taxi di notte (It 1951)
Addio, Mimi [Her Wonderful Life] (It 1951) (produced in 1947)
Messalina (It 1951)
Cavalleria rusticana (It 1953)
Puccini [Two Loves Have I] (It 1953)
Senza veli (It 1953) (also co-script)
Casa Ricordi [House of Ricordi] (It 1954)
Don Camillo e l'onorévole Peppone (It 1955)
Casta diva (It-Fr 1955)
Michele Strogoff (It-Fr-Ger 1956)
Tosca (It 1956)
Polikuska (It 1958)
Cartagine in fiamme [Carthage in Flames] (It 1959)
Don Camillo monsignore ... ma non troppo (It 1961)
Carmen di Trastevere (It-Fr 1962)
La monaca di Monza (It-Fr 1962)

GANCE, ABEL, b. 1889, Paris
Mater dolorosa (Fr 1917) (also script)
La Dixième Symphonie (Fr 1918) (also script)
J'accuse! (Fr 1919) (also script)
La Roue (Fr 1923) (also script)
Au secours! (Fr 1923) (also co-script)
Napoléon (Fr 1927) (also script, titles, editor, actor)

La Fin du monde (Fr 1930) (with Jean Epstein, Walter Rutt-
man, Popoff, Etievant Sauvage, Edmond T. Greville) (also
script, actor)
Mater dolorosa (Fr 1932) (also script)
Le Maître de forges (Fr 1933) (also script)
Poliche (Fr 1934) (also script)
La Dame aux camélias (Fr 1934) (also script)
Napoléon Bonaparte (Fr 1934) (also script, editor, actor)
Le Roman d'un jeune homme pauvre (Fr 1935) (also script)
Lucrèce Borgia (Fr 1935)
Un Grand Amour de Beethoven (Fr 1936) (also script)
Jérôme, Perreau, heros des barricades (Fr 1936)
Le Voleur de femmes (Fr 1936) (also script)
J'accuse! (Fr 1937) (also script, co-dialogue)
Louise (Fr 1938) (also co-script)
Paradis perdu (Fr 1939) (also co-script)
La Vénus aveugle (Fr 1940-41)
Le Capitaine fracasse (Fr 1942) (also co-adaptor, co-dialogue)
La Tour de Nesle [The Tower of Lust] (Fr 1954) (also script,
co-dialogue)
Austerlitz [The Battle of Austerlitz] (Fr-It-Liech-Yug 1960)
(co-script, co-dialogue)
Cyrano et d'Artagan (Fr-It-Sp 1963-64) (also script, dialogue)

GARREL, PHILIPPE, b. 1948
Anémone (Fr 1967) (also script)
Marie pour mémoire (Fr 1968) (also script)
La Révélateur (Fr 1969)
La Concentration (Fr 1969) (also script)
Le Lit de la vierge (Fr 1970) (also script)
La Cicatrice intérieure [Inner Scar] (Fr 1972) (also script,
editor)
L'Athanor (Fr 1973) (also co-script, actor)

GATTI, ARMAND, b. 1924, Monaco
L'Enclos (Fr 1961) (also script)
El otro Cristobal (Cuba 1963) (also script)

GEILFUS, FREDERIC, b. 1917, Brussels
Le Revolver aux cheveux rouges (Bel 1972) (with Denise Geilfus)

GENINA, AUGUSTO, b. Jan. 28, 1892, Rome; d. Sept. 28, 1957
La Parola che uccidi (It 1914)
Il piccolo cerinaio (It 1914)
La fuga degli amanti (It 1914)
Dopo il veglione (It 1914)
L'anello di Siva (It 1914)
Mezzanotte (It 1915) (also story, script)
La gelosia (It 1915)
La doppia ferita (It 1915) (also story, script)
Lulu (It 1915)
Cento HP (It 1916)
La conquista dei diamanti (It 1916)

Abel Gance

L'ultimo travestimento (It 1916)
Il dramma della corona (It 1916)
Il sogno di un giorno (It 1916) (also story)
Il sopravvissuto (It 1916)
La signorina Ciclone (It 1916)
La menzogna (It 1916) (also story, script)
Il presagio (It 1916) (also story, script)
Il siluramento dell'Oceania (It 1917) (also story, script)
Lucciola (It 1917)
Maschiaccio (It 1917) (also story)
Il principe dell'impossible (It 1918) (also script)
Fémmina o Fémina (It 1918) (also story)
L'onesta del peccato (It 1918) (also story)
Kalidaa o La storia di una mummia (It 1918)
Il trono e la seggiola (It 1918)
Addio giovinezza (It 1918) (also script)

I due Crocifissi (It 1918) (also script)
L'emigrata (It 1918)
La maschera e il volto (It 1919)
Lucrezia Borgia (It 1919)
Noris (It 1919) (also story)
Lo scaldino (It 1919)
Bel ami (It 1919)
Debito d'odio (It 1919)
La donna e il cadavere (It 1919) (also story, script)
Le avventure di Bijou (It 1919) (also story)
La douloureuse (It 1920)
I tre sentimentali (It 1920) (also script)
Tre meno due (It 1920) (with L. Antamoro)
I diabolici (It 1920) (also script)
Il castello della malinconia (It 1920)
L'avventura di Dio (It 1920)
La ruota del vizio (It 1920) (also script)
Marito moglie e ... (It 1920) (also story)
La fuggitiva (It 1920) (only supervisor)
L'orizzontale (It 1920) (only story)
L'incatenata (It 1921)
Crisi (It 1921)
L'innamorata (It 1921)
Lucie de Trecoeur (It 1922)
La peccatrice senza peccato (It 1922)
Cìrano di Bergerac (It 1923)
Il corsaro (It 1923) (with Carmine Gallone)
Germaine (It 1923)
Jolly (It 1923) (only story)
La moglie bella (It 1924)
Il focolare spento [Il più grande amore] (It 1925)
L'ultimo Lord (It 1926) (also script)
Addio giovinezza (It 1927) (also script)
Die weisse Sklavin [La schiava bianca] (Ger 1927)
Die Geschichte einer kleiner Parisien [Totte et sa chance] (Fr-Ger 1927)
Die Gefangene von Shanghai [La prigioniera di Shanghai] (Ger 1927)
Scampolo (Ger 1928)
Liebeskarnaval [Mascherata d'amore] (Ger 1928) (also story, script)
Un dramma a 16 anni (It 1929)
Quartier Latin [Quartiere Latino] (Fr 1929)
Prix de beauté [Miss Europa] (Fr 1930)
Les Amants de minuit [Gli amori di mezzanotte] (Fr 1931)
Mitternachtsliebe (Ger version of Les Amants di minuit) (Fr 1931)
Paris-béguin (Fr 1931)
La femme en homme [L'ultimo Lord] (Fr 1931)
Ne sois pas jalouse (Fr 1932) (also story, script)
Nouse ne sommes plus des enfants [Non siamo più ragazzi] (Fr 1934)
Vergiss mich nicht [Non ti scordar di me] (Ger 1935)

Blumen aus Nizza [Fiori di Nizza] (Aus 1926)
La gondole aux chimeres [La gondola della chimere] (It-Fr
    1936)
Squadrone bianco (It 1936) (also co-script)
Frauenliebe, Frauenlied [Amore e dolore di donna] (Ger 1937)
Naples au baiser de feu [Napoli terra d'amore] (Fr 1937)
Castelli in aria (It-Ger 1939)
L'assedio dell'Alcazar (It 1940)
Bengasi (It 1942)
Cielo sulla palude (It 1950)
L'edera (It 1952)
Tre storie proibite (It 1952)
Maddalena (It 1953)
Frou-Frou (Fr-It 1955)

GENTILOMO, GIACOMO, b. April 5, 1909, Trieste
Il carnevale di Venezia (It 1939)
O' sole mio (It 1946)
Tempesta d'anime (It 1946)
Amanti in fuga (It 1947)
I fratelli Karamazoff (It 1948)
Biancaneve e i sette ladri (It 1949)
Atto d'accusa (It 1950)
Lo sparviero del Nilo (It 1951)
Enrico Caruso, leggenda di una voce [The Young Caruso] (It
    1951)
La cieca di Sorrento (It 1952)
Melodie immortali (It 1953)
Appassionatamente (It 1954)
Le due orfanelle (It 1955)
Una voce, una chitarra e un po' di luna (It 1956)
Il cavaliere senza terra (It 1958)
La trovatella di Pompei (It 1958)
Sigfrido (It 1959)
L'ultimo dei vichinghi (It 1961)
Maciste contro il vampiro (It 1961)
I lancieri neri (It 1963)
Le verdi bandiere di Allah (It 1964)
Brenno, il nemico di Roma (It 1964)

GERMI, PIETRO, b. Sept. 14, 1914, Genoa, Italy; d. Dec. 5, 1974
Il testimone (It 1946) (also story, co-script)
Gioventù perduta [Lost Youth] (It 1948) (also story, co-script)
In nome della legge (It 1950) (also co-script)
Il cammino della speranza [The Path of Hope] (It 1950) (also
    co-story, co-script)
La città si difende [Four Ways Out] (It 1951) (also co-script)
La presidentessa (It 1952)
Il brigante di Tacca del Lupo (It 1952) (also co-story, co-
    script)
Gelosia (It 1953) (also co-script)
Amori di mezzo secolo (ep "Guerra 1915-18") (It 1953)
Il ferroviere [The Railroad Man] (It 1956) (also co-script, actor)

L'uomo di paglia (It 1958) (also co-story, co-script, actor)
Un maledetto imbroglio [Facts of Murder] (It 1959) (also co-script, actor)
Divorzio all'italiana [Divorce Italian Style] (It 1961) (also co-story, co-script)
Sedotta e abbandonata [Seduced and Abandoned] (It 1964) (also co-story, co-script)
Signore e signori [The Birds, the Bees and the Italians] (It 1966) (also co-script)
L'immorale (It 1967)
Serafino (It-Fr 1968)
Le castagne sono buone (It 1969) (also co-script)
Alfredo, Alfredo (It 1971)

Pietro Germi

GIL, RAFAEL, b. May 22, 1913, Spain
La semana santa de Murcia (Sp 1935) (with Gonzalo Memedez Pidal)
Semana Santa en Cartagena (Sp 1935) (with Gonzalo Memedez Pidal)
Cinco Minutos de españolada (Sp 1935) (with Gonzalo Memedez Pidal)
El Hombre que so quiso matar (Sp 1941)
Viaje sin destino (Sp 1942)
Huella de luz (Sp 1943)
Elcisa esta debajo de un almendro (Sp 1943)
Lecciones de buen amor (Sp 1943)

El clavo (Sp 1944)
El fantasma y dona Juanita (Sp 1944)
Tierra Sedienta (Sp 1944)
La prodiga (Sp 1946)
Reina Santa (Sp 1946)
Don Quijote de la Mancha (Sp 1947)
La Fé (Sp 1947)
Mare Nostrum (Sp 1948)
La calle sin sol (Sp 1948)
Aventuras de Juan Lucas (Sp 1949)
Una mujer cualquiera (Sp 1949)
La noche del sabado (Sp 1940)
Teatro Apolo (Sp 1950)
El gran galeoto (Sp 1951)
La senora de Fatima (Sp 1951)
De Madrid al cielo (Sp 1952)
Cincuenta anos del Real Madrid (Sp 1952)
Sor Intrepida (Sp 1952)
La Guerra de Dios (Sp 1953)
El Beso de Judas (Sp 1954)
La otra vida del capitan Contreras (Sp 1954)
Murio hace quince anos (Sp 1954)
El canto del Gallo (Sp 1955)
La gran Mentira (Sp 1956)
Un traje blanco (Sp 1956)
Camarote de Lujo (Sp 1957)
Viva lo imposible! (Sp 1958)
La caso de la troya (Sp 1959)
El litri y su sombra (Sp 1959)
Siega verde (Sp 1960)
Carino mio (Sp 1961)
Tu y yo somos tres (Sp 1962)
Rogelia (Sp 1962)
La reina del Cantecler (Sp 1962)
Chantaje a un torero (Sp 1963)
Samba (Sp 1964)
La vida nueva de Pedrito de Andia (Sp 1964)
Currito de la Cruz (Sp 1965)
Es Mi Hombre (Sp 1966)
Camino del Rocio (Sp 1966)
La mujer de otro (Sp 1967)
Verde doncella (Sp 1968)
El marino de los punos de oro (Sp 1968)
Sangre en el ruedo (Sp 1968)
El adulterio decente (Sp 1969)
Sangre en el Ruedo (Sp 197)
El relicario (Sp 1970)
El hombre que se quiso matar (Sp 1970)
El sobre verde (Sp 1971)
Nada menos que todo un hombe (Sp 1971) (also script)
La guerrilla (Sp-Fr 1973)

GILBERT, LEWIS, b. March 6, 1920, London
The Little Ballerina (GFD 1947) (also co-script)
Once a Sinner (Butcher 1950)
There Is Another Sun (Butcher 1951)
Scarlet Thread (Butcher 1951)
Emergency Call [The Hundred Hour Hunt] (Butcher 1952) (also co-script)
Time Gentlemen Please! (ABFD 1952)
Cosh Boy [The Slasher] (IFD 1953) (also co-script)
Johnny on the Run (ABFD-CFF 1953) (with Vernon Harris)
Albert R. N. [Break to Freedom] (Eros 1953)
The Good Die Young (IFD 1954) (also co-script)
The Sea Shall Not Have Them (Eros 1954) (also co-script)
Cast a Dark Shadow (Eros 1955)
Reach for the Sky (RFD 1956) (also co-script)
The Admirable Crichton [Paradise Lagoon] (Modern Screenplays 1957)
Carve Her Name with Pride (RFD 1958) (also co-script)
A Cry from the Streets (Eros 1958)
Ferry to Hong Kong (RFD 1959) (also co-script)
Sink the Bismarck! (20th Br 1960)
Light Up the Sky (Bry 1960)
The Greengage Summer [Loss of Innocence] (Col Br 1961)
H. M. S. Defiant [Damn the Defiant] (Col Br 1962)
The Seventh Dawn (UA 1964)
Alfie (Par Br 1966) (also producer)
You Only Live Twice (UA 1967)
The Adventurers (USA) (Par 1970) (also producer, co-script)
Friends (USA) (Par 1971) (also author, producer)

GILDEMEYER, JOHAN, b. Netherlands
Danstragedie (Dut 1914)
Koningin Elisabeth's dochter (Dut 1915)
Diamant (Dut 1916)
Gloria Transita (Dut 1917)
Gloria Fatalis (Dut 1922)

GILLES, GUY, b. 1940, Algiers
L'Amour à la mer (Fr 1965) (also script, actor)
Au Pan coupé (Fr 1968) (also script)
Clair de terre (Fr 1970) (also script, camera)
Absences repétées (Fr 1972) (also script, dialogue)
Le Jardin qui bascule (Fr 1974) (also script, adaptor, dialogue)

GILLIAT, SIDNEY, b. Feb. 15, 1908, Edgeley, Cheshire
Millions Like Us (GFD 1943) (with Frank Launder) (also co-script)
Waterloo Road (GFD 1945) (also author)
The Rake's Progress [The Notorious Gentleman] (EL 1945)† [co-production company] (also co-producer, co-script)
Green for Danger (GFD 1948)† [co-production company] (also co-producer, co-script)
London Belongs to Me [Dulcimer Street] (GFD 1948)†

[co-production company] (also co-producer, co-script)
State Secret [The Great Manhunt] (BL 1950)† [co-production
   company] (also co-producer, co-script)
The Story of Gilbert and Sullivan [The Great Gilbert and Sulli-
   van] (BL 1953) (also co-producer, co-script)
The Constant Husband (BL 1955)† [co-production company]
   (also co-producer, co-script)
Fortune Is a Woman [She Played With Fire] (Col Br 1957) (also
   co-producer, co-script)
Left, Right and Centre (BL 1959) (also co-producer, co-script)
Only Two Can Play (BL 1962) (also co-producer)
The Great St. Trinian's Train Robbery (BL 1966) (with Frank
   Launder)
Endless Night (BL 1972) (also script)

GILLING, JOHN, b. May 29, 1912
   Escape from Broadmoor (GN 1948) (also script)
   A Matter of Murder (GN 1949) (also script)
   No Trace (Eros 1950) (also script)
   Blackout (Eros 1950) (also co-script)
   The Quiet Woman (Eros 1951) (also script)
   The Frightened Man (Eros 1952) (also script)
   Mother Riley Meets the Vampire [Vampire over London] (Re-
      nown 1952) (also producer)
   The Voice of Merrill [Murder Will Out] (Eros 1952) (also
      script)
   Deadly Nightshade (GFD 1953)
   Recoil (Eros 1953) (also script)
   3 Steps to the Gallows [White Fire] (Eros 1953) (also script)
   Escape by Night (Eros 1954) (also script)
   Double Exposure (GFD 1954) (also script)
   The Embezzler (GFD 1954) (also script)
   The Gilded Cage (Eros 1955)
   Tiger By the Tail [Crossup] (Eros 1955) (also co-script)
   The Gamma People (Col Br 1956) (also co-script)
   Odongo (Col Br 1956) (also script)
   Interpol [Pickup Alley] (Col Br 1957)
   High Flight (Col Br 1957) (also co-script)
   The Man Inside (Col Br 1958) (also co-script)
   Idle on Parade (Col Br 1959)
   The Bandit of Zhobe (Col Br 1959) (also script)
   The Flesh and the Fiends [Mania] (RFI 1960) (also story, co-
      script)
   The Challenge (RFD 1960) (also script)
   Fury at Smuggler's Bay (RFI 1961) (also co-producer, script)
   The Shadow of the Cat (Univ Br 1961)
   The Pirates of Blood River (Col Br 1962) (also co-script)
   The Scarlet Blade (WPD 1963) (also script)
   Panic (Bry 1963) (also co-author, script)
   Brigand of Kandahar (WPD 1965) (also script)
   The Plague of the Zombies (WPD 1965)
   The Reptile (WPD 1965)
   Where the Bullets Fly (GEF 1966)

The Mummy's Shroud (WPD 1967) (also script)
The Night Caller [Blood Beast from Outer Space] (Butcher 1967) (made in 1965)

GIOVANNI, JOSE, b. 1923, Paris
La Loi du survivant (Fr 1967) (also script)
Le Rapace [Birds of Prey] (Fr-It-Mex 1968) (also script)
Dernier Domicile connu (Fr-It 1970) (also script)
Un aller simple (Fr-It 1971) (also script)
Où est passé Tom? (Fr-It 1971) (also adaptor, dialogue)
La Scoumoune (Fr-It 1972) (also script)
Deux Hommes dans la ville (Fr-It 1973) (also script)

GIROLAMI, ENZO (a. k. a. E. G. CASTELLARI)
Ammazzali tutti e torna solo (It-Sp 1968)
Vado l'amazzo e torno (It 1968)
Quella sporca storia del West (It 1968)
La battaglia d'Inghilterra (It-Fr-Sp 1969)
Gli occhi freddi della paura (It-Sp 1970)
Ettore lo fusto (It-Fr-Sp 1971)
La polìzia incrimina, la legge assolve (It-Sp 1971)
Tedeum (It-Sp 1972)
Il cipollaro (It 1974)

GIROLAMI, MARINO (a. k. a. Fred Wilson), b. Rome
La strada buia (It 1949)
Il ladro di Venezia (It 1950)
Amore e sangue (It 1951)
Erà lui sì sì (It 1951)
Milano miliardaria (It 1951)
Mago per forza (It 1952)
Lo sai che i papaveri ... (It 1952)
Noi due soli (It 1953)
Erà lei che lo voleva (It 1953)
Riscatto [Tu sei il mio giùdice] (It 1953)
Oggi sposi (It 1953)
Lasciateci in pace (It 1954)
Il cantante misterioso (It 1955)
Ore io, lezione di canto (It 1955)
Canto per te (It 1956)
La ragazza di via Veneto (It 1956)
Cantando sotto le stelle (It 1956)
Serenate per sedici bionde (It 1957)
Vivendo, contando, che male ti fo? (It 1957)
C'è un sentiero nel cielo (It 1957)
Sette canzoni per sette sorelle (It 1957)
Buongiorno primo amore (It 1958)
La canzone del destino (It 1958)
Il romanzo di un giovane povero (It 1958)
Quando gli angeli pianogono (It 1958)
Quel tesoro di papa (It 1959)
Un canto nel deserto (It 1960)
Il mio amico Jekyll (It 1960)

Caccia al marito (It 1960)
Quanto sei bella Roma (It-Sp 1960)
Ferragosto in bikini (It 1961)
Walter e i suoi cugini (It 1961)
La ragazza sotto il lenzuolo (It 1961)
Un figlio d'oggi (It 1961)
Scandali al mare (It 1961)
Le magnifiche sette (It 1961)
Il medico delle donne (It 1962)
L'assassino si chiama Pompeo (It 1962)
Twist, lolite e vitelloni (It 1962)
L'ira di Achille (It 1962)
Le motorizzate (It 1962)
Siamo tutti pomicioni (It 1963)
Le tardone (It 1964)
Queste pazze, pazze donne (It 1964)
Veneri al sole (It 1965)
Veneri in collegio (It 1965)
I magnifici brutos del West (It 1965)
Il piombe e la carne (It 1965)
Due gringos nel Texas (It 1967)
Spiaggia libera (It 1967)
Granada addio (It 1968)
Franco, Ciccio e le vedove allegre (It 1968)
Anche nel West c'erà una volta Dio (It 1968)

GIVRAY, CLAUDE DE, b. 1933, Nice, France
Tire-au-flanc [The Sad Sack] (Fr 1961)
Une Grosse tête (Fr 1962)
Un Mari à prix fixe (Fr 1964)
L'Amour à la chaîne [Victims of Vice] (Fr 1964)

GLENVILLE, PETER, b. Oct. 28, 1913, London
The Prisoner (Col Br 1955)
Summer and Smoke (USA) (Par 1960)
Term of Trial (WPD 1962) (also script)
Becket (USA) (Par 1964)
Hotel Paradiso (MGM Br 1966) (also producer, co-script)

GODARD, JEAN-LUC, b. Dec. 3, 1930, Paris
A bout de souffle [Breathless] (Fr 1959) (also script, actor)
Le Petit Soldat (Fr 1960) (also script, actor) (Release delayed
    until 1963)
Une Femme est une femme [A Woman Is a Woman] (Fr 1961)
    (also script)
Les Sept Péchés capitaux [Seven Capital Sins] (ep "La Paresse")
    (Fr-It 1962) (also script)
Vivre sa vie [My Life to Live] (Fr 1962) (also script)
Rogopag (ep "Le Nouveaux Monde") (Fr-It 1963) (also script)
Les Carabiniers (Fr-It 1963) (also co-script)
Les Plus Belles escroqueries du monde (ep "Le grand escroc")
    (It-Fr 1964) (also script)
Le Mépris [Contempt] (Fr-It 1963) (also script, actor)

Bande à part [Band of Outsiders] (Fr 1964) (also script, narrator)
Une Femme Mariée [The Married Woman] (Fr 1964) (also script)
Alphaville, une étrange aventure de Lemmy Caution (Fr-It 1965) (also script)
Pierrot le fou (Fr-It 1965) (also script)
Paris vu par ... [Six of a Kind] (ep "Montparnasse-Levallois") (also script)
Masculin féminin (Fr-Swe 1966) (also script)
Made in USA (Fr 1966) (also script, voice)
Deux ou trois choses que je sais d'elle (Fr 1966) (also script)
Le Plus Vieux Métier du monde (ep "L'amour en l'an 2000") (Fr-W Ger-It 1967)
La Chinoise, ou plutôt à la Chinoise (Fr 1967) (also script)
Loin du Vietnam [Far from Vietnam] (Fr 1967) (with Alain Resnais, William Klein, Agnes Varda, Joris Ivens, Claude Lelouch)
Weekend (Fr-It 1967) (also script)
Vangelo '70 (Fr-It 1967) (ep "L'enfant prodigue") (also script)
Le Gai Savoir (Fr-W Ger 1968) (also script)
Un Film comme les autres (Fr 1968) (also script)
One Plus One [Sympathy for the Devil] (GB 1968) (also script)
British Sounds [See You at Mao] (GB 1969) (with Jean-Henri Roger) (also script)
Le Vent d'Est (W Ger-Fr-It 1970) (with Jean-Pierre Gorin) (also co-script)
Pravda (Fr-Czech 1970) (with Jean-Pierre Gorin) (also co-script)
Lotte in Italia (It-Fr 1970) (with Jean-Pierre Gorin) (also co-script)
Jusqu'à la victoire (Fr 1970) (with Jean-Pierre Gorin) (also co-script)
Vladimir et Rosa (Fr-W Ger 1971) (with Jean-Pierre Gorin) (also co-script)
Procès à Chicago [One American Movie/1 a.m.] (Fr-USA 1968-71) (also script)
Tout va bièn (Fr-It 1972) (with Jean-Pierre Gorin) (also co-script)

GOLD, JACK, b. 1930, London
The Bofors Gun (RFD 1968)
The Reckoning (Col Br 1969)
The National Health (Col Br 1973)

GORETTA, CLAUDE, b. June 23, 1929, Geneva
Un Dimance de mai (Swi TV 1953)
Tchekhov ou le miroir des vies perdues (Swi 1964)
Jean-Luc persécuté (Swi TV 1965)
Vivre ici (Swi TV 1968) (also script)
Le Jour des noces (Swi TV 1970) (also script)
Le Fou (Swi 1970) (also script)
Le Temps d'un portrait (Swi 1971) (also script)

Jean-Luc Godard

L'Invitation (Swi 1973) (also script)
Le Fils prodigue (Swi 1974)

GOSSOV, MARRAN, b. Germany
Engelchen oder die Jungfrau von Bamberg (Ger 1967)
Bengelchen liebt Kreuz und quer ... (Ger 1968)
Zuckerbrot und Peitsche (Ger 1968)
Der Kerl liebt mich--und das soll ich glauben? (Ger 1969)
Spiel mit Bulle (Ger 1972)

GOVAR, YVAN, b. France
Nous n'irons plus au bois (Fr 1953)
Le Toubib [Le toubib du gang] (Fr 1955)
Le Circuit de minuit (Fr 1956)
Y en a marre (Bel-Fr 1958)
La Croix des vivants (Fr 1961)
Que Personne ne sorte (Fr 1963)
Un Soir par hasard (Fr 1964)
Deux Heures à tuer (Fr 1965)

GREEN, GUY, b. 1913, Somerset, England
   River Beat (Eros 1954)
   Portrait of Alison [Postmark for Danger] (AA 1955) (also co-
      script)
   Lost [Tears for Simon] (RFD 1956)
   House of Secrets [Triple Deception] (RFD 1956)
   The Snorkel (Col Br 1958)
   Sea of Sand (RFD 1958)
   S. O. S. Pacific (RFD 1959)
   The Angry Silence (BL 1960)
   The Mark (20th Br 1961)
   Light in the Piazza (USA) (MGM 1961)
   Diamond Head (USA) (Col 1962)
   A Patch of Blue (USA) (MGM 1965) (also script)
   Pretty Polly (RFD 1967)
   The Magus (20th Br 1969)
   A Walk in the Spring Rain (USA) (Col 1969)
   Luther (American Film Theatre 1974)

GREENE, DAVID, b. Canada
   The Shuttered Room (WPD 1967)
   Sebastian (Par Br 1968)
   The Strange Affair (Par Br 1968)
   I Start Counting (UA Br 1970)
   The People Next Door (USA) (Avco Emb 1970)
   Madame Sin (Scotia-Barber TV, 1972) (also co-script)
   Godspell (USA) (Col 1973)

GREGORETTI, UGO, b. Sept. 28, 1930, Rome
   I nuovi angeli (It 1961)
   Rogopag (ep "Il pollo ruspante") (It 1962)
   Omicron (It 1962)
   Le più belle truffe del mondo (ep "Folgio di via") (Fr-It 1964)
   Le belle famiglie (Fr-It 1964)

GRIECO, SERGIO (a. k. a. Terence Hathaway), b. Jan. 13, 1917,
      Padua, Italy
   Il sentiero dell'odio (It 1952)
   Non è vero ma ci credo (It 1952)
   I morti non pagano tasse (It 1953)
   Primo premio (It 1953)
   Mariarosa (It 1953)
   La peccatrice dell'isola [Island Sinner] (It 1953)
   Fermi tutti, arrivo io! (It 1953)
   Amarti e il mio peccato (It 1953)
   Tua per la vita (It 1955)
   Lo spadaccino misterioso (It 1956)
   Giovanni dalle bande nere (It 1957)
   Il diavolo nero (It 1957)
   Pia de' Tolomei (It 1958)
   Il pirata dello sparviero nero (It 1958)
   Le notti di Lucrezia [Nights of Lucretia Borgia] (It 1959)
   Ciao ciao bambina (It 1959)

Guy Green, gesturing, with Michael Caine during the filming of The Magus (1968).

Salambò [Loves of Salambo] (It 1960)
La regina dei tartari [The Huns] (It 1960)
La schiava di Roma [Slaves of Rome] (It 1961)
Giulio Cesare contro i pirati (It 1962)
Una spada per l'impero (It 1965)
Agente 077, dall'Oriente con furore (It-Sp-Fr 1965)
Agente 077, missione Bloody Mary (It-Sp-Fr 1965)
Password, uccidete agente Gordon (It-Sp 1966)
Come rubammo la corona d'Inghilterra (It 1967)
Rififi ad Amsterdam (It 1967)
Tiffany memorandum (It 1967)
Il Sergente Klems (It 1971)

GRUNDGENS, GUSTAF, b. 1899, Düsseldorf; d. Oct. 7, 1963
Eine Stadt steht Kopf (Ger 1932)
Die Finanzen des Grossherzogs (Ger 1934)
Capriolen (Ger 1937) (also actor)
Der Schritt vom Wege (Ger 1939)
Zwei Welten (Ger 1940)
Faust (Ger 1960) (also actor) (with a co-director)

GRUNE, KARL, b. Jan. 22, 1890, Vienna; d. Oct. 2, 1962
  Aus eines Mannes Mädchenjahren (Ger 1919) (also co-script)
  Der Mädchenhirt (Ger 1919)
  Menschen in Ketten (Ger 1919) (with F. Zelnik)
  Die Jagd nach der Wahrheit (Ger 1920)
  Nachtbesuch (Ger 1920)
  Nacht ohne Morgen (Ger 1920)
  Mann über Bord (Ger 1921)
  Der Eroberer (Ger 1922)
  Frauenopfer (Ger 1922)
  Der Graf von Charolais (Ger 1922)
  Die Nacht der Medici (Ger 1922)
  Der stärkste Trieb (Ger 1922)
  Schlagende Wetter (Ger 1923)
  Die Strasse (Ger 1923) (also co-script)
  Arabella (Ger 1924)
  Komödianten (Ger 1924)
  Eifersucht (Ger 1925)
  Die Brüder Schellenberg (Ger 1926)
  Am Rande der Welt (Ger 1927) (also co-script)
  Königin Luise (Ger 1927)
  Marquis d'Eon, der Spion der Pompadour (Ger 1928)
  Waterloo (Ger 1928)
  Katherina Knie (Ger 1929)
  Das gelbe Haus des King-Fu (Ger 1931)
  Abdul the Damned (Eng 1935)
  The Marriage of Corbal (Eng 1936)
  Pagliacci (Eng 1936)

GUEST, VAL, b. 1911, London
  Miss London Ltd (GFD 1943) (also co-script)
  Bees in Paradise (GFD 1944) (also co-script)
  Give Us the Moon (GFD 1944) (also script)
  I'll Be Your Sweetheart (GFD 1945) (also co-script)
  Just William's Luck (UA Br 1947) (also script)
  William Comes to Town (UA Br 1948) (also script)
  Murder at the Windmill [Murder at the Burlesque] (GN 1949)
    (also script)
  Miss Pilgrim's Progress (GN 1950) (also script)
  The Body Said No (Eros 1950) (also script)
  Mr Drake's Duck (Eros 1951) (also script)
  Penny Princess (GFD 1952) (also co-producer, script)
  Life With the Lyons [Family Affair] (Ex 1954) (also co-script)
  The Runaway Bus (Eros 1954)† [co-production company] (also
    producer, script)
  Dance Little Lady (Renown 1954) (also co-script)
  Men of Sherwood Forest (Ex 1954)
  The Lyons in Paris (Ex 1955) (also script)
  Break in the Circle (Ex 1955) (also co-script)
  The Quatermass Experiment [The Creeping Unknown] (Ex 1955)
    (also co-script)
  They Can't Hang Me (IFD 1955) (also co-script)
  It's a Wonderful World (Renown 1956) (also script)

The Weapon (Eros 1956)
Quatermass II [Enemy from Space] (UA Br 1957) (also co-
    script)
Carry On Admiral [The Ship Was Loaded] (Renown 1957) (also
    script)
The Abominable Snowman (WB Br 1957)
The Camp on Blood Island (Col Br 1958) (also co-script)
Up the Creek (WB Br 1958) (also co-script)
Further Up the Creek (Col Br 1958) (also co-script)
Life Is a Circus (BL 1958) (also co-script)
Yesterday's Enemy (Col Br 1959)
Expresso Bongo (Britannia 1959) (also co-producer)
Hell Is a City (WPD 1960) (also script)
The Full Treatment (Col Br 1961) (also producer, co-script)
The Day the Earth Caught Fire (Pax 1961) (also co-producer,
    co-script)
Jigsaw (Britannia 1962) (also co-producer, script)
80,000 Suspects (RFD 1963) (also co-producer, script)
The Beauty Jungle [Contest Girl] (RFD 1964) (also producer,
    co-script)
Where the Spies Are (MGM Br 1965)† (also producer, co-
    script)
Casino Royale (Col Br 1967) (with Ken Hughes, John Huston,
    Joseph McGrath, Robert Parrish, Anthony Squire, Richard
    Talmadge)
Assignment K (Col Br 1967) (also co-script)
Toomorrow (FRD 1970) (also script)
When Dinosaurs Ruled the Earth (WB Br 1970) (also script)
Au Pair Girls (LMG 1972) (also co-script)
Confessions of a Window Cleaner (Col 1974) (also co-script)

GUILLERMIN, JOHN, b. Nov. 11, 1925, London
Torment [Paper Gallows] (Adelphi 1949) (also co-producer,
    script)
Smart Alec (GN 1951)
Two on the Tiles (GN 1951)
Four Days (GN 1951)
Song of Paris [Bachelor in Paris] (Adelphi 1952)
Miss Robin Hood (ABFD 1952) (also co-producer)
Operation Diplomat (Butcher 1953) (also co-script)
Adventure in the Hopfields (BL-CFF 1954)
The Crowded Day (Adelphi 1954)
Thunderstorm (BL-CFF 1955)
Town on Trial (Col Br 1957)
The Whole Truth (Col Br 1958)
I Was Monty's Double (ABP 1958)
Tarzan's Greatest Adventure (Par Br 1959) (also co-script)
The Day They Robbed the Bank of England (MGM Br 1960)
Never Let Go (RFD 1960) (also co-author)
Waltz of the Toreadors (RFD 1962)
Tarzan Goes to India (USA) (MGM 1962) (also co-script)
Guns at Batasi (20th Br 1964)
Rapture (USA-Fr) (20th 1965)

Val Guest with actress Yolande Donlan (his wife) on a break from filming Jigsaw (1962).

The Blue Max (20th Br 1966)
P. J. [New Face in Hell] (USA) (Univ 1967)
House of Cards (USA) (Univ 1968)
The Bridge at Remagen (USA) (UA 1968)
El Condor (USA) (National General 1970)
Skyjacked (USA) (MGM 1972)
Shaft in Africa (USA) (MGM 1973)
The Towering Inferno (USA) (20th-WB 1974)

HAANSTRA, BERT, b. 1917, Holten (Twente), Netherlands
Fanfare (Dut 1960) (also co-script, co-editor)
De Zaak M. P. (Dut 1960)
Alleman [The Human Dutch] (Dut 1963)
De Overvaal (Dut 1964) (only script)
De Stem van het Water [The Voice of the Water] (Dut 1965)
Trafic (Dut 1969) (only co-script)
Delta data (Dut 1969) (with John Ferno)
Bij de Beesten Af [Ape and Super-Ape] (Dut 1973)
Doktor Pulder Zaait Papavers (Dut 1975)

HAESAERTS, PAUL, b. Feb. 15, 1901, Boom, Belgium; d. Jan.
    31, 1974
    Rubens (Bel 1948) (also co-script) (with Henry Storck)
    Quatre Peintres belges au travail (Bel 1951) (also script)
    Un Siècle d'or: l'art des primitifs flamands (Bel 1953) (also
        script)
    Architecture, art de l'espace (Bel 195-) (also script)
    Cri et connaissance (Bel 1963) (also co-script) (with Hugo
        Claus)
    Le Clé des chants surrealistes (Bel 1966) (also script)
    Bruegel (Bel 1969) (also script)

HAGGARD, PIERS INIGO, b. 1939, London
    I Can't ... I Can't [Wedding Night] (Eire) (Scotia-Barber 1969)
        (also addition dialogue, song)
    Satan's Skin (Tigon 1971) (also additional script material)

HALL, PETER, b. Nov. 22, 1930, Bary St. Edmunds
    Work Is a Four-Letter Word (RFD 1968)
    A Midsummer Night's Dream (Eagle 1969)
    Three into Two Won't Go (RFD 1969)
    Perfect Friday (London Screenplay 1970)
    The Homecoming (American Film Theatre 1974)

HAMER, ROBERT, b. March 31, 1911, Kidderminster, England;
    d. Dec. 4, 1963
    Dead of Night (ep "The Haunted Mirror") (EL 1945)
    Pink Strings and Sealing Wax (EL 1945) (also co-script)
    It Always Rains on Sunday (GFD 1947) (also co-script)
    Kind Hearts and Coronets (GFD 1949) (also co-script)
    The Spider and the Fly (GFD 1949)
    His Excellency (GFD 1952) (also co-script)
    The Long Memory (GFD 1953) (also co-script)
    Father Brown [The Detective] (Col Br 1954) (also co-script)
    To Paris with Love (GFD 1955)
    The Scapegoat (MGM Br 1959) (also co-script)
    School for Scoundrels (WPD 1960)

HAMILTON, GUY, b. Sept., 1922, Paris
    The Ringer (BL 1952)
    The Intruder (BL 1953)
    An Inspector Calls (BL 1954)
    The Colditz Story (BL 1955) (also co-script)
    Charley Moon (BL 1956)
    Manuela [Stowaway Girl] (RFD 1957) (also co-script)
    The Devil's Disciple (UA 1959)
    A Touch of Larceny (Par Br 1959) (also co-script)
    The Best of Enemies (USA) (Col 1962)
    The Party's Over (Monarch 1963)
    Man in the Middle (20th Br 1963)
    Goldfinger (UA Br 1964)
    Funeral in Berlin (Par Br 1966)
    Battle of Britain (UA Br 1969)

Peter Hall filming <u>Work Is a Four-Letter Word</u> (1968).

Diamonds Are Forever (UA Br 1971)
Live And Let Die (UA Br 1973)

Guy Hamilton (left) with Oliver Reed during the shooting of The
Party's Over (1963).

HANDWERKER, MARIAN, b. Dec. 14, 1944, Talde-Kurgan,
     U. S. S. R.
     Pois, Pois (Bel 1971)
     La Vie à deux (Bel TV 1973)
     La Cage aux ours (Bel 1974)

HANOUN, MARCEL, b. Oct. 26, 1929, Tunis
     Une Simple Histoire (Fr 1958) (also script, camera)
     Le Huitième Jour (Fr 1959) (also co-script)
     Octobre à Madrid (Fr 1966) (also script)
     L'Authentique Procès de Carl-Emmanuel Jung (Fr 1967) (also
          script)
     L'Eté [That Summer] (Fr 1968)
     Le Printemps (Fr 1971) (also co-script)
     L'Hiver (Bel-Fr 1972) (also script)
     L'Automne (Fr 1972) (also script, camera)
     La Vérité sur l'imaginaire (Fr 1974) (also script)

HARTL, KARL ANTON, b. May 10, 1899, Vienna; d. 1974
     Ein Burschenlied aus Heidelberg (Ger 1930)
     Berge in Flammen (Ger 1931) (with Luis Trenker)

Die Gräfin von Monte Cristo (Ger 1932)
Der Prinz von Arkadien (Ger 1932)
F. P. I. antwortet nicht (Ger 1932)
Ihre Durchlaucht, die Verkäuferin (Ger 1933) (also script)
Gold (Ger 1934)
So endete eine Liebe (Ger 1934) (also script)
Zigneunerbaron (Ger 1935)
Ritt in die Freiheit (Ger 1936)
Der Mann, der Sherlock Holmes war (Ger 1937) (also co-
    script)
Die Leuchten des Kaisers [The Emperor's Candlesticks] (Aus
    1936) (also script)
Gastspiel im Paradies (Ger 1938) (also co-script)
Wen die Götter lieben (Ger 1942)
Der weisse Traum (Ger 1943) (Geza von Cziffra directed; Hartl
    supervised)
Der Engel mit der Posaune (Aus 1949)
The Angel with the Trumpet [English version of Der Engel mit
    der Posaune] (BL 1950) (also co-script)
Entführung ins Glück/The Wonder Kid (Aus-GB 1950) (also
    script) [Two versions]
Eroica (Aus 1950) (Walter Kohlm-Veltée directed; Hartl super-
    vised)
Der schweigende Mund (Aus 1951) (also co-script)
Haus des Lebens (Ger 1952) (also co-script)
Liebeskrieg (Ger 1953) (also co-script)
Alles für Papa (Ger 1953) (also co-script)
Weg in die Vergangenheit (Aus 1954)
Reich mir die Hand mein Leben (Aus 1955) (also script)
Rot ist die Liebe (Ger 1957)

HARVEY, ANTHONY, b. June 3, 1931, London
Dutchman (Planet 1966) (also editor)
The Lion in Winter (Avco Emb 1968)
They Might Be Giants (USA) (Univ 1971)
The Abdication (WB 1973)

HAUFLER, MAX, b. June 4, 1910, Basel, Switzerland; d. June 25,
    1965
Farinet ou la fausse monnaie (Swi 1939)
Emil, Me mues halt rede mitenand (Swi 1941) (also script)
Menschen die vorüberziehen (Swi 1942)
Der Teufel hat gut Lachen (Swi-Ger) (only script)

HAYERS, SIDNEY, b. Aug. 24, 1921, Edinburgh
Violent Moment (AA 1959)
The White Trap (AA 1959)
Circus of Horrors (AA 1960)
The Malpas Mystery (AA 1960)
Echo of Barbara (RFD 1961)
Payroll (AA 1961)
Night of the Eagle [Burn Witch Burn] (AA 1962)
This Is My Street (AA 1963)

Three Hats for Lisa (AA 1965)
The Trap (RFD 1966)
Finders Keepers (UA Br 1966)
The Southern Star [L'Etoile du sud] (Col Br 1969)
Mister Jerico (RFD 1970)
Assault (RFD 1971)
The Firechasers (RFD 1971)
Revenge (RFD 1971)
All Coppers Are ... (RFD 1972)

HEPWORTH, CECIL M. (Cecil Milton Hepworth), b. 1874, London;
    d. Feb. 10, 1953
Sweet Lavendar (LIFT 1915)
Iris (Ideal 1915)
Trelawny of the Wells (Butcher 1916)
Sowing the Wind (Hepworth 1916)†
Annie Laurie (Harma 1916)†
The Marriage of William Ashe (Harma 1916)†
Comin' Thro' the Rye (Harma 1916)†
Molly Bawn (Hepworth 1916)†
The Cobweb (Harma 1917)†
The American Heiress (Harma 1917)†
Nearer My God to Thee (Moss 1917)†
The Touch of a Child (Moss 1918)†
Boundary House (Moss 1918)†
The Nature of the Beast (Butcher 1919)†
Sunken Rocks (Butcher 1919)†
Sheba (Butcher 1919)†
The Forest on the Hill (Butcher 1919)†
Anna the Adventuress (National 1920)†
Alf's Button (Hepworth 1920)†
Helen of Four Gates (Hepworth 1920)†
Mrs Erricker's Reputation (Hepworth 1920)†
The Tinted Venus (Hepworth 1921)†
The Narrow Valley (Hepworth 1921)†
Wild Heather (Hepworth 1921)†
Tansy (Hepworth 1921)†
The Pipes of Pan (Hepworth 1923)†
Mist in the Valley (Hepworth 1923)†
Strangling Threads (Ideal 1923)†
Comin' Thro' the Rye (Hepworth 1923)†
The House of Marney (AA 1926)
[†for own production company]

HERMAN, JEAN, b. May 17, 1933, Pagny-sur-Moselle, France
Le Chemin de la mauvaise route (Fr 1962) (also staging)
Le Dimanche de la vie [The Sundays of Life] (Fr-W Ger-It
    1966)
Adieu l'ami (Fr-It 1968) (also co-script)
Popsy Pop [The 21 Carat Snatch] (Fr-It 1971) (also co-adaptor)
L'Oeuf (Fr 1972) (also co-script)

Cecil Hepworth

HERZOG, WERNER, b. Germany
    Lebenszeichen (Ger 1967)
    Die fliegenden Ärzte von Ostafrika (Ger 1968)
    Fata Morgana (Ger 1968-70)
    Auch Zwerge haben klein angefangen (Ger 1970)
    Behinderte zukunft (Ger 1970)
    Land des Schweigens und der Dunkelheit (Ger 1971)
    Aguirre der Zorn Gottes (Ger 1972)
    Die grosse Ekstase des Bildschnitzers Steiner (Ger TV 1974)
    Jeder für sich und Gott gegen Alle (Ger 1974)

HESSLER, GORDON, b. Berlin
    Catacombs (BL 1967) (made in 1964)
    De Sade [Der Marquis De Sade] (USA-W Ger) (AIP 1969) (un-
        credited, with Cy Endfield and uncredited Roger Corman)
    Scream and Scream Again (AIP 1970)
    The Last Shot You Hear (20th Br 1970) (made in 1968)
    The Oblong Box (AIP 1970)
    Cry of the Banshee (AIP 1970) (also producer)
    Murders in the Rue Morgue (AIP 1971)
    Embassy (Hemdale 1972)
    The Golden Voyage of Sinbad (Col 1973)

HEUSCH, PAOLO, b. Feb. 26, 1924, Rome
La morte viene dalla spazio (It 1958)
Un uomo facile (It 1959)
Lycanthropus (It 1962)
Una vita violenta (It 1962)
Il comandante (It 1963)
Una raffica di mitra (It 1967)
Un colpo da mille miliardi (It 1967)
El Che Guevara (It 1968)

HEYDE, NIKOLAI VAN DER, b. Jan. 23, 1936, Leeuwarden,
Netherlands
Een Ochtend van Zes Weken (Dut 1966)
To Grab the Ring (Dut 1968)
Angela (Dut-Bel 1973)
Help, de Dokter Verzupit (Dut 1974)

HICKOX, DOUGLAS, b. Jan. 10, 1929, London
It's All Over Town (BL 1963)
Just for You (BL 1964) (also co-story)
Entertaining Mr. Sloane (WPD 1970)
Sitting Target (MGM-EMI 1972)
Theatre of Blood (UA Br 1973)

HILL, JAMES, b. 1921, Yorkshire, England
The Stolen Plans (ABFD-CFF 1952) (also script)
The Clue of the Missing Ape (ABFD-CFF 1953) (also script)
Peril for the Guy (BL-CFF 1956) (also script)
Mystery in the Mine (CFF 1959) (also co-script)
The Kitchen (BL 1961)
The Dock Brief (MGM Br 1962)
Lunch Hour (Bry 1962)
Every Day's a Holiday [Seaside Swingers] (GN 1964)
A Study in Terror [Fog] (Compton 1965)
Born Free (Col Br 1966)
Die Holle von Macao [The Peking Medallion/ The Corrupt Ones]
(W Ger-Fr-It) (WPD 1966)
Captain Nemo and the Underwater City (MGM Br 1969)
An Elephant Called Slowly (BL 1969) (also co-script)
Black Beauty (Tigon 1971) (also additional dialogue)
The Belstone Fox (20th-Rank 1973) (also script)
The Lion at World's End (EMI 1974) (with Bill Travers) (1971)

HITCHCOCK, ALFRED, b. Aug. 13, 1899, London
Number Thirteen (unfinished 1921)
Always Tell Your Wife (Seymour Hicks Productions 1922) (with
Seymour Hicks)
The Pleasure Garden (GB-Ger) (W & F 1926)
The Mountain Eagle [Fear o' God] (GB-Ger) (W & F 1926)
Downhill [When Boys Leave Home] (W & F 1927)
Easy Virtue (W & F 1927)
The Ring (Wardour 1927) (also story, co-script)
The Farmer's Wife (Wardour 1928) (also co-script)

Champagne (Wardour 1928) (also co-script)
The Manxman (Wardour 1929)
Blackmail (Wardour 1929) (also co-script)
Juno and the Paycock [The Shame of Mary Boyle] (Wardour 1930) (also co-script)
Murder (Wardour 1930) (also co-script)
The Skin Game (Wardour 1931) (also co-script)
Rich and Strange [East of Shanghai] (Wardour 1932) (also co-script)
Waltzes from Vienna [Strauss's Great Waltz] (Gaumont 1933)
The Man Who Knew Too Much (Gaumont 1934)
The 39 Steps (Gaumont 1935)
The Secret Agent (Gaumont 1936)
Sabotage [The Woman Alone] (Gaumont 1936)
Young and Innocent [The Girl Was Young] (GFD 1937)
The Lady Vanishes (MGM Br 1938)
Jamaica Inn (ABPC 1939)
In the U. S. A. :
Rebecca (UA 1940)
Foreign Correspondent (UA 1940)
Mr and Mrs Smith (RKO 1941)
Suspicion (RKO 1942)
Saboteur (Univ 1942) (also author)
Shadow of a Doubt (Univ 1943)
Lifeboat (20th 1943)
Spellbound (UA 1945)
Notorious (RKO 1946)
The Paradine Case (Selznick International 1947)
Rope (WB 1948) (also producer)
Under Capricorn (WB 1949) (also producer)
Stage Fright (WB 1950) (also producer)
Strangers on a Train (WB 1951) (also producer)
I Confess (WB 1952) (also producer)
Dial M for Murder (WB 1953) (also producer)
Rear Window (Par 1954) (also producer)
To Catch a Thief (Par 1955) (also producer)
The Trouble with Harry (Par 1955) (also producer)
The Man Who Knew Too Much (Par 1956) (also producer)
The Wrong Man (WB 1957) (also producer)
Vertigo (Par 1958) (also producer)
North by Northwest (MGM 1959) (also producer)
Psycho (Par 1960) (also producer)
The Birds (Univ 1963) (also producer)
Marnie (Univ 1964) (also producer)
Torn Curtain (Univ 1966) (also producer)
Topaz (Univ 1969) (also producer)
Frenzy (Univ Br 1972) (also producer)

HODGES, MIKE
Get Carter (MGM Br 1971) (also script)
Pulp (UA Br 1972)† [co-production company] (also script)
The Terminal Man (USA) (WB 1974)

Alfred Hitchcock

HOFFMAN, KURT, b. 1910, Freiburg, Germany
   Paradies der Junggesellen (Ger 1939)
   Hurra, ich bin Papa (Ger 1939)
   Quax der Bruchpilot (Ger 1941)
   Kohlhiesels Tochter (Ger 1943)
   Ich vertraue Dir meine Frau an (Ger 1943)
   Das verlorene Gesicht (Ger 1948)
   Heimliches Rendezvous (Ger 1949)
   Fünf unter Verdacht (Ger 1950)
   Der Fall Rabanser (Ger 1950)
   Taxi-Kitty (Ger 1950)
   Fanfaren der Liebe (Ger 1951)
   Königin einer Nacht (Ger 1951)
   Klettermaxe (Ger 1952)
   Liebe im Finanzamt (Ger 1952)
   Musik bei Nacht (Ger 1953)
   Hokuspokus (Ger 1953)
   Moselfahrt aus Liebeskummer (Ger 1953)
   Der Raub der Sabinerinnen (Ger 1954)
   Drei Manner im Schnee (Ger 1954)
   Das fliegende Klassenzimmer (Ger 1954)
   Feuerwerk (Ger 1954)
   Ich denke oft an Piroschka (Ger 1955)
   Heute heiratet mein Mann (Ger 1956)
   Bekenntnisse des Hochstaplers Felix Krull (Ger 1957)
   Salzburger Geschichten (Ger 1957)
   Wir Wunderkinder (Ger 1958)
   Das Wirtshaus im Spessart (Ger 1958)
   Der Engel, der seine Harfe versetzte (Ger 1959)
   Das schöne Abenteuer (Ger 1959)
   Lampenfieber (Ger 1959)
   Das Spukschloss im Spessart (Ger 1960)
   Die Ehe des Herrn Mississippi (Ger 1961)
   Liebe wil gelernt sein (Ger 1962)
   Schneewittchen und die sieben Gaukler (Ger 1963)
   Schloss Gripsholm (Ger 1964)
   Das Haus in der Karpfengasse (Ger 1964)
   Dr. med. Hiob Pratorius (Ger 1965)
   Hokuspokus--oder wie lasse ich meinen Mann verschwinden
     (Ger 1966)
   Liselotte von der Pfalz (Ger 1966)
   Herrliche Zeiten im Spessart (Ger 1967)
   Rheinsberg (Ger 1967)
   Morgens um sieben ist die Welt noch in Ordnung (Ger 1968)
   Ein Tag ist schöner als der andere (Ger 1969) (also co-script)
   Der Kapitän (Ger 1971)

HOLT, SETH (James Holt), b. 1923, Palestine; d. Feb. 13, 1971
   Nowhere to Go (MGM Br 1958) (also co-script)
   Taste of Fear [Scream of Fear] (Col Br 1961)
   Station Six-Sahara (BL 1962)
   The Nanny (WPD 1965)
   Danger Route (USA) (UA 1967)

Diabolique (unfinished 1967)
Monsieur Lecoq (unfinished 1967)
Blood from the Mummy's Tomb (A. P. 1971) (finished by
    Michael Carreras after Holt's death)

HUGHES, KEN, b. Jan. 19, 1922, Liverpool
    Wide Boy (AA 1952)
    The House Across the Lake [Heat Wave] (ABP 1954) (also
        story, script)
    Black 13 (Archway 1954)
    The Brain Machine (AA 1955) (also script)
    Little Red Monkey [Case of the Red Monkey] (AA 1955) (also
        co-script)
    Confession [The Deadliest Sin] (AA 1955) (also script)
    Timeslip [The Atomic Man] (AA 1955)
    Joe Macbeth (Col Br 1955)
    Portrait of Alison (AA 1955) (Guy Green) (co-script only)
    Wicked As They Come (Col Br 1956) (also co-script)
    The Long Haul (Col Br 1957) (also script)
    Jazzboat (Col Br 1960) (also co-script)
    The Trials of Oscar Wilde [The Man with the Green Carnation]
        (Eros 1960) (also script)
    In the Nick (Col Br 1960) (also script)
    The Small World of Sammy Lee (BL 1963) (also author, script)
    Of Human Bondage (MGM Br 1964) (with Henry Hathaway, un-
        credited Bryan Forbes)
    Drop Dead Darling [Arriverderci Baby] (Par British 1966) (also
        script, co-adaptor)
    Casino Royale (Col Br 1967) (with Val Guest, John Huston, Joe
        McGrath, Robert Parrish, Anthony Squire, Richard Tal-
        madge)
    Chitty Chitty Bang Bang (UA Br 1968) (also co-script)
    Cromwell (Col Br 1970) (also script)
    The Internecine Project (BL 1974)

HUGUENOT VAN DER LINDEN, CHARLES A., b. Mar. 24, 1909,
    Amsterdam
    Jonge Harten (Dut 1936) (with H. J. Josephson)

HUISMAN, MICHEL, b. Dec. 21, 1944, Brussels
    Ras-le-bol (1972)

HUNTINGTON, LAWRENCE, b. 1900, London; d. Nov. 29, 1968
    After Many Years (JMG 1929) (also script)
    Romance and Rhythm (MGM Br 1934) (also producer)
    Strange Cargo (Par Br 1936)†
    Two on a Doorstep (B & D-Par Br 1936)
    Cafe Mascot (Par Br 1936)
    Full Speed Ahead (Par Br 1936) (also co-script)
    The Bank Messenger Mystery (Renown 1936)
    Screen Struck (MGM Br 1937)
    Passenger to London (Fox Br 1937)
    Twin Faces (Par Br 1937)

Ken Hughes (right) with Richard Hughes during the filming of
Cromwell (1970).

Dial 999 (Fox Br 1938) (also co-author)
Bad Boy (Radius 1938) (also script)
The Patient Vanishes/This Man Is Dangerous (Pathe 1941)
The Tower of Terror (Pathe 1941)
Suspected Person (Pathe 1942) (also script)
Women Aren't Angels (Pathe 1942) (also co-script)
Warn That Man (Pathe 1943) (also co-script)
Night Boat to Dublin (Pathe 1946) (also co-script)
Wanted for Murder (20th Br 1946)
The Upturned Glass (GFD 1947)
When the Bough Breaks (GFD 1947)
Mr Perrin and Mr Traill (GFD 1948)
Man on the Run (ABP 1949) (also producer, script)
The Franchise Affair (ABP 1951) (also co-script)

There Was a Young Lady (Butcher 1953) (also script)
Contraband Spain (ABP 1955)
Deadly Record (AA 1959) (also co-script)
Stranglehold (RFD 1962)
The Fur Collar (RFD 1962) (also producer, script)
Death Drums Along the River (GB-W Ger) (Planet 1963) (British release 1966)
The Vulture (GB-US-Can) (Par Br 1968)

HURST, BRIAN DESMOND, b. Feb. 12, 1900, Castle Reagh, Co. Down, Ireland
The Tell-Tale Heart [Bucket of Blood] (Fox Br 1934)
Irish Hearts [Norah O'Neale] (MGM Br 1934) (also script)
Riders to the Sea (MGM Br 1935) (also co-script)
Ourselves Alone [River of Unrest] (Wardour 1936) (with Walter Summers)
The Tenth Man (Wardour 1936)
Sensation (ABPC 1937)
Glamorous Night (ABPC 1937)
Prison Without Bars (UA Br 1938)
The Lion Has Wings (UA Br 1939) (with Adrian Brunel, Michael Powell)
On the Night of the Fire [The Fugitive] (GFD 1939) (also co-script)
Dangerous Moonlight [Suicide Squadron] (RKO Br 1941) (also co-script)
Alibi (BL 1942)
The Hundred Pound Window (WB-FN Br 1943)
Men of Arnhem (AFU 1944)
Caesar and Cleopatra (EL 1946) (with Gabriel Pascal)
Hungry Hill (GFD 1947)
The Mark of Cain (GFD 1948)
Trottie True [Gay Lady] (GFD 1949)
Scrooge (Renown 1951)
Malta Story (GFD 1953)
Simba (GFD 1955)
The Black Tent (RFD 1956)
Dangerous Exile (RFD 1957)
Behind the Mask (BL 1958)
His and Hers (Eros 1961)
The Playboy of the Western World (BL 1962) (also script)

HUSSEIN, WARRIS, b. Dec. 9, 1938, Lucknow, India
A Touch of Love (BL 1969)
Quackser Fortune Has a Cousin in the Bronx (USA) (Scotia-Barber 1970)
Melody (BL 1971)
The Possession of Joel Delaney (USA) (Par 1972)
Henry VIII and His Six Wives (MGM-EMI 1972)
Divorce His, Divorce Hers (ABC-TV 1973)

IQUINO, IGNACIO F. (Ignacio Farres Iquino), b. Oct. 25, 1910,
    Valls, Spain
     Sereno y ... Tormenta (Sp 1934)
     Al margen de la ley (Sp 1935)
     Diego Corrientes (Sp 1936)
     Quien me compra un lio? (Sp 1940)
     Alma de Dios (Sp 1941)
     Los ladrones somos gente honrada (Sp 1941)
     El difunto es vun vivo (Sp 1941)
     El pobre rico (Sp 1942)
     Boda accidentada (Sp 1942)
     La culpa del otro (Sp 1942)
     Fin de curso (Sp 1943)
     Viviendo al reves (Sp 1943)
     Un enredo de familia (Sp 1943)
     El hombre de los muñecos (Sp 1943)
     Una sombra en la ventana (Sp 1944)
     Hombres sin honor (Sp 1944)
     Cabeza de hierro (Sp 1944)
     Ni pobre ni rico, sino todo lo contrario (Sp 1945)
     Culpable (Sp 1945)
     El obstaculo (Sp 1945)
     Borrasca de celos (Sp 1946)
     Aquel viejo molino (Sp 1946)
     Noche sin cielo (Sp 1947)
     Sinfonia del hogar (Sp 1947)
     El angel gris (Sp 1947)
     Cancion mortal (Sp 1948)
     El tambor del Bruch (Sp 1948)
     La familia vila (Sp 1949)
     Brigada criminal (Sp 1950)
     Estoria de una escalera (Sp 1950)
     El sistema Pelegrin (Sp 1951)
     La danza del corazon (Sp 1951)
     Tarde de futbol (Sp 1951)
     El Judas (Sp 1952)
     El gofo que vio una estrella (Sp 1953)
     Fuego en la sangre (Sp 1954)
     Good Bye Sevilla (Sp 1954)
     La Pecadora (Sp 1955)
     Quiereme con musica (Sp 1956)
     Los angeles del volante (Sp 1957)
     Secretaria para todo (Sp 1958)
     El nino de las monjas (Sp 1958)
     Buen viaje, Pablo (Sp 1959)
     Juventud a la intemperie (Sp 1961)
     Las Travesuras de morucha (Sp 1962)
     Trigo limpio (Sp 1962)
     Un rincon para quernos (Sp 1964)
     Oeste Nevada Joe [La sfida degli implacabili] (Sp-It 1964)
     07 con el 2 delante (Sp 1965)
     El primer cuartel (Sp 1966)
     La mini Tia (Sp 1967)

De Picos pardos a la ciudad (Sp 1968)
Tres crisantemos (Sp 1969) (also co-script)
Un colt por cuatro cirios (Sp 1971)
Los fabulosos de trinidad (Sp 1973) (also co-script)
Busco tonta para fin de semana (Sp 1973) (also co-script)
Aborto criminol (Sp 1974) (also co-script)

IVENS, JORIS (Georg Henri Anton Ivens), b. Nov. 18, 1898, Nij-
    megen, Netherlands
Wij Bouwen (Dut 1929) (also script, camera, editor)
Zuyderzee (Dut 1930) (also script, camera)
Creosot (Fr 1931) (also editor)
Komsomol (Dut 1933) (also script, co-editor)
The Reichstag Fire (Dut-Rus 1935) (with Dimitrov)
Terre d'Espagne [The Spanish Earth] (Sp 1937) (also co-script)
The Four Hundred Millions (China) (Dut 1939) (also script)
New Frontiers (Unfinished Can 1940)
Our Russian Front (USA) (Harry Ratner Releasing 1942) (also
    co-script) (with Lewis Milestone)
Action Station Four (USA) (also co-script, editor) with Fran-
    çois Villiers)
Indonesia Calling (Australia) (also script, editor)
Pierwsze Lata [The First Years] (Pol-Czech-Bul-Yug 1949)
    (also editor)
Poﾉko j zwyeciezy Swiate [My za Mir, Peace Shall Win] (Pol
    1951) (also co-script) (with Jerzy Bossak)
Naprozod Mﾉoziezy Swiata [Weltjugendfestival] (East Ger-Pol
    1952) (with Ivan Pyriev)
Wyscig Pokoju Warszawa-Berlin-Praha (Pol 1952)
Das Lied der Strome [Song of the Rivers] (East Ger 1954) (also
    co-script)
Les Aventures de Till l'Espiègle (Fr 1956) (only supervisor)
Mein Kind (East Ger 1956) (only supervisor)
L'Italia non è un paese povero (It TV 1959) (also co-script,
    co-editor)
Demain a Nanguila (Mali 1960)
Carnet de viaje [Carta a Charlie Chaplin] (Cuba 1961) (also
    script)
Pueblo en armas (Cuba 1961) (also script)
Vietnam (Vietnam 1965)
Loin du Vietnam (Fr 1967) (also co-producer) (with Alain Res-
    nais, Agnes Varda, Wiliam Klein, Claude Lelouch, Jean-Luc
    Godard)
Le Dix-Septième Parallèle [La Guerra du peuple] (Fr 1968)
    (with Marceline Loridan)
Le peuple et ses fusils: la guerre populaire au Laos (Fr)
    (with co-directors)
Rencontre avec le president Ho Chi Minh (Fr 1969) (with Mar-
    celine Loridan)
Chine (Fr 1973)
The Return of the Flying Dutchman (Fr 1974)

JACKSON, PAT, b. 1916, London
  Western Approaches (CFU 1944)
  Shadow on the Wall (USA) (MGM 1950)
  White Corridors (GFD 1951) (also co-script)
  Encore (ep "Winter Cruise") (GFD 1951)
  Something Money Can't Buy (GFD 1952) (also co-script)
  The Feminine Touch [The Gentle Touch] (RFD 1956)
  Virgin Island (BL 1958) (also co-script)
  Snowball (RFD 1960)
  What a Carve Up! (RFI 1961)
  Seven Keys (AA 1962)
  Don't Talk to Strange Men (Bry 1962)
  Seventy Deadly Pills (CFF 1964) (also script)
  Dead End Creek (CFF 1964) (also co-script)

JACOPETT, GUALTIERO, b. Sept. 4, 1919, Barge, Italy
  Mondo Cane (It 1962)
  La donna nel mondo (It 1962)
  Mondo Cane n. 2 (It 1963) (with Franco Prosperi)
  Africa addio (It 1966)
  Addio Zio Tom (It 1971) (with Franco Prosperi)
  La vita è bella (It 1971) (with Franco Prosperi)

JEFFRIES, LIONEL, b. June 10, 1929, Forest Hill, London
  The Railway Children (MGM-EMI 1970) (also script)
  The Amazing Mr. Blunden (Hemdale 1972) (also script)
  Baxter! (MGM-EMI 1973)

JENNINGS, HUMPHREY, b. 1907, Suffolk, England; d. Sept. 24, 1950
  The Birth of a Robot (Shell Oil Co 1936)
  Penny Journey (GPO 1938)
  Spare Time (GPO 1939) (also script)
  Speaking from America (GPO 1939)
  SS Ionian/Her Last Trip (GPO 1939)
  The First Days (GPO 1939) (? with Harry Watt)
  London Can Take It [Britain Can Take It] (MOI 1940) (with Harry Watt)
  An Unrecorded Victory/Spring Offensive (MOI 1940)
  Welfare of the Workers (MOI 1940) (with Pat Jackson)
  Heart of Britain [This is England] (MOI 1941)
  Words for Battle (MOI 1941) (also script)
  Listen to Britain (MOI 1942) (also co-script, co-editor) (with Stewart McAllister)
  Fires Were Started [I Was a Fireman] (MOI 1943)
  The Silent Village (MOI 1943) (also producer, script)
  The Eight Days (MOI 1944) (also producer)
  The True Story of Lilli Marlene (CFU 1944)
  VI (CFU 1944)
  A Diary for Timothy (CFU 1944-45) (also script)
  A Defeated People (DAK 1946) (also script)
  The Cumberland Story (COI 1947) (also script)
  Dim Little Island (COI) (also producer)
  Family Portrait (Wessex 1950) (also script)

Lionel Jeffries (left) with composer Johnny Douglas studying the score for The Railway Children (1970).

JESSUA, ALAIN, b. Jan. 16, 1932, Paris
    La Vie à l'envers [Life Upside Down] (Fr 1964) (also script)
    Jeu de massacre [Comic Strip Hero] (Fr 1967) (also script)
    Les Panthères blanches (Fr 1971) (also script)
    Traitement de choc (Fr-It 1973) (also script)

JOANNON, LEO, b. Aug. 21, 1904, Aix-En-Provence, France; d.
        March 30, 1969
    Adieu, les copains (Fr 1930) (also script)
    Douaumont (Fr 1930)
    Durand contre Durand (Fr 1931)
    Suzanne (Fr 1932)
    Il a été perdu une mariée (Fr 1932)
    Six cents mille francs par mois (Fr 1933)
    Bibi la puree (Fr 1934)
    Quelle drôle de gosse (Fr 1935)
    Train de plaisir (Fr 1935)
    La Traversee de l'Atlantique (Fr 1935)
    On a trouve une femme nu (Fr c. 1935)
    Arènes joyeuses (Fr c. 1935)

Quand manuit sonnera (Fr 1936)
L'Homme sans coeur (Fr 1936)
Vous n'avez rien à déclarer? (Fr 1936) (with Yves Allegret)
Le Chanteur de minuit (Fr 1937)
Escapade (Fr 1938)
Alerte en Méditerranée [S. O. S. Mediterranean] (Fr 1938) (also
    script)
L'Emigrante (Unfinished Fr 1939) (with Yves Allegret)
Caprices (Fr 1941)
Le Camion blanc (Fr 1942)
Lucrèce (Fr 1943)
La Collection Ménard (Fr 1943)
Le Carrefour des enfants perdus (Fr 1943)
Documents secrets (Fr 1944)
Le 84 prend des vacances (Fr 1949)
Atoll K [Robinson Crusoeland] (Fr 1951)
Drôle de noce (Fr 1951)
Le Défroqué (Fr 1953) (also co-script, co-adaptor, actor)
Le Secret de Soeur Angèle (Fr-It 1955) (also co-dialogue)
L'Homme aux clefs d'or [The Man with Golden Keys] (Fr 1956)
    (also co-script, actor)
Le Désert de Pigalle (Fr 1957) (also actor)
Tant d'amour perdu (Fr 1958) (also co-script)
L'Assassin est dans l'Annuaire (Fr 1961)
Fort du fou (Fr 1962) (also co-adaptor)
Trois enfants dans le désordre (Fr 1966)

JORDA, JOAQUIN, b. Aug. 9, 1935, Santa Coloma de Farnes
    (Gerona), Spain
Dante no es únicamente severo (Sp 1967) (with Jacinto Esteva)
    (also co-story, co-script)

JUTZI, PIEL [also Phil], b. 1894, Rheinpfalz, Germany
Das blinkende Fenster (Ger 1919)
Der maskierte Schrecken (Ger 1919) (also script)
Die Rache des Banditen (Ger 1919)
Die das Licht scheuen ...! (Ger 1920)
Red Bull der letzte Apache (Ger 1920)
Die grosse Gelegenheit (Ger 1925) (only co-camera)
Raub in der Zentralbank (Ger 1925) (only co-camera)
Klass und Datsch, die Pechvöge! (Ger 1926) (also script, cam-
    era)
Kindertragödie (Ger 1927)
Das lebende Leichnam (Ger 1928) (only co-camera)
Unser täglich Brot (Ger 1929)
Hunger in Waldenburg (Ger 1929)
Mutter Krausens Fahrt ins Glück (Ger 1929) (also camera)
Klippen der Ehe (Ger 1929) (only camera)
Berlin-Alexanderplatz (Ger 1931)
Der Kossack und die Nachtigall (Ger 1935)
Lockspitzel Asew (Ger-Aus 1935)
Das Geheimnis des Fräulein Brinx (Polish) (Ger 1936)
Das Gewehr über (Ger 1939) (only camera)
So ein Früchtchen (Ger 1942) (only camera)

KAPLAN, NELLY, b. 1934, Argentina
La Fiancée du pirate [A Very Curious Girl] (Fr 1969) (also co-script, co-adaptor, co-editor)
Papa les petit bateaux (Fr 1971) (also co-script, co-adaptor, co-dialogue)

KARMITZ, MARIN, b. 1940
Sept Jours ailleurs [Seven Days Somewhere Else] (Fr 1968) (also co-script)
Camarades (Fr 1970) (also co-script)
Coup par coup (Fr-W Ger 1972)† [co-production company] (also co-script)

KAST, PIERRE, b. Dec. 22, 1920, Paris
Un Amour de poche (Fr 1957) (also co-script)
Le Bel Age [Love Is When You Make It] (Fr 1958-9) (also co-script)
Merci Natercia (Fr 1959) (also co-script)
La Morte-Saison de amours [The Season for Love] (Fr 1960) (also co-script)
Vacances portugaises (Fr 1962) (also co-script)
Le Grain du sable (Fr-It-W Ger-Port 1965) (also co-script)
La naissance de l'empire romain (Fr TV 1965)
Drôle de jeu (Fr 1968) (also script)
Candomblé et Macumba [Un Drapeau blanc d'Okala] (Fr 1970) (also script)
Les Soleils de l'île de Pâques (Fr-Braz-Chilean 1972) (also script, dialogue)

KÄUTNER, HELMUT, b. March 25, 1908, Düsseldorf, Germany
Kitty und die Weltkonferenz (Ger 1939) (also script)
Die Acnt Entfesselten (Ger 1939)
Frau nach Mass (Ger 1940) (also script)
Kleider machen Leute (Ger 1940) (also script)
Auf Wiedersehen, Franziska (Ger 1941) (also script)
Anuschka (Ger 1942) (also co-script)
Wir machen Musik (Ger 1942) (also script)
Romanze in Moll (Ger 1942) (also co-script)
Grosse Freiheit Nr. 7 (Ger 1944) (also co-script)
Unter den Brücken (Ger 1945) (also co-script)
In jenen Tagen (Ger 1947) (also co-script)
Der Apfel ist Ab (Ger 1948) (also from own play, co-dialogue, co-script, co-lyrics, actor)
Königskinder (Ger 1949) (also co-script, actor)
Epilog (Ger 1950) (also co-script, actor)
Kapt'n Bay-Bay (Aus 1952) (also co-script)
Die letzte Brücke (Ger 1954) (also co-script)
Bildnis einer Unbekannten (Ger 1954) (also co-script)
Glanz und Ende eines Königs [Ludwig II] (Ger 1955)
Des Teufels General [The Devil's General] (Ger 1955) (also co-script)
Himmel ohne Sterne (Ger 1955) (also from own play co-script)
Eine Mädchen aus Flandern [The Girl from Flanders] (Ger 1955)

(also co-script)
Der Hauptmann von Köpenick (Ger 1956) (also co-script)
Die Zürcher Verlobung [The Affairs of Julie] (Ger 1957) (also
     co-script, actor)
Monpti (Ger 1957) (also co-script)
The Restless Years (USA) (Univ 1958)
A Stranger in My Arms (USA) (Univ 1958)
Der Schinderhannes (Ger 1958)
Der Rest ist schweigen (Ger 1959) (also script)
Die Gans von Sedan (Ger 1959) (also co-script)
Das Glas Wasser (Ger 1960) (also script)
Schwarzer Kies (Ger 1961) (also co-script)
Der Traum von Lieschen Müller (Ger 1961)
Die Rote [The Redhead] (Ger 1962)
Das Haus in Montevideo (Ger 1963)
Lausbubengeschichten (Ger 1964)
Die Feuerzangenbowle (Ger 1970)

KIEL, EDITH, b. Belgium
Een Brief Uit Antwerpen (Bel 1941)
Een Aardig Geval (Bel 1942)
Schipperskwartier (Bel 1952)
De Moedige Bruidegom (Bel 1952)
Uit her Zelfdemest (Bel 1952)
Sinjorenbloed (Bel 1953)
De Spotvogel (Bel 1953)
De Hemel op Aarde (Bel 1954)
Min of Meer (Bel 1954)
De Bruid Zonder Bed (Bel 1955)
Boevenprinses (Bel 1956)
Mijn Man Doet dat Niet (Bel 1956)
Voices over land and sea (Bel 1957)
Rendez-vous in't Paradijs (Bel 1957)
Het Meisje en de Madonna (Bel 1958)
Een Zonde Waard (Bel 1959)
De Duivel te Slim (Bel 1960)
Hoe Zotter--Hoe Liever (Bel 1960)
De Stille Genieter (Bel 1961)

KIMMINS, ANTHONY, b. Nov. 10, 1901, Harrow, Middlesex; d.
     May 19, 1964
Bypass to Happiness (Fox Br 1934) (also script)
How's Chances? (Fox Br 1934)
Once in a New Moon (Fox Br 1935)
His Majesty & Co (Fox Br 1935)
All at Sea (Fox Br 1935)
Keep Fit (ABFD 1937)
I See Ice (ABFD 1938) (also co-script)
It's in the Air [George Takes the Air] (ABFD 1938) (also
     script)
Come On George (ABFD 1939) (also co-script)
Trouble Brewing (ABFD 1939) (also co-script)
Mine Own Executioner (BL 1947) (also co-producer)

Bonnie Prince Charlie (BL 1948)
Flesh and Blood (BL 1951)
Mr Denning Drives North (BL 1951) (also co-producer)
Who Goes There! [The Passionate Sentry] (BL 1952) (also producer)
The Captain's Paradise (BL 1953) (also producer, co-script)
Aunt Clara (BL 1954) (also producer)
Smiley (20th Br 1956) (also producer, co-script)
Smiley Gets a Gun (20th Br 1958) (also producer, co-script)
The Amorous Prawn (BL 1962) (also author, co-script)

KING, GEORGE, b. 1899, London; d. June 29, 1966
Too Many Crooks (Fox Br 1930) (also producer)
Leave It to Me (Fox Br 1930) (also producer)
Midnight (Fox Br 1931)†
Number Please (Fox Br 1931)†
Deadlock (Butcher 1931)†
The Professional Guest (Fox Br 1931)†
Two Way Street (UA Br 1931)
Self-Made Lady (UA Br 1932)†
Men of Steel (UA Br 1932)
To Brighton with Gladys (Fox Br 1933)†
Matinee Idol (UA Br 1933)
Too Many Wives (WB Br 1933)
Beware of Women (FN Br 1933)
High Finance (FN Br 1933)
Mayfair Girl (WB Br 1933)
Enemy of the Police (WB Br 1933)
Smithy (WB Br 1933)
Her Imaginary Lover (FN Br 1933)
I Adore You (WB Br 1933)
The Silver Spoon (WB Br 1934)
Oh No Doctor! (MGM Br 1934)†
Murder at the Inn (WB Br 1934)
Little Stranger (MGM Br 1934)†
Guest of Honour (FN Br 1934)
Nine-Forty-Five (WB Br 1934)
To Be a Lady (B & D-Par Br 1934)
Get Your Man (B & D-Par Br 1934)
The Office Wife (WB Br 1934)
The Blue Squadron (GB-It) (FN Br 1934)
Adventure Limited (B & D-Par Br 1934)
Full Circle (WB Br 1935)
Windfall (Radio Br 1935) (also co-producer)
The Man Without a Face (Radio Br 1935) (also co-producer)
Gay Old Dog (Radio 1935) (also co-producer)
Sweeney Todd, the Demon Barber of Fleet Street (MGM Br 1936) (also production company)
The Crimes of Stephen Hawke (MGM Br 1936)†
Reasonable Doubt (MGM Br 1936)
Wanted (SC 1937) (also producer)
Merry Comes to Town (SC 1937) (also producer)
Under a Cloud (Par Br 1937) (also producer)

The Ticket of Leave Man (MGM Br 1937)†
Silver Top (Par Br 1938) (also producer)
Sexton Blake and the Hooded Terror (MGM Br 1938)†
John Halifax Gentleman (MGM Br 1938)†
The Face at the Window (BL 1939) (also producer)
The Chinese Bungalow [Chinese Den] (BL 1940) (also producer)
Crimes at the Dark House (BL 1940) (also producer)
Two for Danger (WB Br 1940)
George and Margaret (WB Br 1940)
The Case of the Frightened Lady [The Frightened Lady] (BL
    1940) (also producer)
Tomorrow We Live [At Dawn We Die] (BL 1942) (also producer)
Candlelight in Algeria (BL 1943)
Gaiety George [Showtime] (WB Br 1946) (also producer)
The Shop at Sly Corner [The Code of Scotland Yard] (BL 1947)
    (also producer)
Forbidden (BL 1949) (also producer)

KLEIN, WILLIAM, b. 1928, New York
Qui êtes-vous Polly Magoo? (Fr 1966) (also script)
Cassius le Grand (Fr 1967) (combination of three shorts filmed
    in 1964-65)
Loin du Vietnam [Far from Vietnam] (Fr 1967) (with Alain Res-
    nais, Joris Ivens, Agnes Varda, Claude Lelouch, Jean-Luc
    Godard)
Mister Freedom (Fr 1968) (also script)
Eldridge Cleaver (Fr 1970) (also co-producer, script, camera,
    co-editor)

KLIMOVSKY, LEON, b. Oct. 16, 1900, Buenos-Aires
El Jugador (Arg 1949)
Se llamaba Carlos Gardel (Arg 1949)
La guitarra de Gardel (Arg 1949)
Marihuana (Arg 1950)
Suburbio (Arg 1951)
La vida color de rosa (Arg 1951)
El Pendiente (Arg 1951)
El Tunel (Arg 1952)
La Parda Flora (Arg 1952)
El Conde de Montecristo (Arg 1953)
Maleficio [Tres citas con el destino] (Arg 1954) (with Fernando
    de Fuentes, Florian Rey)
El juramento de Lagardère (Arg 1954)
El tren expreso (Sp 1954)
La picara molinera (Sp 1955)
Miedo (Sp 1956)
Viaje de novios (Sp 1956)
Los amantes del desierto (Sp-It 1957) (with Goggredo Alessan-
    drini, Fernando Cerchio, Gianni Vernuccio)
Un indiano en moratilla (Sp 1957)
El hombre que perdido el tren (Sp 1958)
S. O. S. abuelita (Sp 1958)
Salto a la gloria (Sp 1959)

Llegaron los Franceses (Sp 1959)
Ama rosa (Sp 1960)
Un bruto para Patricia (Sp 1960)
La paz empieza nunca (Sp 1960)
... Y el cuerpo sigue aguantendo (Sp 1961)
Horizontes de luz (Sp 1961)
Ella y el miedo (Sp 1962)
Escuela de seductoras (Sp 1962)
Todos eran culpables (Sp 1962)
Torrejon City (Sp 1962)
Fuera de la ley (Sp 1963)
La colina de los pequenos diablos (Sp 1964)
Escala en Tenerife (Sp 1964)
Aquella joven de Blanco (Sp 1964)
Los siete bravisimos (Sp 1964)
Una chica para dos (Sp 1965)
Alambradas de violencia (Sp 1966)
Dos mil dolares por Coyote (Sp 1966)
En Gentar se muere facil (Sp 1967)
Un hombre viene a matar (Sp 1967)
Pago cara su muerte (Sp 1967)
El valor de un cobarde (Sp 1968)
Junio 44: desembaracaremos en Normandia [Normandia: Op-
    eracion suicida] (Sp 1968)
Hora O: Operacion Rommel (Sp 1968)
El Puente sobre el Elba (Sp 1968)
No importa morir (Sp-It 1970) (also co-script)
Un dolar y una Tumba (Sp-It 1970) (also co-script)
El hombre que vino del odio (Sp-It 1970)
Los hombres las prefieren viudas (Sp 1970)
La noche de walpurgis (Sp-Ger 1971)
Reverendo Colg (Sp-It 1971)
La casa de las Chivas (Sp 1971)
La saga de los dracula (Sp 1973)
La rebelion de las muertas (Sp 1973)
La orgia nocturna de los vampiras (Sp 1973)

KNOWLES, BERNARD, b. 1900, Manchester, England
A Place of One's Own (EL 1945)
The Magic Bow (GFD 1946)
The Man Within [The Smugglers] (GFD 1947)
Jassy (GFD 1947)
The White Unicorn [Bad Sister] (GFD 1947)
Easy Money (GFD 1948)
The Perfect Woman (GFD 1949) (also co-script)
The Lost People (GFD 1949) (with Muriel Box)
The Reluctant Widow (GFD 1950)
Park Plaza 605 [Norman Conquest] (Eros 1953) (also co-script)
Barbados Quest [Murder on Approval] (RKO Br 1955)
Der Fall X-701 [Frozen Alive] (W Ger-GB) (Butcher 1964) (re-
    leased in GB in 1967)
Spaceflight IC-I (20th Br 1967) (made in 1965)
Hell Is Empty (GB-Czech) (RFD 1970) (with John Ainsworth)

(also co-script) (begun in 1965, finished by Ainsworth in
1967)

KORBER, SERGE, b. 1936
   Le Dix-Septième Ciel (Fr 1966) (also script)
   Un Idiot à Paris [An Idiot in Paris] (Fr 1967) (also co-script)
   La Petite Vertu (Fr 1967)
   L'Homme-orchestre (Fr 1970) (also co-script)
   Sur un arbre perché (Fr 1971) (also co-script)
   Les Feux de la Chandeleur (Fr-It 1972) (also co-adaptor)
   Ursule et Grelu (Fr-It 1973) (also co-script)

KORDA, ALEXANDER (Sándor Kordor), b. Sept. 16, 1893, Turk-
      eye, Hungary; d. Jan. 23, 1956
   Az Egymillio Fontos Bankó [The Million Pound Banknote] (Hun)
      (Corvin 1916)
   Fehér Ejszakák [White Nights] (Hun) (Corvin 1916) (also script)
   Mesék az Irógépról [Tales of the Typewriter] (Hun) (Corvin
      1916) (also script)
   Nagymama [Grandmama] (Hun) (Corvin 1916) (also script)
   A Tiszti Kardbojt [An Officer's Swordknot] (Hun) (Korona 1916)
      (also script)
   Vergődő Szivek [Struggling Hearts] (Hun) (Corvin 1916) (also
      script)
   Faun (Hun) (Corvin 1917)
   A GOlyakalifa [The Stork Caliph] (Hun) (Corvin 1917) (also co-
      script)
   Harrison és Barrison [Harrison and Barrison] (Hun) (Corvin
      1917)
   A Kétszivű Férfi [Man with Two Hearts] (Hun) (Corvin 1917)
   Mágia [Magic] (Hun) (Corvin 1917)
   Mágnás Miska [Mike the Magnate] (Hun) (Corvin 1917)
   Szent Péter Esernyője [St Peter's Umbrella] (Hun) (Corvin 1917)
   A Ketlelku Asszory [Woman with Two Souls] (Hun) (Corvin
      1917)
   Az Aranyember [Man of Gold] (Hun) (Corvin 1918)
   Mary Ann (Hun) (Corvin 1918)
   Se Ki Se Be [Neither In Nor Out] (Hun) (Corvin 1918)
   Ave Caesar (Hun) (Tanacskozt 1919)
   Fehér Rózsa [White Rose] (Hun) (Tanacskozt 1919)
   A III-Es [The Number 11] (Hun) (Corvin 1919)
   Yamata (Hun) (Corvin 1919)
   Prinz und Bettelknabe [The Prince and the Pauper] (Aus) (Sas-
      cha 1920)
   Herren der Meere (Aus) (Sascha 1922)
   Eine versunkene Welt (Aus) (Sascha 1922)
   Samson und Delila (Aus) (Adria 1922)† [co-production company]
      (also co-script)
   Das unbekannte Morgen (Ger) (Ger 1923)† (also author)
   Jedermanns Weib (Aus) (Sascha 1924)
   Tragödie im Hause Habsburg (Ger) (Ger 1924)†
   Der Tänzer meiner Frau (Ger) (Ufa 1925) (also co-script)
   Madame wünscht keine Kinder (Ger) (Ufa 1926)

Eine DuBarry von Heute (Ger) (Ufa 1927)
The Stolen Bride (USA) (FN 1927)
The Private Life of Helen of Troy (USA) (FN 1927)
The Yellow Lily (USA) (FN 1928)
Love and the Devil (USA) (FN 1929)
The Squall (USA) (FN 1929)
Her Private Life (USA) (FN 1929)
The Night Watch (USA) (Fox 1930)
Women Are Willing (USA) (Fox 1930)
Lilies of the Field (USA) (Fox 1930)
The Princess and the Plumber (Fox 1930) (with John Blystone)
Marius (Fr) (Par Fr 1931)
Zum Goldene Anker (Ger) (Par Ger 1931)
Rive Gauche (Fr) (Par Fr 1931)
Die Manner um Lucie (Ger-Fr-US) (Par Ger 1931)
Service for Ladies [Reserved for Ladies] (Par Br 1932) (also
    producer)
Wedding Rehearsal (Ideal 1932)† (also producer)
The Girl from Maxim's (UA Br 1933)† (also co-producer)
The Private Life of Henry VIII (UA Br 1933)† (also producer)
The Private Life of Don Juan (UA Br 1934)† (also producer)
Rembrandt (UA Br 1936)† (also producer)
That Hamilton Woman [Lady Hamilton] (USA) (UA 1941)† (also
    producer) [co-production company]
Perfect Strangers [Vacation from Marriage] (MGM Br-London
    1945)† [co-production company] (also producer)
An Ideal Husband (BL 1948)† (also producer)
Some Hungarian sources also suggest that Korda co-directed the
following three films:
    A Becsapott Ujságíró (Hung) (Tricolor 1914) (with Zilahy
        Gyulaval)
    Tutyu és Totyo (Hung) (Tricolor 1915) (with Zilahy Gyulaval)
    Lyon Lea (Hung) (Nemzeti 1915) (with Miklos Pasztory)

KORPORAAL, JOHN, b. Netherlands
    Rififi in Amsterdam (Dut 1962)
    De Vergeten Medeminnaar (Dut 1963)

KOSTER, HENRY (Hermann Kosterlitz), b. May 1, 1905, Berlin
    Das Abenteuer der Thea Roland [Das Abenteur einer Schönen
        Frau] [Der Storch Hat Uns Getraut] (Ger 1932)
    Das hässliche Mädchen (Ger 1933) (also co-script)
    Peter (Hun-Aus 1934)
    Kleine Mutti [Kismama] (Hun-Aus 1935)
    Das Tagebuch der Geliebten [Maria Baschkirtzeff] [The Affairs
        of Maupassant] (Aus-It 1935)
    Il Dario di una Amata (It version of Das Tagebuch der Gelieb-
        ten) (It 1936)
    Katharina, die Letzte (Aus 1935)
In the U.S.A.:
    Three Smart Girls (Univ 1936)
    One Hundred Men and a Girl (Univ 1937)
    The Rage of Paris (Univ 1938)

First Love (Univ 1939)
Three Smart Girls Grow Up (Univ 1939)
Spring Parade (Univ 1940)
It Started With Eve (Univ 1941)
Between Us Girls (Univ 1942) (also producer)
Music for Millions (MGM 1944)
Two Sisters from Boston (MGM 1946)
The Unfinished Dance (MGM 1947)
The Luck of the Irish (20th 1948)
The Bishop's Wife (RKO 1948)
Come To The Stable (20th 1949)
The Inspector General (WB 1949)
Wabash Avenue (20th 1950)
My Blue Heaven (20th 1950)
Harvey (Univ 1950)
Mr. Belvedere Rings the Bell (20th 1951)
No Highway [In the Sky] (20th Br 1951)
Elopement (20th 1951)
O'Henry's Full House (ep "The Cop and the Anthem") (20th
     1952)
Stars and Stripes Forever (20th 1952)
My Cousin Rachel (20th 1952)
The Robe (20th 1953)
Desiree (20th 1954)
A Man Called Peter (20th 1955)
The Virgin Queen (20th 1955)
Good Morning, Miss Dove (20th 1955)
D-Day the Sixth of June (20th 1956)
The Power and the Prize (MGM 1956)
My Man Godfrey (Univ 1957)
Fraulein (20th 1958)
The Naked Maja (UA 1959)
The Story of Ruth (20th 1960)
Flower Drum Song (Univ 1961)
Mr. Hobbs Takes a Vacation (20th 1962)
Take Her, She's Mine (20th 1963)
Dear Brigitte (20th 1965)
The Singing Nun (MGM 1965)

KOTCHEFF, TED, b. April 7, 1931, Toronto, Ontario
Life at the Top (Col Br 1965)
Two Gentlemen Sharing (AIP 1968)
Outback (Aus) (UA Br 1970)
Billy Two Hats (UA Br 1974)
The Apprenticeship of Duddy Kravitz (Can) (Par 1974)

KRISH, JOHN, b. 1923, London
The Salvage Gang (CFF 1958) (also script)
Unearthly Stranger (AA 1963)
The Wild Affair (Bry 1963) (also script)
Decline and Fall ... of a Bird Watcher (20th Br 1968)
The Man Who Had Power Over Women (Avco Emb 1970)

John Krish shooting Decline and Fall (1968).

KUMEL, HARRY, b. Jan., 1940, Antwerp, Belgium
    Erasmus (Bel 1963)
    Hendrik Conscience (Bel 1964)
    Waterloo (Bel 1965)
    De Grafbewaker (Bel 1965)
    Monsieur Hawarden (Bel 1968) (also co-script)
    Jozef von Sternberg--Een Retrospektieve (Bel TV 1969)
    Les Lèvres rouges [Blut an den Lippen; Daughters of Dark-
       ness] (Bel-Fr-Ger 1971) (also co-script)
    Malpertuis (Bel-Fr 1972)
    De Komst van Joachim Skiller (Bel TV 1974)

KUYPERS, RIK, b. 1925, Belgium
    Meeuwen Sterven in de Haven (Bel 1955) (also co-script) (with
       Roland Verhavert, Ivo Michiels)
    De Obool (Bel 1966)
    Adieu Filippi (Unfinished--Bel 1968)
    Lieven Gevaert, Eerste Arbeider (Bel TV 1969)

LAMPRECHT, GERHARD, b. Oct. 6, 1897, Berlin
    Der Friedhof der Lebenden (Ger 1921) (also co-script)

Fliehende Schatten (Ger 1922) (also co-script)
Die Buddenbrooks (Ger 1923) (also co-script)
Das Haus ohne Lachen (Ger 1923) (also co-script)
Und dennoch kam das Glück (Ger 1923) (also script)
Die Andere (Ger 1924)
Hanseaten (Ger 1925) (also co-script)
Die Verrufenen (Ger 1925) (also co-script)
Menschen untereinander (Ger 1926) (also co-script)
Schwester Veronika (Ger 1926) (also co-script)
Die Unehelichen (Ger 1926) (also co-script)
Der alte Fritz (Ger 1927) (also co-script)
Der Mann mit dem Laubfrosch (Ger 1928) (also co-script)
Unter der Laterne (Ger 1928) (also co-script)
Zweierlei Moral (Ger 1930) (also script)
Zwischen Nacht und Morgen (Ger 1931)
Emil und die Detektive (Ger 1931)
Der schwarze Husar (Ger 1932)
Was wissen denn Männer (Ger 1933)
Spione am Werk (Ger 1933)
Ein gewisser Herr Gran (Ger 1933)
Prinzessin Turandot (Ger 1934)
Einmal eine grosse Dame sein (Ger 1934)
Einer zuviel an Bord (Ger 1935)
Der höhere Befehl (Ger 1935)
Barcarole (Ger 1935)
Ein seltsamer Gast (Ger 1936)
Die gelbe Flagge (Ger 1937)
Madame Bovary (Ger 1937)
Der Spieler (Ger 1938)
Die Geliebte (Ger 1939)
Frau im Strom (Ger 1939)
Mädchen im Vorzimmer (Ger 1940)
Clarissa (Ger 1941)
Diesel (Ger 1942) (also co-script)
Du gehörst mir (Ger 1943)
Kamerad Hedwig (Ger 1945)
Die Bruder Noltenius (Ger 1945)
Irgendwo in Berlin (Ger 1946) (also script)
Madonna im Ketten (Ger 1949)
Quartett zu fünft (Ger 1949)
Meines Vaters Pferde (In two parts) (Ger 1954)
Der Engel mit dem Flammenschwert (Ger 1954)
Oberwachtmeister Borck (Ger 1955)

LAMY, BENOIT, b. Sept. 19, 1945, Arlon, Belgium
Cartoon Circus (Bel 1972) (with Picha)
Home, sweet home (Bel 1974) (also co-script)

LANG, FRITZ, b. Dec. 5, 1890, Vienna
Halbblut (Ger 1919) (also script)
Der Herr der Liebe (Ger 1919)
Die Spinnen (in two parts) (Ger 1919) (also script)
Harakiri (Ger 1919)
Vier um die Frau (Ger 1920) (also co-script)

Das wandernde Bild (Ger 1920) (also co-script)
Der müde Tod (Ger 1921) (also script)
Dr. Mabuse, der Spieler (Ger 1922) (also co-script)
Die Nibelungen (Ger 1924) (also co-script)
Metropolis (Ger 1926) (also co-script)
Spione (Ger 1928) (also producer, co-script)
Die Frau im Mond (Ger 1929) (also producer, co-script)
M (Ger 1931) (also co-script)
Das Testament des Dr. Mabuse (Ger 1933) (also co-script)
Liliom (Fox Europa-Fr 1934)
In the U.S.A. :
    Fury (MGM 1936) (also co-script)
    You Only Live Once (UA 1937)
    You and Me (Par 1938) (also producer)
    The Return of Frank James (20th 1940)
    Western Union (20th 1941)
    Confirm or Deny (20th 1941) (uncredited with Archie Mayo)
    Moontide (20th 1942) (replaced by Archie Mayo)
    Man Hunt (20th 1941)
    Hangmen Also Die (UA 1943) (co-producer, co-story)
    The Ministry of Fear (Par 1944)
    The Woman in the Window (RKO 1944)
    Scarlet Street (Univ 1945) (also producer)
    Cloak and Dagger (WB 1947)
    Secret Beyond the Door (Univ 1948) (also producer)
    House By the River (Rep 1950)
    American Guerrilla in the Philippines (Fox 1950)
    Rancho Notorious (RKO 1952)
    Clash By Night (RKO 1952)
    The Blue Gardenia (WB 1953)
    The Big Heat (Col 1953)
    Human Desire (Col 1954)
    Moonfleet (MGM 1955)
    While the City Sleeps (RKO 1956)
    Beyond a Reasonable Doubt (RKO 1956)
In Germany:
    Der Tiger von Eschnapur (Ger 1958)
    Das indische Grabmal (Ger 1958)
    Die 1000 Augen des Dr. Mabuse (Ger 1960) (also co-script)

LATTUADA, ALBERTO, b. Nov. 13, 1914, Milan
    Giacomo l'idealista (It 1942) (also co-script)
    La nostra guerra (It 1944)
    La Freccia nel fianco (It 1945) (also co-script)
    Il bandito (It 1946) (also story, co-script)
    Il delitto di Giovanni Episcopo [Flesh Will Surrender] (It 1947)
        (also co-script)
    Senza pietà [Without Pity] (It 1948) (also co-script)
    Il mulino del Pò [Mill on the Po] (It 1949) (also co-adaptor)
    Luci del varietà [Variety Lights] (It 1951) (with Federico Fel-
        lini)
    Anna (It 1952)
    Il cappotto (It 1952) (also co-script)
    Amore in città [Love in the City] (ep "Gli italiani si voltano")

Fritz Lang

(It 1953) (also co-story, co-script of episode)
La lupa [The She Wolf] (It 1954) (also co-script, adaptor)
La spiaggia [On the Riviera] (It 1954) (also story, co-script)
Scuola elementare (It 1955) (also story, co-script)
Guendalina (It 1957) (also co-script)
La tempesta [The Tempest] (It 1958)
I dolci inganni (It 1960) (also story, co-script)
Lettere di una novizia (It 1960) (also co-script)
L'imprevisto (It-Fr 1961)
La steppa (It-Fr 1962) (also co-script)
Mafioso (It 1962)
La mandragola [The Love Root] (It 1967)
Don Giovanni in Sicilia (It 1967)
Matchless (It-U.S. 1969) (also co-script)
Fräulein Doktor (It 1969) (also co-script)
L'amica (It 1969)
Venga a prendere il caffè da noi (It 1970)
Bianco, rosso e ... verde (It 1970)
Sono stato io! (It 1972)
Le faro da padre (It 1974)

LAUNDER, FRANK, b. 1907, Hitchen, Herts., England
    Millions Like Us (GFD 1943) (with Sidney Gilliat) (also co-
        script)

Alberto Lattuada at work on Le faro da padre (1974).

2,000 Women (GFD 1944) (also co-script)
I See a Dark Stranger [The Adventuress] (GFD 1946)† [co-pro-
  duction company] (also co-producer, co-script)
Captain Boycott (GFD 1947)† [co-production company] (also co-
  producer, co-script)
The Blue Lagoon (GFD 1949)† [co-production company] (also
  co-producer, co-script)
The Happiest Days of Your Life (BL 1950)† [co-production com-
  pany] (also co-producer, co-script)
Lady Godiva Rides Again (BL 1951) (also co-producer, co-
  script)
Folly to Be Wise (BL 1952) (also co-producer, co-script)
The Belles of St Trinian's (BL 1954) (also co-producer, co-
  script)
Geordie [Wee Geordie] (BL 1955) (also co-producer, co-script)
Blue Murder at St Trinian's (BL 1957) (also co-producer, co-
  script)
The Bridal Path (BL 1959) (also co-producer, co-script)
The Pure Hell of St Trinian's (BL 1960) (also co-producer,
  co-script)
Joey Boy (BL 1965) (also co-producer, co-script)
The Great St Trinian's Train Robbery (BL 1966) (also co-pro-
  ducer, co-script)

LAUTNER, GEORGES, b. 1926, Nice, France
  La Môme aux boutons (Fr 1959)
  Marche ou crève (Fr-Bel 1960)

Arrêtez les tambours (Fr 1960)
Le Monocle noir (Fr 1961)
En plein cirage (Fr 1961)
Le Septième Juré [The Seventh Juror] (Fr 1961)
L'Oeil du monocle (Fr 1962)
Les Tontons Flinguents (Fr-W Ger-It 1963) (also co-adaptor)
Les Pissenlits par la racine [Have Another Bier] (Fr-It 1964)
    (also co-script, co-dialogue)
Le Monocle rit jaune (Fr-It 1964)
Les Barbouzes [Undercover Men] (Fr 1964)
Les Bons Vivants (Fr-It 1965) (with Gilles Grangier)
Galia (It-Fr 1966) (also co-adaptor, co-dialogue)
Ne nous fâchons pas (Fr 1966)
La Grande Sauterelle [The Big Grasshopper] (Fr-W Ger-It
    1967)
Fleur d'oseille (Fr 1967)
Le Pacha [Showdown] (Fr-It 1968) (also co-script)
La route de Salina [Road to Salina] (Fr-It 1969) (also co-script)
Laisse aller, c'est une valse [Troubleshooters] (Fr-It 1971)
    (also co-script)
Il Etait une fois un flic (Fr-It 1972) (also co-script)
Quelques messieurs trop tranquilles (Fr 1973) (also co-script)
La Valise (Fr 1973) (also co-script)
Les Seins de glace (Fr-It 1974) (also adaptor, dialogue)

LAZAGA, PEDRO, b. 1918, Spain
    Encrucijada (Sp 1948)
    Campo Bravo (Sp 1949)
    Hombre Acosado (Sp 1950)
    Maria Morena (Sp 1951) (with José Maria Forqué)
    La Patrulla (Sp 1954)
    Cuerda de Presos (Sp 1955)
    La Vida es Maravillosa (Sp 1955)
    El frente infinito (Sp 1956)
    Torrepartida (Sp 1956)
    Roberto el diablo (Sp 1956)
    El Fotogenico (Sp 1957)
    El aprendiz de malo (Sp 1957)
    La frontera del Miedo (Sp 1957)
    Muchachas de Azul (Sp 1957)
    Ana Dice Si (Sp 1958)
    Luna de Verano (Sp 1958)
    Miss Cuple (Sp 1959)
    Los Tramposos (Sp 1959)
    La Fiel Infanteria (Sp 1959)
    Trio de bamas (Sp 1960)
    Los Economicamente Debiles (Sp 1960)
    Trampa Para Catalina (Sp 1961)
    Martes y trece (Sp 1961)
    La pandilla de los once (Sp 1961)
    Sabian demasiado (Sp 1961)
    Aprendiendo a morir (Sp 1962)

Siete espartanos (Sp 1962)
Fin de semana (Sp 1962)
Eva 63 (Sp 1963)
El calido verano del Senor Rodriguez (Sp 1963)
El timido (Sp 1964)
Dos chicas Locas, Locas (Sp 1964)
El Rostro del asesino (Sp 1964)
Un Vampiro para dos (Sp 1965)
Posicion avanzada (Sp 1965)
La ciudad no es para mi (Sp 1966)
Operacion plus ultra (Sp 1966)
Nuevo en esta plaza (Sp 1966)
La Viudas (ep "Luna de miel") (Sp 1966)
La cicatrices (Sp 1966)
Los guardiamarinas (Sp 1967)
¿Que hacemos con los hijos? (Sp 1967)
Los chicos del preu (Sp 1967)
Novios 68 (Sp 1967)
Sor citroen (Sp 1967)
El Turismo es un gran inveto (Sp 1967)
No desearas la mujer de tu projimo (Sp 1968)
Como sois las mujeres (Sp 1968)
No le busques tres pies (Sp 1968)
La chica de los anuncios (Sp 1968)
Las secretarias (Sp 1968)
Las amigas (Sp 1969)
El abominable hombre de la Costa del Sol (Sp 1969)
El Otro Arbol de guernica (Sp 1969)
Las Secretarias (Sp 1970)
Abuelo [Made in Spain] (Sp-It 1970)
Hora Cero: Operacion Rommel (Sp-It 1970)
A 45 Revoluciones por minuto (Sp 1969)
Verano 70 (Sp 1969)
Las siete vidas del gato (Sp 1970) (also co-script)
El Dinero Tiene Miedo (Sp-Mex 1970)
Vente a elemania, Pepe (Sp 1971)
Blanca por fuera, rosa por dentro (Sp 1971)
La Historia Negra de Peter P. Peter [Black tory] (Sp 1971)
Hay que Educar a papa (Sp 1971)
Vente a ligar al oeste (Sp 1961) (also co-story, co-script)
Mil Millonese para una ruba (Sp 1972) (also co-script)
El Vikingo (Sp 1972)
Paris bien vale una moza (Sp 1973)
El abuelo tiene un plan (Sp-It 1973)
El horo copo (Sp-It 1973)
El amor empieza a medicanoche (Sp 1974)

LEACOCK, PHILIP, b. 1917, London
   Riders of the New Forest (GFD 1946)
   The Brave Don't Cry (ABFD 1952)
   Appointment in London (BL 1953)

The Kidnappers [The Little Kidnappers] (GFD 1953)
Escapade (Eros 1955)
The Spanish Gardener (RFD 1956)
High Tide at Noon (RFD 1957)
Innocent Sinners (RFD 1958)
The Rabbit Trap (USA) (UA 1959)
Take a Giant Step (USA) (UA 1960)
Let No Man Write My Epitaph (USA) (Col 1960)
Hand in Hand (WPD 1960)
13 West Street (USA) (Col 1962)
Reach for Glory (Gala 1962)
The War Lover (Col British 1962)
Tamahine (WPD 1963)

Philip Leacock (left) discusses a scene with Dennis Price on location for Tamahine (1963).

LEAN, DAVID, b. March 25, 1908, Croydon, England
    Major Barbara (GFD 1941) (also editor) (uncredited with Harold
        French, Gabriel Pascal)
    In Which We Serve (BL 1942) (with Noel Coward)
    This Happy Breed (EL 1944) (also co-script)
    Blithe Spirit (GFD 1945) (also co-script)
    Brief Encounter (GFD 1945) (also co-script)
    Great Expectations (GFD 1947) (also co-script)

Oliver Twist (GFD 1948) (also co-script)
The Passionate Friends [One Woman's Story] (GFD 1949) (also
    co-script)
Madeleine (GFD 1950)
The Sound Barrier [Breaking the Sound Barrier] (BL 1952)
Hobson's Choice (BL 1954) (also producer, co-script)
Summertime [Summer Madness] (USA) (UA 1955) (also co-
    script)
The Bridge on the River Kwai (Col Br 1957)
Lawrence of Arabia (Col Br 1962)
Doctor Zhivago (USA) (MGM 1965)
Ryan's Daughter (MGM-EMI 1970)

David Lean with Anthony Wager on the set of Great Expectations
(1947).

LE BON, PATRICK, b. Belgium
S. O. S. Fonske (Bel 1968) (with Robbe de Hert)
Salut en de Kost (Bel 1974)

LECLERE, RENE, b. Belgium
Un Clown dans la rue (Bel 1930)

LEDOUX, PATRICK, b. 1934, Belgium
Klann (Bel 1970) (also co-script, co-music, editor)

LEHMAN, BORIS, b. March 3, 1944, Lausanne, Switzerland
Ne pas stagner (Bel 1973) (also script)
Album 1 (Bel 1974) (also script)

LEITÃO DE BARROS, JOSE (Jose Julio Marques Leitão de Barros),
    b. Oct. 22, 1896; d. June 29, 1967
Malmequer (Por 1918)
Mal de Espanha (Por 1918)
Nazare, praia de pescadores (Por 1929)
Maria do Mar (Por 1930)
Lisboa, crônica anedótica (Por 1930)
A severa (Por 1931) (also co-script)
As pupilas do Senhor Reiter (Por 1935)
Bocage (Por 1936)
Las tres gracias (Sp 1936)
Maria Papoila (Por 1937)
A varanda dos Rouxinois (Por 1939)
Ala arriba (Por 1942)
A pesca do atum (Por 1944)
Lisboa e o problema dos seus acessos (Por 1944)
Inez de Castro (Por-Sp 1945)
Camões (Por 1946) (also co-script)
Vendaval maravilhoso (Por 1949) (also co-script)
A última rainha de Portugal (Por 1950)
Reliquías portuguesas no Brazil (Por 1959)
Comemorações Henriquinas (Por 1960)

LELOUCH, CLAUDE, b. Oct. 30, 1937, Paris
Le Propre de l'homme (Fr 1960)
L'Amour avec des si (Fr 1963)
La Femme spectacle [Paris in the Raw] (Fr 1964)
Une Fille et des fusils [The Decadent Influence] (Fr 1964) (also
    producer, co-script, co-editor)
Les Grands Moments (Fr 1965)
Un Homme et une femme [A Man and a Woman] (Fr 1966)† (also
    co-script, camera)
Vivre pour vivre [Life for Life] (Fr-It 1967) (also co-script, co-
    camera, co-editor)
Loin du Viêtnam [Far from Vietnam] (Fr 1967) (with Jean-Luc
    Godard, William Klein, Alain Resnais, Agnes Varda)
Treize jours en France [Challenge in the Snow] (Fr 1969)†
    (also co-script) (with François Reichenbach)
La Vie, l'amour, la mort [Life, Love, Death] (Fr-It 1968)†
    (also co-script)

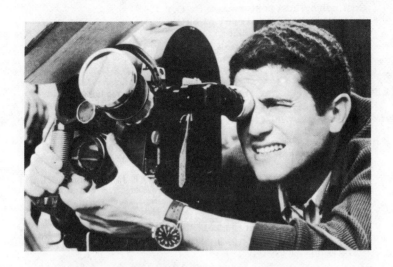

Claude Lelouch

Un Homme qui me plaît (Fr-It 1969)† (also co-script)
Le Voyou [Simon the Swiss] (Fr-It 1970)† [co-production com-
    pany] (also co-script, co-camera)
Smic, smac, smoc [Money, Money, Money] (Fr 1971)† (also
    script, camera)
L'Aventure c'est l'aventure (Fr-It 1972)† (also script, camera)
Visions of Eight (ep "The Losers") (USA) (MGM-EMI 1973)
    (also script)
La Bonne Année (Fr-It 1973)† [co-production company] (also
    producer, co-adaptor, co-dialogue, camera)

LENZI, UMBERTO, b. Aug. 6, 1931, Massa Marittima (Grosseto),
    Italy
Le avventuri di Mary Read (It 1961)
Caterina di Russia (It 1962)
Duello nella sila (It 1962)
Sandokan la tigre di Mompracem (It 1963)
Zorro contro Maciste (It 1963)
L'invincible cavaliere mascherato (It-Fr 1964)
Sandol, il maciste della giungla [Temple of the White Ele-
    phants] (It-Fr 1964)
A 008 operazione sterminio (It-GB 1965)
La montagna di luce (It 1965)
I tre sergenti del Bengali (It-Sp 1965)
L'ultimo gladiator (It 1965)
Attentato ai tre grandi (It-Sp-Ger 1967)
Orgasmo [Paranoia] (It-Fr 1968)
Tutto per tutto (It-Sp 1969)

Così dolce, così perversa (It-Fr-Ger 1969)
La legione dei dannati (It-Ger-Sp 1969)
Un posto ideal per uccidere (It 1971)
Sette orchidee macchiate di rosso (It-Ger 1971)
Milano rovente (It 1972)
L'occhio sbarrato nel buio (It 1974)

LEONE, SERGIO (a. k. a. Bob Robertson), b. 1921, Italy
Il colosso di Rodi [The Colossus of Rhodes] (It-Fr-Sp 1961)
Sodoma e Gomorra [Sodom and Gomorrah] (It 1962) (with Robert
    Aldrich)
Per un pugno di dollari [A Fistful of Dollars] (It 1964)
Per qualche dollari in più [For a Few Dollars More] (It-Ger-Sp
    1965)
Il buono, il brutto, il cattivo [The Good, the Bad and the Ugly]
    (It 1966)
C'erà una volta il West [Once upon a Time in the West] (It
    1968)
Giù la testa [Duck You Sucker] (It 1970)
Il mio nome è nessuno [My Name Is Nobody] (It-Fr-Ger 1974)
    (only producer, story idea)

LESTER, RICHARD, b. Jan. 1932, Philadelphia
It's Trad Dad (Col Br 1962)
The Mouse in the Moon (UA Br 1963)
A Hard Day's Night (UA Br 1964)
The Knack ... and How to Get It (UA Br 1965) (also co-script)
Help! (UA Br 1965)
A Funny Thing Happened on the Way to the Forum (UA Br
    1966)
How I Won the War (UA Br 1969) (also producer)
The Bed Sitting Room (UA Br 1969) (also producer)
The Three Musketeers: The Queen's Diamonds (Panama) (20th
    1973)
Juggernaut (UA Br 1974)
The Four Musketeers: Milady's Revenge (Panama) (20th 1974)

LETHEM, ROLAND, b. Jan. 5, 1942, Brussels
Bandes de cons (Bel 1970) (also script)
Le Saigneur est avec nous (Bel 1974) (also script)

LEWIS, JAY (Jay Gardner Lewis), b. 1914, Warwickshire, England;
    d. June 4, 1969
A Man's Affair (Ex 1949) (also producer, co-script)
The Baby and the Battleship (BL 1956)† (also co-script)
Invasion Quartet (MGM Br 1961)
Live Now--Pay Later (RFI 1962)
A Home of Your Own (BL 1969) (also co-script)

LINDEN, HENK J. VAN DER, b. 1925?, Hoensbroek?, Netherlands
Drie Jongens en een Hond (Dut 1954)
Sjors van de Rebellenclub (Dut 1955)
Trouwe Kameraden (Dut 1957)

De Nieuwe Avonturen van Dik Trom (Dut 1958)
Vier Rakkers en een Oude Jeep (Dut 1959)
Dik Trom en het Circus (Dut 1960)
Avonturen van een Zigeunerjongen (Dut 1960)
Robin Hood en Zijn Schelmen (Dut 1962)
Het Verraad van de Zwarte Roofridder (Dut 1962)
Sjors en Sjimmie op het Pirateneiland (Dut 1962)
De Avonturen van Pietje Bel (Dut 1964)
De Jongen Uit het Wilde Western (Dut 1964)
Vrijbuiters van het Woud (Dut 1965)
Sjors en Sjimmie en de Gorilla (Dut 1966)
Joe Hammond en de Indianen (Dut 1967)
Sjors en Sjimmie in het Land der Reuzen (Dut 1968)
De Man met het Zwarte Masker (Dut 1968)
Een Nederlandse Robinson Crusoe (Dut 1969)
Twee Jongens en een Oude Auto (Dut 1969)
Sjors en Sjimmie en de Toverring (Dut 1971)
Sjors, Sjimmie en de Rebellen (Dut 1972)
Robin en het Robotcomplot (Dut 1972)
Dik Trom en Zijn Dorpsgenoten (Dut 1973)
Lievertjes uit Amsterdam (Dut 1974)
Dik Trom Knapt het Op (Dut 1974)

LINDTBERG, LEOPOLD, b. June 1, 1902, Vienna
Jä-soo (Swi 1935)
Fusilier Wipf (Swi 1938)
Wachtmeister Studer (Swi 1939)
Die missbrauchten Liebesbriefe (Swi 1940)
Landammann Stuaffacher (Swi 1941)
Der Schuss von der Kanzel (Swi 1942)
Marie Louise (Swi 1944)
Die letzte Chance (Swi 1945/46)
Matto regiert (Swi 1947)
Swiss Tour [Four Day's Leave] (Swi-US 1949) (also co-script)
Die Vier im Jeep [Four in a Jeep] (Swi-GB 1951)
Unser Dorf [The Village] (Swi-GB 1953)
Herr und Frau Brandes (Swi TV 1973)
Kein schöner Tag (Swi TV 1974)
Johanna (Swi TV 1974)

LIZZANI, CARLO (a.k.a. Lee Beaver), b. April 3, 1922, Rome
Achtung banditi! (It 1951)
Ai margini della metròpoli (It 1953)
Amore in città [Love in the City] (It 1953)
Crònache di poveri amanti (It 1954)
Lo svitato (It 1956)
La muràglia cinese (It 1956)
Esterina (It 1959)
Il gobbo (It 1960)
Il carabiniere a cavallo (It 1961)
L'oro di Roma (It 1961)
Il processo di Verona (It 1963)
La vita agra (It 1964)

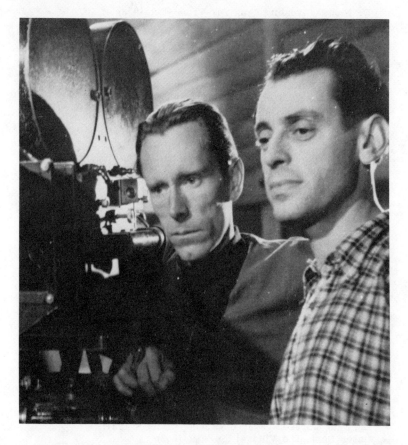

Leopold Lindtberg (right) with cameraman Emil Berna shooting <u>Die letzte Chance</u> (1945/46).

Amori pericolosi (ep "La ronda") (It 1964)
La Celestina P ... R ... (It 1965)
Thrilling (ep "L'autostrada del sole") (It 1965)
La guerra segreta [Dirty War] (Fr-It-Ger 1965) (with Terence Young, Christian-Jacque)
Lutring, svegliata e uccidi (It 1966)
Un fiume di dollari (It 1966)
Requiescant (It 1967)
Banditi a Milano (It 1968)
L'amante di Gramigna (It-Bul 1968)
Amore e ràbbia (ep "L'indifferenza") (It-Fr 1969)
Barbagia (It 1969)
Roma bene (It-Fr-Ger 1971)

Carlo Lizzani

LOACH, KEN, b. June 17, 1936, Nuneaton, Warwickshire, England
   Poor Cow (AA Br 1967) (also co-script)
   Kes (UA Br 1969)† [co-production company] (also co-script)
   Family Life (MGM-EMI 1971)† [co-production company]

LORENTE, GERMAN, b. Nov. 25, 1932, Vinaroz, Spain
   Ante de anochecer (Sp 1962)
   Donte tu estes (Sp 1963)
   Playas de Formentor (Sp 1964)
   Vivir al sol (Sp 1965)
   Su nombre es Daphne (Sp 1966)
   Una dia despues de Agosto (Sp 1966)
   Cover Girl (Sp 1967)
   Sharon vestida de rojo (Sp 1968)
   Las nenas del mini-mini (Sp 1969)
   Coqueluche (Sp-It 1970) (also co-script)
   Una chica casi decente (Sp 1971) (also co-script)
   Que cosas tiene el amor! (Sp 1971) (also co-script)

LOSEY, JOSEPH, b. Jan. 14, 1909, La Crosse, Wisconsin
   The Boy with Green Hair (USA) (RKO 1948)
   The Lawless (USA) (Par 1950)
   M (USA) (Col 1951)
   The Prowler (USA) (UA 1951)
   The Big Night (USA) (UA 1951)

Imbarco a mezzanotte [Stranger on the Prowl] (It 1953)
The Sleeping Tiger (AA Br 1954)
The Intimate Stranger [Finger of Guilt] (AA Br 1956)
Time Without Pity (Eros 1957)
The Gypsy and the Gentleman (RFD 1958)
Blind Date [Chance Meeting] (RFD 1959)
The Criminal [The Concrete Jungle] (AA Br 1960)
The Damned [These Are the Damned] (Col Br 1962)
Eve (RFD 1962)
The Servant (Elstree 1963) (also co-producer)
King and Country (WPD 1964) (also co-producer)
Modesty Blaise (20th Br 1966)
Accident (Lip 1967)
Boom! (RFD 1968)
Secret Ceremony (RFD 1968)
Figures in a Landscape (20th Br 1970)
The Go-Between (MGM-EMI 1971)
L'Assassinat de Trotsky [The Assassination of Trotsky] (Fr-It-GB 1972) (also co-producer)
A Doll's House (GB-Fr) (BL 1973) (also producer)
Galileo (American Film Theatre 1974)

Joseph Losey (right) with Dirk Bogarde on the set of The Servant (1963).

LOY, NANNI, b. Oct. 23, 1925, Cagliari, Italy
Tam tam mayumbe (It 1955) (only second unit director)
Parola di ladro (It 1957) (also co-story, co-script) (with Gianni
Puccini)
Il marito (It 1958) (also co-script) (with Gianni Puccini)
Audace colpo dei soliti ignoti [Fiasco in Milan] (It 1959) (also
co-script)
Un giorno de leoni (It 1961) (also co-story, co-script)
Le guattro giornate di Napoli [The Four Days of Naples] (It
1962) (also co-story, co-script)
Le belle famiglie (ep "Il bastardo della regina") (It 1965) (only
actor)
I complessi (ep "Guglielmo il dentone") (It 1965) (only actor)
Made in Italy (It 1965) (also co-script)
Il padre di famiglia [Head of the Family] (It 1967) (also co-
story, script)
Rosolino Paternò Soldato (It 1968) (also co-script)
Detenuto in attesa di giudizio (It 1971)
Vado, sistemo l'America è torno (It 1972)

LUBITSCH, ERNST, b. Jan. 28, 1892, Berlin; d. Nov. 30, 1947
Blinde Kuh (Ger 1914) (also actor)
Fräulein Seifenschaum (Ger 1914) (also actor)
Auf Eis geführh (Ger 1915) (also actor)
Zucker und Zimt (Ger 1915) (also co-script, co-titles, actor)
(with Ernst Matray)
Wo Ist Mein Schatz? (Ger 1916) (also actor)
Das schönste Geschenk (Ger 1916) (also actor)
Der Kraftmeier (Ger 1916) (also actor)
Der schwarze Moritz (Ger 1916) (also actor)
Schuhpalast Pinkus (Ger 1916) (also actor)
Der gemischte Frauenchor (Ger 1916) (also actor)
Leutnant auf Befehl (Ger 1916) (also actor)
Der GmbH Tenor (Ger 1916) (also actor)
Seine neue Nase (Ger 1917) (also actor)
Der Blusenkönig (Ger 1917) (also actor)
Ein fideles Gefängnis (Ger 1917) (also actor)
Ossis Tagebuch (Ger 1917)
Wenn vier dasselbe Tun (Ger 1917) (also co-script, actor)
Prinz Sami (Ger 1917) (also actor)
Der Rodelkavalier (Ger 1918) (also actor)
Der Fall Rosentopf (Ger 1918) (also actor)
Die Augen der Mumie Ma (Ger 1918) (also actor)
Das Model von Ballett (Ger 1918)
Carmen [Gypsy Blood] (Ger 1918)
Meine Frau, die Filmschauspielerin (Ger 1918) (also co-script)
Meyer aus Berlin (Ger 1918) (also actor)
Das Schwabemädel (Ger 1919)
Die Austernprinzessin (Ger 1919)
Rausch (Ger 1919)
Madame DuBarry [Passion] (Ger 1919)
Die Puppe (Ger 1919) (also co-script)
Ich Möchte kein Mann sein (Ger 1919) (also script)

Ernst Lubitsch

Kohlhiesels Tochter (Ger 1920) (also co-script)
Romeo und Julia im Schnee (Ger 1920) (also co-script)
Sumurun [One Arabian Night] (Ger 1920) (also co-script, actor)
Anna Boleyn [Deception] (Ger 1920)
Die Bergkatze (Ger 1921) (also co-script)
Das Weib des Pharao [The Loves of Pharaoh] (Ger 1921)†
Die Flamme [Montmartre] (Ger 1922)†
In the U. S. A. :
Rosita (UA 1923)
The Marriage Circle (WB 1924)
Three Women (WB 1924) (also co-story)
Forbidden Paradise (Par 1924)
Kiss Me Again (WB 1925)
Lady Windermere's Fan (WB 1925)
So This Is Paris? (WB 1926)
The Student Prince (MGM 1927)
The Patriot (Par 1928)
Eternal Love (UA 1929)
The Love Parade (Par 1929)
Paramount on Parade (ep) (Par 1930)
Monte Carlo (Par 1930)
The Smiling Lieutenant (Par 1931) (also co-script)

Le Lieutenant Souriant (Par 1931) (Fr version of The Smiling
  Lieutenant)
The Man I Killed [Broken Lullaby] (Par 1932)
One Hour With You (Par 1932)
Une Heure Pies de toi (Par 1932) (Fr version of One Hour
  With You)
Trouble in Paradise (Par 1932) (also producer)
If I Had a Million (ep "The Clerk") (Par 1932) (also script in
  episode)
Design for Living (Par 1933)
The Merry Widow (MGM 1934)
La veuve joyeuse (MGM 1934) (Fr version of The Merry Widow)
Angel (Par 1937) (also producer)
Bluebeard's Eighth Wife (Par 1939)
Ninotchka (MGM 1939)
The Shop Around the Corner (MGM 1940)
That Uncertain Feeling (UA 1941)
To Be or Not to Be (UA 1942) (also co-producer, co-story)
Heaven Can Wait (Fox 1943)
Cluny Brown (Fox 1946)
That Lady in Ermine (Fox 1948) (with uncredited Otto Preming-
  er)

LUNTZ, EDOUARD, b. Aug. 8, 1931, La Banle, France
Les Coeurs verts [Naked Hearts] (Fr 1966) (also script)
Le Grabuge (Fr 1969) (also script) (unshown)
Le Dernier Sau (Fr 1970) (also co-script)
L'Humeur vagabonde (Fr 1971) (also co-script, co-adaptor, co-
  dialogue)

LUPO, MICHELE, b. Dec. 4, 1931, Rome
Maciste il gladiatore più forte del mondo (It 1962)
Maciste l'eroe più grande del mondo (It 1963)
Gli schiavi più forte del mondo (It 1964)
Per un pugno nell'occhio (It-Sp 1965)
Sette contro Tutti (It 1965)
Arizona colt (It 1966)
Troppo per vivere ... poco per morire (It 1967)
Colpo maestro al servizio di sua Maestà Britannica (It-Sp 1967)
7 volte 7 (It 1968)
Una storia d'amore (It 1969)
Concerto per pisto solista (It 1970)
Stanza 17-17 palazzo delle tasse, ufficio imposte (It 1970)
Amico stammi lontano almeno in palmo (It 1971)
Dio, sei un vero padreterno (It-Fr 1972)

MacDONALD, DAVID, b. May 9, 1904, Helensburgh, Scotland
Double Alibi (20th Br 1937)
It's Never Too Late to Mend (MGM Br 1937)
When the Poppies Bloom Again (MGM Br 1937)
The Last Curtain (B & D-Par Br 1937)
Death Croons the Blues (MGM Br 1937)
Riding High (BL 1937)

Make It Three (MGM Br 1938)
Dead Men Tell No Tales (ABPC 1938)
Meet Mr Penny (ABPC 1938)
A Spot of Bother (GFD 1938)
This Man Is News (Par Br 1938)
Spies of the Air (ABPC 1939)
This Man in Paris (Par Br 1939)
The Midas Touch (WB Br 1939)
Law and Disorder (RKO Br 1940)
Men of the Lightship (ABFD 1940)
This England [Our Heritage] (Anglo 1941)
The Brothers (GFD 1947) (also co-script)
Snowbound (RKO Br 1948)
Good Time Girl (GFD 1948)
The Bad Lord Byron (GFD 1949)
Christopher Columbus (GFD 1949)
Diamond City (GFD 1949)
Cairo Road (ABP 1950)
The Adventurers [The Great Adventure] (GFD 1951)
The Lost Hours [The Big Frame] (Eros 1952)
Tread Softly (Apex 1952)
Operation Malaya (ABFD 1953)
Devil Girl from Mars (BL 1954)
Alias John Preston (BL 1956)
Small Hotel (ABP 1957)
The Moonraker (ABPC 1958)
A Lady Mislaid (ABP 1958)
Petticoat Pirates (WPD 1961)
The Golden Rabbit (RFD 1962)

MACHIN, ALFRED, b. 1877, Blendecques, France; d. 1929
La Fille de Delft (Bel 1914)
Maudite soit la guerre [Le Moulin maudit] (Bel 1914)
Pervenche (Bel 1921)
L'Enigme du mont Agel (Bel 1924)
Les Heritiers de l'oncle James [Les Millions de l'oncle James]
    (Bel 1924)
Le Coeur des gueux (Bel 1925)
Le Manoir de la peur [L'Homme noir] (Bel 1927)
Le Retour (Bel 1928)

MACKENDRICK, ALEXANDER, b. 1912, Boston, Mass.
Whisky Galore [Tight Little Island] (GFD 1949) (also uncredited
    co-script)
The Man in the White Suit (GFD 1952) (also co-script)
Mandy [Crash of Silence] (GFD 1952)
The Maggie [High and Dry] (GFD 1954)
The Ladykillers (RFD 1955)
Sweet Smell of Success (USA) (UA 1957)
Sammy Going South [A Boy Ten Feet Tall] (Bry-Seven Arts
    1963)
A High Wind in Jamaica (20th 1965)
Don't Make Waves (USA) (MGM 1967)

McNEIL, DAVID, b. June 22, 1946, New York
Overdrive (Bel 1970)
Les Fêtes de Belgique (Bel 1973) (with Henri Storck, Jean
Cleinge)

MAGNI, LUIGI, b. Rome
Faustina (It 1968)
Nell'anno del Signore (It 1970)
Scipione detto anche l'Africano (It 1971)
Eccolo, viene con le nuvole (It 1972)

MALATESTA, GUIDO (a.k.a. James Read), b. Gallarate, Italy
I miliardari (It 1957)
El Alamein (It 1958)
Valeria, ragazza poco seria (It 1958)
Agosto, donne mie non vi conosco (It 1960)
La furia dei barbari [Fury of the Pagans] (It 1960)
Goliath contro i giganti [Goliath Against the Giants] (It 1961)
Maciste contro i mostri [Fire Monsters Against the Sons of
Hercules] (It 1962)
Maciste contro i cacciatori di teste [Colussus and the Head-
hunters] (It 1963)
Zorro contro Maciste (It 1963)
Il vendicatore di Mayas (It 1966)
I predoni del Sahara (It 1966)
Come rubare un quintale di diamanti in Russia (It 1967)
Missione Apocalisse (It 1967)
L'incendio di Roma (It 1968) (produced in 1963)
Samoa la regina della giungla (It 1968)
Tarzana sesso selvaggio (It 1969)
Le calde notti di Poppea (It 1969)
Formula (It-Ger 1970)

MALLE, LOUIS, b. Oct. 30, 1932, Thumeries (Nord), France
Fontaine de Vaucluse (Fr 1953)
Station 307 (Fr 1955)
Le Monde du silence [The Silent World] (Fr 1956) (with Jacques-
Yves Cousteau)
Ascenseur pour l'échafaud [Frantic] [Lift to the Scaffold] (Fr
1957) (also co-script)
Les Amants [The Lovers] (Fr 1958) (also co-script, co-adaptor)
Zazie dans le Métro [Zazie] (Fr 1960) (also co-script, co-
adaptor, co-dialogue)
Vie privée [A Very Private Affair] (Fr-It 1962) (also co-script)
Le Feu follet [The Fire Within] [Will of the Wisp] (Fr-It 1963)
(also co-script, dialogue)
Touriste encore (Fr 1963)
Viva Maria! (Fr-It 1965) (also co-script, co-dialogue)
Le Voleur [The Thief of Paris] (Fr-It 1967) (also co-script, co-
adaptor)
Histoires extraordinaires (ep "William Wilson") [Tales of
Mystery] (Fr-It 1967) (also co-script)
Phantom India (Fr 1968) (also script)

Inde 68 [Louis Malle's India 1969] (Fr TV 1969)
Calcutta (Fr 1969) (also narrator)
Le Souffle au coeur [Murmur of the Heart] (Fr-It-Ger 1971)
 (also script)
Humain trop humain (Fr 1972/73)
Place de la République (Fr 1972/73) (with Fernand Mozskovicz)
Lacombe Lucien (Fr-It-Ger 1974) (also co-script)

Louis Malle (right) with Benoit Ferreux on the set of Le Souffle au
coeur (1971).

MARCELLINI, SIRO (a.k.a. Sean Markson), b. Sept. 16, 1921,
 Rowe
Siamo ricchi e poveri (It 1954)
Un palco all'opera (It 1956)
Ci sposeremo a Capri (It 1956)
Meravigliosa (It-Sp 1960) (with Carlos Arevalos)
Il bacio del sole [Don Vesuvio] (It-Ger 1961)
Il colpo segreto di d'Artagnan [Secret Mask of D'Artagnan]
 (It-Fr 1963)
L'eroe di Babilonia [Beast of Babylon Against the Sons of Her-
 cules] (It-Fr 1963)
Lola Colt (It 1968)
La legge dei gangsters (It 1969)
Quei dannati giorni dell'odio e dell'inferno (It-Sp 1970)

MARCHAL, JUAN XIOL, b. Sept. 14, 1921, Bilbao, Spain
El castillo de Rochal (Sp 1946)
Milagro en la ciudad (Sp 1953)
Avenida Roma, 66 (Sp 1956)
La extranjera (Sp 1958)
Sendas cruzadas (Sp 1961)
Cinco pistolas de Texas [Cinco dollari per Ringo] (Sp-It 1965)
Rio Maldito [Sette pistole per il Gringo] (Sp-It 1966)
El hombre de Caracas (Sp 1968)
La Garsa [Muneca del amor] (Sp 1968)
Las piernas de la serpiente (Sp 1970)
El juego del adulterio (Sp 1974)

MARCHENT, RAFAEL ROMERO, b. 1928, Madrid
Ocaso de un pistolero (Sp 1965)
Dos pistolas gemelas (Sp 1965)
Aqui mando yo (Sp 1966)
Dos crucez en Danger Pass (Sp 1967)
Dos hombres van a morir (Sp 1968)
Uno a uno sin piedad (Sp 1968)
Manos Torpes (Sp 1969)
¿Quien grita venganza? (Sp-It 1969)
Un par de asesions (Sp-It 1970)
Garringo (Sp-It 1970)
Condenados a vivir (Sp 1971)
El Zorro justiciero (Sp-It 1971)
Un dolar de recompensa (Sp-It 1971) (also co-script)
Disco rojo (Sp 1973)

MARGHERITI, ANTONIO (a. k. a. Anthony Dawson, Anthony Daisies),
        b. Sept. 19, 1916, Rome
Space men (It 1960)
Il pianeta degli uomini spenti (It 1961)
L'arciere degli uomini spenti (It 1963)
Il crollo di Roma (It 1964)
I giganti di Roma (It 1964)
Danza macabra (It 1964)
Ursus, il terrore dei Kirghisi (It 1964)
La vergine di Norimberga (It 1964)
Il pelo nel mondo (It 1964)
Anthar l'invincibile (It 1965)
I lunghi capelli della morte (It 1965)
A 007 sfida ai killers (It 1966)
I criminali della galassia (It 1966)
I diafanoidi vengono da Marte (It 1966)
Operazione Goldman (It 1967)
Joe l'implacabile (It 1968)
Io ti amo (It 1968)
Nude ... si muore (It 1968)
E Dio disse a Caino (It-Ger 1969)
Nella stretta morsa del ragno (It-Fr-Ger 1970)
Carne per Frankenstein (It 1972)
Ming, ragazzi! (It 1972)
Novelle galeotte d'amore dal "Decamerone" (It 1972)

MARIEN, MARCEL, b. 1920, Belgium
L'Imitation du cinéma (Bel 1960) (also script)

MARTIN, FRANCIS, b. 1905, Brussels
Le Petite Martyre belge (Bel 1921) (with Paul Flon)
Un Soldat inconnu (Bel 1922) (also actor) (with Paul Flon)
Kermesse sanglante (Bel 1926)
Un Gamin de Bruxelles (Bel 1926) (also script, actor) (with Paul Flon)
On tourne (Bel 1927)
Ça c'est Bruxelles (Bel 1927)
Femmes belges (Bel 1927)
Le Martyre de la petite Yvonne Vieslet (Bel 1929)

MARTINO, SERGIO, b. July 19, 1938, Rome
Dalle ardenne all'inferno (It-Fr-Ger 1969)
Mille peccati ... nessuna virtù (It 1969)
Femmine insaziabili (It-Ger 1969)
America un giorno (It 1970) (also script)
Arizona Colt si scatenò e li fece fuori tutti (It-Sp 1970)
Lo strano vizio della signora Wardh (It-Sp 1970)
I segreti delle città più nude del mondo (only co-script)
I corpi presentano tracce di violenza carnale (It 1972)
Tutti i colori del buio (It-Sp 1972)

MASELLI, FRANCESCO, b. Dec. 9, 1930, Rome
Amore in città (ep "Storia di Caterina") (It 1953)
Gli sbandati (It 1956)
La donna del giorno (It 1957)
I delfini (It 1960)
Le italiane e l'amore (ep "Le adolescenti") (It 1961)
Gli indifferenti [Time of Indifference] (It 1964)
Fai in fretta ad uccidermi ... ho freddo (It 1967)
Ruba al prossimo tuo [A Fine Pair] (It 1968)
Lettera aperta a un giornale della sera (It 1970)

MASTROCINQUE, CAMILLO, b. May 11, 1901, Rome; d. April 23, 1969
Regina della Scala (It 1936) (with G. Salvini)
Voglio vivere con Letizia (It 1937)
L'orologio a cucù (It 1938)
Inventiamo l'amore (It 1938)
Bionda sottochiave (It 1939)
Validità giorni dieci (It 1940)
La danza dei milioni (It 1940)
I mariti (It 1941)
Ridi, pagliaccio! (It 1941)
L'ultimo ballo (It 1941)
Turbine (It 1941)
Oro nero (It 1942)
Fedora (It 1942)
Le vie del cuore (It 1942)
La maschera e il volto (It 1942)

La statua vivente (It 1942)
Il matrimonio segreto (Unfinished Sp 1943)
Il cavaliere del sogno [Donizetti] (It 1946)
Sperduti nel buio (It 1947)
Arrivederci papà [When Love Calls] (It 1948)
Il vento mi ha cantato una canzone (It 1948)
L'uomo dal guanto grigio [Man with the Gray Glove] (It 1949)
La cintura di castità (It 1950)
Duello senza onore [Duel without Honor] (It 1950)
Arejao (It 1951)
Gli inesorabili [Fighting Men] (It 1951)
Attanasio cavallo vanèsio (It 1953)
Il peccato di Anna (It 1953)
Tarantella napoletana (It 1953)
Alvaro piuttosto corsaro (It 1954)
Café-chantant (It 1954)
Totò all'inferno (It 1954)
Figaro, barbiere di Siviglia (It 1955)
Siamo uomini o caporali? (It 1955)
Le vacanze del sor Clemente (It 1955)
La banda degli onesti (It 1956)
Napoli terra d'amore (It 1956)
Totò, lascia o raddoppia? (It 1956)
Totò, Peppino e la ... malafemmina (It 1956)
Totò, Peppino e i fuorilegge (It 1956)
Porta un bacione a Firenze (It 1957)
Totò, vittorio e la dottoressa (It 1957)
Le bellìssime gambe di Sabrina (It 1958)
Domenica è sempre domenica (It 1958)
E arrivata la parigina (It 1958)
Totò a Parigi (It 1958)
La cambiale (It 1959)
Vacanze d'inverno (It 1959)
Anonima cocottes (It 1960)
Il corazziere (It 1960)
Genitori in blue-jeans (It 1960)
Noi duri (It 1960)
Tototruffa '62 (It 1961)
Diciotteni al sole (It 1962)
Gli eroi del doppio gioco (It 1962)
I motorizzati (It 1962)
La cripta e l'incubo (It 1964)
Te lo leggo negli occhi (It 1966)
Un angelo per Satana (It 1967)
Le più bella coppia del mondo (It 1968)

MATARAZZO, RAFFAELLO, b. Aug. 17, 1909, Rome; d. May 17,
    1966
    La fumeria d'oppio (It 1947)
    Lo sciopero dei milioni (It 1948)
    Paolo e Francesca [Legend of Love] (It 1950)
    Catene (It 1951)
    Tormento (It 1951)

I figli di nessuno (It 1951)
Il tenente Giorgio (It 1952)
chi è senza peccato (It 1953)
Giuseppe Verdi (It 1953)
Torna! (It 1954)
La nave dell donne maledette (It 1954)
Vortice (It 1954)
Schiava del peccato (It 1954)
L'angelo bianco (It 1955)
L'intrusa (It 1955)
Guai ai vinti! (It 1957)
L'ultima violenza (It 1957)
Malinconico autunno (It 1958)
Cerasella (It 1960)
Adultero lui, adultera lei (It 1963)

MATTOLI, MARIO, b. Nov. 30, 1898, Toltentino, Italy
Tempo massimo (It 1934)
Amo te sola (It 1935)
Musica in piazza (It 1935)
Sette giorni all'altro (It 1936)
La damigella di Bard (It 1936)
L'uomo che sorride (It 1937)
Questi ragazzi (It 1937)
Gli ultimi giorni di Pompei (It 1937)
Felicità Colombo (It 1937)
Nonna Felicità (It 1938)
La dama bianca (It 1938)
Ai vostri ordini signora (It 1938)
L'ha fatto una signora (It 1939)
Imputato, alzatevi! (It 1939)
Mille chilometri al minuto (It 1939)
Lo vedi come sei? (It 1939)
Eravamo sette vedove (It 1939)
Non me lo dire (It 1940)
Il pirata sono io! (It 1940)
Abbandono (It 1940)
Ore 9 lezione di chimica (It 1941)
Luce nelle tenebre (It 1941)
Voglio vivere così! (It 1941)
Catene invisibili (It 1942)
I tre aquilotti (It 1942)
Labbra serrate (It 1942)
La donna è mobile (It 1942)
Stasera niente di nuovo (It 1942)
Ho tanta voglia di cantare (It 1943)
L'ultima carrozzella (It 1943)
La valle del Diavolo (It 1943)
La vispa Teresa (It 1943)
Circo equestre Za-Bum (It 1945)
Partenza ore sette (It 1945)
La vita ricomincia (It 1945)
I due orfanelli (It 1947)

Fifa e arena (It 1948)
Totò al giro d'Italia (It 1948)
Il fiacre n. 13 (It 1949)
Assunta Spina (It 1949)
I pompieri di Viggiù (It 1949)
Signorinella (It 1950)
Adamo ed Eva (It 1950)
Il vedovo allegro (It 1950)
I cadetti di Guascogna (It 1950)
L'inafferrabile 12 (It 1950)
Totò sceicco (It 1951)
Tototarzan (It 1951)
Accidenti alle tasse (It 1951)
Arrivano i nostri (It 1951)
Il padrone del vapore (It 1951)
Totò terzo uomo (It 1951)
Anema e core (It 1952)
Vendetta sarda (It 1952)
Cinque poveri in automobile (It 1952)
Siamo tutti inquilini (It 1953)
Il più comico spettacolo del mondo (It 1953)
Un turco napoletano (It 1953)
Due notti con Cleopatra (It 1953)
Il medico dei pazzi (It 1954)
Miseria e nobiltà (It 1954)
L'ultimo ammante (It 1956)
Le diciottenni (It 1956)
I giorni più belli (It 1956)
Peppino, le modelle e ... chella la (It 1957)
Come te movi, te fulmino! (It 1958)
Toto, Peppino e le fanatiche (It 1958)
Non perdiamo la testa (It 1959)
Prepontenti più di prima (It 1959)
Guardatele, ma non toccatele! (It 1959)
Tipi da spiaggia (It 1959)
Signori si nasce (It 1960)
Totò, Fabrizi e i giovani d'oggi (It 1960)
Appuntamento ad Ischia (It 1960)
Un mandarino per Teo (It 1960)
Sua ercellenza si fermo a mangiare (It 1961)
Cinque marines per cento ragazze (It 1961)
Appuntamento in riviera (It 1962)
Maciste contro Ercole nella valle dei guai (It 1962)
Obbiettivo ragazze (It 1963)
Cadavere per signora (It 1964)
Per qualche dollaro in meno (It 1966)

MAY, JOE (Joseph Mandel), b. Nov. 7, 1880, Vienna; d. May 5,
    1954
    In der Tiefe des Schachtes (Ger 1912) (also script)
    Vorghiten des Balkanbrandes (Ger 1912) (also script)
    Ein Ausgestossener (Part 1) (Ger 1913)
    Heimat und Fremde (Ger 1913) (also script)

Der verschleierte Bild von Grosz-Kleindorf (Ger 1913)
Entsagungen (Ger 1913)
Die unheilbringende Perle (Ger 1913) (also script)
Der Mann im Kellar (Ger 1914)
Der Spuk in Hause des Professors (Ger 1914)
Das Panzergewölbe (Ger 1914)
Die geheimnisvolle Villa (Ger 1914)
Charley, der Wunderaffe (Ger 1915)
In der Nacht (Ger 1915)†
Das Gesetz der Mine (Ger 1915)† (also co-script)
Sein Schwierigster Fall (Ger 1915)†
Der Geheimsekretär (Ger 1915)† (also co-script)
Die Sünde der Helga Arndt (Ger 1915)† (also co-script)
Die Gespensteruhr (Ger 1915)† (also co-script)
Nebel und Sonne (Ger 1916)†
Ein Blatt Papier (Ger 1916)† (also co-script)
Arme Eva Maria (Ger 1916)†
Wie ich Detektiv wurde (Ger 1916)†
Das rätselhafte Inserat (Ger 1916)† (with Karl Gerhardt)
Die Silhouette des Teufels (Ger 1917)†
Das Geheimnis der leeren Wasserflasche (Ger 1917)†
Der schwarze Chauffeur (Ger 1917)† (also script)
Der Onyxknopf (Ger 1917)
Des Vaters Letzter Wille (Ger 1917)†
Die Hochzeit im Exzentricclub (Ger 1917)†
Die Liebe der Hetty Raymond (Ger 1917)†
Ein Lichtstrahl im Dunkel (Ger 1917)†
Hide Warren und der Tod (Ger 1917)†
Krähen fliegen um den Turm (Ger 1917)†
Das Klima von Vancourt (Ger 1918)†
Das Opfer (Ger 1918)†
Die Kaukasierin (Ger 1918)† (also script) (with Jens W. Krafft)
Ihr grosses Geheimnis (Ger 1918)†
Die Bettelgräfin (Ger 1918)† (also co-script)
Wogen des Schicksals (Ger 1918)†
Sein bester Freund (Ger 1918)†
Veritas Vincit (Ger 1919)†
Die Herrin der Welt (Ger 1919)† (with Jens Krafft, Karl Gerhardt)
Fräulein Zahnarzt (Ger 1919)† (also co-script)
Die Legende von der Heiligen Simplicia (Ger 1920)†
Die Schuld der Lavinia Morland [The Wife Trap] (Ger 1920)†
Das Indische Grabmal (Part I and II) (Ger 1921)†
Tragödie der Liebe (Parts I-IV) (Ger 1923)†
Der Farmer aus Texas (Ger 1925)† (also co-script)
Dagfin (Ger 1926)† (also co-script)
Heimkehr [The Homecoming] (Ger 1929)
Asphalt (Ger 1929)
Ihre Majestät die Liebe (Ger 1930)†
Und das ist die Hauptsache (Ger 1931)†
Zwei in einem Auto (Ger 1932)†
Voyage de noces (Fr version of Hochzeitreise zu Dritt) (Ger 1933)

Ein Lied für Dich (Ger 1933)
Tout pour l'Amour (Fr version of Ein Lied für Dich) (Ger 1933)
Two Hearts in Waltztime (Gaumont 1934) (with Carmine Gallone)
In the U.S.A. :
Music in the Air (Fox 1934)
Confession (WB 1937)
Society Smugglers (Univ 1939)
The House of Fear (Univ 1939)
The Invisible Man Returns (Univ 1940) (also co-script)
The House of Seven Gables (Univ 1940)
You're Not So Tough (Univ 1940)
Hit the Road (Univ 1941)
Johnny Doesn't Live Here Anymore (Mor 1944)

Joe May

MAY, PAUL (Paul Ostermayr), b. May 8, 1909, Munich
Der Edelweisskönig (Ger 1938)
Waldrausch (Ger 1939)
Beates Flitterwochen (Ger 1940)
Links der Isar--rechts der Spree (Ger 1940)
Violanta (Ger 1942)
Die unheimliche Wandlung des Alex Roscher (Ger 1943)
Duell mit dem Tod (Aus 1949) (also story, script)

König fur eine Nacht (Ger 1950)
Zwei Menschen (Ger 1952)
Junges herz voll liebe (Ger 1953)
08/15 (Ger 1953)
Phantom des grossen Zeltes (Ger 1953)
08/15 (part 2) (Ger 1955)
08/15 in der Heimat (Ger 1955)
Oberarzt Dr. Solm (Ger 1955)
Weil Du arm bist, musst Du früher sterben (Ger 1956)
Flucht in die Tropennacht (Ger 1957)
Der Fuchs von Paris (Ger 1957)
Weisser Holunder (Ger 1957)
Die Landärztin (Ger 1958)
Heisse Ware (Ger 1958)
Und ewig singen die Wälder (Aus 1959)
Heimat--deine Lieder (Ger 1959)
Soldatensender Calais (Ger 1960)
Freddy und der Millionär (Ger 1961)
Via Mala (Ger 1961)
Waldrauch (Ger 1962)
Scotland Yard jagt Dr. Mabuse (Ger 1963)

MEISEL, KURT, b. 1912, Vienna
Verspieltes Leben (Ger 1949) (also actor)
Tragödie einer Leidenschaft (Ger 1949)
Liebe auf Eis (Ger 1950) (also actor)
Dämonische Liebe (Ger 1951) (also actor)
Die Todesarena (Ger 1953)
Das Sonntagskind (Ger 1956)
Vater sein dagegen sehr (Ger 1957) (also actor)
Drei Mann auf einem Pferd (Ger 1957) (also actor)
Madeleine--Tel. 13 61 11 (Ger 1958)
Kriegsgericht (Ger 1959)
Liebe verboten--heiraten erlaubt (Ger 1959)
Die rote Hand (Ger 1960) (also actor)
Der Verschwender (Ger 1964)

MELVILLE, JEAN-PIERRE (Jean-Pierre Grunbach), b. Oct. 20,
    1917, Paris; d. Aug. 2, 1973
    Le Silence de la mer (Fr 1948)† (also script, dialogue, co-
        editor)
    Les Enfants terribles (Fr 1949)† (also co-adaptor, designer)
    Quand tu liras cette lettre (Fr 1953)
    Bob le flambeur (Fr 1956)† [co-production company] (also
        script, dialogue, co-camera)
    Léon Morin, prêté (Fr-It 1961) (also script, dialogue)
    Le Doulos (Fr-It 1962) (also script, dialogue)
    L'Aîné des Ferchaux (Fr-It 1963) (also script, dialogue)
    Le Deuxième Souffle [Second Breath] (Fr 1966) (also script, co-
        dialogue)
    Le Samourai [The Samourai] (Fr-It 1967) (also script)
    L'Armée des ombres (Fr-It 1969) (also script)
    Le Cercle rouge (Fr-It 1970) (also production manager, script)

(2 versions)
Un Flic [Dirty Money] (Fr-It 1972) (also script)

MERCANTI, PINO, b. Palermo, Italy
All'ombra della gloria (It 1963)
Malcarne (It 1947) (with co-director)
I cavalieri dalla maschera nera (It 1948)
Il principe ribelle (It 1950)
La vendetta di una pazza (It 1952)
Serenata amara (It 1953)
La carovana del peccato (It 1953)
La voce del sangue (It 1954)
I cinque dell'Adamello (It 1955)
Agguato sul mare (It 1956)
Primo applauso (It 1957)
Ricordati di Napoli (It 1958)
L'ultima canzone (It 1958)
Il cavaliere dai cento volti (It 1960)
Il duca nero (It 1963)
Il vendicatore mascherato [I piombi di Venezia] (It 1964)

MESNIL, CHRISTIAN, b. Jan. 11, 1940, Brussels
Psychedelissimo [Delices d'amour] (Bel 1968)
L'Amoureuse (Bel 1972) (also co-script)

MEYER, PAUL, b. Sept. 29, 1920, Limal, Belgium
De Klinkaart (Bel TV 1956) (also script)
Déjà s'envole le fleur maigre [Les enfants du Borinage] (Bel 1960) (also script)
Wallonie 67--La sidérurgie (Bel TV 1967)

MICHIELS, IVO, b. Belgium
Meeuwen Sterven in de Haven (Bel 1955) (also co-script) (with Roland Verhavert, Rik Kuypers)

MILES, CHRISTOPHER, b. April 19, 1939, London
Up Jumped a Swagman (Elstree 1965)
The Slow Race (unreleased, made 1968) (also script)
The Virgin and the Gypsy (London Screenplays 1970)
A Time for Loving [A Room in Paris] (USA) (Hemdale 1972)

MITCHELL, OSWALD, b. 18??, England; d. 1949
Danny Boy (Butcher 1934) (also co-producer, co-script) (with Challis Sanderson)
Cock o' the North (Butcher 1935) (also producer, script) (with Challis Sanderson)
Stars on Parade (Butcher 1936) (also producer, co-script) (with Challis Sanderson)
King of Hearts (Butcher 1936) (also co-producer) (with Walter Tennyson)
Shipmates o' Mine (Butcher 1936) (also co-script)
Variety Parade (Butcher 1936)
Rose of Tralee (Butcher 1937) (also co-author, script)

Old Mother Riley (Butcher-Hyde-Bell 1937)
Lily of Laguna (Butcher 1938) (also co-script)
Almost a Gentleman (Butcher 1938) (also co-script)
Little Dolly Daydream (Butcher 1938) (also script)
Old Mother Riley in Paris (Butcher 1938)
Night Journey (Butcher 1938)
Music Hall Parade (Butcher 1939) (also co-script)
Old Mother Riley MP (Butcher 1939) (also co-script)
Jailbirds (Butcher 1939)
Pack Up Your Troubles (Butcher 1940)
Sailors Don't Care (Butcher 1940)
Danny Boy (Butcher 1941) (also co-script)
Bob's Your Uncle (Butcher 1941) (also co-script)
Asking for Trouble (Anglo 1942) (also co-script)
The Dummy Talks (Anglo 1943)
Old Mother Riley Overseas (Anglo 1943) (also producer)
Old Mother Riley at Home (Anglo 1943) (also co-script)
Loyal Heart (Anglo 1946)
The Mysterious Mr. Nicholson (Ambassador 1947) (also co-script)
Black Memory (Ambassador 1947)
The Greed of William Hart (Ambassador 1948)
House of Darkness (BL 1948)
The Temptress (Ambassador 1949)
The Man from Yesterday (Renown 1949)

MOCKY, JEAN-PIERRE, b. July 6, 1929, Nice, France
Les Dragueurs [The Young Have No Morals] (Fr 1959) (also script, co-adaptation)
Un Couple [The Love Trap] (Fr 1960) (also co-script)
Snobs (Fr-Swi 1961) (also script, co-adaptation)
Les Vierges [The Virgins] (Fr 1963) (also co-script)
Un Drôle de paroissien [Heaven Sent] (Fr 1963) (also co-adaptor)
La Cité de l'indicible peur/La Grande Frousse (Fr 1964) (also co-script)
La bourse et la vie [Money or Your Life] (Fr-Ger-It 1965) (also co-script, co-adaptor)
Les Compagnons de la marguerite [Order of the Daisy] (Fr-It 1966) (also script)
Les Grande Lessive (Fr 1968) (also co-script)
Solo [Moral Love] (Fr-Belg 1970) (also actor, script)
L'Etalon (Fr 1970) (also actor, script)
L'Albatros [Love Hate] (Fr 1971) (also co-producer, co-script, actor)
Chuk (Fr 1971) (also co-script, actor)
L'Ombre d'une chance (Fr 1973) (also script, actor)
Un Linceul n'a pas de poches (Fr 1974) (also co-adaptor, co-dialogue, actor)

MOERMAN, ERNEST, b. 1897, Belgium; d. 1943
Monsieur Fantômas (Bel 1937) (also script)

MONICELLI, MARIO, b. May 15, 1915, Rome
Co-directed with Stefano Vanzina (Steno)
    Toto cerca casa (It 1949)
    Al diavolo la celebrità (It 1949)
    Vita da cani (It 1949)
    E arrivato il cavaliere (It 1950)
    Guardie e ladri (It 1951)
    Totò e i re di Roma (It 1952)
    Totò e le donne (It 1952)
    Le infedeli [The Unfaithfuls] (It 1953)
Directed alone:
    Proibito [Forbidden] (It 1955) (also co-script)
    Totò e Carolina (It 1955) (also co-script)
    Donatella (It 1956)
    Un eroe di nostri tempi (It 1956) (also co-story)
    Il medico e lo stregone (It 1957)
    Padri e figli (It 1957)
    I soliti ignoti [Persons Unknown] (It 1957) (also co-script)
    La grande guerra (It 1959) (also co-script)
    Risate di gioia [The Passionate Thief] (It 1960) (also co-script)
    Boccaccio '70 (ep "Renzo e Luciana") (It 1961) (also co-script of episode)
    I compagni [The Organizer] (It 1963) (also co-script)
    Alta infedeltà [High Infidelity] (ep "Gente moderna") (It 1964)
    Casanova '70 (It 1965)
    L'armata Brancaleone (It 1966) (also co-script)
    Le fate [The Queens] (ep "fata Armenia") (It 1966)
    Capriccio all'Italiana (ep "La bambinaia") (It 1968)
    La ragazza con la pistola (It 1968)
    To! è morta la nonna! (It 1969) (also co-script)
    Brancaleone alle crociate (It 1970)
    Le coppie (ep "Il frigidaire") (It 1970)
    La mortadella [Lady Liberty] (It-Fr 1971) (also co-script)
    Vogliamo i colonelli (It 1972)

MONTERO, ROBERTO BIANCHI (a.k.a. M. Robert White), b. Dec. 17, 1907, Rome
    I contrabbandieri del mare (It 1949)
    La figlia della madonna (It 1949)
    Sono io l'assassino! (It 1949)
    Faddija [La legge della vendetta] (It 1950)
    La scogliera del peccato (It 1951)
    L'amante del male (It 1952)
    Una madre ritorna (It 1953)
    Addio Napoli (It 1954)
    Il mostro dell'isola (It 1954)
    Nessuno ha tradito (It 1954)
    Piccola santa (It 1954)
    Giuramento d'amore (It 1955)
    Cantate con noi (It 1956)
    Dramma nel porto (It 1956)
    Arriva la zia d'America (It 1957)
    Orizzonte infuocato (It 1957)

Mario Monicelli

Donne, amori e matrimoni (It 1958)
Gagliardi e pupe (It 1958)
La zia d'America va a sciare (It 1958)
La duchessa di Santa Lucia (It 1959)
La Pica sul Pacifico (It 1959)
La sceriffa (It 1959)
Il terribile Teodoro (It 1961)
Un alibi per morire (It 1962)
I due della legione (It 1962)
Notti calde d'oriente (It 1962)
Superspettacoli nel mondo (It 1962)
Tharus figlio di Attila [Tarus, Son of Attila] (It 1962)
Universo proibito (It 1962)
I rinnegati di capitan Kidd (It 1963)
Sexy Nudo (It 1963)
La belva di Saigon (It 1964)
Il ranch degli spietati (It-Sp-Ger 1965) (with Jesus Balcozar)
Agente Z 55, missions disperato (It 1965)
Tecnica di un massacro (It 1967)
Le due facce del dollaro (It 1968)
Quella donnata pattuglia (It 1969)
L'òcchio del ragno (It 1971)
I senza Dio (It 1971) .
Rivelazione di un maniaco sessuale al Capo della squadra mo-
    bile (It 1972)

MORE O'FERRALL, GEORGE see O'FERRALL, GEORGE

MOREL, FRANÇOIS XAVIER, b. Belgium
    Brigade anti-sex (Bel 1970) (also script) (under the name J. W.
        Rental)
    Ma soeur ne pense qu'à ça [Pornoschwestern] (Bel-Ger 1971)
    Du côté de chez Pauline (Bel TV 1972)

MORRIS, ERNEST, b. 1915, London
    Operation Murder (ABP 1957)
    Three Sundays to Live (UA Br 1957)
    Son of a Stranger (UA Br 1957)
    The Betrayal (UA Br 1958)
    A Woman of Mystery (UA Br 1958)
    On the Run (UA Br 1958)
    Three Crooked Men (Par Br 1958)
    Night Train for Inverness (Par Br 1960)
    The Tell-Tale Heart (WPD 1960)
    Strip Tease Murder (Par Br 1961)
    Highway to Battle (Par Br 1961)
    Tarnished Heroes (WPD 1961)
    Transatlantic (UA Br 1961)
    The Court Martial of Major Keller (WPD 1961)
    The Spanish Sword (UA Br 1962)
    Three Spare Wives (UA Br 1962)
    What Every Woman Wants (UA Br 1962)
    Masters of Venus (CFF 1962)
    Night Cargoes (CFF 1962)
    Operation Stogie (UA Br 1962)
    Echo of Diana (Butcher 1963)
    Shadow of Fear (Butcher 1963)
    The Sicilians (Butcher 1964)
    Five Have a Mystery to Solve (CFF 1964)
    The Return of Mr. Moto (20th Br 1965)

MOULLET, LUC, b. 1941, St. Cyrice (Seine)
    Brigitte et Brigitte (Fr 1966) (also script)
    Les Contrebandières (Fr 1968)† (also script, adaptor, dialogue)
    Une Aventure de Billy le Kid [A Girl Is a Gun] (Fr 1971) (also
        script, lyrics)

MURNAU, F. W. (Friedrich Wilhelm Murnau or F. W. Plumpe),
        b. Dec. 28, 1888, Bielefeld (Westphalia), Germany; d. March
        11, 1931
    Der Knabe in Blau (Ger 1919)
    Satanas (Ger 1919)
    Abend ... Nacht ... Morgen (Ger 1920)
    Der Bucklige und die Tänzerin (Ger 1920)
    Der Gang in die Nacht (Ger 1920)
    Der Januskopf (Ger 1920)
    Sehnsucht (Ger 1920)
    Marizza, genannt die Schmugglermadonna (Ger 1921)
    Schloss Vogelöd (Ger 1921)

Der brennende Acker (Ger 1922)
Nosferatu, eine Symphonie des Grauens (Ger 1922)
Phantom (Ger 1922)
Die Austreibung (Ger 1923)
Die Finanzen des Grossherzogs (Ger 1923)
Der letzte Mann (Ger 1924)
Tartuff (Ger 1924)
Faust (Ger 1926)
Sunrise (USA) (Fox 1927)
Four Devils (USA) (Fox 1927)
City Girl (USA) (Fox 1930)
Tabu (USA) (Par 1931) (also co-producer, co-script) (with
    Robert Flaherty)

NEAME, RONALD, b. April 23, 1911, London
Take My Life (GFD 1947)
Golden Salamander (GFD 1950) (also co-script)
The Card [The Promoter] (GFD 1952)
The Million Pound Note [Man with a Million] (GFD 1954)
The Man Who Never Was (20th Br 1956)
Windom's Way (RFD 1957)
The Horse's Mouth (UA Br 1959)
Tunes of Glory (UA Br 1960)
Escape from Zahrain (USA) (Par 1961)
I Could Go On Singing (UA Br 1962)
The Chalk Garden (Univ Br 1963)
Mister Moses (USA) (UA 1965)
A Man Could Get Killed (USA) (Univ 1966) (with Cliff Owen)
Gambit (USA) (Univ 1966)
The Prime of Miss Jean Brodie (20th Br 1969)
Scrooge (20th Br 1970)
The Poseidon Adventure (USA) (20th 1972)

NIE, RENE VAN, b. 1938, Netherlands
Viji van de Vierdaagse (Dut 1974)
Kinf van de Zon (Dut 1975)

NORMAN, LESLIE, b. 1911, London
Too Dangerous to Live (FN Br 1939) (with Anthony Hankey)
The Night My Number Came Up (GFD 1955)
X the Unknown (Ex 1956)
The Shiralee (MGM Br 1957)
Dunkirk (MGM Br 1958)
Summer of the Seventeenth Doll (USA) (UA 1959)
The Long and the Short and the Tall (WPD 1961)
Spare the Rod (Bry 1961)
Mix Me a Person (BL 1962)

NYS, GUIDO J., b. Belgium
Pandore [Cierges d'amour] (Bel 1968)
In Love with Death (Bel 1969) (also camera)
The Naked D (Bel 1970) (also camera, editor)

Ronald Neame

O'CONNOLLY, JAMES, b. 1926
    The Hi-Jackers (Butcher 1964) (also script)
    Smokescreen (Butcher 1964) (also script)
    The Little Ones (Bl 1965) (also script)
    Berserk! (Col Br 1967)
    The Valley of Gwangi (USA) (WB 1968)
    Crooks and Coronets (WPD 1969) (also script)
    Tower of Evil [Horror of Snape Island] (GB-US) (MGM-EMI
        1972) (also script)
    Mistress Pamela (MGM-EMI 1973) (also script)

O'FERRALL, GEORGE MORE, b. 1906
    Angels One Five (ABP 1952)
    The Holly and the Ivy (BL 1952)
    The Heart of the Matter (BL 1953)
    The Green Scarf (BL 1954)
    Three Cases of Murder (ep "Lord Mountdrago") (BL 1955)
    The Woman for Joe (RFD 1955)
    The March Hare (BL 1956)

O'HARA, GERALD, b. Boston, Mass.
    That Kind of Girl (Compton 1963)
    Game for Three Losers (AA 1965)
    The Pleasure Girls (Compton 1965)

Maroc 7 (RFD 1966)
Amsterdam Affair (Lip 1968)
All the Right Noises (20th Br 1971) (also script) (made in 1969)

OLIVIER, SIR LAURENCE KERR, b. May 22, 1907, Dorking, Sur-
    rey, England
Henry V (EL 1945) (also producer, co-script, actor)
Hamlet (GFD 1948) (also producer, actor)
Richard III (IFD 1956) (with Anthony Bushell) (also producer,
    actor)
The Prince and the Showgirl (WB Br 1957) (with Anthony Bu-
    shell) (also co-producer, actor)
The Entertainer (Bry 1960) (also actor)
Three Sisters (BL 1970) (also actor)

OLMI, ERMANO, b. July 24, 1931, Bergamo, Italy
Il tempo si è fermato (It 1960)
Il posto (It 1961)
I fidanzati (It 1963)
... e venne un uomo (It 1965)
Un certo giorno (It 1968)

OLSEN, ROLF
Hochzeit am Neusiedler (Aus 1963)
Heiss weht der Wind [Mein Freund Shorty] (Ger-Aus 1964)
Der letzte Ritt nach Santa Cruz (Ger-Aus 1964)
In Frankfurt sind die Nächte heiss (Aus 1966)
Spukschloss im Salzkammergut (Ger 1965) (with Hans Billian)
Heubodengeflüster (Ger 1967)
Der Arzt von St. Pauli (Ger 1968)
Paradies der flotten Sünder (Ger 1968)
Auf der Reeperbahn Nachts um halb eins (Ger 1969)
Käpt'n Rauhbein aus St. Pauli (Ger 1971)
Die Kompanie der Knallkoppe (Ger 1971)
Blutiger Freitag (Ger-It 1972)
Unsere Tante ist das letzte (Ger 1973)

OPHULS, MAX (Max Oppenheimer), b. May 6, 1902, Saarbrücken,
    Saarland (Germany); d. March 26, 1957
Dann schon lieber Lebertran (Ger 1930) (also co-script)
Die verliebte Firma (Ger 1931)
Die verkaufte Braut (Ger 1932)
Die lachenden Erben (Ger 1932)
Liebelei (Ger 1932)
Une Histoire d'amour (Fr version of Liebelei) (Fr 1933)
On a volé un homme (Fr 1933)
La signora di tutti (It 1934) (also co-script)
Divine (Fr 1935) (also co-script)
Komedie om Geld (Dut 1936) (also co-script)
La Tendre Ennemie (Fr 1936) (also co-script)
Yoshiwara (Fr 1937) (also co-script)
Werther (Fr 1938) (also co-script)
Sans lendemain (Fr 1939) (also co-script)

De Mayerling à Sarajevo (Fr 1939) (also co-script)
L'Ecole des femmes (unfinished Fr 1940)
The Exile (USA) (Univ 1947)
Letter from an Unknown Woman (USA) (Univ 1948)
Caught (USA) (MGM 1949)
The Reckless Moment (USA) (Col 1949)
Vendetta (RKO 1950) (uncredited, with credited Mel Ferrer, and
    uncredited Stuart Heisler, Howard Hughes, Preston Struges)
La Ronde (Fr 1950) (also co-script)
Le Plaisir (Fr 1952) (also co-script)
Madame de (Fr-It 1953) (also co-script)
Lola Montès (Fr 1955) (also co-script)

Max Ophuls

OURY, GERARD (Max-Gérard Houry Tannenbaum), b. April 24,
    1919, Paris
    La Main chaude [Eternal Ecstasy] (Fr-It 1959) (also co-script,
        co-dialogue)
    La Menace (Fr-It 1961) (also co-script)
    Le Crime ne paie pas [The Gentle Art of Murder] (Fr-It 1961)

    (also co-script)
Le Corniaud [The Sucker] (Fr-It 1965) (also co-script)
La Grande Vadrouille [Don't Look Now ... We're Being Shot
    At!] (Fr 1966) (also script, co-adaptor)
Le Cerveau [The Brain] (Fr-It 1969) (also co-script)
La Folie des grandeurs (Fr-It-Sp-Ger 1971) (also co-script,
    co-adaptor, co-dialogue)
Les Aventures de Rabbi Jacob [The Mad Adventures of 'Rabbi'
    Jacob] (Fr-It 1973) (also co-script)

OWEN, CLIFF, b. April 22, 1919, London
Offbeat (BL 1960)
A Prize of Arms (Bry 1961)
The Wrong Arm of the Law (BL 1962)
That Riviera Touch (RFD 1966)
A Man Could Get Killed (USA) (Univ 1966) (with Ronald Neame)
The Magnificent Two (RFD 1967)
The Vengeance of She (WPD 1968)
Steptoe and Son (MGM-EMI 1972)
Ooh ... You Are Awful (BL 1972)
No Sex Please--We're British (Col Br 1973)

PABST, GEORG WILHELM, b. Aug. 27, 1885, Raudnitz, Bohemia;
    d. May 29, 1967
Der Schatz (Ger 1923) (also script)
Graefin Donelli (Ger 1924)
Die Freudlose Gasse [The Joyless Street] (Ger 1925)
Geheimnisse einer Seele (Ger 1926)
Man Spielt nicht mit der Liebe! (Ger 1926)
Die Liebe der Jeanne Ney (Ger 1927)
Abwege (Ger 1928)
Die Büchse der Pandora [Pandor's Box] (Ger 1929)
Das Tagebuch einer Verlorenen [Diary of a Lost Girl] (Ger
    1929)
Die weisse Hölle von Piz Palü (Ger 1929) (with Arnold Fanck)
Prix de Beauté (Fr 1930) (only co-script)
Westfront (Ger 1930)
Skandal um Eva (Ger 1930)
Die Dreigroschenoper (Ger 1931)
L'Opéra de quat' sous (Fr version of Die Dreigroschenoper)
    (Ger-Fr 1931)
Kameradschaft (Ger 1931)
La Tragédie de la mine (Fr version of Kameradschaft) (Ger-Fr
    1932)
Die Herrin von Atlantis (Ger 1932)
L'Atlantide (Fr version of Die Herrin von Atlantis) (Ger 1932)
Don Quichotte (Fr 1933)
Don Quixote (Eng version of Don Quichotte) (UA Br 1933)
Du Haut en bas (Fr 1933)
La Nuit (Fr 1933) (only supervisor)
A Modern Hero (USA) (WB 1934)
Mademoiselle Docteur (Fr 1936)
Le Drame de Shanghai (Fr 1938)

L'Esclave blanche (Fr 1938) (only supervisor, producer)
Jeunes filles in détresse (Fr 1939)
Feuertaufe (Ger 1940)
Komödianten (Ger 1941) (also co-script)
Paracelsus (Ger 1943)
Meine Vier Jungens (Ger 1944)
Der Fall Molander (Ger 1945) (uncredited)
Der Prozess (Aus 1948)
Geheimnisvolle Tiefe (Aus 1949)
Duell Mit Dem Tode (Aus 1950) (only supervisor, co-script)
Ruf Aus dem Äther (Aus 1951) (only supervisor)
La Voce del silenzio (It 1952) (also co-script)
Cose Da Pazzi (It 1953) (also co-script)
Das Bekenntnis der Ina Kahr (Ger 1954)
Der Letzte Akt (Aus 1955)
Es Geschah am 20 Juli (Ger 1955)
Rosen Für Bettina (Ger 1956)
Durch die Wälder, Durch die Auen (Ger 1956)

PAGNOL, MARCEL, b. 1895, Aubagne (Bouches-du-Rhônes), France
Topaze (Fr 1932) (only script)
Direct au coeur (Fr 1933) (also script)
Le Gendre de M. Poirier (Fr 1933) (also script)
Léopold le bien-aimé (Fr 1933) (also script)
Angèle (Fr 1934) (also script)
Jofroi (Fr 1934) (also script)
Merlusse (Fr 1935) (also script)
Gigalon (Fr 1935) (also script)
César (Fr 1936) (also based on his play, script)
Regain (Fr 1937) (also script)
Le Schpountz (Fr 1938) (also script)
La Femme du boulanger (Fr 1938) (also script)
La Fille du puisatier (Fr 1940) (also script)
Nais (Fr 1946) (also script)
La Belle Meunière (Fr 1948) (also script)
Topaze (Fr 1951) (also script)
Manon des sources (Fr 1952) (also script)
Les Lettres de mon moulin [Letters from My Windmill] (Fr 1954) (also script)

PAOLELLA, DOMENICA, b. Oct. 15, 1915, Foggia, Italy
Un ladro in paradiso [Thief in Paradise] (It 1952)
Canzoni di mezzo secolo [Half a Century of Songs] (It 1952)
Canzoni, canzoni, canzoni [Cavalcade of Songs] (It 1953)
Gran varietà [Great Vaudeville] (It 1954)
Rosso e nero (It 1954)
Il coraggio (It 1955)
Flucht in die Dolomiten [Il prigioniero della montagna] (Ger-Gr-It 1955) (with G. Bassino, Luis Trenker)
Destinazione Piovarolo (It 1955)
Canzoni di tutta Italia (It 1956)
Sanremo canta (It 1956)
Non sono più guaglione (It 1958)

Destinazione Sanremo (It 1959)
Madri pericolose (It 1960)
I pirati della costa (It 1960)
I teddy boys della canzone (It 1960)
Il segreto dello sparviero nero (It 1961)
Il terrore dei mari (It 1961)
Il giustiziere dei mari (It 1962)
Maciste contro lo sceicco [Samson against the Sheik] (It 1962)
Le prigioniere dell'isola del diavolo (It 1962)
Ursus gladiatore ribelle [Rebel Gladiator] (It 1963)
Maciste nel'inferno di Genghis Khan [Hercules Against the Barbarians] (It 1964)
Maciste contri i mongoli (It 1964)
Il gladiatore che sfida l'impero [Challenge of the Gladiators] (It 1965)
Odio per odio (It 1967)
Execution (It 1968)
La ragazza del prete (It 1970)
La preda (It 1974)

PAROLINI, GIANFRANCO (a. k. a. Frank Kramer)
La furia di Ercole [The Fury of Hercules] (It 1962)
Sansone [Samson] (It 1962)
Anno 79, la distruzione di Ercolano [79 A. D.] (It-Fr 1963)
Il vecchio testamento (It-Fr 1963)
I dieci gladiatori [The Ten Gladiators] (It 1964)
Johnny West il mancino (It-Fr-Sp 1965)
La sfida viene da Bangkok (It-Fr-Ger 1965)
... Ehi, amico, c'è Sabata ... hai chiuso! (It 1969)
Cinque per l'inferno (It 1969)
Indio Black (It 1970)

PARRA, PIM DE LA, b. Jan. 5, 1940, Paramaribo, Surinam
Megalopolis 1 (Dut 1963)
Obsessions (Dut 1969)
Rubia's Jungle (Dut 1970)
Frank en Eva (Dut 1973)
Mijn Nachten met Susan, Olga, Albert, Julie, Piet en Sandra (Dut 1975)

PASOLINI, PIER PAOLO, b. March 5, 1922, Bologna, Italy;
    d. November 1, 1975
Accattone (It 1962) (also script)
Mamma Roma (It 1963) (also script)
La rabbia (It 1963) (also script)
Rogopag (cp "La ricotta") (It 1963) (also story, script for episode)
Il vangelo secondo Matteo [The Gospel According to St. Matthew] (It 1964) (also script)
Comizi d'amore (It 1965) (also script)
Uccellacci e uccellini [The Hawks and the Sparrows] (It 1966) (also script)
Le streghe (ep "La terra vista dalla luna") (It 1967) (also script for episode)

Edipo re [Oedipus Rex] (It 1967) (also script, actor)
Capriccio all'italiana (ep "Che cosa sono le nuvole?") (It 1968)
    (also script for episode)
Teorema (It 1968) (also from own novel, script)
Amore e rabbia (ep "La fiore di campo") (It 1969) (also script
    for episode)
Medea (It-Fr-Ger 1969) (also script)
Porcile [Pigsty] (in two parts) (It 1970) (also script)
Il decamerone (It 1970) (also script, actor)
I racconti di Canterbury (It 1971)
I muri di sana (It 1972)
I Fiori delle 1001 notte (It 1974)

PATINO, BASILEO MARTIN, b. 1936, Lumbrales, Salamanca
Neuve cartas a Berta (Sp 1967) (also script)
Del amor y otras soledades (Sp 1969) (also co-script)

PAVEL, SAMY, b. Nov. 5, 1944, Cairo, Egypt
Les Deux Saisons de la vie (Bel 1972) (also co-script, actor)
Miss O'Gynie et les hommes-fleurs (Bel 1973) (also co-script)

PEARSON, GEORGE, b. 1875, London; d. Feb. 8, 1973
The Fool (Pathé 1913) (also script)
The Sentence of Death (Pathé 1913) (also script)
Heroes of the Mine [The Great Mine Disaster] (Pathe 1913)
    (also co-script)
The Live Wire (Pathe 1914)
A Study in Scarlet (Moss 1914)
Incidents of the Great European War (Royal 1914) (also script)
The Life of Lord Roberts V C (Imperial 1914) (also co-script)
A Cinema Girl's Romance (Royal 1915)
The True Story of the Lyons Mail (Moss 1915)
John Halifax, Gentleman (Moss 1915)
Ultus, the Man from the Dead [Ultus 1: The Townsend Mystery,
    Ultus 2: The Ambassador's Diamonds] (Gaumont-Victory
    1915) (also co-script)
Sally Bishop (Gaumont 1916) (also script)
Ultus and the Grey Lady [Ultus 3: The Grey Lady, Ultus 4:
    The Traitor's Fate] (Gaumont-Victory 1916) (also script)
Ultus and the Secret of the Night [Ultus 5: The Secret of the
    Night] (Gaumont-Victory 1916) (also script)
Ultus and the Three-Button Mystery [Ultus 6: The Three But-
    ton Mystery, Ultus 7] (Gaumont-Victory 1917) (also script)
The Better 'Ole: or, the Romance of Old Bill [Carry On]
    (Jury 1918) (also co-script)
The Kiddies in the Ruins (Jury 1918)† (also producer, script)
Garry Owen (Welsh-Pearson 1920)† (also producer, script)
Nothing Else Matters (Jury 1920)† (also producer, script)
Mary-Find-the-Gold (Jury 1921)† (also producer, script)
Squibs (Jury 1921)† (also producer, co-script)
Mord Em'ly [Me and My Girl] (Jury 1922)† (also producer)
The Wee MacGregor's Sweetheart (Jury 1922)† (also producer,
    script)

Squibs Wins the Calcutta Sweep (Jury 1922)† (also producer,
   script)
Life, Love and Laughter (Gaumont 1923)† (also producer,
   script)
Squibs M P (Gaumont 1923)† (also producer, co-script)
Squibs' Honeymoon (Gaumont 1923)† (also producer, co-script)
Reveille (Gaumont 1924)† (also producer, script)
Satan's Sister (W & F 1925) (also co-producer, script)
The Little People (Butcher 1926)† (also co-producer, co-script)
Blinkeyes (Gaumont 1926)† (also producer, script)
Huntingtower (Par Br 1927)† [co-production company]
Love's Option (Par Br 1928)† [co-production company] (also script)
Auld Lang Syne (Par Br 1929)† [co-production company] (also
   script)

East Lynne on the Western Front (Gaumont 1931)† (also co-
   author)
The Third String (Gaumont 1932)† (also co-producer, co-script)
A Shot in the Dark (Radio 1933)
The Pointing Finger (Radio 1933)
The River Wolves (Radio 1934)
Four Masked Men (Univ Br 1934)
Whispering Tongues (Radio 1934)
Open All Night (Radio 1934)
The Ace of Spades (Radio 1935)
That's My Uncle (Univ Br 1935)
Gentleman's Agreement (B & D-Par Br 1935)
Once a Thief (B & D-Par Br 1935)
Jubilee Window (B & D-Par Br 1935) (also co-script)
Checkmate (B & D-Par Br 1935)
The Secret Voice (B & D-Par Br 1936)
Wednesday's Lunch (B & D-Par Br 1936)
Murder By Rope (B & D-Par Br 1936)
Midnight at Madame Tussaud's [Midnight at the Wax Museum]
   (Par Br 1936)
The Fatal Hour (B & D-Par Br 1936)

PELISSIER, ANTHONY, b. 1912, London
The History of Mr. Polly (GFD 1949) (also script)
The Rocking Horse Winner (GFD 1949) (also script)
Night Without Stars (GFD 1951)
Encore (ep "Gigolo and Gigolette") (GFD 1951)
Meet Me Tonight (GFD 1952)
Personal Affair (GFD 1953)
Meet Mr. Lucifer (GFD 1953)

PERIER, ETIENNE, b. Dec. 11, 1931, Brussels
Bobosse (Bel 1959)
Meurtre en 45 tours (Bel 1960) (also co-script)
Bridge to the Sun (Bel 1961)
Lo spadaccino di Siena [Le Mercenaire, The Swordsman of
   Siena] (It-Fr 1962)
Dis-moi qui tuer (Bel 1965)

Des garçons et des filles (Bel 1968)
Rublo de dos caras [Le Rouble a deux Faces] (Sp-Fr 1969)
Zeppelin (WB 1971)
When Eight Bells Toll (Cin 1971)
Un Meurtre est un meurtre (Bel 1973)
La main à couper (Bel 1974)

PETRI, ELIO (Eraclio Petri), b. Jan. 29, 1929, Rome
L'assassino (It 1961) (also co-script)
I giorni contati (It 1962) (also co-script)
Il maestro di Vigevano (It 1963) (also co-script)
Alta infedeltà [High Infidelity] (ep "Peccato nel pomeriggio")
    (It 1964) (also co-script for episode)
La decima vittima [The Tenth Victim] (It 1965) (also co-script)
A ciascuno il suo (It 1967) (also co-script)
Un tranquillo posto di campagna (It 1968) (also co-story, co-
    script)
Indagine su un cittadino al di sopra di ogni sospetto [Investiga-
    tion of a Citizen Above Suspicion] (It 1969) (also co-script)
La classe operaia va in Paradiso (It 1971) (also co-script)
La proprietà non è più un furto (It 1972) (also co-script)

PHILIPP, HARALD, b. Germany
Das alte Försterhaus (Ger 1956)
Heute blau und morgen blau (Ger 1957)
Siebenmal in der Woche (Ger 1957)
Der Czardas-König (Ger 1958)
Rivalen der Manege (Ger 1958)
Tausend sterne leuchten (Ger 1959)
Strafbataillon 999 (Ger 1960)
Division Brandenburg (Ger 1960)
Unter Aufschluss der Öffentlichkeit (Ger 1961)
Auf Wiedersehen (Ger 1962)
Mordnacht in Manhattan (Ger 1965)
Winnetou und das Halbblut Apanatschi (Ger-Dan-Yug 1966)
Blonde Köder für den Morder (Ger 1970)
Ehemänner Report [Seilensprung Report] (Ger 1970)
Hurra, wir sind Mal wider Junggesellen (Ger 1971)
Die Tote aus der Themse (Ger 1971)

PIALAT, MAURICE, b. Aug. 21, 1925, Cunihat (Puy-de-Dome)
Village d'enfants (Fr 1969) (also script)
L'Enfance nue (Fr 1969) (also script, co-adaptor)
Nous ne veillirons pas ensemble (Fr-It 1972) (also co-producer,
    story, script)
La maison des bois (Fr TV 1973)
La Gueule ouverte (Fr 1973) (also producer, script)

PICAZO, MIGUEL, b. 1927
Oscuros sueños de Agosto (Sp 1968)
Homenaje para Adriana (Sp 1970)

PICK, LUPU, b. Jan. 2, 1886, Jassy, Romania; d. March 7, 1931
Der Liebe des Van Royk (Ger 1918)
Die Tolle Heirat von Lalo (Ger 1918)
Der Herr über Leben und Tod (Ger 1919)
Kitsch (Ger 1919)
Misericordia (Ger 1919)
Seelenverkaufer (Ger 1919)
Marionetten der Leidenschaft (Ger 1919)
Mein Wille ist Gesetz (Ger 1919)
Der Dummkopf (Ger 1920) (also actor)
Das lachende Grauen (Ger 1920)
Niemand weiss es (Ger 1920) (also actor)
Oliver Twist (Ger 1920)
Tötet nicht mehr (Ger 1920) (also actor)
Grausige Nächte (Ger 1921)
Scherben (Ger 1921)
Zum Paradies der Damen (Ger 1922)
Sylvester (Ger 1923)
Weltspiegel (Ger 1923)
Das Haus der Lüge (Ger 1925)
Das Panzergewölbe (Ger 1926)
Napoleon auf St. Helena (Ger 1929)
Gassenhauer (Ger 1931)

PIEL, HARRY, b. 1892, Düsseldorf, Germany; d. July 12, 1963
Das amerikanische duell (Ger 19--) (also actor)
Die Rache der Grafin Barnetti (Ger 19--)
Sein Todfeind (Ger 19--)
Der stumme Zeuge (Ger 19--)
Zur Strecke gebracht (Ger 19--)
Ben Ali Bey (Ger 1913)
As actor and director:
Police 1111 (Ger 1916)
Unter heisser Sonne (Ger 1916)
Das Auge des Götzen (Ger 1919)
Das Geheimnis des Zirkus Barre (Ger 1920)
Der grosse Coup (Ger 1919)
Über den Wolken (Ger 1919)
Das geheimnisvolle Telephon (Ger 1921)
Luftpiraten (Ger 1921)
Der brennende Berg (Ger 1921)
Das fliegende Auto (Ger 1921)
Der Fürst der Berge (Ger 1921)
Das Gefangnis auf dem Meeresgrunde (Ger 1921)
Das Geheimnis der Katakomben (Ger 1921)
Das lebende Ratsel (Ger 1921)
Panik (Ger 1921)
Der Ritt unter Wasser (Ger 1921)
Die Todesfalle (Ger 1921)
Unus, der Weg in die Welt (Ger 1921)
Der Verachter des Todes (Ger 1921)
Das schwarze Kouvert (Ger 1922)
Das verschwundene Haus (Ger 1922) (also producer)

Abenteuer einer Nacht (Ger 1923) (also co-producer)
Die letzte Kampf (Ger 1923)
Menschen und Masken (Ger 1923)
Rivalen (Ger 1923)
Auf gefährlichen Spuren (Ger 1924)
Der Mann ohne Nerven (Ger 1924) (also producer)
Abenteuer im Nachtexpress (Ger 1925)
Schneller als der Tod (Ger 1925)
Zigaro, der Brigant von Monte Diavolo (Ger 1925) (also producer)
Achtung Harry! Augen auf! (Ger 1926)
Der schwarze Pierro 26 (also co-script)
Was ist los im Zirkus Beely? (Ger 1926)
Rätsel einer Nacht (Ger 1927)
Sein grosster Bluff (Ger 1927)
Mann gegen Mann (Ger 1928)
Panik (Ger 1928)
Seine stärkste Waffe (Ger 1929)
Männer ohne Beruf (Ger 1929)
Die Mitternachts-Taxe (Ger 1929)
Sein bester Freund (Ger 1929)
Achtung! Auto-Diebe! (Ger 1930)
Menschen im Feuer (Ger 1930)
Er oder ich (Ger 1930)
Bobby geht los (Ger 1931)
Schatten der Unterwelt (Ger 1931)
Der Geheimagent (Ger 1932)
Jonny stiehlt Europa (Ger 1932)
Das Schiff ohne Hafen (Ger 1932)
Sprung in den Abgrund (Ger 1933)
Ein Unsichtbarer geht durch die Stadt (Ger 1933)
Der Herr der Welt (Ger 1934) (only director)
Die Welt ohne Maske (Ger 1934)
Artisten (Ger 1935)
90 Minuten Aufenthalt (Ger 1936)
Der Dschungel raft (Ger 1936)
Sein bester Freund (Ger 1937)
Menschen, Tiere, Sensationen (Ger 1938)
Der unmögliche Herr Pitt (Ger 1938)
Gesprengte Gitter (Ger 1940)
Panik (Ger 1940-1943)
Der Mann im Sattel (Ger 1945)
Der Tiger Akbar (Ger 1950)

PIEROTTI, PIERO (a.k.a. Peter E. Stanley), b. Jan. 1, 1912,
    Pisa, Italy
    L'arciere nero (It 1959)
    La scimitarra del saraceno (It 1959)
    Calvalcata selvaggia (It 1960)
    Marco Polo (It 1962)
    Una regina per Cesare (It 1963)
    Napoleone a Firenza (It 1964)
    Golia e il cavaliere mascherato (It 1964)

Il ponte dei sospiri (It 1964)
Ercole contro Roma (It 1964)
Zorro il ribelle (It 1966)
Sansone e il tesoro degli Incas (It 1968)
Assalto al tesore di stato (It 1968)
Testa o croce (It 1969)

PIETRANGELI, ANTONIO, b. Jan. 19, 1919, Rome, d. July 12,
    1968
    Il sole negli occhi (It 1953) (also story, script)
    Amori di mezzo secolo (ep "1910") (It 1954) (also co-story,
        co-script for episode)
    Lo scapolo (It 1956) (also co-story, co-script)
    Souvenir d'Italie [It Happened in Rome] (It 1957) (also co-
        script)
    Nata di marzo (It 1960) (also co-story, co-script)
    Adua e la compagne [Love a la Carte] (It 1960) (also co-script)
    Fantasmi a Roma [Ghosts of Rome] (It 1961) (also co-script)
    La parmigiana (It 1963) (also co-script)
    La visita (It 1964) (also co-story, co-script)
    Il magnifico cornuto [The Magnificent Cuckold] (It-Fr 1964)
    Io la conoscevo bene (It-Ger-Fr 1965) (also co-story, co-
        script)
    Le fate [The Queens] (ep "Fata maria") (It 1966)
    Come, Quando e perché (It 1968)
    L'Assoluto naturale (It 1969)

PLATTS-MILLS, BARNEY
    Bronco Bullfrog (BL 1970) (also script)
    Private Road (Maya 1971) (also script)

POLLET, JEAN-DANIEL, b. June 20, 1936, Paris
    Mediteranée (Fr 1963) (also script)
    La Ligne de mire (Unfinished Fr 1959-1963)
    Paris vu par ... [Six in Paris] (ep "Rue Saint-Denis") (Fr
        1964) (also script)
    Un Balle au coeur [A Shot in the Heart] (Fr 1965) (also co-
        script)
    Tu imagines Robinson (Fr 1969) (also script)
    L'Amour c'est gai, l'amour c'est triste (Fr 1970) (also script)
    Le Maître du temps (Fr 1970) (also script)

POLLOCK, GEORGE, b. 1907, Leicester
    Stranger in Town (Eros 1957)
    Rooney (RFD 1958)
    Sally's Irish Rogue (BL 1958)
    Broth of a Boy (BL 1959)
    Don't Panic Chaps! (Col Br 1959)
    And the Same to You (Eros 1960)
    Murder She Said (MGM Br 1961)
    Village of Daughters (MGM Br 1962)
    Kill or Cure (MGM Br 1962)
    Murder at the Gallop (MGM Br 1963)

Murder Most Foul (MGM Br 1964)
Murder Ahoy (MGM Br 1964)
Ten Little Indians (WPD 1965)

PONTECORVO, GILLO (Gilberto Pontecorvo), b. Nov. 19, 1919,
    Pisa, Italy
La grande strada azzurra (It 1957)
Kapò (It 1960)
La battaglia di Algeri (It 1966)
Queimada (Burn) (It 1969)
Cristo non voleva morire (It 1972)

POWELL, MICHAEL (Michael Latham Powell), b. Sept. 30, 1905,
    Canterbury, Kent, England
Two Crowded Hours (Fox Br 1931)
Rynox (Ideal 1931)
My Friend the King (Fox Br 1931)
The Rasp (Fox Br 1931)
The Star Reporter (Fox Br 1931)
Hotel Splendide (Ideal 1932)
C. O. D. (UA Br 1932)
His Lordship (UA Br 1932)
Born Lucky (MGM Br 1932)
The Fire Raisers (W & F 1933) (also co-script)
The Night of the Party (Gaumont 1934)
Something Always Happens (WB Br 1934)
The Girl in the Crowd (FN Br 1934)
Red Ensign [Strike!] (Gaumont 1934) (also co-script)
Lazybones (Radio Br 1935)
The Love Test (Fox Br 1935)
Some Day (WB Br 1935)
The Phantom Light (Gaumont 1935)
Her Last Affaire (PDC 1935)
The Price of a Song (Fox Br 1935)
The Brown Wallet (FN Br 1936)
Crown vs. Stevens (WB Br 1936) (made in 1934)
The Man Behind the Mask (MGM Br 1936)
Edge of the World (BIED 1937) (also script)
The Lion Has Wings (UA Br 1939) (with Brian Desmond Hurst,
    Adrian Brunel)
The Spy in Black [U-Boat 29] (Col Br 1939)
The Thief of Bagdad (UA Br 1940) (with Ludwig Berger, Tim
    Whelan)
Contraband [Blackout] (Anglo 1940) (also co-script)
49th Parallel [The Invaders] (GFD 1941) (also co-producer)
One of Our Aircraft is Missing (Anglo 1942) (with Emeric
    Pressburger) (also co-producer, co-script)
The Life and Death of Colonel Blimp [Colonel Blimp] (GFD
    1943) (with Emerie Pressburger) (also co-producer, co-
    script)
The Volunteer (Anglo 1943) (with Emeric Pressburger) (also
    co-producer, co-script)
A Canterbury Tale (EL 1944) (with Emeric Pressburger) (also

co-producer, co-script)
I Know Where I'm Going (GFD 1945) (with Emeric Pressburger)
(also co-producer, co-script)
A Matter of Life and Death [Stairway to Heaven] (GFD 1946)
(with Emeric Pressburger) (also co-producer, co-script)
Black Narcissus (GFD 1947) (with Emeric Pressburger) (also co-
producer, co-script)
The Red Shoes (GFD 1948) (with Emeric Pressburger) (also co-
producer, co-script)
The Small Back Room (BL 1949) (with Emeric Pressburger)
(also co-producer, co-script)
Gone to Earth [The Wild Heart] (BL 1950) (with Emeric Pressburger and uncredited Reuben Mamoulian) (also co-script)
The Elusive Pimpernel (BL 1950) (with Emeric Pressburger)
(also co-script)
Tales of Hoffman (BL 1951) (with Emeric Pressburger) (also
co-producer, co-script)
Oh, Rosalinda!! (ABP 1955) (with Emeric Pressburger) (also
co-producer, co-script)
The Battle of the River Plate [Pursuit of the Graf Spee] (RFD
1956) (with Emeric Pressburger) (also co-producer, co-
script)
Ill Met by Moonlight [Night Ambush] (RFD 1957) (with Emeric
Pressburger) (also co-producer, co-script)
Luna de Miel [Honeymoon] (Sp-GB 1958) (also co-producer, co-
script)
Peeping Tom (AA 1960) (also producer, actor)
The Queen's Guards (20th Br 1961) (also producer)
Bluebeard's Castle (Aus TV 1964)
They're a Weird Mob (Aust-GB 1966) (also producer)
Age of Consent (Aust 1968) (also co-producer)
The Boy Who Turned Yellow (CFF 1972)

PREVERT, PIERRE, b. May 26, 1906, Paris
L'Affaire est dans le sac (Fr 1932) (also actor)
Adieu Léonard (Fr 1943) (also co-story, co-script, co-dia-
logue, actor)
Voyage-surprise (Fr 1946) (also co-story, co-script, actor)

PUCCINI, GIANNI, b. Nov. 9, 1914, Milan; d. Dec. 3, 1968
Il capitano di Venezia (It 1952)
Parola di ladro (It 1957)
Il marito (It 1958)
Carmela è una bambola (It 1958)
Il nemico di mia moglie (It 1959)
L'impiegato (It 1959)
Il carro armato dell'8 settembre (It 1960)
L'attico (It 1963)
Cuori infranti (ep "E vissero felici") (It 1963)
Amore facile (It 1964)
L'idea fissa (ep "La prima notte è Sabata 18 luglio") (It 1964)
Amore in quattro dimensioni (ep "Amore e arte") (It 1964)
Io uccido, tu uccidi (It 1965)

I soldi (It 1965) (with Giorgio Cavedon)
Racconti a due piazze (ep) (It 1966)
Ballata da un miliardo (It 1967)
Dove si spara di più (It 1967)
I settle fratelli Cervi (It 1968)

QUILICI, FOLCO, b. April 9, 1930, Ferrara, Italy
Sesto continente (It 1954)
L'ultimo paradiso (It 1957)
Tam tam mayumbe (It 1958) (with co-director)
Dagli Appennini alle Ande (It 1959)
Ti-Kojo e il suo pescecane (It 1962)
Le schiave esistono ancora (It 1964)
Una spiagga lontana (It 1970)
Oceano (It 1971)

RABENALT, ARTHUR MARIA, b. May 15, 1905, Vienna
Pappi (Ger 1934) (also co-script)
Eine Siebzehnjährige (Ger 1934)
Was bin ich ohne Dich (Ger 1934)
Ein Kind, ein Hund, ein Vagabund (Ger 1934)
Das Frauenparadies (Ger 1936)
Die Liebe des Maharadscha (Ger 1936)
Millionenerbschaft (Ger 1937)
Liebelei und Liebe (Ger 1937)
Männer mussen so sein (Ger 1939)
Johannisfeuer (Ger 1939)
Flucht ins Dunkel (Ger 1939)
Weisser Flieder (Ger 1940)
Achtung! Feind hört mit! (Ger 1940)
Die 3 Codonas (Ger 1940)
Leichte Muse (Ger 1941)
... reitet für Deutschland (Ger 1941)
Fronttheater (Ger 1941)
Meine Frau Teresa (Ger 1942)
Liebespremiere (Ger 1943)
Zirkus Renz (Ger 1943)
Die Schuld der Gabriele Rottweil (Ger 1944)
Am Abend nach der Oper (Ger 1944)
Regimentsmusik (Ger 1945)
Wir beide liebten Katharina (Ger 1945)
Chemie und Liebe (Ger 1948)
Morgen ist alles besser (Ger 1948)
Anonyme Briefe (Ger 1949)
Das Mädchen Christine (Ger 1949)
Martina (Ger 1949)
Nächte am Nil (Ger 1949)
Die Frau von gestern Nacht (Ger 1950)
O Ohr 15, Zimmer 9 (Ger 1950)
Hochzeit im Heu (Ger 1951)
Unvergangliches Licht (Ger 1951)
Die Försterchristil (Ger 1952)
Das weisse Abenteuer (Ger 1952)

Alraune (Ger 1952)
Wir tanzen auf dem Regenbogen (Ger 1952) (with C. Gallone)
Die Fiakermilli (Ger 1953)
Lavendel (Ger 1953) (also co-script)
Der letzte Walzer (Ger 1953)
Der Vogelhändler (Ger 1953)
Der unsterbliche Lump (Ger 1953)
Die Sonne von St. Moritz (Ger 1954)
Der Zigeunerbaron (Ger 1954)
Der Zarewitsch (Ger 1954)
Solang' es hübsche Mädchen gibt (Ger 1955)
Unternehmen Schlafsack (Ger 1955)
Liebe ist ja nur ein Märchen (Ger 1955)
Die Ehe des Dr. med. Danwitz (Ger 1956)
Tierarzt Dr. Vlimmen (Ger 1956)
Zwischen Zeit und Ewigkeit (Ger 1956)
Glücksritter (Ger 1957)
Frühling in Berlin (Ger 1957)
Für zwei Groschen Zärtlichkeit (Ger 1957)
Eine Frau, die weiss was sie will (Ger 1958) (also co-script)
Das haut einen Seemann doch nicht um (Ger 1958)
Vergiss mein nicht (Ger 1958)
Geliebte Bestie (Ger 1958)
Lass mich am Sonntag nicht allein (Ger 1959)
Das grosse Wunschkonzert (Ger 1960)
Der Held meiner Träume (Ger 1960)
Mann im Schatten (Ger 1961)

RACIOPPI, ANTONIO, b. 1928, Rome
Tempo di villeggiature (It 1956)
La congiura dei Borgia (It 1958)
La donna di ghiaccio (It 1961)
Tempo di credere (It 1962)
K. O. va e uccidi (It 1967) (only script)
Brucia, ragazzo, brucia (It 1967) (only story, script)
Mio padre Monsignore (It 1970)
La "mano nera," prima della mafia, più della mafia (It 1972)
Le mille e una notte all'italiana (It 1972)

RADEMAKERS, FONS, b. Sept. 5, 1920, Roosendael (Brabant),
    Netherlands
Dorp aan de Rivier [Doctor in the Village] (Dut 1957)
Makkers, Staakt uw Wild Gerass [That Joyous Eve] (Dut 1959)
Het Mes [The Knife] (Dut 1961)
Als Twee Druppels Water [The Spitting Image] (Dut 1963) (also
    producer)
De Dans van de Reiger [The Dance of the Heron] (Dut-Fr-Yug
    1966) (also co-producer, script)
Mira--De Teleurgang van der Waterhoek (Bel-Dut 1971)
Niet Voor de Poesen [Because of the Cats] (Dut-Bel 1973) (also
    producer)
Max Havelaar (Dut-Indonesian 1975)

REED, CAROL (SIR), b. Dec. 30, 1906, Putney, London
   It Happened in Paris (ABFD 1935) (with Robert Wyler)
   Midshipman Easy [Men of the Sea] (ABFD 1935)
   Laburnum Grove (ABFD 1936)
   Talk of the Devil (UA Br 1936) (also co-author, co-script)
   Who's Your Lady Friend? (ABFD 1937)
   Bank Holiday [Three on a Weekend] (GFD 1938)
   Penny Paradise (ABFD 1938)
   Climbing High (MGM Br 1938)
   A Girl Must Live (20th Br 1939)
   The Stars Look Down (GN 1939)
   Night Train to Munich [Night Train] (MGM Br 1940)
   The Girl in the News (MGM Br 1940)
   Kipps [The Remarkable Mr. Kipps] (20th Br 1941)
   The Young Mr. Pitt (20th Br 1942)
   The New Lot (Army Kinematograph Unit 1943)
   The Way Ahead (EL 1944)
   The True Glory (MOI 1945) (with Garson Kanin)
   Odd Man Out (GFD 1947) (also producer)
   The Fallen Idol (BL 1948) (also co-producer)
   The Third Man (BL 1949)
   Outcast of the Islands (BL 1951) (also producer)
   The Man Between (BL 1953) (also producer)
   A Kid for Two Farthings (IFD 1955) (also producer)
   Trapeze (USA) (UA 1956) (also producer)
   The Key (Col Br 1958)
   Our Man in Havana (Col Br 1960) (also co-producer)
   Mutiny on the Bounty (USA) (MGM 1962) (uncredited, replaced
      by Lewis Milestone; also uncredited reputedly George Seaton,
      Richard Thorpe, Billy Wilder, Andrew Marton, Marlon
      Brando)
   The Running Man (Col Br 1963) (also co-producer)
   The Agony and the Ecstasy (US-It) (20th 1965) (also producer)
   Oliver! (Col Br 1968)
   Flap [The Last Warrior] (USA) (WB 1970)
   Follow Me! (RFD 1971)

REEVES, MICHAEL, b. 1944, London(?); d. Feb. 11, 1969
   Il castello dei morti vivi [Castle of the Living Dead] (It-Fr
      1964) (direction on English prints credited to Herbert Wise
      [pseud. of Luciano Ricci], but other sources credit the
      writer Warren Kiefer with direction and suggest that Reeves
      completed the final two weeks of shooting.)
   La sorella di Satana [The Revenge of the Blood Beast] (It 1965)
   The Sorcerors (Tigon 1967) (also co-script)
   Witchfinder General [The Conqueror Worm] (Tigon 1968) (also
      co-script)

REGUEIRO, FRANCISCO, b. Aug. 2, 1934, Valladolid, Spain
   El primer amor (Sp 1962)
   El buen amor (Sp 1963) (also script)
   Amador (Sp 1965) (also script)
   Si volvemos a vernos [Smashing Up!] (Sp 1967) (also co-script)

Carol Reed (right) with Sir Ralph Richardson on the set of The
Fallen Idol (1948).

    Me anveneno de azules (Sp 1969) (also co-script)
    Carta de amor de un asesino (Sp 1974)

REICHENBACH, FRANÇOIS, b. July 3, 1924, Paris
    L'Amérique insolite [America the Unexpected] (Fr 1960)
    Un coeur gros comme ça! [The Winner] (Fr 1962)
    Les Amoureux du France (Fr-It 1964) (with Pierre Grimblat)
    Treize Jours en France [Challenge in the Snow] (Fr 1968) (with
       Claude Lelouch)
    Arthur Rubenstein: l'amour de la vie [Love of Life] (Fr 1969)
    La Caravane d'amour [We Have Come for Your Daughters] (Fr-
       US 1971)
    Johnny Hallyday (Fr 1971)
    Monte-Carlo (Fr 1972)
    La Raison du plus fou (Fr 1973) (also co-script)

REINL, HARALD, b. 1908, Bad Ischl, Germany
  Bergkristall (Ger 1949) (also co-script)
  Gesetz ohne Gnade (Ger 1950)
  Fegefeuer der Liebe (Ger 1951) (also script)
  Der Herrgrottschnitzer von Ammergau (Ger 1952)
  Hinter Klostermauern (Ger 1952) (also script)
  Der Klosterjager (Ger 1953)
  Rosen-Resli (Ger 1954) (also co-script)
  Der schweigende Engel (Ger 1954) (also co-script)
  Ein Herz schlägt für Erika (Ger 1955)
  Solange du lebst (Ger 1955) (also co-script)
  Die Fischerin vom Bodensee (Ger 1956) (also co-script)
  Johannisnacht (Ger 1956)
  Die Prinzessin von St. Wolfgang (Ger 1957) (also co-script)
  Almenrausch und Edelweiss (Ger 1957)
  Die Zwillinge vom Zillertal (Ger 1957) (also co-script)
  Die grünen Teufel von Monte Cassino (Ger 1958)
  Romarei, das Mädchen mit den grünen Augen (Ger 1958)
  U 47--Kapitänleutnant Prien (Ger 1958)
  Der Frosch mit der Maske [The Face of the Frog] (Ger 1959)
  Paradies der Matrosen (Ger 1959)
  Die Bande des Schreckens [The Terrible People] (Ger 1960)
  Der Fälscher von London [The Forger of London] (Ger 1960)
  Im Stahlnetz des Dr. Mabuse (Ger 1961)
  Der Schatz im Silbersee (Ger 1962)
  Teppich des Grauens (Ger-It-Sp 1962)
  Die unsichtbaren Krallen des Dr. Mabuse (Ger 1962)
  Die weisse Spinne (Ger 1963)
  Winnetou I (Ger-Yug 1963)
  Der Würger von Schloss Blackmoor (Ger 1963)
  Winnetou II (Ger-Fr-Yug 1964)
  Zimmer 13 [Room 13] (Ger 1964)
  Der letzte Mohikaner (Ger-It 1965)
  Der unheimliche Mönch (Ger 1965)
  Winnetou III (Ger-Yug 1965)
  Die Nibelungen I & II (Ger 1967) (also co-script)
  Die Schlangengrube und das Pendel (Ger 1967)
  Dynamit in grüner Seide (Ger-It 1968)
  Todeschüsse am Broadway (Ger 1968)
  Der Tod im roten Jaguar (Ger-It 1968)
  Winnetou und Shatterhand im Tal der Toten (Ger-It-Yug 1968)
    (also co-script)
  Die Lümmel von der ersten Bank (Teil 3) [Wir Hau'n die Pauker
    in die Pfanne] (Ger 1970)
  Kommissar X jagt die roten tiger (Ger-It 1971)
  Wer zuletzt lacht, lacht am besten (Ger 1971)
  Grün ist die Heide (Ger 1972)
  Sie Liebten sich einen Sommer (Ger-It 1972)
  Die blutigen Geier von Alaska (Ger 1973)

REISZ, KAREL, b. 1926, Czechoslovakia
  We Are the Lambeth Boys (RFD 1958)
  Saturday Night and Sunday Morning (Bry 1960)

Night Must Fall (MGM Br 1964) (also co-producer)
Morgan--a Suitable Case for Treatment (BL 1966)
Isadora [The Loves of Isadora] (RFD 1969)
The Gambler (USA) (Par 1974)

RENOIR, JEAN, b. Sept. 15, 1894, Paris
La Fille de l'eau (Fr 1924) (also producer, set designer)
Nana (Fr 1926) (also producer, co-titles)
Charleston (Fr 1927) (also producer)
Marquitta (Fr 1927) (also producer)
La Petite Marchande d'allumettes (Fr 1928) (also co-producer,
    script, adaptor) (with Jean Tedesco)
Tire-au-flanc (Fr 1928) (also co-adaptor)
Le Tournoi (Fr 1929) (also script)
Le Bled (Fr 1929)
On Purge bébé (Fr 1931) (also script, dialogue)
La Chienne (Fr 1931) (also script, dialogue)
La Nuit de careefour (Fr 1932) (also script, dialogue)
Boudu sauvé des eux [Boudu Saved from Drowning] (Fr 1932)
    (also script, dialogue)
Chotard et Cie (Fr 1933) (also script, dialogue)
Madame Bovary (Fr 1934) (also script, adaptor, dialogue)
Toni (Fr 1934) (also co-script)
Le Crime de Monsieur Lange (Fr 1935) (also co-adaptor)
Une partie de campagne (Unfinished Fr 1936) (also script, dia-
    logue, actor) (released 1946)
La Vie est à nous (Fr 1936) (also co-script)
Les Bas-Fonds (Fr 1936) (also co-adaptor, co-dialogue)
La Grande Illusion (Fr 1937) (also co-script, co-dialogue)
La Marseillaise (Fr 1938) (also co-script, co-dialogue)
La Bête humaine (Fr 1938) (also script, dialogue, actor)
La Règle du jeu (Fr 1939) (also co-script, co-dialogue, actor)
La Tosca (It 1940) (also co-script) (film begun by Renoir, but
    finished by Carl Koch)
Swamp Water (USA) (20th 1941)
This Land Is Mine (USA) (RKO 1943) (also co-script)
The Southerner (USA) (UA 1945) (also script, dialogue)
The Diary of a Chambermaid (USA) (UA 1946) (also co-adaptor)
The Woman on the Beach (USA) (RKO 1946) (also co-adaptor,
    co-dialogue)
The River (India 1950) (also co-adaptor, co-dialogue)
La carrozza d'oro [Le Carrosse d'or; The Golden Coach] (It-
    Fr 1952) (also co-adaptor, co-dialogue)
French Cancan (Fr-It 1955) (also script, dialogue)
Eléna et les hommes [Paris Does Strange Things] (Fr-It 1956)
    (also script, co-adaptor, co-dialogue, song lyrics)
Le Déjeuner sur l'herbe (Fr 1959)† [co-production company]
    (also script, dialogue)
Le Testament du Dr. Cordelier (Fr 1959) (also script, narrator)
Le Caporal épinglé [The Vanishing Corporal] (Fr 1962) (also co-
    script, co-dialogue)
Le Petit Théâtre de Jean Renoir (Fr-It-W Ger TV 1969) (also
    producer, script, dialogue, narrator)

RESNAIS, ALAIN, b. June 3, 1922, Vannes
  Schema d'une identification ouvert pour cause d'inventaire (Fr
    1945) (A 16mm feature, all copies of which are lost)
  Hiroshima mon amour (Fr-Japan 1959)
  L'Année dernière à Marienbad [Last Year at Marienbad] (Fr-It
    1961)
  Muriel ou le temps d'un retour [Muriel] (Fr-It 1964)
  La Guerre est finie [The War Is Over] (Fr-Sw 1965)
  Loin du Vietnam [Far from Vietnam] (Fr 1967) (with William
    Klein, Joris Ivens, Agnes Varda, Claude Lelouch, Jean-Luc
    Godard)
  Je t'aime, je t'aime (Fr 1967)
  Stavisky (Fr 1974)

RIBEIRO, ANTONIO LOPES, b. April 16, 1908, Lisbon
  Fraulein Lausbub (Por-Ger 1933) (with Max Nosseck)
  Gado Bravo (Por 1933)
  Revolução de Maio (Por 1936) (also producer)
  Feitico do imperio (Por 1940)
  O pai tirano (Por 1941) (also co-script)
  Frei Luis de Sousa (Por 1950)
  O primo basilio (Por 1959)

António Lopes Ribeiro

RICHARDSON, TONY, b. June 5, 1928, Shipley, Yorkshire, England
  Look Back in Anger (ABP 1959)
  The Entertainer (Bry 1960)

Sanctuary (USA) (20th 1961)
A Taste of Honey (Bry 1961) (also co-script)
The Loneliness of the Long Distance Runner (Bry 1962) (also co-producer)
Tom Jones (UA British 1963) (also producer)
The Loved One (USA) (MGM 1965)
Mademoiselle (GB-Fr) (UA Br 1966)
The Sailor from Gibraltar (UA Br 1967) (also co-script)
The Charge of the Light Brigade (UA Br 1968)
Ned Kelly (UA Br 1970) (also co-script)
Dead Cert (UA Br 1974) (also co-script)
A Delicate Balance (American Film Theatre 1973)

Tony Richardson (right) and cameraman Desmond Davies planning the next shot on The Loneliness of the Long Distance Runner (1962).

RIEFENSTAHL, LENI (HELENE, BERTHA AMALIE), b. Aug. 22, 1922, Berlin
Das blaue Licht (Ger 1932) (also producer, story, actress)
Der Sieg des Glaubens (Ger 1933)
Triumph des Willens (Ger 1934)
Tag der Freiheit--unsere Wehrmacht (Ger 1935)
Fest der Völker (Ger 1936) (also script)

Fest der Schönheit (Ger 1936) (also script)
Tiefland (Ger 1945) (also producer, script, camera, actress)
     (released in 1954)
Schwarze Fracht (unfinished) (Ger 1956)

RIGHELLI, GENNARO, b. Dec. 12, 1886, Salerno, Italy; d. Jan.
     6, 1949
Giovanna la pallida (It 1911) (also script)
La fidanzata di Messina (It 1911)
La vita di una chanteuse (It 1911)
La portatrice di pane (It 1911) (only actor)
Due destini (It 1911)
Andreuccio da Perugia (It 1911)
Decamerone (It 1911)
L'eroica fanciulla di Derna (It 1911)
Lotta nella tenebre (It 1911)
Per la tua bambina (It 1911)
Tugendbund (It 1911)
Il capriccio di un principe (It 1913)
Hussein il pirata (It 1913)
Primo ed ultimo bacio (It 1916)
Febbre di gloria (It 1916)
L'articolo IV (It 1916)
Come le foglie (It 1916)
Per tutta la vita (It 1917)
C'erà una volta (It 1917)
Un'ombra che passa (It 1917)
200 all'ora (It 1917)
Demonietta (It 1917)
Il veleno del piacere (It 1917)
La regina del carbone (It 1918)
Le avventure di Doloretta (It 1918)
Quando tramonta il sole (It 1918)
La peccatrice casta (It 1919)
La signora della perle (It 1919)
La vergine folle (It 1919)
La casa di vetro (It 1920)
L'orrizzontale (It 1920)
Caina (It 1920)
Il richiamo (It 1920)
La canaglia di Parigi (It 1921)
Amore rosso (It 1921) (also script)
Il viaggio (It 1921)
La cassa sotto le neve (It 1921)
L'incognita (It 1922)
Orient (Ger 1923)
La Vie de Bohème [La Bohème] (Ger 1923)
Una moglie e ... due mariti (It 1924)
Transatlantisches [Il transatlantico] (Ger 1925)
Ivangorod [La fortezza di Ivangorod] (Ger 1925)
Catene (Ger 1925)
Der Meister des Welt [Il campione del mondo] (Ger 1925)
Das Mädchen mit der Protektion [Il ragattiere di Amsterdam]

Heimweh [Gli esiliati del Volga] (Ger 1927)
Svengali [Il dominio delle tenebre] (Ger 1927)
Trapezio [Il cerchio dei pugnali] (Ger 1928)
Frauenraub in Marokko [Il rovente Sahara] (Ger 1928)
Der geheime Kurier [Le rouge et le noir] (Ger 1928)
Der Präsident [Il presidente di Costanueva] (Ger 1928)
Il rapido siberiano [Il direttissimo della Siberia] (Ger 1928)
La canzone dell'amore (It 1930)
La scala (It 1931)
Patatrac (It 1931)
L'armata azzurra (It 1932)
Al buio insieme (It 1933)
Il presidente della Ba. Ce. Cre. Mi (It 1933)
Il signore desidera? (It 1933)
La fanciulla dell'altro mondo (It 1934)
L'ultimo dei Bergerac (It 1934)
Quei due (It 1935)
Re burlone (It 1935)
La luce del mondo (It 1935)
Aria del continente (It 1935)
Amazzoni bianche (It 1936)
Lo smemorato (It 1936)
Pensaci Giocomino! (It 1936)
Gatta ci cova (It 1937)
Lasciate ogni speranza! (It 1937)
L'allegro cantante (It 1938)
Hanno rapito un uomo (It 1938)
Il destino in tasca (It 1938)
Fuschi d'artificio (It 1938)
La voce senza volto (It 1938)
L'ultimo scugnizzo (It 1938)
Il cavaliere di San Marco (It 1939)
Il barone di Corbo (It 1939)
Due occhi per non vedere (It 1939)
Le educan le Saint'Cyr (It 1939)
L'eredità in corsa (It 1939)
Forse eri tu l'amore (It 1940)
Manovre d'amore (It 1940)
Il pozzo dei miracoli (It 1941)
L'attore scomparso (It 1941)
Orizzonte di sangue (It 1942)
Colpi di timone (It 1942)
Tempesta sul golfo (It 1942)
La storia di una capinera (It 1943)
Abbasso la miseria! (It 1946)
Abbasso la ricchezza! (It 1946)
Il corriere del re (It 1947)

RILLA, WOLF, b. 1920, Germany
    Noose for a Lady (AA 1953)
    Glad Tidings (Eros 1953) (also script)
    Marilyn (Butcher 1953) (also script)
    The Large Rope (UA Br 1953)

The End of the Road (BL 1954)
The Black Rider (Butcher 1954)
Stock Car (Butcher 1955)
The Blue Peter [Navy Heroes] (Bl 1955)
Pacific Destiny (BL 1956)
The Scamp (GN 1957)
Bachelor of Hearts (RFD 1958)
Witness in the Dark (RFD 1959)
Village of the Damned (MGM Br 1960) (also co-script)
Piccadilly Third Stop (RFD 1960)
Jessy (Renown 1961)
Watch It Sailor! (Col Br 1961)
Cairo (MGM Br 1962)
The World Ten Times Over (WPD 1963)† [co-production com-
pany] (also script)
Secrets of a Door to Door Salesman (New Realm 1973)

RISI, DINO, b. Dec. 23, 1926, Milan
Vacanze col gangster [Vacation with a Gangster] (It 1952) (also
co-story, co-script)
Il viale della speranza (It 1953) (also co-producer, co-story,
co-script)
Amore in città [Love in the City] (ep "Paradiso per quattro
ore") (It 1953)
Il segno di Venere (It 1955)
Pane, amore e ... [Scandal in Sorrento] (It 1955) (also co-
story, co-script)
Poveri ma belli [Poor but Handsome] (It 1956) (also co-story,
co-script)
La Nonna Sabella (It 1957) (also co-script)
Bella ma povere [Irresistible] (It 1958) (also co-script)
Venezia, la luna e tu (It 1958) (also co-script)
Pòveri milionàri (It 1959) (also co-story, co-script)
Il vedovo (It 1960) (also co-story, co-script)
Il mattatore [Love and Larceny] (It 1960)
Un amore e Roma (It-Fr 1960) (also co-story)
Una vita difficile (It 1961)
Il sorpasso [The Easy Life] (It 1962)
La marcia su Roma (It 1962) (also co-script)
I mostri (It 1963) (also co-script)
il giovedì [Thursday] (It 1963) (also co-script)
Il gaucho (It 1964)
Le bambole [Four Kinds of Love] (ep "La telefonata") (It 1965)
I complessi (ep "Una giornata decisiva") (It 1965)
I nostri marita (ep "Il marito di Attilia) (It 1966)
L'ombrellone [Weekend Italian Style] (It 1966) (also co-script)
Operazione San Gennaro (It-Fr-Ger 1966) (also co-story, co-
script)
Il tigre [The Tiger and the Pussycat] (It 1967) (also co-story)
Il profeta [Mr. Kinky] (It 1968)
Straziami, ma di baci saziami (It 1968) (also co-story, co-
script)
Il giovane normale (It 1969) (also co-script)

Vedo nudo (It 1969)
La moglie del prete [The Priest's Wife] (It 1970)
In nome del popolo italiano (It 1971)
Mordi e fuggi (It-Fr 1972)
Sessomatto (It 1973)
Profumo di donna (It 1974)

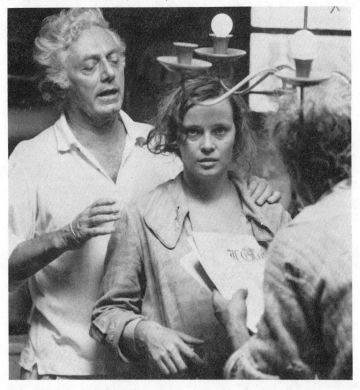

Dino Risi with actress Laura Antonelli on the set of Sessomatto (1973).

RISI, NELO, b. 1920, Milan
Andremo in città (It 1966)
Diario di una schizofrenica (It 1968)
Ondata di calore (It 1969)
Una stagione all'inferno (It 1971)
Eloisa e Abelardo (It 1972)

RITTER, KARL, b. 1888, Wurzburg, Germany
Weiberregiment (Ger 1936)
Verräter (Ger 1936)

Internehmen Michael (Ger 1937) (also co-script)
Urlaub auf Ehrenwort (Ger 1937)
Patrioten (Ger 1937) (also co-script)
Pour le mérite (Ger 1938) (also co-script)
Legion Condor (Ger 1939) (also co-script)
Capriccio (Ger 1939)
Die Hochzeitsreiser (Ger 1939) (also co-script)
Bal paré (Ger 1940) (also co-script)
Kadetten (Ger 1941) (also co-script)
Über alles in der Welt (Ger 1941) (also co-script)
Stukas (Ger 1941) (also co-script)
G. P. U. (Ger 1942) (also co-script)
Dora (Ger 1943) (also co-script)
Sommernachte (Ger 1944)
Das Leben geht weiter (Ger 1945) (only co-script)
Ball der Nationen (Ger 1954)
Staatsanwaltin Corda (Ger 1954)

RIVETTE, JACQUES, b. March 1, 1928, Rouen, France
Paris nous appartient (Fr 1960) (also co-script, co-dialogue)
La Religieuse (Fr 1966) (also co-adaptor, co-dialogue)
L'Amour fou [Mad Love] (Fr 1969) (also co-script)
Out One (Fr 1971) (also co-script) (with Suzanne Schiffman)
Out one: Spectre (Fr 1972) [Shortened version of Out One]
Céline et Julie vont en bateau [Celine and Julie Go Boating]
    (Fr 1974) (also co-script)

ROBBE-GRILLET, ALAIN, b. Aug. 18, 1922, Brest, France
L'Immortelle (Fr-It-Turk 1963) (also script)
Trans-Europ-Express [Trans Europe Express] (Fr 1967) (also
    script)
L'Homme qui ment [The Man Who Lies] (Fr-Czech 1968) (also
    script)
L'Eden et après [Eden and After] (Fr-Czech 1970) (also script)
Glissements progressifs du plaisir (Fr 1973) (also script)
Le Jeu avec le feu (Fr-It 1974) (also script, dialogue)

ROBERT, YVES, b. June 19, 1920, Saumur, France
Les Hommes ne pensent qu'à ça (Fr 1953) (also co-script)
Ni vu ni connu (Fr 1958) (also co-adaptor)
Signé Arsène Lupin (Fr-It 1959) (also actor, co-script)
La Famille Fenouillard (Fr 1961) (also co-script)
La Guerre des boutons [The War of the Buttons] (Fr 1962)
    (also co-adaptor)
Bébert et l'omnibus (Fr 1963)† [co-production company]
Les Copains (Fr 1965)† [co-production company]
Monnaie de singe (Sp-It 1965)
Alexandre le bienheureux (Fr 1968)† [co-production company]
    (also co-script)
Clérambard (Fr 1969)† [co-production company] (also co-script)
Le Grand Blond avec une chaussure noire (Fr 1972)† [co-pro-
    duction company] (also co-script)
Salut l'artiste (Fr 1973)† [co-production company] (also

co-script)
Le Retour du grand blond (Fr 1974)

ROBISON, ARTHUR (ROBINSON), b. June 25, 1888, Chicago; d.
     1935?
Nacht des Grauens (Ger 1915)
Schatten (Ger 1922) (also co-script)
Zwischen Abends und Morgen (Ger 1923) (also script)
Pietro, der Korsar (Ger 1925) (also script)
Manon Lescaut (Ger 1926) (also script)
Der letzte Walzer (Ger 1927) (also co-script)
Looping the Loop (Ger 1928) (also co-script)
Frauenschicksal (Ger 1929)
The Informer (BIP 1929)
Jenny Lind (Fr version of A LADY'S MORALS) (USA) (MGM
     1930)
Mordprozess Mary Dugan (Ger version of THE TRIAL OF
     MARY DUGAN) (USA) (MGM 1931)
Quand on est belle (Fr version of THE EASIEST WAY) (USA)
     (MGM 1931)
Des jungen Dessauers grosse Liebe (Ger 1933)
Fürst Woronzeff (Ger 1934)
Le Secret des Woronzeff (Fr version of Fürst Woronzeff) (Ger
     1934)
Mach' mich glücklich (Ger 1935)
Tambour battant (Fr version of Des jungen Dessauers grosse
     Liebe) (Fr-Ger 1935)
Epoux célibataires (Fr 1933)
Monsieur le marquis (Fr 1933)
Der Student von Prag (Ger 1935)

ROCHA, RAULO, b. 1935, Porto, Portugal
Os verdes anos (Por 1963) (also script)
Mudar de vida (Por 1966) (also script)
Pousada das chagas (Por 1971) (also script)

ROEG, NICHOLAS, b. Aug. 15, 1928
Performance (WB Br 1970) (also camera) (made in 1968) (with
     Donald Cammell)
Walkabout (Australia 1970) (also camera)
Don't Look Now (GB-It) (BL 1973)

ROHMER, ERIC (Jean Marie Maurice Scherer), b. April 4, 1920,
     Nancy, France
Le Signe du Lion [The Sign of Leo] (Fr 1959) (also script)
La Carrière de Suzanne (Fr 1963) (also script)
Paris vu par ... [Six of a Kind] (ep "Place de l'Etoile") (Fr
     1964) (also script)
La Collectionneuse (Fr 1966) (also script)
Ma nuit chez Maud [My Night with Maud] (Fr 1969) (also
     script)
Le Genou de Claire [Claire's Knee] (Fr 1970) (also script)
L'Amour, l'après-midi [Love in the Afternoon] (Fr 1972) (also
     script)

Arthur Robison

ROSI, FRANCESCO, b. Nov. 15, 1922, Naples, Italy
    Camicie rosse [Red Shirts] (It 1953) (with Goffredo Alessandro,
      Franco Rossi)
    La sfida (It 1957)
    I magliardi (It 1959)
    Salvatore Giulano (It 1962)
    Le mani sulla città (It 1963)
    Il momento della verità [The Moment of Truth] (It 1964)
    C'era una volta (It 1967)
    Uomini contro (It 1970)
    Il caso matlei (It 1972)
    Lucky Luciano (It 1973)

ROSSELLINI, ROBERTO, b. May 8, 1906, Rome
    La nave bianca (It 1941) (with Francesco de Robertis) (also co-
      script)
    I Tre aguilotti (It 1942) (with Mario Mattoli)

Un pilota ritorna (It 1942)
L'invasore (It 1943) (supervised only)
L'uomo della croce (It 1943) (also co-script)
Roma, città aperta [Open City] (It 1945) (also co-script)
Desiderio (It 1946) (also co-script) (with Marcello Pagliero)
Paisa [Paisan] (It 1947) (also producer, co-story, co-script)
L'amore (ep "Una voca umana") (It 1948) (also co-script of
    episode)
Germania, anno zero [Germany Year Zero] (It-Ger 1948) (also
    co-story, co-script)
Francesco, giullare di dio [Flowers of St. Francis] (It 1950)
    (also co-script)
Stromboli, terra di dio [Stromboli] (It 1951)† (also story, co-
    script)
I sette peccati capitali [The Seven Capital Sins] (ep "L'invidia")
    (It-Fr 1952) (also story, co-script for episode)
Europa '51 [The Greatest Love] (It 1952) (also script)
La macchina ammazzacattivi (It 1952) (also script)
Siamo donne (ep "Ingrid Bergman") (It 1953)
Dov'è la libertà? (It 1954)
Viaggio in Italia [The Lonely Woman] (It 1954) (also co-script)
Amori di mezzo secolo (ep "Napoli '43") (It 1954)
Giovanna d'Arco al rogo (It 1954) (also script)
La paura [Angst/Fear] (It-Ger 1954)
Le psychodrame (It 1957)
Il generale della Rovere (It 1959) (also script)
India (It 1959-1960) (also producer)
Era notte a Roma (It 1960) (also co-script)
Viva l'Italia (It 1961) (also co-script)
Torino nei centi Anni (It TV 1961)
Vanina Vanini [The Betrayer] (It 1961)
Benito Mussolini (It 1962) (supervised only)
Anima nera (It 1962) (also script)
Rogapag (ep "Illibatezza") (It 1963) (also script for episode)
L'eta del ferro (It TV 1964)
La prise du pouvoir par Louis XIV (It TV 1966)
Idea di un'isola (It TV 1967)
Gli Atti degli Apostoli (It TV 1968)
El Mommua (Egy 1969) (supervised only)
La lotta dell'uorro per le sopra vivenza (It TV 1970)
Socrate (It TV 1970) (also co-script)
Sant'agostino (It TV 1972)
Pascal (It TV 1972)
L'amora vanti anni (It-Fr 1972)
L'eta di cosimo (It TV 1973)
The Age of the Medicins (It TV 1973)
Il messia (It 1974)
Cartesio (It TV 1974)
Anni Caldi (It 1974)

ROSSI, FRANCO, b. April 28, 1919, Firenze, Italy
I falsari (It 1952) (also co-script)
Camicie rosse [Red Shirts] (It 1953) (with Goffredo Alessandro,

Francesco Rosi)
Il seduttore (It 1954) (also co-script)
Amici per la pelle (It 1955)
Solo per te Lucia (It 1956)
Amore a prima vista (It 1958)
Calypso (It 1959) (also co-story, co-script) (with Leonardo
    Benvenuti, Golfiero Colonna)
Tutti innamorati (It 1959) (only supervisor)
Morte di un amico (It 1959) (also co-script)
Odissea nuda (It 1961) (also co-story, co-script)
Smog (It 1962) (also co-story, co-script)
Controsesso (ep "Cocaina di domenica") (It 1964)
Tre notti d'amore (e' "Moglie bambina") (It 1964)
Alta infedeltà [High Infidelity] (ep "Scandaloso") (It 1964)
I complessi (ep "I complessi della schiava nubiana") (It 1965)
Le bambole [Four Kinds of Love] (ep "La minestra") (It 1965)
Le streghe [The Witches] (ep "La siciliana") (It 1967) (also
    script for episode)
Una rosa per tutti (It 1967)
Non faccio la guerra, faccio l'amore [Don't make War, Make
    Love] (It 1967)
Le avventure di Ulisse (It 1969)
Giovinezza, giovinezza (It 1969)
Porgi l'altra guancia (It 1974)

ROUCH, JEAN, b. May 31, 1917, Paris
Les Fils de l'eau (Fr 1955) (also script, camera) (combination
    of 5 shorts made 1948-1951)
Moi un noir (Fr 1959) (also script, camera)
La Pyramide humaine (Fr 1961) (also script, camera)
Chronique d'un été (Fr 1961) (also co-script) (with Edgar
    Morin)
La Punition (Fr 1963) (also script) (with Roberto Rossellini)
La Fleur de l'âge/Les Adolescents (ep "Véronique et Marie-
    France") (Can-Fr-Jap-It 1971) (also script) (filmed in 1965)
Paris vu par ... [Six of a Kind] (ep "Gare du Nord") (Fr 1964)
La Chasse au lion à l'arc (Fr 1965) (also script, camera)
Jaguar (Fr 1953-67) (also script, camera)
Petit à Petit (Fr 1970) (also co-script)
Cocorico Monsieur Poulet (Fr 1974) (also script)

ROY, JEAN-LOUIS, b. 1938, Geneva
L'Inconnu de Shandigor (Swi 1966) (also script)
Black-Out (Swi 1970) (also script)

ROZIER, JACQUES, b. Nov. 10, 1926, Paris
Adieu Phillipine (Fr-It 1963) (also co-script)
La Méduse (Fr 1968) (also script)
Dix filles qui se lèvent à midi (Fr 1969) (also script)
Chichifrichi (Fr 1970) (also script)
Du côte d'Orouet (Fr 1973)
Les Naufrages de l'île de la Tortue (Fr 1974) (also script,
    dialogue)

Franco Rossi

RUSSELL, KEN (Henry Kenneth Alfred Russell), b. July 3, 1927, Southampton, England
   French Dressing (WPD 1964)
   Billion Dollar Brain (UA Br 1967)
   Women in Love (UA Br 1969)
   The Music Lovers (UA Br 1970)†
   The Devils (WB Br 1971)† [co-production company] (also script)
   The Boy Friend (MGM-EMI 1971)† (also script)
   Savage Messiah (MGM-EMI 1972)†
   Mahler (VPS 1974)† [co-production company] (also script)

RUTTEN, GERARD, b. July 19, 1912, Den Haag
   Terra Nova (Dut 1932)
   Dood Water (Dut 1934)
   Rubber (Dut 1936)
   Sterren Stralen Overal (Dut 1953)
   Het Wonderlijke Leven van Willem Parel (Dut 1955)
   De Vliegende Hollander (Dut 1957)
   Wederzijds (Dut 1963)

RYE, STELLAN, b. July 4, 1880, Randers, Germany; d. Nov. 14,
    1914
    Bedingung: kein Anhang (Ger 1913)
    Sommernachtstraum (Ger 1913)
    Der Student von Prag (Ger 1913)
    Die Verführte (1913) (with C. L. Schleich)
    Die Augen des Ole Brandes (Ger 1914) (with co-director)
    Erlenkönigs Tochter (Ger 1914)
    Evintrude, die Geschichte eines Abenteurers (Ger 1914) (also
        co-script) (with co-director)
    Das Haus ohne Fenster und Türen (Ger 1914)
    Serenissimus lernt Tango (Ger 1914)
    Peter Schlemihl (Ger 1915)

SALA, VITTORIO, b. July 1, 1918, Palermo, Italy
    Donne sole (It 1956)
    Costa azzurra (It 1959)
    La regina della amazzoni (It 1960)
    I dongiovanni della Costa azzurra (It 1963)
    Il trento del sabato (It 1964)
    L'intrigo (It 1964)
    Berlino, appuntamento per le spie (It 1965)
    Ischia, operazione amore (It 1966)
    Ray Master l'inafferrabile (It 1967)

SALCE, LUCIANO, b. Sept. 25, 1922, Rome
    Uma pulga na balança (Por 1953)
    Floradas na Serra (Por 1953)
    Le pillole di Ercole (It 1960)
    Il federale (It 1961)
    La voglia matta (It 1962)
    La cuccagna (It 1962)
    Le ore dell'amore (It 1963)
    Le monachine (It 1963)
    Alta infedeltà [High Infidelity] (ep "La sospirosa") (It 1964)
    Slalom (It 1965)
    Le bambole (ep "Il trattamento di eugenetica") (It 1965)
    Come imparai ad amare le done (It 1965)
    El Greco (It 1965)
    Le fate (It 1966)
    Ti ho sposato per allegria (It 1967)
    La pecora nera (It 1968)
    Colpo di stato (It 1969)
    Il Prof. Dott. Guido Tersilli primario della Clinica Villa Ce-
        leste convenzionata don de mutue (It 1970)
    Basta guardaria (It 1970)
    Il provinciale (It 1971)
    Il sindacalista (It 1972)

SAMPERI, SALVATORE, b. 1945, Padua, Italy
    Grazie zia (It 1968)
    Cuore di mamma (It 1968)
    Malizia (It 1972)
    La sbandata (It 1974)

SAMUELSON, GEORGE BERTHOLD, b. July 6, 1888, London(?);
    d. April 17, 1947
    The Admirable Crichton (Jury 1918)†
    The Way of an Eagle (Jury 1918)†
    The Bridal Chair (FBO 1919)† (also co-script)
    The Winning Goal (General 1920)†
    The Game of Life (G B Samuelson 1922)† (also producer, co-
      script)
    I pagliacci (Napoleon 1923) (also producer) (with Walter Sum-
      mers)
    Afterglow (Napoleon 1923) (also producer) (with Walter Sum-
      mers)
    Motherland (Reciprocity 1927) (also script) (with Rex Davis)
    Two Little Drummer Boys (Victoria 1928)†
    For Valour (Victoria 1928) (also producer)
    The Forger (Ideal 1928)
    Valley of the Ghosts (JMG 1928)
    Spanish Eyes (MGM Br 1930)
    The Other Woman (UA Br 1931)
    Jealousy (FN Br 1931)
    The Wickham Mystery (UA Br 1931)†
    Inquest (FN Br 1931)
    Collision (UA Br 1932)†
    Threads (UA Br 1932)†
    The Callbox Mystery (UA Br 1932)†
    The Crucifix (Univ Br 1934) (also co-script)

SANGSTER, JIMMY
    The Horror of Frankenstein (MGM-EMI 1970) (also producer,
      co-script)
    Lust for a Vampire (MGM-EMI 1970)
    Fear in the Night (MGM-EMI 1972) (also producer, co-script)

SASDY, PETER, b. Budapest
    Taste the Blood of Dracula (WPD 1969)
    Countess Dracula (RFD 1970) (also co-story)
    Hands of the Ripper (RFD 1971)
    Doomwatch (Tigon 1972)
    Nothing but the Night (20th-Rank 1973)

SAURA, CARLOS (Carlos Altares Saura), b. Jan. 4, 1932, Huesca,
    Spain
    Cuenca (Sp 1958) (also script, co-camera, co-commentary)
    Los golfos (Sp 1959) (also co-script, actor)
    Llanto por un Bandido (Sp-It-Fr 1963) (also co-story, co-script)
    La caza (Sp 1965) (also co-story, script)
    Peppermint Frappé (Sp 1967) (also story, co-script)
    Stress es tres, tres (Sp 1968) (also story, co-script)
    La madriguera (Sp 1969) (also story, co-script)
    El jardin de las délicias (Sp 1970) (also story, co-script)
    Ana y los lobos (Sp 1971) (also story, co-script)
    La prima angélica (Sp 1973) (also story, co-script)

SAUTER, CLAUDE, b. 1924, Montrouge, France
Bonjour sourire (Fr 1955) (supervising director Robert Dhery)
Classe tous risques [The Big Risk] (Fr-It 1959) (also co-script)
L'Arme à gauche [Guns for the Dictator] (Fr-Sp-It 1964) (also
    co-script)
Les Choses de la vie [The Things of Life] (Fr-It 1969) (also
    co-script)
Max et les ferrailleurs (Fr 1971) (also co-script, co-dialogue)
César et Rosalie [César and Rosalie] (Fr-It-W Ger 1972) (also
    co-script)
Vincent, François, Paul et les autres (Fr 1974) (also co-
    script)

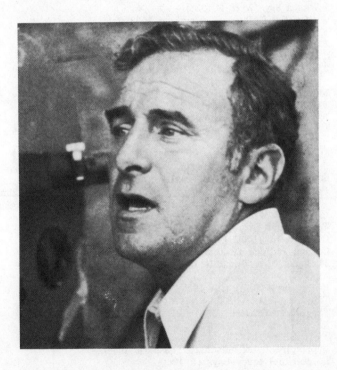

Claude Sauter

SAVILLE, PHILIP, b. London
Stop the World--I Want to Get Off (WPD 1966)
Oedipus the King (RFD 1967) (also co-script)
The Best House in London (MGM British 1968)
Secrets (Satori 1971) (also story)

SAVILLE, VICTOR, b. Sept. 25, 1897, Birmingham, England
   Conquest of Oil (Anglo American Oil Company 1921)
   The Arcadians (Gaumont 1927) (also co-producer)
   Tesha (Wardour 1928) (also producer, co-script)
   Kitty (Wardour 1929) (also producer)
   Woman to Woman (W & F 1929) (also co-producer, script)
   The 'W' Plan (Wardour 1930) (also producer, co-script)
   A Warm Corner (Ideal 1930) (also co-script)
   The Sport of Kings (Ideal 1931)
   Michael and Mary (Ideal 1931)
   Hindle Wakes (Gaumont 1931) (also co-script)
   Sunshine Susie [The Office Girl] (Ideal 1931) (also co-script)
   The Faithful Heart [Faithful Heart] (Ideal 1932) (also co-script)
   Love on Wheels (W & F 1932) (also co-script)
   The Good Companions (Gaumont-Welsh-Pearson 1933)
   I Was a Spy (W & F 1933)
   Friday the Thirteenth (Gaumont 1933)
   Evergreen (Gaumont 1934)
   Evensong (Gaumont 1934)
   The Iron Duke (Gaumont 1935)
   The Love Affair of the Dictator [The Loves of a Dictator]
      (Gaumont 1935)
   Me and Marlborough (Gaumont 1935)
   First a Girl (Gaumont 1935)
   It's Love Again (Gaumont 1936)
   Dark Journey/ The Anxious Years (UA Br 1937)† [co-production
      company]
   Storm in a Teacup (UA Br 1937)† [co-production company]
      (also producer) (with Ian Dalrymple)
   South Riding (UA Br 1938) (also co-producer)
   Forever and a Day (USA) (RKO 1943) (with René Clair, Edmund
      Goulding, Cedric Hardwicke, Frank Lloyd, Robert Stevenson,
      Herbert Wilcox)
   Tonight and Every Night (USA) (Col 1944) (also producer)
   Conspirator (USA) (MGM 1949)
   Calling Bulldog Drummond (MGM Br 1951)
   24 Hours of a Woman's Life [Affair in Monte Carlo] (ABP
      1952)
   I, the Jury (USA) (UA 1953) (also producer)
   The Long Wait (USA) (UA 1954) (also producer)
   The Silver Chalice (USA) (WB 1955) (also producer)

SAVONA, LEOPOLDO (a. k. a. L. Colman), b. Latina, Italy
   Il principe della màschera rossa (It 1956)
   Le notti dei teddy-boys (It 1960)
   I mongoli (It 1961)
   Accatone (It 1961) (with Pier Paolo Pasolini)
   Io bacio ... tu baci (It 1962) (with co-director)
   La guerra continua (It 1962)
   La leggenda de Fra' Diavolo (It 1962)
   L'ultima carica (It 1964)
   I diavoli di Spartivento (It 1964)
   Due perdoni la mia pistola (It 1969)

Killer Kid (It 1967)
Un uomo chiamato Apocalisse Joe (It-Sp 1970)

SCHELL, MAXIMILIAN, b. Aug. 12, 1930, Vienna
First Love (Avco Emb 1970) (also co-producer, co-script,
    actor)
Der Fussgänger (Swi-Ger-Israeli 1973) (also script)

SCHLESINGER, JOHN, b. 1926, London
A Kind of Loving (AA 1962)
Billy Liar! (AA 1963)
Darling (AA 1965)
Far from the Madding Crowd (WPD 1967)
Midnight Cowboy (USA) (UA 1969)
Sunday, Bloody Sunday (UA 1971)
Visions of Eight (ep "The Longest") (USA) (MGM-EMI 1973)
    (also script)

SCHLÖNDORFF, VOLKER, b. 1939, Wiesbaden, Germany
Der junge Törless (Ger 1966) (also script)
Mord und Totschlag (Ger 1967) (also co-script)
Michael Kohlhaas--Der Rebell (Ger 1969) (also co-script)
Der plötzliche Reichtum der armen Leute von Kombach (Ger
    1971)
Die Moral der Ruth Halbfass (Ger 1972)
Strohfeuer (Ger 1972)

SCHMID, DANIEL, b. 1941, Flims, Switzerland
Thut Alles im Finstern, eurem Herrin das Licht zu ersparen
    (Swi 1971) (also script)
Heute Nacht oder nie (Swi 1972) (also script)
La Paloma (Swi 1974) (also script)

SCHNYDER, FRANZ, b. March 5, 1910, Burgdorf (Bern), Switzer-
    land
Gilberte de Courgenay (Swi 1940)
Gespensterhaus (Swi 1942)
Wilder Urlaub (Swi 1943)
Uli der Knecht (Swi 1954)
Heidi und peter (Swi 1954)
Uli der Pächter (Swi 1955)
Zwischen und die Berge (Swi 1956)
Der 10. Mai (Swi 1957) (also script)
Die Käserei in der Vehfreude (Swi 1958)
Anne Bäbi Jowäger (Swi 1960)
Jakobli und Meyeli (Swi 1961) (also script)
Der Sittlichkeitsverbrecher (Swi 1963)
Geld und Geist [La reconciliation] (Swi 1964)
Sechs Kümmer buber (Swi TV 1968)

SCHOENDORFER, PIERRE, b. 1928, Chamaillières, France
Ramuntcho (Fr 1959)
Pêcheur d'Islande (Fr 1959) (also co-script)

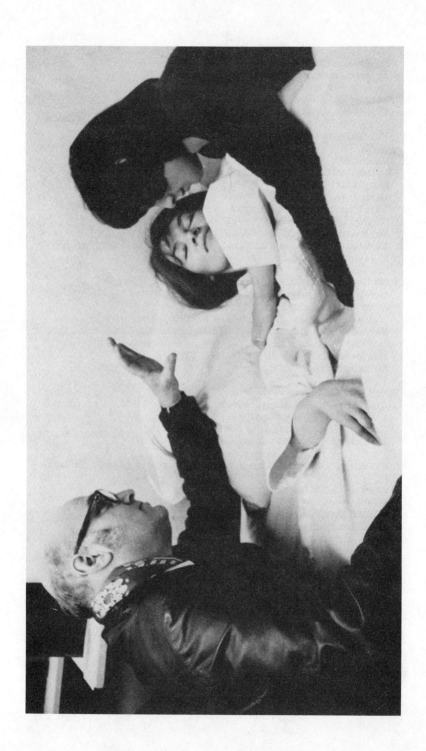

La Passe du Diable (Fr 1959) (with Jacques Dupont)
La 317e section (Fr 1965) (also co-script)
Objectif 500 millions (Fr 1966) (also script)
La patrouille Anderson (Fr 1967) (also script)
Le Désert des Tartares (Fr 1971) (also script)

SCHOUKENS, GASTON, b. Feb. 5, 1901, Brussels; d. April 7,
    1961
Monsieur mon chauffeur (Bel 1926) (also script, camera)
Tu ne sauras jamais (Bel 1927)
Les Croix de l'Yser (Bel 1928) (with Paul Flon)
La famille Klepkens (Bel 1929) (with Paul Flon)
De Familie Klepkens (Flemish version of La Famille Klepkens)
    (Bel 1929)
Le Plus Joli Rêve (Bel 1931)
Le Cadavre n⁰ 5 (Bel 1932)
Si tu vois mon oncle (Bel 1933) (also script)
Un Séducteur (Bel 1933)
Un Gosse pour cent mille francs (Bel 1933)
Les Quatre Mousquetaires (Bel 1934)
En avant la musique [Au roi de la pomme de terre frite] (Bel
    1935)
C'était le bon temps (Bel 1936)
Gardons notre sourire [Ersatz et Kommandantur] (Bel 1937)
Mon père et mon papa (Bel 1937)
Bossemans et Coppenolle (Bel 1938)
Ceux qui veillent (Bel 1939)
Les Invités de huit heures (Bel 1944)
Un "Soir" de joie (Bel 1954)
L'Amour est quelque part (Bel 1955)
La Drôle de guerre de 44 (Bel 1956)
Un Week-end fantastique (Bel 1959) (also script)
Scandale à la Belgique joyeuse (Bel 1959) (also script)

SELPIN, HERBERT, b. Germany; d. July 31, 1942
Chauffeur Antoinette (Ger 1931)
Der Traum vom Rhein (Ger 1933)
Mädels von heute (Ger 1933)
Zwischen zwei Herzen (Ger 1934)
Der Springer von Pontresina (Ger 1934)
Die Reiter von Deutsch-Ostafrika (Ger 1934)
Ein idealer Gatte (Ger 1935)
Der grüne Domino (Ger 1935)
Skandal um die Fledermaus (Ger 1936)
Spiel an Bord (Ger 1936)
Die Frau des Anderen (Ger 1936)
Alarm in Peking (Ger 1937)
Heiratsschwindler (Ger 1937)
Ich liebe dich (Ger 1938)

Facing page: John Schlesinger (left) with Glenda Jackson and
Murray Head filming Sunday, Bloody Sunday (1971).

Sergeant Berry (Ger 1938)
Wasser für Canitoga (Ger 1939)
Ein Mann auf Abwegen (Ger 1940)
Trenck der Pandur (Ger 1940)
Carl Peters (Ger 1941)
Geheimakte WB I (Ger 1942)
Titanic (Ger 1943) (completed by Werner Kliner)

SEQUI, MARIO, b. June 30, 1910, Cagliari, Italy
L'isola di Montecristo (It 1950)
Monastero di Santa Chiara (It 1951)
Altura (It 1951)
Incantesimo tragico [Olivia] (It 1951)
Cronaca di un delitto (It 1953)
Gioventù di notte (It 1962)
Gli uomini dal passo pesante (It 1966)
Il cobra [Cobra] (Sp-It 1967)
Le tigri di Mompracem (It-Sp 1970)

SEWELL, VERNON, b. 1903, London
The Medium (MGM Br 1934) (also script)
Breakers Ahead/As We Forgive (GFD 1938)
The Silver Fleet (GFD 1943) (also co-script) (with Gordon
    Wellesley)
The World Owes Me a Living (Anglo 1945) (also co-script)
Latin Quarter (Anglo 1945) (also script)
The Ghosts of Berkeley Square (Pathé 1947)
Uneasy Terms (Pathé 1948)
The Jack of Diamonds (Ex 1949)
Trek to Mashomba (GFD 1951)
The Dark Light (Ex 1951) (also script)
Black Widow (Ex 1951)
Ghost Ship (AA 1952) (also producer, script)
Counterspy [Undercover Agent] (AA 1953)
The Floating Dutchman (AA 1953) (also script)
Dangerous Voyage [Terror Ship] (AA 1954) (also author)
Radio Cab Murder (Eros 1954)
Where There's a Will (Eros 1955)
Johnny, You're Wanted (AA 1956)
Soho Incident [Spin a Dark Web] (Col Br 1956)
Home and Away (Eros 1956) (also co-script)
Rogue's Yarn (Eros 1957) (also co-script)
Battle of the V I [Unseen Heroes] (Eros 1958)
Wrong Number (AA 1959)
Urge to Kill (AA 1960)
The Wind of Change (Bry 1960)
House of Mystery (AA 1961) (also script)
The Man in the Back Seat (AA 1961)
Strongroom (Bry 1962)
A Matter of Choice (Bry 1963) (also co-script)
Strictly for the Birds (RFD 1963)
Some May Live (Butcher 1967)
The Blood Beast Terror (Tigon 1968)

Curse of the Crimson Altar [Crimson Cult] (Tigon 1968)
Burke and Hare (UA Br 1971)

SHARP, DON, b. April 22(?), 1922, Australia
    The Stolen Airliner (BL-CFF 1955) (also script)
    The Golden Disc [The Inbetween Age] (ABP 1958)
    The Adventures of Hal 5 (CFF 1958) (also script)
    The Professionals (AA 1960)
    Linda (Bry 1960)
    The Kiss of the Vampire [Kiss of Evil] (Univ Br 1962)
    It's All Happening (Magna 1963)
    The Devil-Ship Pirates (WPD 1964)
    Witchcraft (20th Br 1964)
    The Curse of the Fly (20th Br 1965)
    The Face of Fu Manchu (WPD 1965)
    Rasputin the Mad Monk (WPD 1965)
    Our Man in Marrakesh [Bang Bang You're Dead] (AA 1966)
    The Brides of Fu Manchu (AA 1966)
    Jules Verne's Rocket to the Moon [These Fantastic Flying
        Fools] (AA 1967)
    Taste of Excitement (Crispin 1969) (also co-script)
    Psychomania (Scotia-Barber 1972)
    Callan (EMI 1974)

SIMMONS, ANTHONY, b.
    Your Money or Your Wife (RFD 1960)
    Four in the Morning (West One 1965) (also script)
    The Optimists of Nine Elms (Scotia-Barber 1973) (also story,
        co-script)

SIMON, JEAN-DANIEL, b. 1942, France
    La Fille d'en face [The Girl Across the Way] (Fr 1967)
    Adelaïde [The Depraved] (Fr-It 1968) (also co-script)
    Ils (Fr 1970) (also co-adaptor)
    Fontaine le guyon (Fr 1973) (also co-script)
    Il pleut toujours où c'est mouillé (Fr 1974)

SIMONELLI, GIORGIO, b. Nov. 23, 1901, Rome
    Guerra alla guerra (It 1946) (with co-director)
    Dove sta Zaza? (It 1948)
    Undici uomini e un pallone (It 1948)
    Accidenti alla guerra (It 1949)
    Se fossi deputato (It 1949)
    Le due madonne (It 1950) (with co-director)
    Amori e veleni (It 1950)
    La bisarca (It 1950)
    Io sono il capataz (It 1951)
    Auguri e figli maschi (It 1951)
    La paura fa 90 (It 1951)
    Io, Amleto (It 1953)
    Era lei che lo voleva (It 1953) (with co-director)
    Saluti e baci (It 1953)
    Canzone appassionata (It 1954)

Accadde al commissariato (It 1954)
Io sono la primola rossa (It 1954)
Canzone d'amore (It 1954)
La moglie è uguale per tutti (It 1955)
Il campanile d'oro (It 1956)
Al sud niente di nuovo (It 1956)
Guaglione (It 1956)
Napoli, sole mio! (It 1956)
Non cantare, baciami (It 1957)
Perfide ... ma belle (It 1958)
Marinai, donne e guai (It 1958)
Fantasmi e ladri (It 1959)
Noi siamo due evasi (It 1959)
I baccanali di Tibertio (It 1969)
Un dollaro di fifa (It 1960)
Che femmina! ... e che dollari (It 1961)
Robin Hood e i pirati (It 1961)
I magnifici tre (It 1961)
Gerarchi si muove (It 1962)
I tre nemici (It 1962)
I trombini di Fra' Diavolo (It 1962)
Due samurai per cento geishe (It 1963)
Ursus nella terra di fuoco (It 1963)
I due toreri (It 1964)
I due Mafiosi (It 1964)
Due Mafiosi nel Far West (It 1964)
I due sergenti del generale Custer (It 1965)
Due Mafiosi contro Goldginger (It 1965)
Due Mafiosi control Al Capone (It 1966)
I due sanculotti (It 1966)
I due figli di Ringo (It 1967)

SIODMAK, CURT (Kurt Siodmak), b. August 10, 1902, Dresden,
     Germany
     Bride of the Gorilla (USA) (Realart 1951) (also script)
     The Magnetic Monster (USA) (UA 1953) (also script)
     Curucu, Beast of the Amazon (Univ 1956) (also script)
     Love Slaves of the Amazon (Univ 1957) (also producer, script)
     The Devil's Messenger (Herts-Lion 1962) (also co-script) (with
          Herbert L. Storck)
     Ski Fever (USA) (AA 1969) (also co-script)

SIODMAK, ROBERT, b. August 8, 1900, Memphis, Tenn.; d.
     March 10, 1973
     Menchen am Sonntag (Ger 1929) (also story, co-script) (with
          Edgar G. Ulmer)
     Abschied [So Sind die Menschen] (Ger 1930)
     Der Mann, der Seinen Morder Sucht (Ger 1931)
     Voruntersuchung (Ger 1931)
     Autour d'une enquête (Fr 1931) (Fr version of Voruntersuchung)
          (supervisor only)
     Stürme der Leidenschaft [Tempest] (Ger 1932)
     Quick (Ger 1932) (also Fr version 1932)

Brennendes Geheimmis [The Burning Secret] (Ger 1933)
Le Sexe Faible (Fr 1934)
La Crise est finie [The Slump Is Over] (Fr 1934)
La Vie parisienne (Fr 1936)
Mister Flow [Compliments of Mr. Flow] (Fr 1936)
Cargaison blanche [Woman Racket] (Fr 1937)
Mollenard [Hatred] (Fr 1938)
Ultimatum (Fr 1938)
Pièges [Personal Column] (Fr 1939)
West Point Widow (USA) (Par 1941)
Fly by Night (USA) (Par 1942)
The Night Before the Divorce (USA) (20th 1942)
My Heart Belongs to Daddy (USA) (Par 1942)
Someone to Remember (USA) (Rep 1943)
Son of Dracula (USA) (Univ 1943)
Cobra Woman (USA) (Univ 1944)
Phantom Lady (USA) (Univ 1944)
Christmas Holiday (USA) (Univ 1944)
The Suspect (USA) (Univ 1945)
Conflict (USA) (WB 1945) (also co-story treatment)
The Strange Affair of Uncle Harry (USA) (Univ 1945)
The Spiral Staircase (USA) (RKO 1945)
The Killers (USA) (Univ 1946)
The Dark Mirror (USA) (Univ 1946)
Time Out of Mind (USA) (Univ 1947)
Cry of the City (USA) (20th 1948)
Criss Cross (USA) (Univ 1949)
The Great Sinner (USA) (MGM 1949)
The File on Thelma Jordan (USA) (Par 1950)
Deported (USA) (Univ 1950)
The Whistle at Eaton Falls (USA) (Col 1951)
The Crimson Pirate (USA) (WB 1952)
Le Grand Jeu [Flesh and the Woman] (Fr 1954)
Die Ratten (Ger 1955)
Mein Vater, der Schauspieler (Ger 1956)
Nachts, wenn der Teufel kam [The Devil Strikes at Night] (Ger 1957)
Dorothea Angermann (Ger 1959)
The Rough and the Smooth [Portrait of a Sinner] (Renown 1959)
Katya [Magnificent Sinner] (Ger 1960)
Affäre Nina B (Fr-It-Ger 1961)
Der Schut (Ger-Fr-It 1964)
Der Schatz der Azteken (Ger-Fr-It 1965)
Die Pyramide des Sonnengottes (Ger-Fr-It 1965)
L'Homme de Marrakech (Fr-Sp-It 1966) (replaced by Jacques Deray)
Custer of the West (Cin 1967)
Der Kampf um Rom (Ger-It; released in two parts in 1968 and 1969)

SIRK, DOUGLAS (Dietlef Hans Sierck), b. April 26, 1900, Hamburg
'T was één April [It Was in April] (Dut version of April, April) (Ger 1935)

April, April (UFA 1935)
Das Mädchen vom Moorhof (UFA 1935)
Stützen der Gesellschaft (Ger 1935)
Schlussakkord (Ger 1936)
Das Hofkonzert (Ger 1936)
La Chanson du souvenir [Fr version of Das Hofkonzert] (Ger 1936)
Zu neuen Ufern (Ger 1937)
La Habanera (Ger 1937)
Accord Final (Ger-Fr 1939)
Boefje (Dut 1939)
In the U. S. A. :
Hitler's Madman (MGM 1943)
Summer Storm (UA 1944) (also co-script)
A Scandal in Paris (UA 1946)
Lured (UA 1947)
Sleep, My Love (UA 1948)
Siren of Atlantis (UA 1948) (uncredited, with Gregg Tallas)
Shockproof (Col 1949)
Slightly French (Col 1949)
Mystery Submarine (Univ 1950)
The First Legion (UA 1951) (also co-producer)
Thunder on the Hill (Univ 1951)
The Lady Pays Off (Univ 1951)
Weekend with Father (Univ 1951)
No Room for the Groom (Univ 1952)
Has Anybody Seen My Gal? (Univ 1952)
Meet Me at the Fair (Univ 1952)
Take Me to Town (Univ 1953)
All I Desire (Univ 1953)
Taza, Son of Cochise (Univ 1954)
Magnificent Obsession (Univ 1954)
Sign of the Pagan (Univ 1954)
Captain Lightfoot (Univ 1955)
All That Heaven Allows (Univ 1955)
There's Always Tomorrow (Univ 1956)
Never Say Goodbye (Univ 1956) (uncredited, with Jerry Hopper)
Battle Hymn (Univ 1957)
Interlude (Univ 1957)
The Tarnished Angels (Univ 1957)
A Time to Love and a Time to Die (Univ 1958)
Imitation of Life (Univ 1959)

SLUIZER, GEORGE, b. Aug. 25, 1932, Paris
João (Dut-Braz 1972)

SOLDATI, MARIO, b. Nov. 17, 1906, Turin, Italy
La principessa Tarakanova (It 1938) (with Fedor Ozep)
Due milioni per un sorriso (It 1939) (with C. Borghesio)
Dora Nelson (It 1939)
Tutta per la donna (It 1940)
Piccolo mondo antico (It 1941)
Tragica notte (It 1942)

Malombra (It 1942)
Quartieri alti (It 1943)
Le miserie del signor Travet [His Young Wife] (It 1946)
Mio figlio professore (It 1946) (only actor)
Eugenia Grandet (It 1947)
Daniele Cortis (It 1947)
Fuga in Francia [Flight into France] (It 1948)
Quel bandito sono io [The Taming of Dorothy] (It-GB 1950)
Botta e risposta (It 1950)
Donne e briganti (It 1951)
E l'amor che mi rovina (It 1951)
O. K. Nerone [O. K. Nero] (It 1951)
Il sogno di Zorro (It 1952)
Le avventure di Mandrin (It-Fr 1952)
I tre corsari [The Three Pirates] (It 1952)
Jolanda, la figlia del Corsaro Nero [Yolanda] (It 1953)
La provinciale [The Wayward Wife] (It 1953)
La mano dello straniero [The Stranger's Hand] (It-GB 1954)
Questa è la vita (ep "Il ventaglio") (It 1954)
La donna del fiume [Women of the River] (It 1955)
Guerra e pace [War and Peace] (It-US 1956) (second unit director)
Era di venerdì (It 1956)
Italia piccola (It 1957)
Policarpo ufficiale di scrittura (It 1959)
La Bibbia [The Bible] (It-Amer 1966) (only co-script)

SOLLIMA, SERGIO (a.k.a. Simon Sterling), b. April 14, 1921, Rome
Amore difficile (ep "L'avaro") (It 1962)
Agente 3S3, passaporto per l'inferno (It-Fr-Sp 1965)
Agente 3S3, massacro al sole (It-Fr-Sp 1966)
Requiem per un agente segreto (It-Ger-Sp 1966)
El halcón y la presa (Sp 1966)
Faccia a Faccia (It-Sp-Fr 1967)
La resa dei conti (It 1967)
Corri, uomo, corri (It-Fr 1968)
Città violenta (It-Fr 1970)
Il diavolo nel cervello (It 1971)
Revolver (It-Fr-Ger 1972)

SORDI, ALBERTO, b. June 15, 1919, Rome
Fumo di Londra (It 1966)
Scusi, lei è favorevole o contrario? (It 1966)
Un Italiano in America (It 1967)
Amore mio, aiutami (It 1969)
Le coppie (ep "La camerae") (It 1970)
Togliattigrad (It 1971)

SOUTTER, MICHEL, b. June 2, 1932, Geneva
La Lune avec les dents (Swi 1966) (also script)
Haschisch (Swi 1968) (also script)
La Pomme (Swi 1969) (also script)

James ou pas (Swi 1970) (also script)
Les Arpenteurs (Swi 1972) (also script)
L'escapade (Swi 1973) (also script)

SPEYER, JAAP, b. Nov. 29, 1891, Amsterdam; d. Sept. 18, 1952
  Wenn Frauen lieben und hassen (Ger 1917)
  Das gestohlene Hotel (Ger 1918)
  Der Teilhaber (Ger 1918)
  Der gelbe Schatten (Ger 1919)
  "Lilli" und "Lillis Ehe" (Ger 1919)
  Das eherne Gesetz (Ger 1920)
  Das Recht der freien Liebe (Ger 1920)
  Entblätterte Blüten (Ger 1920)
  Gefolterte Herzen 1. Teil (Ger 1920)
  Gefolterte Herzen 2. Teil (Ger 1920)
  Un den Bruchteil einer Sekunde (Ger 1920)
  Die röte Nacht (Ger 1921)
  Strandgut der Leidenschaft (Ger 1921)
  Das blonde Verhängnis (Ger 1921)
  Jimmy, ein Schicksal von Mensch und Tier (Ger 1922)
  Der allmächtige Dollar (Ger 1923)
  Der Frauenkönig (Ger 1923)
  Die Puppe vom Lunapark (Ger 1924)
  Die Blumenfrau vom Postdamer Platz (Ger 1925)
  Elegantes Pack (Ger 1925)
  Die Moral der Gasse (Ger 1925)
  Die drei Mannequins (Ger 1926)
  Liebeshandel (Ger 1926)
  Mädchenhandel (Ger 1926)
  Bigamie (Ger 1927)
  Hotelratten (Ger 1927)
  Valencia (Ger 1927)
  Die drei Frauen von Urban Hell (Ger 1928)
  Fräulein Chauffeur (Ger 1928)
  G'schichten aus dem Wienerwald (Ger 1928)
  Die Sache mit Schorrsiegel (Ger 1928)
  Jennys Bummel durch die Männer (Ger 1929)
  Ein kleiner Vorschusz auf die Seligkeit (Ger 1929)
  Zapfenstreich am Rhein (Ger 1930)
  De Jantjes (Dut 1934)
  Kermisgasten (Dut 1936)
  Op een Avond in Mei (Dut 1936)
  Een Koninkrijk voor een Huis (Dut 1949)

STAUDTE, WOLFGANG, b. 1906, Saarbrucken, Saarland, Germany
  Akrobat schö-ö-ön (Ger 1943) (also script)
  Ich hab' von Dir geträumt (Ger 1944)
  Der Mann, dem man den Namen stahl (only co-script)
  Die Mörder sind unter uns (Ger 1946) (also script)
  Die seltsamen Abenteuer des Herrn Fridolin B. (Ger 1948)
    (also script)
  Rotation (Ger 1949) (also co-script)
  Schicksal aus zweiter Hand (Ger 1949) (also script)

Der Untertan (Ger 1951) (also co-script)
Die Geschichte des kleinen Muck (Ger 1953) (also co-script)
Leuchtfeuer (Ger 1954) (also co-script)
Ciske--Ein Kind braucht Liebe (Ger 1955) (also script)
Rose Bernd (Ger 1957)
Kanonen-Serenade (Ger 1958) (also co-script)
Madeleine und der Legionär (Ger 1958)
Der Maulkorb (Ger 1958)
Kirmes (Ger 1960) (also script)
Der letzte Zeuge (Ger 1960)
Die glücklichen Jahre der Thorwalds (Ger 1962) (with John
    Olden)
Die Dreigroschenoper [The Three Penny Opera] (Ger-Fr 1963)
Herrenpartie (Ger 1964)
Das Lamm (Ger 1964)
Ganovenehre (Ger 1966)
Heimlichkeiten (Ger 1968) (also co-script)

STEIN, PAUL LUDWIG, b. Feb. 4, 1892, Vienna; d. 1952
    Der Teufel der Liebe (Ger 1919)
    Gewalt gegen Recht (Ger 1919)
    Das Martyrium (Ger 1920)
    Die geschlossene Kette (Ger 1920)
    Arme Violetta [The Red Peacock] (Ger 1920)
    Der Schauspieler der Herzogin (Ger 1920)
    Ehrenschuld (Ger 1921)
    Das Opfer der Ellen Larsen (Ger 1921)
    Sturmflut des Lebens (Ger 1921)
    Der ewige Kampf (Ger 1921)
    Es leuchtet meine Liebe (Ger 1922)
    Nacht der Versuchung (Ger 1921)
    Die Kette (Ger 1923)
    Der Löwe von Venedig (Ger 1923)
    Ein Traum vom Glück (Ger 1924)
    Ich liebe dich (Ger 1924)
    Liebesfeuer (Ger 1925)
    Die Insel der Träume [Eine anstandige frau] (Ger 1925)
    Fünfuhrtee in der Ackerstrasse (Ger 1926)
    My Official Wife (USA) (WB 1926)
    Don't Tell the Wife (USA) (WB 1927)
    The Climbers (USA) (WB 1927)
    The Forbidden Woman (USA) (Pathé 1927)
    Man-Made Woman (USA) (Pathé 1928)
    Ehre deine Mutter (Ger 1928)
    Show Folks (USA) (Pathé 1928)
    Her Private Affair (USA) (Pathé 1929)
    This Thing Called Love (USA) (Pathé 1929)
    One Romantic Night (USA) (UA 1930)
    Sin Takes a Holiday (USA) (Pathé 1930)
    The Lottery Bride (USA) (UA 1930)
    Born to Love (USA) (Pathé 1931)
    A Woman Commands (USA) (RKO 1932)
    Lily Christine (Par Br 1932)

Breach of Promise (Sono Art-World Wide 1932)
The Song You Gave Me (Col Br 1934)
Red Wagon (Wardour 1934)
Blossom Time (Wardour 1934)
Mimi (Wardour 1935)
Heart's Desire (Wardour 1935)
Faithful (Wardour 1936)
Cafe Colette [Danger in Paradise] (ABFD 1937)
Just Like a Woman (ABPC 1937)
Black Limelight (ABPC 1938)
Jane Steps Out (ABPC 1938)
The Outsider (ABPC 1939)
A Gentleman of Venture [It Happened to One Man] (RKO Br
1940)
Poison Pen (ABPC 1941)
The Saint Meets the Tiger (RKO Br 1941)
Talk About Jacqueline (MGM Br 1942)
Kiss the Bride Goodbye (Butcher 1944) (also producer, story)
Waltz Time (BIP 1945)
Twilight Hour (BIP 1945)
The Lisbon Story (BIP 1946)
The Laughing Lady (BIP 1947)
Counterblast (Pathé 1948)
The Twenty Questions Murder Mystery (GN 1950)

STEINHOFF, HANS, b. March 10, 1882, Pfaffenhofen, Germany; d.
1945
Bräutigam auf Kredit (Ger 1921)
Der Bettelstudent (Ger 1922)
Biribi (Ger 1922) (also script)
Der falsche Dimitri (Ger 1922) (also co-script)
Kleider machen Leute (Ger 1922) (also co-script)
Inge Larsen (Ger 1923)
Mensch gegen Mensch (Ger 1924)
Gräfin Mariza (Ger 1925)
Der Mann, der sich verkauft (Ger 1925) (also co-script)
Der Herr des Todes (Ger 1926)
Die Tragödie eines Verlorenen (Ger 1926)
Wien-Berlin (Ger 1926)
Schwiegersöhne (Ger 1926) (also co-script)
Familientag im Hause Prellstein (Ger 1927)
Das Frauenhaus von Rio (Ger 1927)
Die Sandgräfin (Ger 1927)
Ein Mädel und drei Clowns (Ger 1928)
Das Spreewaldmädel (Ger 1928)
Nachtgestalten (Ger 1929)
Rosenmontag (Ger 1930)
Die Pranke (Ger 1931)
Kopfüber ins Glück (Ger 1931)
Die Faschingsfee (Ger 1931)
Mein Leopold (Ger 1931)
Der wahre Jakob (Ger 1931)
Scampolo, ein Kind der Strasse (Ger 1932)

Mutter und Kind (Ger 1933)
Liebe muss verstanden sein (Ger 1933)
Madame wünscht keine Kinder (Ger 1933)
Hitlerjunge Quex (Ger 1933)
Freut euch des Lebens (Ger 1934)
Die Insel (Ger 1934)
Lockvogel (Ger 1934)
Der alte und der junge König (Ger 1935)
Der Ammenkönig (Ger 1935)
Eine Frau ohne Bedeutung (Ger 1936)
Ein Volksfreund (Ger 1937) (also co-script)
Tanz auf dem Vulkan (Ger 1938) (also story, co-script)
Robert Koch (Ger 1939)
Die Geierwally (Ger 1940)
Ohm Krüger (Ger 1941)
Rembrandt (Ger 1942) (also co-script)
Gabriele Dambrone (Ger 1943) (also co-script)
Melusine (Ger 1944) (also co-script)
Shiva und die Galgenblume (Ger 1945) (also co-script)

STENO (pseud.) see VANZINA, STEFANO

STEVENSON, ROBERT, b. 1905, London
Happy Ever After (Ger-GB 1932) (German version directed by
    Paul Martin)
Falling for You (W & F 1933) (with Jack Hulbert)
Jack of All Trades [The Two of Us] (Gaumont 1936)
Tudor Rose [Nine Days a Queen] (Gaumont 1936) (also co-
    script)
The Man Who Changed His Mind [The Man Who Lived Again]
    (Gaumont 1936)
King Solomon's Mines (GFD 1937)
Non-Stop New York (GFD 1937)
Owd Bob [To the Victor] (GFD 1938)
The Ware Case (ABFD 1938) (also co-script)
Young Man's Fancy (ABFD 1939) (also story)
Return to Yesterday (ABFD 1940) (also co-script)
Tom Brown's Schooldays (USA) (RKO 1940)
Back Street (USA) (Univ 1941)
Joan of Paris (USA) (RKO 1942)
Forever and a Day (USA) (RKO 1943) (also co-producer) (with
    René Clair, Edmund Goulding, Sir Cedric Hardwicke, Frank
    Lloyd, Victor Saville, Herbert Wilcox)
Jane Eyre (USA) (20th 1944) (also co-script)
Dishonoured Lady (USA) (UA 1947)
To the Ends of the Earth (USA) (Col 1948)
I Married a Communist [The Woman on Pier 13] (USA) (RKO
    1949)
Walk Softly Stranger (USA) (RKO 1950)
My Forbidden Past (USA) (RKO 1951)
The Las Vegas Story (USA) (RKO 1952)
Johnny Tremain (USA) (BV 1957)
Old Yeller (USA) (BV 1957)

Darby O'Gill and the Little People (USA) (BV 1959)
Kidnapped (USA) (BV 1960) (also script)
The Absent-Minded Professor (USA) (BV 1961)
In Search of the Castaways (USA) (BV 1962)
Son of Flubber (USA) (BV 1963)
The Misadventures of Merlin Jones (USA) (BV 1963)
Mary Poppins (USA) (BV 1964)
The Monkey's Uncle (USA) (BV 1964)
That Darn Cat! (USA) (BV 1965)
The Gnome-Mobile (USA) (BV 1966)
Blackbeard's Ghost (USA) (BV 1967)
The Love Bug (USA) (BV 1968)
The Mickey Mouse Anniversary Show (USA) (BV 1968) (with
    Ward Kimball)
My Dog, the Thief (USA) (BV 1969)
Bedknobs and Broomsticks (USA) (BV 1971)

STORCK, HENRI, b. Sept. 5, 1907, Ostende, Belgium
Symphonie paysanne (Bel 1944)
Rubens (Bel 1948) (with Paul Haesaerts)
Le Banquet des fraudeurs (Bel 1951)
Hermann Teirlinck (Bel 1953)
Les Fêtes de Belgique (Bel 1970) (with Jean Cleinge, David Mc-
    Neil)

SUAREZ, GONZALO, b. 1934
Ditirambo (Sp 1967) (also co-producer, script, actor)
El extrano caso del Doctor Fausto (Sp 1969) (also story, script,
    actor)
Morbos (Sp 1971)
Aoom (Sp 1971) (also co-script, story)
Diego y Alicia (Sp 1972)
El secreto de Penatu Rocanegra (Sp-Licht 1973)
Al diablo con amor (Sp 1974)

SUMMERS, MANUEL, b. 1935, Seville, Spain
EOC: El viejecito (Sp 1959)
Del rosa al amarillo (Sp 1963) (also script)
La nina de luto (Sp 1963)
El juego de la oca (Sp 1964) (also script)
Juguetes rotas (Sp 1966) (also script)
No somos de piedra (Sp 1967) (also script)
El eterno triangulo (Sp 1967) (also script)
Por que te engaña tu marido (Sp 1969) (also script)
Urtain, el rey de la selva (Sp 1970) (also script, story)
Adios, Cigueña, Adios (Sp 1970) (also co-script)
El niño es nuestro (Sp 1973) (also story, script)

SUMMERS, WALTER, b. Sept. 2, 1896, Barnstaple, England
I pagliacci (Napoleon 1923) (also script) (with G. B. Samuelson)
Afterglow (Napoleon 1923) (also script) (with G. B. Samuelson)
A Couple of Down and Outs (Napoleon 1923) (also script)

The Unwanted (Napoleon 1924) (also script)
The Cost of Beauty (Napoleon 1924) (also script)
Who Is This Man? (Napoleon 1924) (also script)
Ypres (New Era 1925) (also script)
Mons (New Era 1926) (also script)
Nelson (New Era 1926) (also script)
The Battles of the Coronel and Falkland Islands/The Deeds
    Men Do (British Instructional-British Projects 1927)
Bolibar (Pro Patria 1928) (also script)
The Lost Patrol (Fox Br 1929) (also script)
Chamber of Horrors (PDC 1929) (also script)
Raise the Roof (FNP Br 1930) (also script)
Suspense (Wardour 1930) (also script)
The Man from Chicago (Wardour 1930) (also co-script)
The Flying Fool (Wardour 1931) (also script)
Men Like These [Trapped in a Submarine] (Wardour 1931) (also
    co-script)
The House Opposite (Pathé 1931) (also script)
Timbuctoo (Wardour 1933) (also script) (with Arthur Woods)
The Warren Case (Pathé 1934) (also script)
The Return of Bulldog Drummond (Wardour 1934) (also script)
What Happened Then? (Wardour 1934) (also script)
McGlusky the Sea Rover [Hell's Cargo] (Wardour 1935) (also
    script)
Music Hath Charms (Wardour 1935) (with Thomas Bentley,
    Alexander Esway, Arthur Woods)
Ourselves Alone·[River of Unrest] (Wardour 1936) (with Brian
    Desmond Hurst)
The Limping Man (Pathé 1936) (also script)
The Price of Folly (Pathé 1937) (also co-script)
Premiere [One Night in Paris] (ABPC 1938)
At the Villa Rose [House of Mystery] (ABPC 1939)
Dark Eyes of London [The Human Monster] (Pathé 1939) (also
    co-script)
Traitor Spy [The Torso Murder Mystery] (Pathé 1939) (also co-
    script)

SYKES, PETER
    The Committee (Planet 1968) (also co-script)
    Demons of the Mind (MGM-EMI 1972)
    The House in Nightmare Park (MGM-EMI 1973)
    Steptoe and Son Ride Again (MGM-EMI 1973)
    Venom (Mark Associates 1974) (made in 1971)

SZULZINGER, BORIS, b. Sept. 20, 1945, Brussels
    Nathalie après l'amour (Bel 1970) (also script) (under the name
        Michael B. Sanders)
    Les Tueurs fous [Lonely Killers] (Bel 1972)

TANNER, ALAIN, b. Dec. 6, 1929, Geneva
    Les Apprentis (Swi 1964) (also script)
    Une Ville à Chandigarh (Swi 1966) (also script)
    Charles mort ou vif (Swi 1969) (also script)

La Salamandre (Swi 1971) (also script)
Le Retour d'Afrique (Swi 1973)
Le Milieu du monde (Swi 1974)

TATI, JACQUES, b. Oct. 9, 1908, Pecq (Seine-et-Oise), France
Jour de fête (Fr 1947) (also script, actor)
Les Vacances de Monsieur Hulot [Monsieur Hulot's Holiday]
(Fr 1952) (also script, actor)
Mon Oncle (Fr 1958) (also script, actor)
Playtime (Fr 1968) (also script, actor)
Trafic [Traffic] (Fr 1971) (also script, actor)

TELDERS, WIMS, b. Belgium
Naar het groeide (Bel 1958)
Onschuldig Verlangen (Bel 1959)
Vertrapte Schoonheid (Bel 1959)
Samen Leven ... Samen Sterven (Bel 1959)
'Te Geheim Document (Bel 1962)
De Grap (Bel 1968)
Zum Foch (Bel 1968)

TENNYSON, PENROSE, b. 1912, London; d. 1940
There Ain't No Justice (ABFD 1939) (also co-script)
The Proud Valley (ABFD 1940)
Convoy (ABFD 1940) (also co-script)

TERPSTRA, ERIK, b. 1937, Amsterdam
De Verloedering van de Swieps (Dut 1967)
Daniël (Dut 1971)

TESSARI, DUCCIO, b. Oct. 11, 1926, Genoa, Italy
Arrivano i titani [Sons of Thunder] (It 1962) (also co-script)
Il fornaretto di Venezia [The Scapegoat] (It-Fr 1963) (also
script)
La sfinge sorride prima di morire, stop, Londra (It-Ger 1964)
(also co-script)
Una vòglia da morire (It 1965) (also script)
Il ritorno di Ringo (It 1965) (also script)
Kiss, Kiss ... bang bang (It 1965) (also script)
Per amore ... per magia [For Love ... for Magic] (It 1967)
(also script)
I bastardi [The Cats] (It-Ger 1967) (also co-script)
Meglio vedova [Better a Widow] (It 1967) (also co-script)
Vivi o preferibilmente morti (It 1969) (also co-script)
Matchball (It 1970) (also co-script)
Quella pìccola differenza [That Little Difference] (It 1970) (also
co-script)
Forza G (It 1970) (also co-script)
La morte risale a ieri sera [Death Occurred Last Night] (It
1970) (also co-script)
Tony Arzenta (It 1972) (also co-script)
Zorro (It 1974) (also co-script)

THIELE, ROLF, b. March 7, 1918, Redlice, Czechoslovakia
   Primanerinnen (Ger 1951) (also script)
   Der Tag vor der Hochzeit (Ger 1952) (also script)
   Geliebtes Leben (Ger 1953) (also script)
   Sie (Ger 1954) (also producer, script)
   Mamitschka (Ger 1955) (also co-script)
   Die Barrings (Ger 1955) (also co-script)
   Friederike von Barring (Ger 1956) (also script)
   Skandal in Ischl (Ger 1957)
   El Hakim (Ger 1957)
   Der tolle Bomberg (Ger 1957)
   Das Mädchen Rosemarie (Ger 1958) (also co-script)
   Die Halbzarte (Ger 1959)
   Labyrinth (Ger 1959) (also co-script)
   Auf Engel schiesst mann nicht (Ger 1960) (also script)
   Der liebe Augustin (Ger 1960)
   Man nennt es Amore (Ger 1961) (also co-script)
   Lulu (Ger 1962) (also script)
   Das schwarz-weiss-rote Himmelbett (Ger 1962)
   Moral 63 (Ger 1963) (also script)
   Venusberg (Ger 1963) (also script)
   DM-Killer (Ger 1964) (also co-script)
   Tonio Kröger (Ger-Fr 1964)
   Wälsungenblut (Ger 1964)
   Die Herren (Ger 1965) (co-dir.)
   Das Liebeskarussell (Ger 1965) (co-dir.)
   Grieche sucht Griechin (Ger 1966)
   Der Tod eines Doppelgängers (Ger 1966) (also script)
   Der Lügner und die Nonne [The Liar and the Nun] (Ger 1967)
     (with Joseph Cezch)
   Die Ente klingelt um 1/2-8 (Ger-It 1968)
   Komm nur, mein liebstes Vögelein ... (Ger 1968) (also co-
     script)
   Grimms Märchen von lusternen Pärchen (Ger 1969)
   Ohrfeigen (Ger 1969) (also script)
   Komm nach Wien--ich zeig Dir was (Ger 1969)
   Bleib sauber, liebling! (Ger 1971)
   Die scharfe Heinrich--die bumsfidelen Abenteuer einer jungen
     Ehe (Ger 1971)
   Gelobt sei, was hart macht (Ger 1972)
   Versuchung im Sommerwind (Ger 1973)

THIELE, WILHELM (William Thiele), b. May 10, 1890, Vienna
   Fiat Lux (Aus 1923)
   Carl Michael Ziehrers Märchen auf Alt-Wien (Aus 1923) (also
     co-script)
   Franz Lehar (Aus 1923) (with Hans Torre)
   Das Totenmahl auf Schloss Begalitza (Ger 1923) (also script)
   Orient Express (Ger 1927) (also script)
   Der Anwalt des Herzens (Ger 1927) (also co-script)
   Die Dame mit der Maske (Ger 1928)
   Hurrah! Ich Liebe (Ger 1928)
   Adieu, Mascotte (Ger 1929)
   Liebeswalzer (Ger 1930)

Rolf Thiele

Valse d'Amour [Fr version of Liebeswaltzer] (Ger 1930) (with
  Germaine Dulac)
Die Drei von der Tankstelle (Ger 1930)
Le Chemin du Paradis [Fr version of Die Drei von der Tank-
  stelle] (Ger 1930) (with Max de Vaucorbeil)
Die Privatsekretärin (Ger 1930)
Dactylo [Fr version of Die Privatesekretärin] (Ger 1930) (with
  Richard Pottier)
Der Ball (Ger 1931)
Le Bal [Fr version of Der Ball] (Ger 1931)
Madame hat Ausgang (Ger 1931) (also co-script)
L'Amoureuse Aventure [Fr version of Madame hat Ausgang]
  (Ger 1931)
Zwei Herzen und ein Schlat (Ger 1932)
Le Fille et le garçon [Fr version of Zwei Herzen und ein
  Schlag] (Ger 1932)
Mädchen zum Heiraten (Ger 1932)
Marry Me [English version of Mädchen zum Heiraten] (Ger 1932)
Waltz Time (Gaumont 1932)
Grossfürstin Alexandra (Aus 1933)
Lottery Lover (USA) (Fox 1935)
Don't Get Personal (USA) (Univ 1936)
The Jungle Princess (USA) (Par 1936)
London by Night (USA) (MGM 1937)
Beg, Borrow or Steal (USA) (MGM 1937)
Bad Little Angel (USA) (MGM 1939)
Bridal Suite (USA) (MGM 1939)
The Ghost Comes Home (USA) (MGM 1940)
Tarzan's Triumph (USA) (RKO 1943)
Tarzan's Desert Mystery (USA) (RKO 1943)
The Madonna's Secret (USA) (Rep 1946)
Der letzte Fussgänger (Ger 1960)
Sabine und die 100 Männer (Ger 1960)

THOMAS, GERALD, b. Dec. 10, 1920, Hull, England
  Circus Friends (BL-CFF 1956)
  Time Lock (IFD 1957)
  The Vicious Circle [The Circle] (IFD 1957)
  The Duke Wore Jeans (AA 1958)
  Carry On Sergeant (AA 1958)
  Chain of Events (RL 1958)
  The Solitary Child (BL 1958)
  Carry On Nurse (AA 1959)
  Carry On Teacher (AA 1959)
  Please Turn Over (AA 1959)
  Carry On Constable (AA 1960)
  Watch Your Stern (AA 1960)
  No Kidding [Beware of Children] (AA 1960)
  Carry On Regardless (AA 1961)
  Raising the Wind (AA 1961)
  Twice Round the Daffodils (AA 1962)
  Carry On Cruising (AA 1962)
  The Iron Maiden (AA 1962)
  Nurse on Wheels (AA 1963)

Carry On Cabby (AA 1963)
Carry On Jack (AA 1963)
Carry On Spying (AA 1964)
Carry On Cleo (AA 1964)
The Big Job (AA 1965)
Carry On Cowboy (AA 1965)
Carry On Screaming (AA 1966)
Don't Lose Your Head (RFD 1966)
Follow That Camel (RFD 1967)
Carry On Doctor (RFD 1968)
Carry On--Up the Khyber (RFD 1968)
Carry On Camping (RFD 1969)
Carry On Again, Doctor (RFD 1969)
Carry On Up the Jungle (RFD 1970)
Carry On Loving (RFD 1970)
Carry On Henry (RFD 1971)
Carry On At Your Convenience (RFD 1971)
Carry On Matron (RFD 1972)
Carry On Abroad (20th-Rank 1972)
Bless This House (20th-Rank 1973)
Carry On Girls (20th-Rank 1973)
Carry On Dick (20th-Rank 1974)

THOMAS, RALPH, b. Aug. 10, 1915, Hull, England
Once Upon a Dream (GFD 1949)
Helter Skelter (GFD 1949)
Traveller's Joy (GFD 1949)
The Clouded Yellow (GFD 1950)
Appointment with Venus [Island Rescue] (GFD 1951)
Venetian Bird [The Assassin] (GFD 1952)
A Day to Remember (GFD 1953)
The Dog and the Diamonds (ABFD-CFF 1953)
Doctor in the House (GFD 1954)
Mad About Men (GFD 1954)
Above Us the Waves (GFD 1955)
Doctor at Sea (RFD 1955)
The Iron Petticoat (IFD 1956)
Checkpoint (RFD 1956)
Doctor at Large (RFD 1957)
Campbell's Kingdom (RFD 1957)
A Tale of Two Cities (RFD 1958)
The Wind Cannot Read (RFD 1958)
The 39 Steps (RFD 1959)
Upstairs and Downstairs (RFD 1959)
Conspiracy of Hearts (RFD 1960)
Doctor in Love (RFD 1960)
No Love for Johnnie (RFD 1961)
No, My Darling Daughter (RFD 1961)
A Pair of Briefs (RFD 1962)
The Wild and the Willing (RFD 1962)
Doctor in Distress (RFD 1963)
Hot Enough for June [Agent 8 3/4] (RFD 1963)
The High Bright Sun [McGuire Go Home!] (RFD 1964)

Doctor in Clover (RFD 1965)
Deadlier Than the Male (RFD 1966)
Nobody Runs Forever (RFD 1968)
Some Girls Do (RFD 1969)
Doctor in Trouble (RFD 1970)
Percy (MGM-EMI 1971)
Quest for Love (RFD 1971)
It's a 2' 6" above the Ground World (BL 1972)† [co-production
    company]
Percy's Progress (EMI 1974)† [co-production company]

THOMPSON, J(OHN) LEE, b. Aug. 1, 1914, Bristol, England
Murder Without Crime (ABP 1950) (also script)
The Yellow Balloon (ABP 1952) (also co-script)
The Weak and the Wicked (ABP 1954) (also co-script)
For Better for Worse [Cocktails in the Kitchen] (ABP 1954)
    (also co-script)
As Long As They're Happy (GFD 1955)
An Alligator Named Daisy (RFD 1955)
Yield to the Night [Blonde Sinner] (ABP 1956)
The Good Companions (ABPC 1957)
Woman in a Dressing Gown (ABP 1957)
Ice Cold in Alex (ABP 1958) (also co-script)
Tiger Bay (RFD 1959)
No Trees in the Street (ABP 1959)
North West Frontier [Flame Over India] (RFD 1959)
I Aim at the Stars (USA) (Col 1960)
The Guns of Navarone (Col Br 1961)
Cape Fear (USA) (Univ 1962)
Taras Bulba (USA) (UA 1962)
Kings of the Sun (USA) (UA 1963)
What a Way to Go (USA) (20th 1963)
Return from the Ashes (UA Br 1965) (also co-producer)
Eye of the Devil (MGM Br 1966) (with uncredited Michael An-
    derson)
Before Winter Comes (Col Br 1969)
Country Dance (MGM-EMI 1971) (made in 1969)
Huckleberry Finn (USA) (UA 1974)

TOURJANSKY, VICTOR, b. March 4, 1892, Kiev, Russia
Simfonija ljubvi i smerti (Rus 1914) (with S. Jur'ev)
Bratja Karamazovy (Rus 1915) (also script)
Ljubov' pod maskoj (Rus 1915)
Po trupam k scast'ju (Rus 1915) (acted also)
Kak Kubyskin stal kinoakterom (Rus 1915)
Poimet kto ljubit (Rus 1915) (also acted)
Skazka morja (Rus 1915)
Syn strany gde carstvo mraka (Rus 1915) (also actor)
Velikij Magaraz (Rus 1915) (also actor) (with A. Kamenskij)
Zenscinavampir (Rus 1915) (also actor)
Magaraz (Rus 1916)
Ljubov', sirokuju, kak more vinestit' ne mogut zizni berega
    (Rus 1916)

Yvette (Rus 1917)
Ostrov zaben'ja (Rus 1917) (also actor)
Prazdnik noci (Rus 1917)
Skertso diavola (Rus 1918)
Surogaty ljubvi (Rus 1918) (also story, script, actor)
Obmanutaja Eva (Rus 1918)
Balgospoden (Rus 1919)
Irene Negludov (Rus 1919)
L'ordonnance (Fr 1920)
Les contes de Mille et une Nuits (Fr 1921)
Le 15, prélude de Chopin (Fr 1922)
Nuit de Carnaval (Fr 1922)
Le chant de l'amour triomphant (Fr 1923)
Calvaire d'amour (Fr 1923)
Ce cochon de Morin (Fr 1924)
La Dame masquée (Fr 1924)
Le Prince charmant (Fr 1924)
Michel Strogoff (Fr 1926)
The Gallant Gringo [The Adventurer] (USA) (MGM 1928) (completed by W. S. Van Dyke II)
Wolga Wolga (Ger 1928)
Manolescu (Ger 1929)
Der Herzog von Reichstadt (Ger 1931)
L'Aiglon (Fr 1931) [Fr version of Der Herzog von Reichstadt]
Le Chanteur inconnu (Fr 1932)
L'hotel des etudiants (Fr 1932)
The Battle [English version of La bataille] (Fr 1933)
L'Ordonnance (Fr 1934)
Volga en flammes (Czech-Fr 1934)
Les Yeux noirs (Fr 1935)
Die ganze Welt dreht sich um Liebe (Ger 1935)
Vertige d'un soir (Fr 1935)
Stadt Anatol (Ger 1936)
Puits en flammes (Fr version of Stadt Anatol) (Ger 1936)
La Mensonge de Nina Petrowna (Fr 1937)
Nostalgie (Fr 1937)
Der Blaufuchs (Ger 1938)
Geheimzeichen LB 17 (Ger 1938)
Verklungene Melodie (Ger 1938)
Eine Frau wie Du (Ger 1939)
Der Gouverneur (Ger 1939)
Feinde (Ger 1940) (also co-script)
Die keusche Geliebte (Ger 1940)
Illusion (Ger 1941) (also co-script)
Die goldene Brücke (Ger 1942)
Liebesgeschichten (Ger 1942)
Tonelli (Ger 1943) (also co-script)
Orient-Express (Ger 1944) (also co-script)
Dreimal Komödie (Ger 1945) (also co-script)
Si te hubieras casada (Sp 1948)
Der blaue Strohut (Ger 1949) (also co-script)
Der Mann, der Zweimal Leben wollte (Ger 1950)
Vom Teufel gejagt (Ger 1950) (also co-script)

Mutter sein dagegen sehr (Ger 1951)
Ehe für eine Nacht (Ger 1952)
Salto mortale (Ger 1953)
Arlette erlobert Paris (Ger 1955)
Morgengrauen (Ger 1954)
Die Toteninsel (Ger 1955) (also co-script)
Königswalzer (Ger 1955)
Beichtgeheimnis (Ger 1956)
Herz ohne Gnade (Ger 1958)
La Venere di Cheronea (It 1957)
I battelieri del Volga (It 1958)
Eroe il grande (It 1959) (with A. Genoino)
I cosacchi (It 1959) (with D. Damiani)
La donna dei faraoni (It 1960) (with G. Rivalta)
Michel Strogoff [Le Triomphe de Michel Strogoff] (It-Fr-Yug
   1961)
Una regina per Cesare (It 1962)

TOYE, WENDY, b. May 1, 1917, London
The Teckman Mystery (BL 1954)
Raising a Riot (BL 1955)
Three Cases of Murder (ep "In the Picture") (BL 1955)
All for Mary (RFD 1955)
True as a Turtle (RFD 1957)
We Joined the Navy (WPD 1962)

TRENKER, LUIS, b. Oct. 4, 1892, Ulrich, Germany
Berg im Flammen (Ger 1931) (also actor) (with Karl Hartl)
Der Rebell (Ger 1932) (also actor) (with Kurt Berhnhardt)
Der verlorene Sohn (Ger 1934) (also script, actor)
Der Kaiser von Kalifornien (Ger 1936) (also script, actor)
Condottieri (It-Ger 1937) (also co-script, actor)
Der Berg ruft (Ger 1937) (also co-script, actor)
Liebesbriefe aus dem Engadin (Ger 1938) (also co-script) (with
   co-director)
Der Feuerteufel (Ger 1940)
Flucht in die Dolomiten [Il prigioniero della montagna] (Ger-
   Fr-It 1955) (also co-script) (with G. Bassino, Pier Paolo
   Pasolini)
Von der Liebe besiegt (Ger 1956) (also actor)
Wetterleuchten um Maria (Ger 1957)
Sein bester Freund (Ger 1962)

TROMMER, HANS, b. Dec. 18, 1904, Zürich
Romeo und Julia auf dem Dorfe (Swi 1941) (with Valerian
   Schmidely)
Lucerne et son festival international de musique (Swi 1946-1947)
Das Kabel (Swi 1951-1952)
Landschaft in Umbruch (Swi 1956)
Zum goldenen Ochsen (Swi 1958)
Zürcher Impressionen (Swi 1961)
Begegnungen (Swi 1964)

TRONSON, ROBERT (Robert De Coudre Tronson), b. May 18,
1924, Chilmark, Wiltshire, England
Man at the Carlton Tower (AA 1961)
Man Detained (AA 1961)
Never Back Losers (AA 1961)
Number Six (AA 1962)
The Traitors (RFD 1962)
On the Run (AA 1963)
Farewell Performance (AA 1963)
Ring of Spies (AA 1963)

TRUFFAUT, FRANÇOIS, b. Feb. 6, 1932, Paris
Les 400 coups [The 400 Blows] (Fr 1959) (also script, co-
adaptor)
Tirez sur le pianiste [Shoot the Painist] (Fr 1960) (also script,
co-adaptor, dialogue)
Jules et Jim (Fr 1961) (also script, co-adaptor)
L'amour à vingt ans (ep "Antoine et Colette") [Love at Twenty]
(Fr 1962) (also script)
La Peau douce [Silken Skin] (Fr 1964) (also co-script, co-dia-
logue)
Fahrenheit 451 (GB) (RFD 1966) (also co-script)
La Mariée était en noir [The Bride Wore Black] (Fr-It 1967)
(also co-script)
Baisers volés [Stolen Kisses] (Fr 1968) (also co-script)
La Sirène du Mississippi [Mississippi Mermaid] (Fr-It 1969)
(also script)
L'Enfant sauvage [The Wild Child] (Fr 1969) (also co-script,
actor)
Domicile conjugal [Bed and Board] (Fr-It 1970) (also co-script)
Les Deux Anglaises et le Continent [Anne and Muriel] (Fr 1971)
(also co-script, narrator)
Une Belle Fille comme moi [Such A Gorgeous Kid Like Me]
(Fr 1972) (also co-script)
La Nuit américaine [Day for Night] (Fr-It 1973) (also co-script,
actor)

UCICKY, GUSTAV, b. 1898, Vienna; d. 1961
Cafe Electric (Aus 1927)
Pratermizzi (Aus 1927) (with co-director)
Tingel-Tangel (Ger 1927)
Ein Besserer Herr (Ger 1928)
Herzen ohne Ziel (Ger 1928) (with co-director)
Der Sträfling aus Stambul (Ger 1929)
Vererbte Triebe (Ger 1929)
Das Flötenkonzert von Sanssouci (Ger 1930)
Hokuspokus (Ger 1930)
Der unsterbliche Lump (Ger 1930)
Yorck (Ger 1930)
Im Geheimdienst (Ger 1931)
Mensch ohne Namen (Ger 1932)
Un homme sans nom (Fr 1932) (Fr version of Meusch ohne
Namen)

François Truffaut

Morgenrot (Ger 1933)
Flüchtlinge (Ger 1933)
Der junge Baron Neuhaus (Ger 1934) (also script)
Das Mädchen Johanna (Ger 1935)
Unter heissem Himmel (Ger 1936)
Savoy-Hotel 217 (Ger 1936)
Der zerbrochene Krug (Ger 1937)
Frau Sixta (Ger 1938)
Mutterliebe (Ger 1939)
Aufruhr in Damaskus (Ger 1939)
Der Postmeister (Ger 1940)
Ein Leben lang (Ger 1940)
Heimkehr (Ger 1941)
Späte Liebe (Ger 1943)
Am Ende der Welt (Ger 1943)
Der gebieterische Ruf (Ger 1944)

Das Herz muss schweigen (Ger 1944)
Singende Engel (Ger 1949) (also co-script)
Der Seelenbräu (Ger 1950)
Cordula (Ger 1950) (also co-script)
Bis wir uns wiederseh'n (Ger 1952)
Der Kaplan von San Lorenzo (Ger 1952)
Ein Leben für Do (Ger 1953)
Die Hexe (Ger 1954) (also co-script)
Zwei blaue Augen (Ger 1955)
Die Heilige und ihr Narr (Ger 1957)
Der Jager von Fall (Ger 1957)
Der Edelweisskönig (Ger 1957)
Das Mädchen vom Moorhof (Ger 1958)
Der Priester und das Mädchen (Ger 1958)
Das Erbe von Björndal (Ger 1960)

USTINOV, PETER, b. April 16, 1921, London
School for Secrets (GFD 1946) (also script, actor)
Vice Versa (GFD 1948) (also co-producer, script, actor)
Private Angelo (ABP 1949) (with Michael Anderson) (also pro-
    ducer, co-script, actor)
Romanoff and Juliet (USA) (Univ 1961) (also producer, script,
    actor)
Billy Budd (RFD 1962) (also co-script, actor)
Hammersmith Is Out (USA) (Cin 1972) (also actor)

VADIM, ROGER (Roger Vadim Plemiannikov), b. Jan. 26, 1928,
    Paris
Et Dieu créa la femme [And God Created Woman] (Fr 1956)
    (also co-script, co-adaptor, co-dialogue)
Sait-on jamais (Fr-It 1957) (also script, dialogue)
Les Bijoutiers du clair de lune [Heaven Fell That Night] (Fr
    1957) (also co-script, co-dialogue)
Les Liaisons dangereuses (Fr 1959) (also script, co-adaptor)
Et mourir de plaisir [Blood and Roses] (Fr-It 1960) (also
    script, co-adaptor)
La Bride sur le cou [Please, Not Now!] (Fr 1961) (begun by
    Jean Aurel)
Les Sept Péchés capitaux (ep "L'orgueil") [Seven Capital Sins]
    (Fr 1962) (also script)
Le Vice et le vertu [Vice and Virtue] (Fr-It 1962) (also co-
    script, co-adaptor)
Château en Suède (Fr-It 1963) (also script, co-adaptor)
La Ronde (Fr-It 1964)
La Curée [The Game Is Over] (Fr 1966) (also script, co-
    adaptor)
Barbarella (Fr-It 1967) (also co-script)
Histoires extraordinaires [Tales of Mystery] (ep "Metzenger-
    stein") (Fr-It 1967) (also co-script)
Pretty Maids All in a Row (USA) (MGM-EMI 1971)
Hellé (Fr 1972) (also script, co-adaptor, co-dialogue)
Don Juan 1973 (Fr-It 1973) (also script, co-adaptor)
La Jeune Fille assassinée [Charlotte] (Fr-W Ger-It 1974) (also
    script, adaptor, dialogue)

Flinke Kerels (Bel 1938)
Engel van en Man (Bel 1939)
den Helm Geboren (Bel 1939)
Nieuwe Levensvreugd (Bel 1939)
sens Tegen Peeters (Bel 1939)
s Troof (Bel 1940)
ens en Peeters Dikke Vrienden (Bel 1940)
Geluk, Monika (Bel 1941)
de Fliere Flinker (Bel 1942)

STEFANO (a.k.a. Steno), b. Jan. 19, 1915, Rome
   with Mario Monicelli
olo la celebrità [Fame and the Devil] (It 1949)
rca casa (It 1949)
ato il cavaliere (It 1950)
cani (It 1950)
e ladri (It 1951)
re di Roma (It 1952)
donne (It 1952)
lori (It 1952)
i [The Unfaithfuls] (It 1953)

bestia e la virtù (It 1953)
ltri tempi (It-Fr 1953)
pretura (It 1954)
o a Roma (It 1954)
e di Giacomo Casanova [Sins of Casanova] (It-Fr

(It 1955)
rone (It-Fr 1956)
volte (It-Sp 1956)
panna (It 1957)
iziotto (It 1958)
e cameriera (It 1958)
(It 1958)
pennello proibito (It-Fr-Sp 1959)
i vampiri [Uncle Was a Vampire] (It 1959)
ldo (It 1960)
e (It 1960)
ezzo (It 1960)
1960)
ille mesi (It 1961)
t 1962)
mare [Musketeers of the Sea] (It-Fr 1962)
(It 1962)
1962)
ro (It 1963)
It-Sp 1963)
(It 1964)
965)
t 1966)
elica (It-Fr-Sp 1966)
1968)

Peter Ustinov with Anthony Newley shooting Vice Versa (1947).

VADJA, LADISLAO, b. Aug. 18, 1905, Budapest; d. March 25,
   1965
   The Beggar Student (BL 1931)
   Where Is This Lady? (BL 1932) (with Victor Hanbury)
   Hallo Budapest! (Hun 1934)
   Ember a hid alatt (Hun 1936)
   Szenzacio (Hun 1936) (with Istvan Szekely)
   Wings over Africa (RKO Br 1936)
   Harom Saekany (Hun 1936)
   The Wife of General Ling (Eng 1937)

A kokcsonkert kastely (Hun 1937)
Az en lanyom nem olyan (Hun 1937)
Rozsa Bokor (Hun 1937)
Magdat kicsapiak (Hun 1938)
Donto pillanat (Hun 1938)
Fekete gyemantok (Hun 1938)
Pentek Rezi (Hun 1938)
Rozmaring (Hun 1938)
Giuliano de' Medici (It 1940)
La zia smemorata (It 1941) (also script)
Se vende un palacio (Sp 1943)
Doce lunas de miel (Sp 1943)
Te quiero para mi (Sp 1944)
El testamento del Virrey (Sp 1944)
Cinco lobitos (Sp 1945)
Tres espejos (Sp 1947)
Barrio (Sp 1947)
Sin uniforme (Sp 1948)
The Call of the Blood [Il richiamo del sangue] (GB-It 1948)
The Golden Madonna [La madonna d'oro] (GB-It 1949)
The Woman with No Name [Her Panelled Door] (ABP 1950)
   (also co-script)
Septima pagina (Sp 1950)
Ronda española (Sp 1951)
Dona Francisquita (Sp 1952) (also co-script)
Carne de horca (Sp-It 1953)
Adventuras del barbero de Sevilla (It-Sp 1954)
Marcelino, pan y vino (Sp-It 1955) (also co-story, co-script)
Tarde de toros (Sp 1955)
Mio tio Jacinto [Pepote] (It-Sp 1956) (also co-script)
Un angel paso por Brooklyn (Sp-It 1957) (also co-script)
Es geschah am hellichten Tage [It Happened in Broad Daylight]
   (Ger-Swi 1958) (also co-script)
Ein Mann geht durch die Wand (Ger 1959)
Maria, matricula de Bilboa (Sp 1960)
Der Lügner (Ger 1961)
Die Schatten werden langer [Girls in the Shadows] (Ger 1962)
   (also co-script)
Das Feuerschiff (Ger 1963)
La signora di Beirut (Unfinished; It 1965)

VALERE, JEAN, b. May 21, 1925, Paris
   La Sentence [The Verdict] (Fr 1959) (also co-script)
   Les Grandes Personnes (Fr-It 1960) (also co-script)
   Le Gros Coup (Fr-It 1964) (also co-script)
   La Femme écarlate (Fr-It 1969) (also co-script)
   Mont-Dragon (Fr 1971) (also co-script)

VANCINI, FLORESTANO (a.k.a. Stan Vance), b. Aug. 24, 1936,
      Ferrara, Italy
   La lunga notte dell '43 (It 1960)
   Le Italiane e l'amore (ep "Le separazione legale") (It 1961)
   La banda Casaroli (It 1962)

La calda vita (It 1964)
Le stagioni del nostro amore (It 196
I lunghi giorni della vendetta (It 19
Un'estate in quattro (It 1969)
Violenza al sole (It 1970)
Commissione Parlamentare d'inch
   Mafia in Sicilia (It 1971)
La Vendetta (It 1972)
Il delitto Matteotti (It 1972)
Amore amara (It 1974)

VAN DER HEY
   Nether
Een Octe
   Fr 1
To Gra

VANDERH
   19
De V
Alle
Uil
De
H

Dri
Een
Met
Naa
Jans
Wit
Jans
Veel
Anton

VANZINA,
Co-directed
   Al diav
   Totò ce
   E arriva
   Vita da
   Guardie
   Totò e i
   Totò e le
   Totò e co
   Le infedel
Directed Alone
   L'uomo, la
   Cinema d'a
   Un giorni i
   Un america
   Le avventu
      1954)
   Piccola posta
   Mio figlio Ne
   Femmine tre
   Susanna tutta
   Mia nonna pol
   Guardia, ladro
   Totò nella luna
   Totò, Eva e il
   Tempi duri per
   A noi piace fre
   Letto a tre piaz
   Un militare e m
   Psycosissimo (It
   Le ragazza di m
   Totò Diabolicus
   I moschettieri de
   Copacabana palac
   I due colonnelli (I
   Totò contro i quat
   Gli eroi del West (
   Un mostro e mezz
   Letti sbagliati (It 1
   Amore all'Italiana (
   Rose rosse per Ang
   La feldmarescialla (

Capriccio all'Italiana (ep "Il Maestro della domenica") (It 1968)
Arriva Dorelik (It 1968)
I trapianto (It-Sp 1969)
Cose di "Cosa Nostra" (It-Fr 1970)
Il vichingo venuto dal Sud (It-Fr 1971)
Anastasia mio fratello presunto capo dell'Anonima assassini
    (It 1972)
Il terrore con gli occhi storti (It 1972)
L'uccello migratore (It 1972)

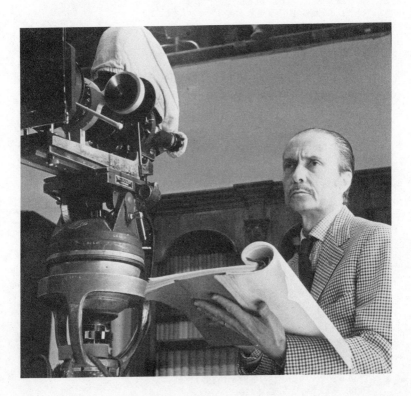

Stefano Vanzina ("Steno")

VARDA, AGNES, b. May 30, 1928
    La Pointe-Courte (Fr 1955) (also script, dialogue)
    Cléo de 5 à 7 (Fr 1962) (also script, dialogue)
    Le Bonheur (Fr 1965) (also script, dialogue)
    Loin du Vietnam [Far from Vietnam] (Fr 1967) (with William
        Klein, Alain Resnais, Joris Ivens, Claude Lelouch, Jean-Luc
        Godard)
    Les Créatures (Fr-Swe 1966) (also script, dialogue)
    Lions Love (USA) (Max Raab 1969) (also producer, script)

VARI, GIUSEPPE (a. k. a. Jack Warren)
   Infame accusa (It 1952)
   Mamma perdonami (It 1954)
   Due lacrime (It 1954)
   Addio sogni di gloria (It 1955)
   Il ricatto di un padre (It 1957)
   Giovane canaglia (It-Sp 1958)
   Spavaldi e innamorati (It 1959)
   I normanni [Attack of the Normans] (It-Fr 1962)
   Canzoni in ... bikini (It 1963)
   Roma contro Roma (It 1964)
   Deguejo (It 1966)
   L'ultimo killer (It 1967)
   Un buco in fronte (It 1968)
   Un posto all'inferno (It 1969)
   Terza impotesi su un caso di perfetta strategia criminale (It
     1972)
   Il lupo dei mari (It 1974)

VARNEL, MARCEL, b. Oct. 16, 1894, Paris; d. July 13, 1947
   Silent Witness (USA) (Fox 1932) (with R. L. Hough)
   Chandu the Magician (USA) (Fox 1932) (with William Cameron
     Menzies)
   Infernal Machine (USA) (Fox 1933)
   Freedom of the Seas (Wardour 1934)
   Girls Will Be Boys (Wardour 1934)
   Dance Band (Wardour 1935)
   No Monkey Business (GFD 1935)
   I Give My Heart (Wardour 1935)
   Public Nuisance Number 1 (GFD 1936)
   All In (GFD 1936)
   Good Morning Boys [Where There's a Will] (Gaumont 1937)
   Okay for Sound (GFD 1937)
   Oh, Mr. Porter! (GFD 1937)
   Convict 99 (GFD 1938)
   Alf's Button Afloat (GFD 1938)
   Hey! Hey! USA! (GFD 1938)
   Old Bones of the River (GFD 1938)
   Ask a Policeman (MGM Br 1939)
   Where's That Fire? (20th 1939)
   The Frozen Limits (GFD 1939)
   Band Waggon (GFD 1940)
   Let George Do It (ABFD 1940)
   Gasbags (EFS 1940)
   Neutral Port (GFD 1940)
   The Ghost of St. Michael's (ABFD 1941)
   Turned Out Nice Again (UA Br 1941)
   I Thank You (GFD 1941)
   Hi Gang! (GFD 1941)
   South American George (GFD 1941)
   Much Too Shy (Col Br 1942)
   King Arthur Was a Gentleman (GFD 1942)
   Get Cracking (Col Br 1943)

Bell-Bottom George (Col Br 1943)
He Snoops to Conquer (Col Br 1944)
I Didn't Do It (Col Br 1945) (also co-producer)
George in Civvy Street (Col Br 1946) (also co-producer)
This Man Is Mine (Col Br 1946) (also producer)

VERHAVERT, ROLAND, b. May 1, 1927, Melsele-Waas, Belgium
Meeuwen Sterven in de Haven (Bel 19   ) (also co-script) (with
Rik Kuypers, Ivo Michiels)
Kerkhofblommen (Bel 1964)
Het Afscheid (Bel 1966)
Maurice Maeterlinck (Bel TV 1969)
Is Dat Recht Vaardig (Bel TV 1971)
Rolande met de Bles (Bel 1972)
De Loteling (Bel 1973)

VERHOEVEN, MICHAEL, b. Germany
Paarungen (Ger 1967)
Engelchen macht weiter--hope, hoppe Reiter (Ger 1968)
Der Bettenstudent, oder. Was mach' ich mit den Mädchen (Ger
1969)
OK (Ger 1970)
Wer in Glashaus liebt ... der Graben (Ger 1971)

VERHOEVEN, PAUL, b. 1938, Netherlands
Floris (Dut TV series) (1968-1969)
Wat Zien Ik [Business Is Business] (Dut 1972)
Turkish Delight (Dut 1973)
Keetje Tippel (Dut 1975)

VERNEUIL, HENRI, b. Oct. 15, 1920, Rhodes
La Table aux creves [The Village Feud] (Fr 1951) (also co-
script)
Brelan d'as [Full House] (Fr 1952)
Le Fruit défendu [Forbidden Fruit] (Fr 1952) (also co-script)
Le Boulanger de Valorgue [The Baker of Valorgue] (Fr-It 1953)
Carnaval (Fr 1953)
L'Ennemi public no. I [Public Enemy No. 1] (Fr-It 1953)
Le Mouton à 5 pattes [The Sheep Has 5 Legs] (Fr 1954) (also
co-script)
Les Amants du Tage [The Lovers of Lisbon] (Fr 1954)
Des Gens sans importance (Fr 1955) (also co-script)
Paris-Palace Hôtel (Fr-It 1956) (also co-script)
Une Manche et la belle (Fr 1957) (also co-script)
Maxime (Fr 1958)
Le Grand Chef [The Big Chief] (Fr-It 1958) (also co-script)
La Vache et le prisonnier [The Cow and I] (Fr-W Ger 1959)
(also co-script)
La Française et l'amour [Love and the Frenchwoman] (ep
"L'Adultère") (Fr 1960)
L'Affaire d'une nuit (Fr 1960)
Le Président (Fr-It 1961) (also co-script)
Les Lions sont lâchés [The Lions Are Loose] (Fr-It 1961)

Un Singe en hiver (Fr 1962)
Mélodie en sous-sol [The Big Snatch] (Fr-It 1962) (also co-script)
100,000 dollars au soleil (Fr-It 1963) (also co-script)
Weekend à Zuydcoote [Weekend at Dunkirk] (Fr-It 1964)
La Vingt-cinquième heure [The 25th Hour] (Fr-It-Yug 1967) (also co-script)
La Bataille de San Sebastian [Guns for San Sebastian] (Fr-Mex-It 1967) (also uncredited co-adaptor)
Le Clan de Siciliens [The Sicilian Clan] (Fr 1968) (also co-script)
Le Casse [The Burglars] (Fr-It 1971) (also co-script)
Le Serpent [The Serpent] (Fr-It-W Ger 1973) (also producer, co-script)

VERSTAPPEN, WIM, b. Apr. 15, 1937, Gemert, Netherlands
De Minder Gelukkige Terugkeer van Jozef Katus Naar het Land van Rembrandt (Dut 1966)
Confessions of Loving Couples (Dut 1967) (with Pim de la Parra)
Liefdesbekentenissen (Dut 1967)
Tag der offenen Tür (Ger TV 1967) (with Pim de la Parra)
Drop Out (Dut 1969)
Festival of Love (Dut 1970)
Blue Movie (Dut 1971)
V. D. (Dut 1972)
Dakota (Dut 1974)
Alicia (Dut 1974)
Wraak (Dut 1975)

VIERTEL, BERTHOLD, b. June 28, 1885, Vienna; d. Sept. 25, 1953
Nora (Ger 1923) (also co-script)
Die Perücke (Ger 1924) (also script)
Die Abenteuer eines Zehnmarkscheines (Ger 1926)
The One Woman Idea (USA) (Fox 1929)
Seven Faces (USA) (Fox 1929)
Man Trouble (USA) (Fox 1930)
The Spy (USA) (Fox 1931)
The Magnificent Lie (USA) (Par 1931)
Die heilige Flamme [Ger version of The Sacred Flame] (USA) (WB 1931) (also co-script)
The Wiser Sex (USA) (Par 1932)
The Man From Yesterday (USA) (Par 1932)
Little Friend (Gaumont 1934)
The Passing of the Third Floor Back (Gaumont 1935)
Rhodes of Africa (Gaumont 1936)

VIGO, JEAN, b. April 26, 1905, Paris; d. Oct. 5, 1934
À propos de Nice (Fr 1930) (also producer, script, editor)
Zéro de conduite (Fr 1933) (also producer, script, editor)
L'Atalante (Fr 1934) (also producer, co-script)

VISCONTI, LUCHINO, b. Nov. 2, 1906, Milan
   Osessione (It 1942) (also co-script)
   Giorni di Gloria (ep) (It 1945)
   La terra trema (It 1948) (also script)
   Bellissima (It 1951) (also co-script)
   Appunti su un fatto di cronaco (It 1951)
   Siamo donne [We the Women] (ep) (It 1953)
   Senso [The Wanton Contessa] (It 1954) (also co-script)
   Le notti bianche [White Nights] (It 1957) (also co-script)
   Rocco e i suoi fratelli [Rocco and His Brothers] (It 1960) (also
   Il gattopardo [The Leopard] (It 1963) (also co-script)
   Vaghe stelle dell'Orsa [Sandra] (It 1965) (also co-script)
   Le streghe (ep "La strega bruciata via") (It 1967)
   Lo straniero [The Stranger] (It 1967) (also co-script)
   La caduta degli dei [Götterdammerung: The Damned] (It 1969)
     (also co-script)
   Morte a Venezia [Death in Venice] (It-Fr 1970) (also producer,
     co-script)
   Ludwig (It 1972) (also co-story, co-script)
   Grupo di famiglia in un interno (It 1974)

Luchino Visconti

VIVARELLI, PIERO (a. k. a. Donald Murray)
   Sanremo la grand sfida (It 1960)
   Io bacio ... tu baci (It 1960)
   Oggi a Berlini (It 1962)
   Il vuolto (It 1963)
   Rita la figlia americana (It 1965)

Mister X (It 1967)
Satanik (It 1968) (also actor)
Il Decamerone nero (It-Fr 1969)

VOHRER, ALFRED, b. 1918, Stuttgart
Schmutziger Engel (Ger 1958)
Meine Bräute (Ger 1958)
Verbrechen nach Schulschluss (Ger 1959)
Mit 17 weint man nicht (Ger 1960)
Bis dass das Geld euch scheidet (Ger 1960)
Unser Haus in Kamerun (Ger 1961)
Die toten Augen von London [The Dead Eyes of London] (Ger 1961)
Die Tür mit den sieben Schlössern [The Door with Seven Locks] (Ger 1961)
Das Gasthaus an der Themse [The Inn on the river] (Ger 1962)
Ein Alibi zerbricht (Ger 1963)
Der Zinker [The Squeaker] (Ger 1963)
Das indische Tuch [The indian scarf] (Ger 1963)
Der Hexer [The Mysterious Magician] (Ger 1964)
Unter Geiern [Among Vultures] (Ger-It-Fr-Yug 1964)
Wartezimmer zum Jenseits (Ger 1964)
Neues vom Hexer (Ger 1965)
Old Surehand I [Flaming Frontier] (Ger-Yug 1965)
Lange Beine--lange Finger (Ger 1966)
Winnetou und sein Freund Old Firehand (Ger-Yug 1966)
Der Bucklige von Soho (Ger 1966)
Die blaue Hand (Ger 1967)
Der Mönch mit der Peitsche (Ger 1967)
Der Hund von Blackwood Castle (Ger 1967)
Im Banne des Unheimlichen (Ger 1968)
Der Gorilla von Soho (Ger 1968)
Der Mann mit dem Glasauge (Ger 1968)
Sieben Tage Frist (Ger 1969)
Herzblatt, oder Wie sag ich's Meiner Tochter (Ger 1969)
Das gelbe Haus am Pinnasberg (Ger 1970)
Liebe ist nur ein Wort (Ger 1971)
Und der Regen verwischt jede Spur (Ger-Fr 1972)
Der Stoff, aus dem die Träume sind (Ger 1972)
Alle Menschen werden Brüder (Ger 1973)
Gott schützt die Liebenden (Ger 1973)

VON BOLVARY, GEZA (Geza Maria von Bolvary-Zahn), b. Dec. 27, 1897, Budapest; d. Aug. 10, 1961
Ketarev Asszony (Hun 1920)
Lengyelver (Hun 1920)
Tavaszi Szerelem (Hun 1921)
Egy Fiunak a Fele (Hun 1922)
Mutterherz (Ger 1923)
Der Weg zum Licht (Ger 1923) (also script) (with Kurt Rosen)
Wüstenrausch (Ger 1923)
Hochstapler Wider Willen (Ger 1924)
Mädchen, die man nicht heiratet (Ger 1924)

Der Königsgrenadier (Ger 1925)
Frauen, die nicht lieben dürfen (Ger 1925)
Die Liebe der Bajadere (Ger 1926)
Die Fürstin der Riviera (Ger 1926)
Das deutsche Mutterherz (Ger 1926)
Fräulein Mama (Ger 1926)
Die Gefangene von Shanghai (Ger 1927) (?with Augusto Genina)
Der Geisterzug [The Ghost Train] (Ger-GB 1927)
Artisten (Ger 1928)
Der fesche Husar (Ger 1928)
Haus Nummer 17 [Number Seventeen] (Ger-GB 1928)
The Wrecker (GB-Ger 1928)
Champagner (Aus-GB 1929)
The Vagabond Queen (GB-Ger 1929)
Vater und Sohn (Ger 1929)
Der Erzieher meiner Tochter (Ger 1930)
Zwei Herzen im dreiviertel Takt [Two Hearts in Waltz Time]
    (Ger 1930)
Delikatessen (Ger 1930)
Ein Tango für dich (Ger 1930)
Das Lied ist aus (Ger 1930)
Der Herr auf Bestellung (Ger 1930)
Die Lustigen Weiber von Wien (Ger 1931)
Der Raub der Mona Lisa (Ger 1931)
Liebeskommando [Love's Command] (Ger 1931)
Ein Lied, ein Kuss, ein Mädel (Ger 1932)
Ich will nicht wissen wer du bist (Ger 1932)
Ein Mann mit Herz (Ger 1932)
Was Frauen träumen (Ger 1933)
Die Nacht der grossen Liebe (Ger 1933)
Skandal in Budapest (Ger-Hun 1933) (with Stefan Szekely)
Pardon Tevedtem (Hun version of Skandal in Budapest) [Romance
    in Budapest] (Ger-Hun 1933) (with Stefan Szekely)
Das Schloss im Süden (Ger 1933)
Chateau de rêve (Fr version of Das Schloss im Suden) (Ger
    1933)
Ich kenn' dich nicht und liebe dich (Ger 1934)
Toi que j'adore (Fr version of Ich kenn' dich nicht und liebe
    dich) (Ger 1934)
Abschiedswalzer (Ger 1934)
La Chanson de l'adieu (Fr version of Abschiedswalzer) (Ger
    1934)
Frühjahrsparade (Ger-Aus 1935)
Tavoszi Parade (Hun version of Frühjahrsparade) (Ger-Aus
    1935)
Winternachtstraum (Ger 1935)
Stradivari (Ger 1935)
Stradivarius (Fr version of Stradivari) (Ger 1935)
Es flüstert die Liebe (Aus 1935)
Die Entführung (Ger 1936)
Das Schloss in Flandern (Ger 1936)
Mädchenpensionat/Prinzessin Dagmar (Aus 1936)
Die Julika/Ernte (Aus 1936)

Lumpazivagabundus (Aus 1937)
Premiere (Aus 1937)
Der Unwiderstehliche (Ger 1937)
Zauber der Bohème (Aus 1937)
Die unruhigen Mädchen (Aus 1938)
Spiegel des Lebens (Ger 1938)
Zwischen Strom und Steppe/ Pusztaliebe (Ger 1939) (also co-
   script)
Tiszavirag (Hun version of Zwischen Strom und Steppe) (Ger
   1939) (also co-script)
Maria Ilona (Ger 1939)
Opernball (Ger 1939)
Wiener G'schichten (Ger 1940)
Traummusik (Ger-It 1940)
Rosen in Tirol (Ger 1940)
Dreimal Hochzeit (Ger 1941)
Schicksal (Ger 1942)
Die heimliche Gräfin (Ger 1942)
Der dunkel Tag (Ger 1943)
Ein Mann mit Grundsätzen? (Ger 1943)
Schrammeln (Ger 1944)
Die Fledermaus (Ger 1945)
Die tolle Suzanne (Ger 1945) [unfinished]
Addio Mimi (It 1948) (uncredited with Carmine Gallone)
Wer bist du, den ich liebe? (Ger 1949)
Hochzeitsnacht in Paradies (Ger 1950)
Schwarze Augen (Ger 1951)
Meine Frau macht Dummheiten (Ger 1952)
Fritz und Friederike (Ger 1952)
Dalmatinische Hochzeit/ Einmal kehr' ich wieder (Ger-Yug 1953)
Die Tochter der Kompanie (Ger-It 1953) (with Tullio Covaz)
La figlia del reggimente (It version of Die Tochter der Kom-
   panie) (Ger-It 1953) (with Tullio Covaz)
Ja, ja, die Liebe in Tirol (Ger 1955)
Ein Herz bleibt allein/ Mein Leopold (Ger 1955)
Das Donkosakenlied (Ger 1956)
Was die Schwalbe sang (Ger 1956)
Schwarzwaldmelodie (Ger 1956)
Unsterbliche Liebe (Ger 1956)
Hoch droben auf dem Berg (Ger 1957)
Es wird alles wieder gut (Ger 1957)
Schön ist die Welt (Ger 1957)
Zwei Herzen im Mai (Ger 1958)
Schwarzwälder Kirsch (Ger 1958)
Das gab's nur einmal (Ger 1958) (compilation)
Hoch klingt der Radetzky-marsch (Aus 1958)
Ein Lied geht um die Welt (Ger 1958)

VRIJMAN, JAN (Jan Hulsebos), b. Feb. 12, 1925, Amsterdam
   Op de Bodem van de Hemel (Dut 1966)
   Het Gangstermeisje (Dut 1966) (only co-script) (with Franz
   Weisz)

WALKER, PETER, b. 1938, London
  I Like Birds (Border 1967) (also producer, script)
  Strip Poker/The Big Switch (Miracle 1968)† (also producer,
    script)
  School for Sex (Miracle 1968)† (also producer, script)
  Man of Violence (Miracle 1970)† (also producer, co-script)
  Cool It Carol (Miracle 1970)† (also producer)
  Die Screaming, Marianne (London Screen Distributors 1971)†
    (also producer)
  The Four Dimensions of Greta (Hemdale 1972)† (also producer,
    actor)
  The Flesh and Blood Show (Tigon 1972)† (also producer, actor)
  Tiffany Jones (Hemdale 1973)† (also producer)
  House of Whipcord (Heritage 1974) (also producer, story)

WATKINS, PETER, b. Norbiton, Surrey, England
  The War Game (BFI 1966) (also script)
  Privilege (RFD 1967) (also additional dialogue)
  Gladiatorena [Peace Games] (Swe 1969) (also co-script)
  Punishment Park (USA) (1971) (also co-script, co-editor)

WATT, HARRY, b. Oct. 18, 1906, Edinburgh
  Nine Men (UA Br 1943) (also script)
  Fiddlers Three (Ealing 1944)
  The Overlanders (Australian 1946) (also script)
  Eureka Stockade (Australian 1949) (also story, co-script)
  Where No Vultures Fly [Ivory Hunter] (GFD 1951) (also story)
  West of Zanzibar (GFD 1954) (also story)
  The Siege of Pinchgut (ABP 1959) (also co-script)

WEIDENMANN, ALFRED, b. May 10, 1916, Stuttgart
  Hände hoch (Ger 1942) (also script)
  Junge Adler (Ger 1944) (also co-script)
  Die Schenke zur ewigen Liebe (Ger 1945) (also co-script)
  Wir bummeln um die Welt (Ger 1949) (co-dir & co-script)
  Ich und Du (Ger 1953) (also co-script)
  Canaris (Ger 1954)
  Der Himmel ist nie ausverkauft (Ger 1955) (also co-script)
  Alibi (Ger 1955)
  Kitty und die grosse Welt (Ger 1956)
  Der Stern von Afrika (Ger 1958)
  Scampolo (Ger 1958)
  Solange das Herz schlägt (Ger 1958)
  Buddenbrooks (Ger 1959)
  Ich bin auch nur eine Frau (Ger 1962)
  Julia du bist zauberhaft [Adorable Julia] (Ger-Aus-Fr 1962)
  Das grosse Liebesspiel [And So to Bed] (Ger-Aus 1963)
  Verdammt zur Sünde (Ger 1964)
  Die Herren (Ger 1965) (with co-director)
  Das Liebeskarussell (Ger-Aus 1965)
  Schüsse in 3/4 Takt (Ger 1965)
  Ich suche einen Mann (Ger 1966)
  Maigret und sein grösster Fall (Ger-Aus-It 1966)

Peter Watkins (right) directing Gladiatorena [Peace Games] (1969).

Pistol Jenny (Ger 1969)
Unter den dächern von St. Pauli (Ger 1970)
Das Freudenhaus (Ger 1971)

WEISZ, FRANZ, b. July 23, 1938, Berlin
   Het Gangstermeisje (Dut 1966) (also co-script) (with Jan Vrij-
      man)
   De Inbreker [The Frame Up] (Dut 1972)
   Naakt Over de Schutting [The Lady on the Fence] (Dut 1973)
   Rooie Sien (Dut 1975)

WERTMÜLLER, LINA (Arcangela Wertmüller von Elgg), b. Aug.
   14, 1928, Rome
   I basilischi (It 1963)

Questa volta parliamo di uomini (It 1965)
Rita la zanzara (It 1962) (only script)
Non stuzzicate la zanzara (It 1967)
Mimi metallurgico, ferito nell'onore [The Seduction of Mimi]
    (It 1971)
Film d'amore e d'anarchia, ovvero stamattina alle 10 in Via
    dei Fiori, nella casa di tolleranza [Love and Anarchy]
    (It 1972)
Quando le donne persero la coda (It 1962) (also co-script)
Travolti da un insito nell'azzurro mare di agosto [Swept Away]
    (It 1974) (also co-script)
Tutto a posto e niente in orchine (It 1974) (also co-script)

WEYERGANS, FRANÇOIS, b. Belgium
    Aline (Bel 1967)
    Baudelaire Is Gestorven in de Zomer (Bel 1967)
    Un film sur quelqu'un (Bel 1972)
    Je t'aime, tu danses (Bel 1974)

WICKI, BERNHARD, b. Oct. 28, 1919, Sankt-Polten, Austria
    Warum sind sie gegen uns (Ger 1958) (also script)
    Die Brücke (Ger 1959)
    Das Wunder des Malachias (Ger 1961) (also co-script)
    The Longest Day (20th 1963) (with Ken Annakin, Andrew Mar-
        ton, and uncredited Darryl F. Zanuck)
    The Visit (20th 1964)
    Saboteur: Code Name Morituri (20th 1964)
    Transit (Unfinished 1965)

WIENE, ROBERT, b. 1881, Sasku; d. July 17, 1938
    Arme Eva (Ger 1914) (with W. A. Berger)
    Er rechts, sie links (Ger 1915)
    Die Konservenbraut (Ger 1915)
    Der Liebesbrief der Königin (Ger 1916)
    Der Mann im Spiegel (Ger 1916)
    Die Räuberbraut (Ger 1916)
    Der Sekretär der Königin (Ger 1916)
    Das wandernde Licht (Ger 1916)
    Ein gefährliches Spiel (Ger 1919) (also script)
    Das Kabinett der Dr. Caligari [The Cabinet of Dr. Caligari]
        (Ger 1919)
    Die drei Tänze der Mary Wilford (Ger 1920)
    Genuine (Ger 1920)
    Die Nacht der Königin Isabeau (Ger 1920) (also script)
    Die Rache einer Frau (Ger 1920)
    Höllische Nacht (Ger 1921)
    Das Spiel mit dem Feuer (Ger 1921) (with Georg Kroll)
    Salome (Ger 1922)
    Tragikomödie (Ger 1922) (also co-producer)
    I. N. R. I. (Ger 1923) (also script)
    Der Puppenmacher von Kiang-Ning (Ger 1923)
    Raskolnikoff (Ger 1923) (also script)

Bernhard Wicki

Orlacs Hände (Ger 1925)
Pension Groonen (Ger 1925)
Der Gardeoffizier (Ger 1926)
Die Königin vom Moulin-Rouge (Ger 1926)
Der Rosenkavalier (Ger 1926) (also co-script)
Die berühmte Frau (Ger 1927)
Die Geliebte (Ger 1927)
Die Frau auf der Folter (Ger 1928)
Die grosse Abenteuerin (Ger 1928)
Leontines Ehemänner (Ger 1928)
Unfug der Liebe (Ger 1928)
Der Andere (Ger 1930)
Panik in Chikago (Ger 1931)
Der Liebesexpress (Ger 1931)
Polizeiakte 909 (Ger 1934) (also script)

Eine Nacht in Venedig (Ger 1934) (also script)
The Robber Symphony (Concordia 1936) (only producer)
Ultimatum (Fr 1938) (died during making of film; finished by
  R. Siodmak)

WILCOX, HERBERT, b. April 19, 1892, Cork, Eire
  Chu Chin Chow (Graham-Wilcox 1923)† [co-production company]
    (also producer, script)
  Southern Love [A Woman's Secret] (Graham-Wilcox 1923)†
    [co-production company] (also producer, script)
  Decameron Nights (GB-Ger) (Graham-Wilcox-Decla 1924)† [co-
    production company] (also co-producer, co-script)
  The Only Way (FN Br 1925)† (also producer, script)
  Nell Gwynne (FN Br 1926) (also producer, script)
  London (Par Br 1926)
  Tiptoes (Par Br 1927)
  Mumsie (W & F 1927)† (also producer)
  Dawn (W & F 1928) (also producer, co-script)
  The Bondman (W & F 1929) (also producer)
  The Woman in White (W & F 1929)
  The Loves of Robert Burns (W & F 1930) (also producer, co-
    script)
  The Chance of a Night Time (W & F 1931) (with Ralph Lynn)
    (also producer)
  Carnival [Venetian Nights] (W & F 1931) (also producer)
  The Blue Danube (W & F 1932) (also producer)
  Goodnight Vienna [Magic Night] (W & F 1932) (also producer)
  Yes Mr Brown (W & F 1933) (with Jack Buchanan) (also pro-
    ducer)
  The King's Cup (W & F 1933) (with Robert J. Cullen, Alan
    Cobham, Donald Macardie) (also producer)
  The Little Damozel (W & F 1933) (also producer)
  Bitter Sweet (UA Br 1933) (also producer, co-script)
  The Queen's Affair [Runaway Queen] (UA Br 1934) (also pro-
    ducer)
  Nell Gwynn (UA Br 1934) (also producer)
  Peg of Old Drury (UA Br 1935) (also producer)
  Limelight [Backstage] (GFD 1936)
  The Three Maxims [The Show Goes On] (GFD 1936)
  This'll Make You Whistle (GFD 1936) (also producer)
  London Melody [Girls in the Street] (GFD 1937) (also producer)
  Victoria the Great (RKO Br 1937) (also producer)
  Sixty Glorious Years [Queen of Destiny] (RKO Br 1938) (also
    producer)
  Nurse Edith Cavell (USA) (RKO 1939) (also producer)
  No, No Nanette (USA) (RKO 1940) (also producer)
  Irene (USA) (RKO 1940) (also producer)
  Sunny (USA) (RKO 1941) (also producer)
  They Flew Alone [Wings and the Woman] (RKO Br 1942) (also
    producer)
  Yellow Canary (RKO Br 1943) (also producer)
  Forever and a Day (USA) (RKO 1943) (with René Clair, Edmund
    Goulding, Sir Cedric Hardwicke, Frank Lloyd, Victor

Saville, Robert Stevenson) (also co-producer)
I Live in Grosvenor Square [A Yank in London] (Pathé 1945)
    (also producer)
Piccadilly Incident (Pathé 1946) (also producer)
The Courtneys of Curzon Street [The Courtney Affair] (BL
    1947) (also producer)
Spring in Park Lane (BL 1948) (also producer)
Elizabeth of Ladymead (BL 1949) (also producer)
Maytime in Mayfair (BL 1949) (also producer)
Odette (BL 1950) (also producer)
Into the Blue [The Man in the Dinghy] (BL 1951) (also co-pro-
    ducer)
The Lady With the Lamp (BL 1951) (also producer)
Derby Day [Four Against Fate] (BL 1952) (also co-producer)
Trent's Last Case (BL 1952) (also producer)
Laughing Anne (Rep Br 1953) (also producer)
Trouble in the Glen (Rep Br 1954) (also producer)
Lilacs in the Spring [Let's Make Up] (Rep Br 1954) (also pro-
    ducer)
King's Rhapsody (BL 1955) (also producer)
My Teenage Daughter [Teenage Bad Girl] (BL 1956) (also pro-
    ducer)
These Dangerous Years [Dangerous Youth] (ABP 1957)
The Man Who Wouldn't Talk (BL 1958) (also producer)
Wonderful Things! (ABP 1958)
The Lady Is a Square (ABP 1959) (also co-producer)
The Heart of a Man (RFD 1959)

WINAR, ERNST (Wilhelm Eichhorn), b. Leiden, Netherlands
De Man op de Achtergrond (Dut 1923)
Der Neffe aus Amerika (Ger 1927)
Das Haus am Krogel (Ger 1927)
Paragraph 182--Minderjährig (Ger 1927)
Wochenendbraut (Ger 1928)
Der Hafenbaron (Ger 1928)
Op Stap (Dut 1935)
De Kirbbebijter (Dut 1935) (with Hermann Kosterlitz)
De Laatste Dagen van een Eiland (Dut 1938)
Vijftig Jaren (Dut 1948)
Dik Trom en Zijn Dorpsgenoten (Dut 1948)
Trowe Kamerarden (Dut 1950)
Kees, de Zoon van de Stroper (Dut 1950)

WINNER, MICHAEL, b. 1936, London
Climb Up the Wall (New Realm 1960) (also co-script)
Shoot to Kill (New Realm 1961) (also script)
Old Mac (Carlyle 1961)
Some Like It Cool (SF Films 1961) (also script)
Out of the Shadow (New Realm 1961) (also script)
Play It Cool (AA 1962)
The Cool Mikado (UA Br 1963) (also co-script)
West 11 (WPD 1963)
The System [The Girl Getters] (Bry 1964)

You Must Be Joking! (Col Br 1965)
The Jokers (RFD 1966)
I'll Never Forget What's 'is Name (RFD 1967) (also producer)
Hannibal Brooks (UA Br 1969) (also producer, co-story)
The Games (20th Br 1969)
Lawman (USA) (UA 1970)† (also producer)
The Nightcomers (Avco-Emb 1972)† (also producer)
Chato's Land (UA Br 1972)† (also producer)
The Mechanic (USA) (UA 1972)
The Stone Killer (1973)
Scorpio (USA) (UA 1972)†
Death Wish (USA) (CIC 1974)

WISBAR, FRANK (Franz Wysbar), b. 1899, Tilsit, Germany; d.
    March 17, 1967
  Im Banne des Eulenspiegels (Ger 1932)
  Anna und Elisabeth (Ger 1933) (also co-script)
  Rivalen der Luft (Ger 1933)
  Hermine und die sieben Aufrechten (Ger 1935) (also co-script)
  Die Werft zum grauen Hecht (Ger 1935) (also co-script)
  Fährmann Maria (Ger 1936) (also co-script)
  Die Unbekannte (Ger 1936) (also co-script)
  Ball im Metropol (Ger 1937) (also co-script)
  Petermann ist dagegen (Ger 1937) (also co-script)
  Strangler of the Swamp (USA) (PRC 1935) (also co-story, script)
  Devil Bat's Daughter (USA) (PRC 1946) (also co-producer, co-
    story)
  Lighthouse (USA) (PRC 1946)
  Secrets of a Sorority Girl (USA) (PRC 1946)
  The Prairie (USA) (Screen Guild 1947)
  The Mozart Story (USA) (Screen Guild 1948)
  Haie und Kleine Fische (Ger 1957)
  Nasser Asphalt (Ger 1958)
  Hunde, wolt ihr ewig Leben! [Battle Inferno] (Ger 1959) (also
    co-script)
  Nacht fiel über Gotenhafen (Ger 1959) (also co-script)
  Fabrik der Offiziere (Ger 1960)
  Barbara (Ger 1961)
  Marcia o Crepa [Sprung in die Hölle] (It-Ger 1962) (also co-
    script)
  Durchbruch Lok 234 (Ger 1963)

WOODS, ARTHUR, b. 1904, Liverpool; d. 1940
  Timbuctoo (Wardour 1933) (with Walter Summers)
  On Secret Service [Secret Agent] (Wardour 1933) (also co-
    script)
  Give Her a Ring (Pathé 1934)
  Radio Parade of 1935 [Radio Follies] (Wardour 1934) (also co-
    script)
  Drake of England [Drake the Pirate] (Wardour 1935)
  Music Hath Charms (Wardour 1935) (with Thomas Bentley,
    Alexander Esway, Walter Summers)
  Once in a Million [Weekend Millionaire] (Wardour 1936)

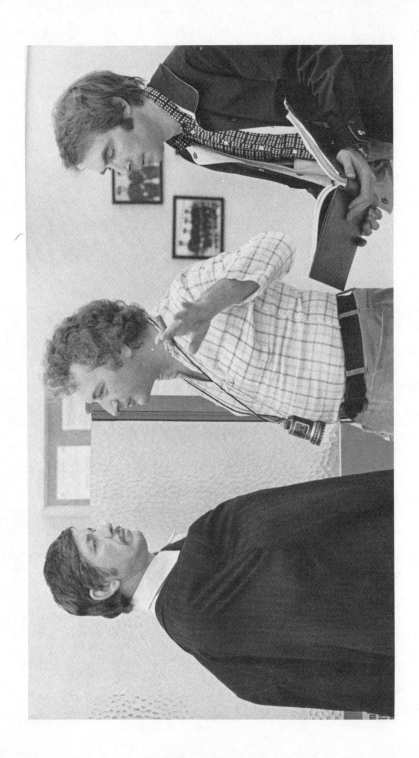

Where's Sally (FN Br 1936)
Rhythm in the Air (Fox Br 1936)
Irish for Luck (FN Br 1936)
Mayfair Melody (WB Br 1937)
Don't Get Me Wrong (FN Br 1937) (with Reginald Purdell)
The Windmill (FN Br 1937)
The Compulsory Wife (WB Br 1937)
You Live and Learn (WB Br 1937)
The Dark Stairway (WB Br 1938)
The Singing Cop (WB Br 1938)
Mr Satan (FN Br 1938)
Glamour Girl (WB Br 1938)
Thistledown (WB Br 1938)
Dangerous Medicine (FN Br 1938)
The Return of Carol Deane (WB Br 1938)
They Drive By Night (FN Br 1938)
The Nursemaid Who Disappeared (WB Br 1939)
Q Planes [Clouds Over Europe] (Col Br 1939) (with Tim Whelan)
Confidential Lady (FN Br 1939)
Busman's Honeymoon [Haunted Honeymoon] (MGM Br 1940)

WRIGHT, BASIL, b. June 12, 1907, London
Windmill in Barbados (EMI 1930)
O'er Hill and Dale (EMI 1931)
The Country Comes to Town (EMI 1932)
Cargo for Jamaica (EMI 1933)
Liner Cruising South (EMI 1933)
Song of Ceylon (GPO 1934)
Night Mail (GPO 1936) (with Harry Watt)
Children at School (RFU 1937)
The Face of Scotland (RFU 1938)
This Was Japan (GF 1945)
The Story of Omolo (MOI 1946)
Waters of Time (FOB 1951)
World without End (UNESCO 1953)
The Immortal Land (Contemporary 1958) (also co-producer)
Greek Sculpture (Contemporary 1958) (with Michael Ayrton) (also co-producer)
A Place for Gold (BL 1960) (also producer)

WUYTS, HERMAN, b. Belgium
Princes (Bel 1968)
General Massacre (Bel 1970) (with Burr Jerger)

YATES, PETER, b. July 24, 1929
Summer Holiday (WPD 1963) (with Herbert Ross)
One Way Pendulum (UA Br 1964)
Robbery (Par Br 1967)

Facing page: Michael Winner (center) with Charles Bronson (left) on the set of The Stone Killer (1973).

Bullitt (USA) (WB 1968)
John and Mary (USA) (20th 1969)
Murphy's War (London Screen Distributors 1971)† [co-produc-
  tion company]
The Hot Rock [How to Steal a Diamond in Four Easy Lessons]
  (USA) (20th 1972)
The Friends of Eddie Coyle (USA) (Par 1973)

Peter Yates

YORK, EUGEN, b. Nov. 26, 1912, Rybinsk, Russia
  Heidesommer (Unfinished) (Ger 1945)
  Morituri (Ger 1948)
  Die letzte Nacht (Ger 1949)
  Schatten der Nacht (Ger 1950)
  Die Schatten des Herrn Monitor (Ger 1950)
  Export in Blond (Ger 1950)
  Lockende Gefahr (Ger 1951)
  Das Fräulein von Scuderi (Ger 1955)
  Ein Herz kehrt heim (Ger 1956)
  Das Herz von St. Pauli (Ger 1957)
  Mann im Strom (Ger 1958)

Der Greifer (Ger 1958)
Das Mädchen mit den Katzenaugen (Ger 1958)
Nebelmorder (Ger 1964)

YOUNG, TERENCE (Shaun Terence Young), b. June 20, 1915,
    Shanghai
    Men of Arnhem (AFU 1944) (with Brian Desmond Hurst)
    One Night with You (GFD 1948)
    Corridor of Mirrors (GFD 1948)
    Woman Hater (GFD 1948)
    They Were Not Divided (GFD 1950) (also script)
    Valley of the Eagles (GFD 1951)
    Tall Headlines/The Frightened Bride (GN 1952)
    The Red Beret [Paratrooper] (Col Br 1953)
    That Lady (20th Br 1955)
    Storm Over the Nile (IFD 1955) (with Zoltan Korda)
    Safari (Col Br 1956)
    Zarak (Col Br 1956) (with Yakima Canutt)
    Action of the Tiger (MGM Br 1957)
    No Time to Die [Tank Force] (Col Br 1958) (also co-script)
    Serious Charge (Eros 1959)
    Too Hot to Handle (WPD 1960)
    Un, deux, trois, quatre! [Black Tights] (Fr 1960)
    Dr. No (UA Br 1962)
    From Russia with Love (UA Br 1963)
    The Amorous Adventures of Moll Flanders (Par Br 1965)
    Thunderball (UA Br 1965)
    Danger Grows Wild/The Poppy Is Not a Flower (UNESCO 1966)
    Triple Cross (Fr-GB 1967)
    Wait Until Dark (USA) (WB 1967)
    Mayerling (Fr-GB 1968) (also script)
    L'Arbre de Noël [The Christmas Tree] (Fr-US 1969) (also
        script)
    De la part des copains [Cold Sweat] (Fr-It 1970)
    Soleil rouge [Red Sun] (Fr-It-Sp 1971)
    Cosa nostra [The Valachi Papers] (Fr-It 1972)

ZAMPA, LUIGI, b. Jan. 2, 1905, Rome
    L'attore scomparso (It 1941) (also co-script)
    Fra diavolo (It 1942) (also co-script)
    Signorinette (It 1942) (also co-script, editor)
    C'è sempre un Ma (It 1942) (also co-story, co-script)
    L'abito nero da sposa (It 1943) (also co-script)
    Un americano in vacanza [A Yank in Rome] (It 1945) (also
        adaptor)
    Vivere in pace [To Live in Peace] (It 1946) (also co-story, co-
        script)
    L'onorevole Angelina [Angelina] (It 1947) (also co-script)
    Anni difficili (It-Fr 1948) (also co-script)
    Campane a martello (It 1949) (also co-script)
    Cuori senza frontiere [The White Line] (It 1950)
    E più facile che un camelo [His Last 12 Hours] (It 1951)
    Signori in carrozza! (It 1951) (also co-script)

Terence Young on a break from shooting Triple Cross (1967).

Processo alla città [The City Stands Trial] (It 1952)
Anni facili (It 1953) (also co-script)
Siamo donne (ep) (It 1953) (also co-script)
Questa è la vita (ep "La patente") (It 1954) (also co-script of
   episode)
La romana [Woman of Rome] (It 1954) (also co-script)
L'arte di arrangiarsi (It 1954) (also co-script)
Ragazze d'oggi (It 1955) (also story, script)
La ragazza del Palio [The Love Specialist] (It 1957) (also co-
   script)
Ladro lui, ladra lei (It 1958) (also story)
Il magistrato (It 1959) (also story, co-script)
Il vigile (It 1960) (also co-script)
Anni ruggenti (It 1962) (also co-story, co-script)
Frenesia dell'estate (It 1963)
Una questione d'onore (It 1966) (also co-script)
I nostri mariti (ep "Il marito di Olga") (It 1966)
Le dolci signore [Anyone Can Play] (It 1967)

Il medico della mutua (It 1968) (also co-script)
Contestazione Generale (It 1969)
Bello, onesto, emigrato Australia sposerebbe compaesana illibata (It 1971)
Bisturi, la Mafia bianca (It 1972)

ZAMPI, MARIO, b. Nov. 1903, Rome; d. Dec. 1, 1963
Thirteen Men and a Gun (GB-It) (BIED 1938) (also producer)
Spy for a Day (Par Br 1940) (also producer)
The Phantom Shot (IFR 1947) (also producer)
The Fatal Night (Col Br 1948) (also producer)
Come Dance with Me (Col Br 1950) (also producer)
Shadow of the Past (Col Br 1950) (also co-producer)
Laughter in Paradise (ABP 1951) (also producer)
Top Secret [Mr. Potts Goes to Moscow] (ABP 1952) (also producer)
Happy Ever After [Tonight's the Night] (ABP 1954) (also producer)
Now and Forever (ABP 1956) (also producer)
The Naked Truth [Your Past Is Showing] (RFD 1957) (also producer)
Too Many Crooks (RFD 1959) (also co-producer)
Bottoms Up! (WPD 1960) (also producer)
Five Golden Hours (Col Br 1961) (also co-producer)

ZEFFIRELLI, FRANCO, b. Feb. 23, 1923, Florence, Italy
Camping (It 1958)
La bisbetica domata [The Taming of the Shrew] (It-US 1967) (also co-producer, co-script)
Romeo e Giulietta [Romeo and Juliet] (It-GB 1968) (also co-script)
Fratello sole, sorella luna [Brother Sun, Sister Moon] (It-GB 1971) (also co-script)

ZEGLIO, PRIMO (a. k. a. Omar Hopkins; Anthony Creepy), b. July 8, 1906, Buronzo, Italy
Genoveffa di Brabante (It 1947)
La figlia del diavolo (It 1953)
Nerone e Messalina (It 1954)
La vendetta del corsaro (It 1954)
Capitan Fantasma (It 1954)
Dimentica il mio passato [Consuelo] (It 1954)
Il figlio del Corsaro rosso (It 1960)
Morgan il pirata (It 1960)
Le sette sfide (It 1961)
Il dominatore dei sette mari [Sir Francis Drake] (It 1962)
Io, Semiramide (It 1963)
L'uomo della valle maledetta (It 1964)
I due violenti (It 1965)
I quatro inesorabili (It 1966)
4...3...2...1...morte (It 1967)
Killer adios (It 1968)

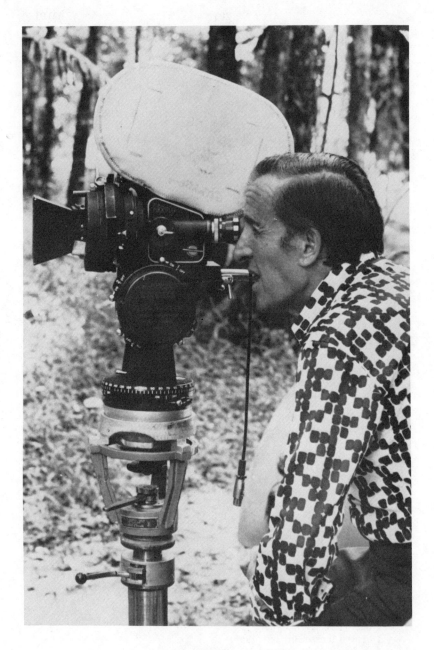

Luigi Zampa sighting

ZURLINI, VALERIO, b. Mar. 19, 1926, Bologna, Italy
   Le ragazze di San Frediano (It 1954)
   Estate violenta (It 1959)
   La ragazza con la valigia (It 1961)
   Cronaca familiare (It 1962)
   Le soldatesse (It 1965)
   Seduto alla sua destra (It 1968)
   I gabbiani d'inverno o l'Inverno sull'Adriatico (It 1972)

ABOUT THE COMPILERS:

JAMES ROBERT PARISH, New York-based free-lance writer, was born near Boston. He attended the University of Pennsylvania and graduated as a Phi Beta Kappa with a degree in English. A graduate of the University of Pennsylvania Law School, he is a member of the New York Bar. As president of Entertainment Copyright Research Co., Inc., he headed a major researching facility for the film and television industries. Later he was a reporter for Motion Picture Daily and Variety. He is the author of such books as The Fox Girls, The RKO Gals, Hollywood's Great Love Teams, The Tough Guys, Elvis Presley Scrapbook, Actors' Television Credits (1950-1972). Among his co-authorship credits are: The Cinema of Edward G. Robinson, Liza!, The Glamour Girls, The Great Spy Pictures, and Film Directors: A Guide to their American Pictures.

KINGSLEY CANHAM, London-based free-lance writer, was born in Port Elizabeth, South Africa, on February 18, 1945. A film buff from early childhood, he attended St. Andrew's College in Grahamstown and in 1962 came to England. He has contributed to many cinema journals, including Film, Focus on Film, Films in Review, Films and Filming, and Screen. His cinema research has been published by Tantivy Press, The British Film Institute, and the National Film Archive. He is the author of a number of books in the Hollywood Professional series. He is currently the London correspondent for Filmguia, a Spanish cinema journal.

LORENZO CODELLI, a student in political sciences and a free-lance writer and translator, is based in Trieste, Italy. He is a regular essay and interview contributor to the French film monthly, Positif. He also writes for the British magazine Monogram and is a very active participant in the field of Italian cultural film exhibition. He is an avid collector books, magazines, and has an extensive cinema still collection.

HERVE DUMONT was born in February 1943 in Berne, Switzerland, and attended schools in Sweden, Germany, and Spain, receiving his PhD in 1970. For the cinema journal Travelling he has provided several articles, and has contributed to such Spanish film publications as Film Ideal and El Cine. He is associated with the Swiss National Film Archive in Lausanne, Switzerland and is the author of W. S. Van Dyke (1975).

PIERRE GUINLE was born in the Catalan-speaking part of France in 1940 and became a movie devotee at the late age of 16. He is currently employed as a translator for a Brussels-based organization. He was one of the founders of the French film magazine Présence du Cinema and has contributed researching information for many cinema journals in Europe and the United States. He is an extensive world traveler; his hobbies are film memorabilia, vintage wines, and haute cuisine.

NORMAN MILLER is employed by a New York City bank and has been a film buff all his life. He maintains a large private reference library of cinema materials from all over the world, providing a basis for his assistance to cinema scholars everywhere. Side interests in music, art, literature, and castles serve to highlight his film researching activities.

JEANNE PASSALACQUA was born in New York City and graduated from Baruch College. She has always been interested in the cinema and is a contributor to several cinema journals. Her first job was working in a secretarial capacity for a major film company. At present she is associated with one of the city libraries. She is married and has one daughter.

FLORENCE SOLOMON, born in New York, attended Hunter College and then joined Ligon Johnson's copyright research office. Later she was appointed director for research at Entertainment Copyright Research Co., Inc. and is presently a reference supervisor at A. S. C. A. P. 's Index division. Ms. Solomon has collaborated on such works as The American Movies Reference Book, TV Movies, The Great Movie Series, and The Debonairs. She is the niece of the noted sculptor, the late Sir Jacob Epstein.